THE ROLE OF 'EXPERTS' IN INTERNATIONAL AND EUROPEA DECISION-MAKING PROCESSES

Experts are increasingly relied on in decision-making processes at inte national and European levels. Their involvement in those processe however, is contested. This timely book on the role of 'experts' provid a broad-gauged analysis of the issues raised by their involvement i decision-making processes. The chapters explore three main recurrin themes: the rationales for involving experts and ensuing legitimac problems; the individual and collective dimensions of expert involv ment in decision making; and experts and politics, and the politics expertise. With contributions from leading scholars and practitioner they theorize the experts' involvement in general and address their role i the policy areas of environment, trade, human rights, migration, finan cial regulation and agencification in the European Union.

MONIKA AMBRUS is a lecturer in public international law at th University of Groningen, the Netherlands.

KARIN ARTS is Professor of International Law and Development at th International Institute of Social Studies of Erasmus Universit Rotterdam, the Netherlands.

ELLEN HEY is Professor of Public International Law at the Erasmu School of Law, Rotterdam, the Netherlands.

HELENA RAULUS is Assistant Professor at the Erasmus School of Law Rotterdam, the Netherlands.

THE ROLE OF 'EXPERTS' IN INTERNATIONAL AND EUROPEAN DECISION-MAKING PROCESSES

Advisors, Decision Makers or Irrelevant Actors?

Edited by

MONIKA AMBRUS

KARIN ARTS

ELLEN HEY

and

HELENA RAULUS

CAMBRIDGE
UNIVERSITY PRESS

CAMBRIDGE
UNIVERSITY PRESS

University Printing House, Cambridge CB2 8BS, United Kingdom

Cambridge University Press is part of the University of Cambridge.

It furthers the University's mission by disseminating knowledge in the pursuit of education, learning and research at the highest international levels of excellence.

www.cambridge.org
Information on this title: www.cambridge.org/9781107074781

First published 2014

Printed in the United Kingdom by Clays, St Ives plc

A catalogue record for this publication is available from the British Library

Library of Congress Cataloguing in Publication data
The role of 'experts' in international and European decision-making processes : advisors, decision makers or irrelevant actors? / edited by Monika Ambrus, Karin Arts, Ellen Hey, and Helena Raulus.
pages cm
ISBN 978-1-107-07478-1 (hardback)
1. Decision making. 2. Consultants. 3. Specialists. I. Ambrus, Monika.
HD30.23.R65 2014
320.6–dc23
2014006990

ISBN 978-1-107-07478-1 Hardback

CONTENTS

FIGURES AND TABLES

Figures

Tables

CONTRIBUTORS

MONIKA AMBRUS
Lecturer in Public International Law, Faculty of Law, University of Groningen, the Netherlands and Managing Editor of the *Netherlands Yearbook of International Law.*

STEINAR ANDRESEN
Research Professor, Fridtjof Nansen Institute and Adjunct Professor, Pluricourts Center of Excellence, University of Oslo, Norway.

KARIN ARTS
Professor of International Law and Development, International Institute of Social Studies (ISS), The Hague, the Netherlands, part of Erasmus University Rotterdam.

E. MADALINA BUSUIOC
Fellow in Risk and Regulation, Centre for Analysis of Risk and Regulation, London School of Economics and Political Science, UK.

MICHELLE EVERSON
Professor, Birkbeck College, University of London, UK.

LUKASZ GRUSZCZYNSKI
Assistant Professor of Law, Institute of Law Studies, Polish Academy of Sciences, Warsaw, Poland and Managing Co-Editor of the *Polish Yearbook of International Law.*

JOYEETA GUPTA
Professor of Environment and Development in the Global South, group on Governance and Inclusive Development, Amsterdam Institute of Social Science Research, University of Amsterdam, the

Netherlands and at the UNESCO-IHE Institute for Water Education, Delft, the Netherlands.

PETER M. HAAS
Professor of Political Science, Department of Political Science, University of Massachusetts Amherst, USA.

JEFF HANDMAKER
Assistant Professor in Law, Human Rights and Development, International Institute of Social Studies (ISS), The Hague, the Netherlands, part of Erasmus University Rotterdam.

ALEXIA HERWIG
Assistant Professor, Faculty of Law, University of Antwerp, Belgium.

ELLEN HEY
Professor of Public International Law, Erasmus School of Law, Erasmus University Rotterdam, the Netherlands and Visiting Professorial Fellow, School of Law, University of New South Wales, Sydney, Australia (2013–15).

JAN KLABBERS
Academy Professor (Martti Ahtisaari Chair), University of Helsinki, Finland.

KARIM KNIO
Assistant Professor in Politics, International Institute of Social Studies (ISS), The Hague, the Netherlands, part of Erasmus University Rotterdam.

JESSICA LAWRENCE
PhD candidate, Department of Transnational Legal Studies, Faculty of Law, VU University Amsterdam, the Netherlands.

CLAUDIA MORA
Research Director, Faculty of Social Sciences, Universidad Andrés Bello, Santiago, Chile.

HELENA RAULUS
Assistant Professor in European Union Law, Erasmus School of Law, Erasmus University Rotterdam, the Netherlands.

SOPHIE SCHOLTEN
Lecturer/Researcher, Police Academy, School for Police Investigation and PhD candidate, Centre for Migration Law and Institute for Sociology of Law, Faculty of Law, Radboud University Nijmegen, the Netherlands.

ADRIAAN SCHOUT
Deputy Director Research and Senior Research Fellow, Clingendael Netherlands Institute for International Relations, The Hague, the Netherlands.

LORNA SCHREFLER
Research Fellow and Head of Regulatory Policy, Centre for European Policy Studies, Brussels, Belgium.

BERND SIEBENHÜNER
Professor of Ecological Economics and Vice-President for Graduate Education and Quality Management, Carl-von-Ossietzky University of Oldenburg, Germany.

JAAP SLEIFER
Senior Policy Advisor with Actal, The Hague, the Netherlands.

SURYA P. SUBEDI
Professor of International Law, University of Leeds, UK and United Nations Special Rapporteur for Human Rights in Cambodia.

ASHLEY TERLOUW
Professor of Sociology of Law, Centre for Migration Law and Institute for Sociology of Law, Faculty of Law, Radboud University Nijmegen, the Netherlands.

WOUTER G. WERNER
Professor of Public International Law, Department of Transnational Legal Studies, Faculty of Law, VU University, Amsterdam, the Netherlands.

1

The role of experts in international and European decision-making processes: setting the scene

MONIKA AMBRUS, KARIN ARTS, ELLEN HEY AND HELENA RAULUS

Analyses of the significance of knowledge in present-day society,[1] also referred to as knowledge society, fuelled our curiosity about the role that experts play in international and European decision-making processes. This interest prompted us to ask the question reflected in the title of this book: are experts in these decision-making processes advisors, decision makers or irrelevant actors? A literature survey illustrated that, while analysis of knowledge utilization is – and has been – readily available in the social sciences,[2] there is only scant analysis of *how* experts relate to decision-making processes at the international and European levels.[3] This realization in turn prompted us to bring together a group of, yes, 'experts' to discuss the above-mentioned

We gratefully acknowledge the financial contributions for the organization of a seminar in support of this project from the COST Action IS 1003: International Law Between Constitutionalization and Fragmentation: The Role of Law in the Post-national Constellation, Erasmus School of Law, the International Institute of Social Studies and the Vereniging Trustfonds Erasmus University Rotterdam. We also gratefully acknowledge the valuable contributions to the editorial process provided by Lindsay van den Bergh, Loes van der Graaf, Sacha Grievink, Sander van de Laar, Edwin van 't Pad and Vera Willems, student assistants at the Department of International and European Union Law at the Erasmus School of Law, Rotterdam, the Netherlands.

[1] We include only a few examples: U. Beck, *Risk Society, Towards a New Modernity* (London: Sage, 1992); N. Caplan, 'The Two-Communities Theory and Knowledge Utilization', *Public Administration Review*, 39 (1979), 459–70; P. M. Haas, 'Introduction: Epistemic Communities and International Policy Coordination', *International Organization*, 46 (1992), 1–37; N. Stehr, *Knowledge Societies* (London: Sage, 1994); R. Grundmann and N. Stehr, *Experts: The Knowledge and Power of Expertise* (London: Routledge, 2001).

[2] See references in note 1 and Schrefler, Chapter 4, this volume.

[3] Some fairly recent examples include: L. Botcheva, 'Expertise and International Governance: Eastern Europe and the Adoption of European Union Environmental Legislation', *Global Governance*, 7 (2001), 197–224, which addresses concerns about

question at a two-day seminar held in June 2011, which is at the origin of this book.

From the outset, one could ask why the contributors to this book qualify as 'experts'. Is it because as an individual, each is 'a person who has [or is deemed or claimed to have] extensive skill or knowledge in a particular field'?[4] Or is it because they belong to expert communities that share a common knowledge base, accepted methods for presenting their findings and certain values? As illustrated below and in the chapters of this book, both the individual and collective elements are relevant for identifying who might qualify as an expert. Honesty about where we and the authors come from also requires us to unveil that most of the contributors to this project participate in various international or European decision-making processes as experts, thereby bringing hands-on experience of what it means to be an expert to the book. Are we being self-referential in that we are studying ourselves in our roles as experts? To some degree, this might be the case.

To sum up, for the purposes of the project we initially adopted the above-cited plain-language definition of the term 'expert',[5] thereby referring to the individual dimension of what it means to be an expert. However, as noted above, there is also a collective dimension to being an expert.[6] Moreover, who qualifies as an expert may be the result of a

the sources of credibility and policy influence of expert information in environmental governance; G.J. Brandsma, 'Backstage Europe: Comitology, Accountability and Democracy in the European Union', unpublished PhD thesis, Utrecht University (2010), available at: http://igitur-archive.library.uu.nl/dissertations/2010-0204-200144/brandsma.pdf, which focuses on the particular institutional setting of the EU; K. Conca, *Governing Water: Contentious Transnational Politics and Global Institution Building* (Cambridge, MA: MIT Press, 2006), which maps the processes of institution-building in water governance, including the role of networking among experts and professionals; C.E. Foster, *Science and the Precautionary Principle in International Courts and Tribunals: Expert Evidence, Burden of Proof and Finality* (Cambridge University Press, 2011), which deals with the role of expert witnesses and advisors in international legal proceedings; A. Gornitzka and U. Sverdrup, 'Access of Experts: Information and EU Decision-Making', *West European Politics*, 34 (2011), 48–70, which examines patterns of participation in the expert group system of the European Commission; and M. Halme-Tuomisaari, *Human Rights in Action: Learning Expert Knowledge* (Leiden: Martinus Nijhoff, 2010), which explores the activities of a network of Nordic human rights experts.

[4] Adjusted version of a definition of the term 'expert' provided in *Collins Concise Dictionary*, www.collinsdictionary.com/dictionary/english/expert.

[5] See note 4. [6] See Haas, Chapter 2 and Werner, Chapter 3, both this volume.

political process, which in turn may predetermine the nature of the outcome of the expert process.[7]

In terms of policy areas, we chose to focus on the role of experts in decision-making processes regarding environment, trade (with a focus on trade and health-related risks), human rights and migration, and financial regulation, the latter particularly from the perspective of the European Union (EU). In addition, in relation to the EU we also included chapters on expert involvement in European Commission processes and national administrations, and on the so-called agencification process, because we suggest that these processes epitomize the involvement of experts in decision making and aptly illustrate legitimacy problems that expert involvement may lead to. We chose the above-mentioned policy areas on the basis of our experience that the involvement of experts in these areas is contested, both in theory and in practice. This book thus does not present a comprehensive overview of all policy areas in which experts are involved in international or European decision-making processes, an impossible endeavour by any account.

In terms of the status of the decisions resulting from the decision-making processes in which experts participate, we chose to focus on those processes that result in decisions that impact the lives of individuals and groups in society, regardless of whether those decisions are legally binding. Think of United Nations (UN) human rights special mandate-holders whose work does not generally lead to binding decisions in international law, but whose decisions may have consequences for individuals, vulnerable and other groups or governments.[8] Furthermore, in some cases the fact that there is no binding decision to contest may be part of the problem.[9] Moreover, in most international environmental regimes, expert input is linked to decisions taken by the conference of the parties, which are not legally binding.[10] Yet, we suggest that expert involvement in international environmental regimes illustrates some traits that also feature in expert involvement in decision-making processes that may result in binding decisions, such as in the World Trade Organization (WTO) and the EU.[11]

[7] See Herwig, Chapter 10 and Knio, Chapter 16, both this volume.
[8] See Subedi, Chapter 12, this volume.
[9] See Scholten and Terlouw, Chapter 14, this volume.
[10] See Part II, this volume.
[11] See Parts III and V, this volume.

The methodological approach adopted in this book is eclectic in that we asked the authors to reflect on the role of experts on the basis of their own methodological preferences. We chose this approach above all because we were curious about the insights that the various narratives would generate.[12] The result is a multifaceted 'picture' of experts and their involvement in international and European decision-making processes. The chapters in this book illustrate that a variety of methodologies, ranging from classical legal and policy analyses to critical Foucauldian analyses, are relevant for understanding how experts relate to these decision-making processes. Does such an eclectic approach lead to contradictions? Yes. However, we submit that it first and foremost results in a wealth of insights, both substantively and methodologically. This wealth is illustrated by, for example, the treatment of the notion of epistemic community developed by Haas on the basis of constructivist political science theories[13] and further explored in several chapters.[14] Many of the chapters themselves add further methodological insights on how experts might be studied. These chapters engage with knowledge utilization literature,[15] Aristotelian virtue ethics,[16] institutional learning theory,[17] the notion of semi-autonomous fields,[18] the French *Régulation* School[19] and perspectives from public management.[20]

In this introductory chapter we discuss the following themes. First, we consider the rationales for involving experts in international and European decision-making processes and the legitimacy problems that ensue.[21] Second, we highlight the individual and collective aspects of involving experts in decision making. Third, we discuss the political dimensions of involving experts in decision making. Fourth, we briefly address the question that inspired this book. Lastly, we provide a short overview of the structure of the book.

[12] L. Lixinski, 'Narratives of the International Legal Order and Why they Matter', *Erasmus Law Review*, 6 (2013), 2–5.

[13] Haas, Chapter 2, this volume.

[14] See Werner, Chapter 3, this volume. Werner explores the relevance of the concept of epistemic communities for international lawyers as experts.

[15] Schrefler, Chapter 4, this volume.

[16] Klabbers, Chapter 5, this volume.

[17] Siebenhüner, Chapter 7, this volume.

[18] Scholten and Terlouw, Chapter 14, this volume.

[19] Knio, Chapter 16, this volume.

[20] Schout and Sleifer, Chapter 17, this volume.

[21] For the sake of brevity from hereon in, reference is to 'decision-making processes', omitting the clarification 'international and European', unless the qualification is conceptually necessary.

Prior to engaging with the above-mentioned themes, we thank the authors involved in the project for sharing their thoughts with us and, in particular, their intellectual curiosity about the role of experts in decision-making processes, as well as for their commitment to the project.

1.1 Rationales for involving experts and ensuing legitimacy problems

Experts are called upon to provide input into ever more complex decision-making processes. They are involved in policy making, law-making, and implementation and enforcement efforts. Two reasons for involving experts in decision-making processes at the international and European levels appear prominently in the literature; both concern the legitimacy of governance.[22]

First, it is suggested that involving experts in decision making enhances the quality, and thus the legitimacy, of the decisions taken by providing scientific – presumably neutral – solutions to technical problems. Traditionally, this reason for involving experts in decision making is particularly prominent in those areas where expertise in the natural sciences plays an important role, such as in decision making regarding environmental issues or health risks.[23] Increasingly, input from other disciplines, such as law, economics and other social sciences, is also qualified as expert involvement. For instance, in 2012 Piccone referred to the independent experts that carry out the Special Procedures for Human Rights in the UN as 'the bricks and mortar that have helped keep this house standing' and as 'dedicated experts [who] . . . carry out the unheralded legwork that the system has come to depend on for credible reporting and advice'.[24] Relying on expertise then is regarded as bringing credibility to and depoliticizing the decision-making process. However, as Beck has shown, expertise, including expertise in the natural sciences, can become

[22] D. Bodansky, 'The Legitimacy of International Governance: A Coming Challenge for International Environmental Law?', *American Journal of International Law*, 93 (1999), 596–624.

[23] See Haas, 'Introduction: Epistemic Communities'; Haas, Chapter 2, this volume.

[24] T. Piccone, *Catalysts for Change: How the UN's Independent Experts Promote Human Rights* (Washington DC: Brookings Institution Press, 2012), at 4.

contested.[25] This observation is aptly illustrated by the predicament in which the Intergovernmental Panel on Climate Change (IPCC) and its expert members were involved in 2010.[26]

Second, including experts in decision-making processes has been justified because it is thought to enhance the legitimacy of these processes themselves by increasing transparency as well as providing for more inclusive decision making through the participation of experts. Nanz and Steffek, for instance, suggest that 'legitimation can be generated by means of deliberation between a variety of social actors (e.g., government officials from different national communities, scientific experts, NGOs, etc.)'.[27] Accordingly: 'Well-informed and consensus-seeking discussion in expert committees that are embedded in international decision-making procedures has been suggested as an effective remedy to the legitimation problems of international governance.'[28] Buchanan and Keohane also point out that 'legitimacy [in international decision-making processes] depends crucially upon the activities of external epistemic actors in what might be called the transnational civil society channel of accountability'.[29]

The above-mentioned arguments entail that experts and their expertise are resorted to for enhancing both input and output legitimacy of decision-making processes. Input legitimacy refers to the claim that expert involvement (input) in decision-making processes is likely to engender debate and broader participation, which in turn generate decisions that, as such, are more likely to be regarded as legitimate.[30] Output legitimacy refers to the claim that expert involvement in decision making generates better-quality decisions and that it is the content of those decisions (output) that generates legitimacy. Input and output legitimacy may also inter-relate in the sense that if the legitimacy of the decision-making process (input legitimacy) is contested, its outcome (output legitimacy) may be more easily challenged as well. Consequently, the relationship between input and

[25] See below, notes 70 and 71. [26] See Siebenhüner, Chapter 7, this volume.

[27] P. Nanz and J. Steffek, 'Global Governance, Participation and the Public Sphere', *Government and Opposition*, 39 (2004), 314–35, at 315.

[28] *Ibid.*, 320.

[29] A. Buchanan and R. O. Keohane, 'The Legitimacy of Global Governance Institutions' in R. Wolfrum and V. Röben (eds.), *Legitimacy in International Law* (Berlin: Springer, 2008), 25–62, at 59.

[30] On input and output legitimacy, see F. W. Scharpf, *Governing in Europe: Effective and Democratic?* (Oxford University Press, 1999).

output legitimacy is a reoccurring theme in the chapters of this book, with most contributors pointing to the need for enhanced input legitimacy in order to generate output that better meets standards of justice and generates compliance pull, that is, incentives that foster compliance.

A good example of the tense relationship between expert involvement in decision making and legitimacy can be derived from the experiences of the EU. It has been argued that the EU has no great legitimacy problem because it takes decisions in policy areas where there is 'low electoral salience'.[31] In this view, the EU attains legitimacy by adopting better decisions, that is, by concentrating on the objective outcome of the decision-making processes (output legitimacy). The EU decision-making processes, accordingly, should be perceived as regulatory processes, where parliamentary involvement could be seen as interfering with or undermining legitimacy.[32] Increased expert involvement in the EU, also by adding new layers of experts through the agencification process, fits within this view. However, it is precisely these developments that have given rise to challenges regarding the accountability of the regulatory decision-making processes, both from democratic[33] and judicial perspectives.[34] Consequently, it must be recognized that expert involvement can provide only a limited answer to the legitimization of decision making.[35]

As a result of these legitimacy concerns, demands regarding the accountability of expert involvement arise as well. These concerns relate especially to the selection of experts and the openness of expert

[31] A. Moravcsik, 'In Defence of the "Democratic Deficit": Reassessing Legitimacy in the European Union', *Journal of Common Market Studies*, 40 (2002), 603–24, in particular at 615–16. See also Schout and Sleifer, Chapter 17, this volume.

[32] A. Føllesdal and S. Hix, 'Why There is a Democratic Deficit in the EU: A Response to Majone and Moravcsik', *Journal of Common Market Studies*, 44 (2006), 533–62, in which the authors refer specifically to Moravcsik, 'In Defence of the "Democratic Deficit"' and G. Majone, 'Europe's Democratic Deficit: The Question of Standards', *European Law Journal*, 4 (1998), 5–28; G. Majone, 'The European Commission: The Limits of Centralization and the Perils of Parliamentarization', *Governance*, 15 (2002), 375–92.

[33] See references in note 32; and Y. Papadopoulos, 'Problems of Democratic Accountability in Network and Multilevel Governance', *European Law Journal*, 13 (2007), 469–86. See also Everson, Chapter 15, this volume.

[34] See Busuioic, Chapter 18, this volume.

[35] For instance, C. Scott, 'Governing without Law or Governing without Government? New-ish Governance and the Legitimacy of the EU', *European Law Journal*, 15 (2009), 160–73.

communities and their views to public scrutiny and critique. Expert involvement is thereby becoming subject to similar expectations as the decision-making processes themselves, with questions being raised in relation to how to create forms of accountability to govern these expert processes. Various contributors to this book offer different ways out of this conundrum, including further regulation of expert involvement,[36] limiting the role of the experts,[37] enhancing civil society involvement[38] and returning to Aristotelian virtue ethics.[39]

1.2 Experts and expert communities

Given the characterization of contemporary society as an information or knowledge society, the widespread involvement of experts in international and European decision-making processes does not come as a surprise. However, this finding quickly leads to the realization that the answer to the question of who is an expert is not straightforward. The chapters in this book illustrate that, in order to unveil the role of experts in decision making, 'using the methods and approaches of the natural sciences' does not suffice as a selection criterion.[40] How then might experts and expertise be qualified? As the chapters in this book demonstrate, in some policy areas the regimes themselves provide some degree of clarification as to who might qualify as an expert, while in other cases experts seem to emerge by default.[41]

Terms for selecting experts and regulating their modus operandi are in place, in particular in international regimes regarding the environment,[42] trade and health-related risks,[43] and in the EU,[44] while contentious attempts to further formalize the selection and role of UN human rights special mandate-holders are ongoing.[45] Gruszczynski, in

[36] Schrefler, Chapter 4, Gupta, Chapter 8, Gruszczynski, Chapter 11, Herwig, Chapter 10, Subedi, Chapter 12, Schout and Sleifer, Chapter 17 and Busuioc, Chapter 18, all this volume.
[37] Everson, Chapter 15, this volume.
[38] Gupta, Chapter 8 and Siebenhüner, Chapter 7, both this volume.
[39] Klabbers, Chapter 5, this volume.
[40] See also Grundmann and Stehr, *Experts*.
[41] Scholten and Terlouw, Chapter 14 and Handmaker and Mora, Chapter 13, both this volume.
[42] Andresen, Chapter 6 and Siebenhüner, Chapter 7, both this volume.
[43] Herwig, Chapter 10 and Gruszczynski, Chapter 11, both this volume.
[44] Schout and Sleifer, Chapter 17, Busuioc, Chapter 18 and Everson, Chapter 15, all this volume.
[45] Subedi, Chapter 12, this volume.

illustrating the progressive formalization of expert involvement in WTO dispute settlement proceedings related to health risks, makes the point that 'the output of adjudication can only be as good as the underlying process'.[46]

At the same time, other contributors emphasize that the formalization of expert involvement often prioritizes certain expertise. For instance, Herwig submits that the Agreement on Sanitary and Phytosanitary Measures (SPS Agreement) fails to 'involve a sufficiently broad range of experts who could address all justice-related aspects in risk policy-making'.[47] Knio in turn shows that the appointment of a homogeneous group of experts, consisting of persons who are associated with the (financial) system that they are requested to review, will not necessarily yield significant and necessary inputs on how to change the system. Rather, their involvement is likely to result in certain, predictable approaches to the financial crises.[48]

Considerations similar to those that inform Herwig prompt Gupta to suggest that more structured, participatory and integrated assessments – or what she refers to as civic science, involving civil society members – may be required to increase the compliance pull of decisions in environmental decision making.[49] Siebenhüner similarly suggests that lay-learning should be integrated into the IPCC process. His chapter also illustrates how organizational learning has led to the further formalization of the working methods of the IPCC and improved the quality of its output.[50] Subedi's chapter, besides pointing to the advantages of attempts to further formalize and regulate the involvement of UN human rights special mandate-holders, also reveals an important disadvantage: further polarization of the decision-making process.[51]

However, requirements for expert involvement may also remain unspecified or informal. Handmaker and Mora, for example, in discussing the role of migration experts, point out that there seems to be an informal group of policy advisors and implementers who share common beliefs and as a result reproduce existing hierarchies, thereby 'out-lawing' so-called irregular migrants.[52] Similarly, Scholten and Terlouw illustrate that airline carriers can be characterized as a group

[46] Gruszczynski, Chapter 11, this volume, at 218.
[47] Herwig, Chapter 10, this volume, at 215. [48] Knio, Chapter 16, this volume.
[49] Gupta, Chapter 8, this volume. [50] Siebenhüner, Chapter 7, this volume.
[51] Subedi, Chapter 12, this volume. [52] Handmaker and Mora, Chapter 13, this volume.

of migration experts in situations in which private actors are called upon to implement migration policies.[53]

The above-mentioned findings regarding experts lead us to the collective aspect of what it means to be an expert. This collective dimension prompted Oscar Schachter as early as 1977 to refer to international legal experts involved in decision making as 'a kind of invisible college dedicated to a common intellectual enterprise ... engaged in a continuous process of communication and elaboration'.[54] The invisibility of the college indirectly also points to a problem that today is associated with the involvement of expert communities in decision making: their lack of transparency. Thus, while on the one hand, it is argued that involving experts in decision making enhances transparency, especially in relation to public administration processes and consultations,[55] on the other hand, it is submitted in various chapters of this book that expert communities themselves may not be transparent.

In 1992 Peter Haas found that the manner in which experts in the natural sciences operate can be explained in terms similar to those used by Schachter for international lawyers. He coined the term 'epistemic communities'.[56] This conceptualization has been further developed by Haas since, in particular with respect to how natural science experts operate in environmental regimes. Haas characterizes epistemic communities as:

> networks – often transnational – of knowledge-based experts with an authoritative claim to policy relevant knowledge within their domain of expertise. Their members share knowledge about the causation of ... phenomena ... and a common set of normative beliefs about what actions will benefit human welfare in such a domain. Members are experts with professional training who enjoy social authority based on their reputation for impartial expertise.[57]

Haas maintains that international lawyers do not form an epistemic community, even if they may be part of an epistemic community also involving natural scientists. This stance seems to be due to the

[53] Scholten and Terlouw, Chapter 14, this volume.

[54] O. Schachter, 'The Invisible College of International Lawyers', *Northwestern University Law Review*, 72 (1977), 217–26, at 217.

[55] See above, notes 27 *et seq.*

[56] Haas, 'Introduction: Epistemic Communities'.

[57] P. M. Haas, 'Epistemic Communities' in D. Bodansky, J. Brunnée and E. Hey (eds.), *The Oxford Handbook of International Environmental Law* (Oxford University Press, 2007), 791–806, at 793.

impartiality that he attributes to experts in the natural sciences and to their expertise. Instead, he argues that international lawyers are better characterized as norm entrepreneurs.[58] Werner engages with the notion of epistemic communities and identifies the challenges that both natural science and legal experts have had to face regarding their neutrality and their ability to communicate 'truth'. He suggests that experts, both in the natural sciences and in law, mediate between the production and application of knowledge and in the process constitute the knowledge they pass on, thereby also engaging in the politics of their expertise. He also points out that, even if international lawyers cannot readily be classified as an epistemic community, structurally the two domains of expertise share an important trait: they can impact political decision making only when they are 'grounded in some shared criteria of validity'.[59]

As Schachter pointed out for international lawyers, expert communities tend to encompass both academics and policy makers,[60] thereby blurring the lines between advice and decision making. This point and the ensuing problem, in terms of delegitimizing decision making, is illustrated by Schrefler's chapter on the role of expertise in regulatory policy making. Schrefler points to the need to embed expertise in specific procedural, organizational and incentive-based contexts when delegating regulatory powers to experts.[61] Similar points are made by Schout and Sleifer in discussing the better regulation system of the EU.[62] Moreover, Busuioc points to the fact that the de facto relegation of risk management responsibilities by the European Commission to agencies has resulted in the Court of Justice of the European Union opening the door at least for a procedural review (as opposed to a substantive review) of decisions taken. The Court, at least to some extent, has thereby stepped in to regulate the agencification process.[63]

Lawrence makes the point that the WTO 'is founded on the privileging of expert knowledge'.[64] She also suggests that it might not be possible to change this, since: 'Experts are not something that can be "added to" or "subtracted from" the WTO in order to tweak input or output legitimacy. Instead their [inputs] . . . are the fabric from which the organization is cut.'[65]

[58] Haas, Chapter 2, this volume. [59] Werner, Chapter 3, this volume, at 62.
[60] Schachter, 'The Invisible College', at 217. [61] Schrefler, Chapter 4, this volume.
[62] Schout and Sleifer, Chapter 17, this volume. [63] Busuioc, Chapter 18, this volume.
[64] Lawrence, Chapter 9, this volume, at 174. [65] *Ibid.*, at 193.

Klabbers draws us back to the individual expert. He advocates a focus on Aristotelian virtue ethics and the need to consider the ethics of the individual expert when appointing or selecting experts. He suggests that further regulation of the position of experts may not be sufficient to legitimize their role. Moreover, he questions whether further regulation is desirable as it runs the risk of resulting in an 'audit society' 'based, in essence, on a total lack of trust [which] as such [is] unsustainable'.[66]

Borrowing from others and based on the chapters in this book, we suggest that an expert involved in international and European decision-making processes can be characterized as follows. An expert is a person who has, or is deemed or claimed to have, extensive skill or knowledge in a particular field and who is part of a wider group consisting of persons holding similar expertise. The group operates on the basis of a common knowledge base and shared values, and uses accepted methods to present its findings. Note that this definition does not entail that scientists by definition are experts, since the generation of knowledge as such is excluded from the definition. As to the role that experts play in decision-making processes, we suggest that the characterization employed by Werner appropriately describes their role: they mediate between the production and application of knowledge and in the process constitute the knowledge they pass on, thereby also engaging in the politics of their expertise. This last point brings us to the next theme that we touch upon in this introduction.

1.3 Experts and politics and the politics of expertise

As Andresen illustrates, natural science experts in international environmental regimes may in some contexts have a limited influence on decision making, amongst other things, due to high political conflict. He suggests that:

> Generally, scientific expertise is most important in the agenda-setting phase, and gradually declines in significance as politics and governments take control over the relevant decision-making processes, notably in regimes facing 'malign' political problems ... When there are deep political conflicts, including conflicts over value judgments, scientific

[66] Klabbers, Chapter 5, this volume, at 87.

> expertise has scant room for influence. Thus, we see that the substance of the response is determined essentially by politics, not by scientific expertise.[67]

This finding points to the tension between, on the one hand, the desire for scientific reasoning to inform decision making and, on the other hand, the need for decision makers to ground their decisions in some degree of political awareness. Simply put, the output generated by experts may not harmonize with the highly political issues up for consideration by decision makers. As a result, experts may find themselves in the challenging position of having to balance between remaining autonomous and being involved,[68] or even between credibility and saliency.[69]

According to Ulrich Beck, the challenging position in which experts find themselves has increased the political nature of the natural sciences in what he refers to as 'risk society'. Beck submits that the sciences 'have become a branch office of politics, ethics, business and judicial practice in the grab of numbers'.[70] He also contends that 'it will become a central insight for the role of all sciences that one requires an institutionally strengthened and protected moral and political backbone in order to be able to conduct respectable research at all'.[71] He thus refers to two elements that reoccur in various chapters in this book: the need for further institutionalization of the role of experts and the need for enhanced moral reflection upon their role.

Similar to Beck, David Kennedy points to the role of, in particular, legal experts, who function in what he refers to as the 'background', where they frame the contours of political decision making by curtailing the political (re)distributive choices that politicians are able to make.[72] He thus refers to the political nature of legal expert opinion, urging researchers to focus on uncovering the background. He also cautions against a too one-sided focus of legal research on how to make governance arrangements more accountable. In fact, he urges us to uncover the politics of, in his case, legal expertise.[73]

[67] Andresen, Chapter 6, this volume, at 124. [68] Andresen, Chapter 6, this volume.

[69] Siebenhüner, Chapter 7, this volume. [70] Beck, *Risk Society*, at 82. [71] *Ibid.*

[72] D. Kennedy, 'Challenging Expert Rule: The Politics of Global Governance', *Sydney Journal of International Law*, 27 (2005), 5–28, available at: www.law.harvard.edu/faculty/dkennedy/publications.

[73] *Ibid.* See also D. Kennedy, 'Law and the Political Economy of the World', *Leiden Journal of International Law*, 26 (2013), 7–48.

Several of the chapters in this book take on the challenge posed by Kennedy by analysing the role of legal experts.[74] Others focus on expert communities consisting of natural scientists,[75] financial experts[76] or on the role of experts in general.[77] Werner highlights the political nature of legal expert advice by pointing out that:

> While legal experts are needed to disclose the requirements of international law, it is widely recognized that their advice is based on a particular way of framing and prioritizing issues; the more international law expands and fragments, the more room there is for such legalistic politics.[78]

Schrefler furthermore points out that there is no such thing as a purely technical use of power, whether in the hands of experts (bureaucrats) or politicians. She remarks that:

> The traditional dichotomy between neutral or bureaucratic and political decision making has increasingly fewer supporters. Arguably, it cannot be upheld. Regulatory policy making is better depicted as a continuum ranging from 'government by experts' to 'government by politicians'. In this context, there is no such thing as a neutral policy appraisal. Nor is it, consequently, realistic to conceive that a purely technical use of power exists.[79]

How the politics of engaging experts in the exercise of technocratic public power may operate is illustrated by Schrefler's own chapter, as well as the chapters in this volume by Everson on the EU method of employing regulatory power and the chapter by Knio on the de Larosière Commission, part of the system for EU financial supervision.[80] Everson, for instance, points to the radical scientification of the social which 'entails a negation, not of political steering capacity, but of political subjectivity itself'.[81] Lawrence makes a similar point with respect to the

[74] Werner, Chapter 3, Subedi, Chapter 12 and Handmaker and Mora, Chapter 13, all this volume.

[75] Andresen, Chapter 6, Siebenhüner, Chapter 7, Gupta, Chapter 8 (even if also more broadly), Herwig, Chapter 10 and Gruszczynski, Chapter 11, all this volume.

[76] Knio, Chapter 16, this volume.

[77] Klabbers, Chapter 5, Schrefler, Chapter 4, Everson, Chapter 15 and Busuioc, Chapter 18, all this volume.

[78] Werner, Chapter 3, this volume, at 62.

[79] Schrefler, Chapter 4, this volume, at 76.

[80] Knio, Chapter 16, this volume.

[81] Everson, Chapter 15, this volume, at 338.

WTO when she suggests that we need to critically rethink what this regime 'means in terms of our ability to participate in the system that governs us'.[82]

1.4 Are experts advisors, decision makers or irrelevant actors?

What answers have we found to the question that inspired this project? At the outset we can safely conclude that experts are not irrelevant, even if their input, in certain contexts or phases of decision-making processes, may not resound in the decisions that are taken.[83] From there on, the chapters in this book show that the answer to the question is: 'it depends', even within one organization. Lawrence, for example, shows that in the WTO experts of various disciplines are decision makers.[84] Herwig, however, illustrates that in the same WTO food safety experts who provide advice to the (expert) decision makers in the SPS Agreement and the Codex Alimentarius are best characterized as advisors, even if they exercise important roles in decision making.[85]

Overall, we conclude that in the variety of institutional settings, including privatized ones,[86] experts with a range of disciplinary backgrounds exert significant influence on decision making and on the formulation of the decisions taken. Their impact seems to be particularly influential where they participate in the exercise of regulatory powers, such as in the WTO and the EU. In these cases, they may act as de facto decision makers, even if de jure the decisions are taken by others.

These findings raise questions regarding how individuals and groups in society may gain influence over international and European decision-making processes involving experts. They also invite us to re-engage with politics, the politics of expertise in particular.

1.5 Mapping the book

The themes raised in this introductory chapter are explored further in the five parts of this book. The chapters in Part I theorize expert involvement in decision-making processes in general terms. Part I includes chapters by Peter Haas on epistemic communities; by Wouter Werner

[82] Lawrence, Chapter 9, this volume, at 193. [83] See text at note 67.
[84] Lawrence, Chapter 9, this volume. [85] Herwig, Chapter 10, this volume.
[86] Scholten and Terlow, Chapter 14 and Handmaker and Mora, Chapter 13, both this volume.

on the politics of expertise, including international legal experts; by Lorna Schrefler on the various roles that expertise plays in regulatory policy making; and by Jan Klabbers on the virtues of expertise.

The subsequent three parts explore the role of expertise in different international policy areas. Part II contains chapters on experts in international environmental regimes. Contributions to this part are by Steinar Andresen on the role of natural science expertise in multilateral environmental agreements; by Bernd Siebenhüner on organizational learning in the IPCC; and by Joyeeta Gupta on the development of a science–policy interface ladder. Part III focuses on the role of experts in the WTO. It contains contributions by Jessica Lawrence on expert participation in WTO decision-making processes; by Alexia Herwig on experts in decision making within the SPS Agreement and the Codex Alimentarius; and by Lukasz Gruszczynski on the role of experts in health-related trade disputes. Part IV focuses on experts in human rights related policy areas, with chapters by Surya Subedi on the UN system of special human rights mandate-holders; by Jeff Handmaker and Claudia Mora on the role of experts in defining irregular migration; and by Sophie Scholten and Ashley Terlouw on private carriers as experts in immigration control.

Finally, Part V focuses on experts and decision making in the EU. Two chapters take as their focal point the solutions to the financial crisis, with Michelle Everson analysing the traditional EU model of using a technology of expertise and Karim Knio discussing the de Larosière Commission. The other two chapters of this part consider the use of expertise in the EU more generally. Adriaan Schout and Jaap Sleifer focus on the interaction between European and national experts. Finally, Madelina Busuioc considers the approach taken by the Court of Justice of the European Union to the agencification process.

PART I

Theorizing expert involvement in international and European decision making

2

Ideas, experts and governance

PETER M. HAAS

> The ideas of economists and political philosophers, both when they are right and when they are wrong, are more powerful than is commonly understood. Indeed the world is ruled by little else. Practical men, who believe themselves to be quite exempt from any intellectual influence, are usually the slaves of some defunct economist. Madmen in authority, who hear voices in the air, are distilling their frenzy from some academic scribbler of a few years back. I am sure that the power of vested interests is vastly exaggerated compared with the gradual encroachment of ideas.
>
> (John Maynard Keynes, *The General Theory of Employment, Interest and Money* (1935), at 383)

2.1 Introduction

International relations have changed dramatically over the last 40 years. The international system has become more globalized and complex.[1] The growth in the number and types of actors, as well as the interdependence of their interactions, has led to a setting of increased uncertainty for decision makers regarding the nature of the policy environment, the consequences of their actions and the interests/preferences and even identity of their strategic partners. Concomitantly, constructivist analysis of international relations moved to take account of the ideas that shape individual and collective understandings of this new political landscape. Given that ideas provide the maps of the uncertain landscape of international journeys, the following

My thanks to the participants at the Conference on Experts for their comments on my preliminary presentation and to Ardeshir Pezeshk for illuminating discussions on this topic.

[1] U. Beck, *Risk Society* (London: Sage, 1992); R. Jervis, *System Effects* (Princeton University Press, 1997); D. Held, A. McGrew, D. Goldblatt and J. Perraton, *Global Transformations* (Stanford University Press, 1999); A. Giddens, *Runaway World* (London: Routledge, 2000).

question arises: which ideas are likely to be selected and by what mechanisms do they shape subsequent behaviour? With the spread of policy communities and substantive international regimes, it has increasingly become clear that the distribution of power and understandings varies from issue to issue. The key research questions are how do actors come to recognize the context in which they operate? What is the national interest, is cooperation necessary to achieve it, who should participate and what policies are appropriate to achieve the national goals?

Constructivism, as a theory of politics, provides a means of understanding and explaining contemporary events characterized by uncertainty and complexity. It is a research programme in international relations and comparative politics that focuses on broad questions of identity formation and collective understandings that guide choices through processes of social learning and normative deliberation.[2] It assumes that notions of identity and behavioural choices are formed through interactions with the international system[3] and that different actors shape frames of reference adopted by states and other political actors.[4] How actors perceive themselves and others is constructed through a variety of mechanisms. Constructivists focus on a number of primary mechanisms: language, social frames or narratives, theoretical blinders by analysts, causal arguments and normative arguments.

Here I focus primarily on the latter two constructivist factors – causal and normative arguments – as they involve agency and expertise in the creation of social frames in which problems are understood by analysts

[2] M. Blyth, 'Any More Bright Ideas? The Ideational Turn in Comparative Politics', *Comparative Politics*, 29 (1997), 229–50; J. G. Ruggie, 'What Makes the World Hang Together? Neo-utilitarianism and the Social Constructivist Challenge', *International Organization*, 52 (1998), 855–85; M. Blyth, 'Structures Do Not Come with an Instruction Sheet: Interests, Ideas, and Progress in Political Science', *Perspectives*, 1 (2003), 695–706; M. Blyth, 'Powering, Puzzling, or Persuading? The Mechanisms of Building Institutional Orders', *International Studies Quarterly*, 51 (2007), 761–77; V. Pouliot, '"Sobjectivism": Towards a Constructivist Methodology', *International Studies Quarterly*, 51 (2007), 359–84; R. Abdelal, M. Blyth and C. Parsons (eds.), *Constructing the International Economy* (Ithaca, NY: Cornell University Press, 2010); E. Adler, 'Seizing the Middle Ground: Constructivism in World Politics', *European Journal of International Relations*, 3 (1997), 319–63; S. Guzzini, 'A Reconstruction of Constructivism in International Relations', *European Journal of International Relations*, 6 (2000), 147–82.

[3] A. Wendt, 'The Agent-Structure Problem in International Relations Theory', *International Organization*, 41 (1987), 335–70; A. Wendt, 'Anarchy is What States Make of it', *International Organization*, 46 (1992), 391–425.

[4] P. M. Haas, 'Introduction: Epistemic Communities and International Policy Coordination', *International Organization*, 46 (1992), 1–37.

and actors, as well as the understanding by actors of their own goals and identities. This chapter concentrates more narrowly on the role of expertise: who is deemed responsible for articulating policy-relevant ideas in contemporary international relations. According to constructivists, experts interpret the world for decision makers and thus the governance arrangements which decision makers negotiate. While experts are the agents to the principal decision makers, the principals delegate a great deal of authority to and exercise minimal strategic control over them. This happens due to the principals' underlying lack of understanding about the policy space for which the experts are consulted. As a consequence, experts highlight issues for the agenda, frame the meaning of those issues relative to pre-existing issues, help to illuminate state interests, privilege policies and shape the international bargaining space through their influence over actors' preferences and the attendant payoff matrices. Experts potentially shape both the consequence and appropriateness for the principals who rely on their advice. While states remain the primary decision makers, framing and advice come from experts. Experts, moreover, often operate within transnational epistemic communities, in which they engage in learning processes with the aim of impacting international relations.

This chapter first provides a general argument about epistemic communities and their role in constructing international relations, and an intellectual history of their study. While epistemic communities arise nationally, their effects are stronger when they occur in multiple countries and in international organizations. Thus, they are seen as transnational actors, since the individuals act in concert with others in other countries or institutional venues. Thereafter, it contrasts two patterns of construction: the first one involves learning through epistemic communities in the domain of environmental protection, while the second one involves norm entrepreneurs and norm application in the area of human rights.

This chapter presents the concept of epistemic communities and the context in which insights about these communities were developed, i.e., constructivism. Its main claim is that in order to be influential, expertise needs to be organized and self-organized in terms of epistemic communities. The chapter furthermore differentiates experts who operate within epistemic communities and those who operate as norm entrepreneurs. International lawyers, I suggest, can be part of an epistemic community or norm entrepreneurs. Finally, section 2.4 addresses research frontiers.

2.2 Constructivism

Constructivism focuses on the multiple political and social processes by which actors in the international system seek to understand an ambiguous and confusing world. Katzenstein, Keohane and Krasner differentiate between radical and softer strands of constructivism.[5]

Radical constructivism considers the role of language in shaping collective understandings through the social development of broad ideas that rest on constitutive processes of actor deliberation, linguistic manipulation and language.[6] Alexander Wendt talks of 'turtles all the way down',[7] in which collective understanding is based on linguistic operations and deep-seated, taken-for-granted assumptions about the world, such as the immutable nature of anarchy and sovereignty.[8] Radical construction, with its origins in social theory, is summarized by Pouliot as follows:

> Constructivism constitutes a 'style of reasoning' of its own in social science . . . based on three tenets: first, that knowledge is socially constructed (an epistemological claim); second, social reality is constructed (an ontological claim); and third, knowledge and reality are mutually constitutive (a reflexive claim).[9]

Softer forms of constructivism focus on agency and the role of causal and normative ideas in guiding collective behaviour. They address the roles of actors in creating social facts and strategic choices through the use of rhetorical language and persuasion in order to bolster and institutionalize their prior worldviews.[10] Softer constructivism is more agnostic than its radical counterpart about the depth of its analysis. It maintains that not all ideas are fully socially constituted and that the social science analyst, as opposed to political actors, may not be as fully socially influenced, or at

[5] P. J. Katzenstein, R. O. Keohane and S. D. Krasner, 'International Organization and the Study of World Politics', *International Organization*, 52 (1998), 645–86.

[6] M. Shapiro (ed.), *Language and Politics* (New York University Press, 1984); F. V. Kratochwil, *Rules, Norms, and Decisions* (Cambridge University Press, 1989); S. Pinker, *The Stuff of Thought* (New York: Penguin, 2007); J. Friedrichs and F. Kratochwil, 'On Acting and Knowing', *International Organization*, 63 (2009), 701–32.

[7] A. Wendt, *Social Theory of International Politics* (Cambridge University Press, 1999), Chapter 3.

[8] T. Hopf, 'The Promise of Constructivism in International Relations Theory', *International Security*, 23 (1998), 171–200; Wendt, *Social Theory of International Politics*; Guzzini, 'A Reconstruction of Constructivism'.

[9] Pouliot, '"Sobjectivism"', at 361.

[10] Ruggie, 'What Makes the World Hang Together?', at 879.

least is influenced by different mechanisms.[11] While any interpretation of the social world is subject to prior social factors, these factors operate differently on political actors, such as diplomats, and on social science analysts, such as international relations scholars. Whereas diplomats pursue bureaucratic advancement and seek to accrue security and wealth for their countries, academics operate subject to the social influences of academic advancement and confirmation of their analysis.

The analysis of these different mechanisms (language, causal ideas and normative ideas) is difficult to synthesize, as it rests on incommensurate epistemological and ontological assumptions. Current research on European integration and identities captures many of the dynamics and theoretical approaches developed by both strands of constructivists.[12] This chapter employs a soft constructivism approach.

2.2.1 *Constructivism: the role of frames and science*

Constructivism has many independent origins. Philosophers and sociologists of science demonstrated that the world is not directly accessible, implying that our understanding of the world is mediated by pre-existing ideas about it.[13] Social psychology recognized the role of frames. Kenneth Boulding noted that conventional microeconomics assumes stable and fixed preferences, whereas preferences are in fact changeable and subject to social construction.[14] American pragmatism has elaborated the interplay between theorists and the world and has developed consensual models of knowledge accumulation through evolutionary epistemologies.[15] Robert Jervis and Janice Stein illustrated how foreign

[11] P. M. Haas and E. B. Haas, 'Pragmatic Constructivism and the Study of International Relations', *Millennium: Journal of International Studies*, 31 (2002), 573–601.

[12] B. Rosamond, 'Constructing Globalization' in K. M. Fierke and K. E. Jorgensen (eds.), *Constructing International Relations* (Armonk, NY: M. E. Sharpe, 2001), 201–19; N. Fligstein, *Euro-Clash* (Oxford University Press, 2008); J. A. Caporaso and S. Tarrow, 'Polanyi in Brussels', *International Organization*, 63 (2009), 593–620; J. T. Checkel and P. J. Katzenstein (eds.), *European Identity* (Cambridge University Press, 2009); T. Risse, *A Community of Europeans?* (Ithaca, NY: Cornell University Press, 2010).

[13] P. L. Berger and T. Luckmann, *The Social Construction of Reality* (New York: Doubleday Anchor, 1967); B. Holzner and J. H. Marx, *Knowledge Application: The Knowledge System in Society* (Boston: Allyn & Bacon, 1979).

[14] K. Boulding, *The Image: Knowledge in Life and Society* (Ann Arbor: University of Michigan Press, 1956), Chapter 6.

[15] S. Toulmin, *Human Understanding* (Princeton University Press, 1972); D. T. Campbell, *Methodologies and Epistemology for Social Sciences* (University of Chicago Press, 1988).

policy decision makers' perspectives varied from more objective descriptions of the policy environment, and how these perspectives shaped their decisions.[16] Research on cognitive maps and operational codes provided methodological techniques for demonstrating the internal logic of actors' belief systems.[17] Decision analysis revealed that actors make cognitive short-cuts when making choices, and thus purely rational models of political choice are incomplete and often irrelevant to describe the manner in which decisions are made. Subjective understanding, satisficing, discounting costs in prospect theory, framing and bounded rationality all play roles in making choices.[18] The policy studies literature complements decision analysis by focusing on the role of distinct sets of actors in representing the world in which decision makers find themselves.[19] Gramsci and Gramscian analysis focused on networks of transnational intellectuals in educating the populace and instructing the state.[20]

Social Studies of Knowledge (SSK) clarified that science enjoys a social cachet in the modern world and noted that the practice of scientific discovery seldom corresponded to the ideal type of the social method. Moreover, it showed that scientific justifications masked underlying normative commitments, largely through distributional consequences

[16] R. Jervis, *The Logic of Images in International Relations* (Princeton University Press, 1970); R. Jervis, *Perception and Misperception in International Politics* (Princeton University Press, 1976); J. G. Stein and R. Tanter, *Rational Decision-Making: Israel's Security Choices 1967* (Columbus: Ohio State University Press, 1980).

[17] O. Holsti, 'The "Operational Code": Approach to the Study of Political Leaders', *Canadian Journal of Political Science*, 3 (1970), 123–57; R. Axelrod, *Structure of Decision: The Cognitive Maps of Political Elites* (Princeton University Press, 1976); O. Holsti, *The 'Operational Code' as an Approach to the Analysis of Belief Systems* (Arlington, VA: National Science Foundation, 1977); S. G. Walker, 'Operational Code Analysis as a Scientific Research Program' in C. Elman and M. Elman (eds.), *Progress in International Relations Theory* (Cambridge, MA: MIT Press, 2003), 245–76.

[18] D. Braybrooke and C. E. Lindblom, *A Strategy of Decision* (New York: Free Press, 1963); D. Kahneman, P. Slovic and A. Tversky (eds.), *Judgment under Uncertainty: Heuristics and Biases* (Cambridge University Press, 1982); H. A. Simon, *Reason in Human Affairs* (Stanford University Press, 1983); H. A. Simon, 'Human Nature in Politics: The Dialogue of Psychology with Political Science', *American Political Science Review*, 79 (1985), 293–304; J. March, *A Primer on Decision Making: How Decisions Happen* (New York: Free Press, 1994).

[19] D. A. Stone, 'Causal Stories and the Formation of Policy Agendas', *Political Science Quarterly*, 104 (1989), 281–300; J. Kingdon, *Agendas, Alternatives and Public Policy* (Boston: Addison-Wesley, 1995).

[20] K. Mannheim, *Ideology and Utopia* (London: Routledge, 1936); S. Gill (ed.), *Gramsci, Historical Materialism and International Relations* (Cambridge University Press, 1993).

but also by accepting only the participation of more elite actors.[21] Still, most SSK writers recognize that there is a continuum between science and non-science: even if the scientific extreme in practice does not correspond to the version taught in primary school or even necessarily at universities, it does have stronger claims to impartiality than less scientific claims.

This broad literature review of constructivism's various strands underscores that political actors' understanding of the world is not objective, but subject to the influence of diverse social groups of experts. Still, it is possible to provide plausible hypotheses about the forms of construction that will occur and persist subject to the influence and beliefs of different groups, including groups of experts.

2.2.2 *The role of scientific expertise: domains of knowledge and governance*

We can conceive of different domains of knowledge in which construction occurs. In each domain there are different experts and social dynamics through which decisions and social construction are made.

Philosophers of science differentiate between domains of knowledge – each with its own dynamics.[22] They distinguish three such domains based on the nature of facts. *Brute facts* are those that are ultimately consensual observations supported by verification. This is where nature bites back, which is the traditional realm of natural science and engineering. *Hybrid facts* are those that stretch the reach of the expert community. This refers to the domain of knowledge where the implications of the beliefs exceed the technical groundwork on which the facts are built. For instance,

[21] M. Polanyi, 'The Republic of Science', *Minerva*, 1 (1962), 54–72; M. Foucault, *The Archaeology of Knowledge* (New York: Pantheon Books, 1972); B. Barnes and D. Edge, *Science in Context* (Cambridge, MA: MIT Press, 1982); S. Woolgar, *Science: The Very Idea* (London: Tavistock, 1988); S. Jasanoff and Society for Social Studies of Science, *Handbook of Science and Technology Studies* (Thousand Oaks, CA: Sage, 1995); B. Barnes, D. Bloor and J. Henry, *Scientific Knowledge: A Sociological Analysis* (University of Chicago Press, 1996); J. Ziman, *Real Science: What it is, and What it Means* (Cambridge University Press, 2000); S. Jasanoff, 'Technologies of Humility: Citizen Participation in Governing Science', *Minerva*, 41 (2003), 223–44; S. Jasanoff, *States of Knowledge: The Co-production of Science and Social Order* (New York: Routledge, 2004); S. Maasen and P. Weingart, 'What's New in Scientific Advice to Politics?' in S. Maasen and P. Weingart (eds.), *Democratization of Expertise?* (Dordrecht: Springer, 2005), 1–19.

[22] G. E. M. Anscombe, 'On Brute Facts', *Analysis*, 18 (1958), 69–72; R. Harre and P. Secord, *The Explanation of Social Behaviour* (Oxford: Blackwell, 1972); Kratochwil, *Rules, Norms, and Decisions.*

in the realm of ecology, experts may be asked to advise on sustainable limits to human activities or report on when ecosystems may be in danger.[23] Finally, *social facts* constitute the domain of knowledge that derives largely from the thoughts of observers of political processes. This domain relies on concepts we use routinely in offering descriptions and interpretations of political events and behaviour, yet they remain context-dependent and controversial within their policy arenas. Examples of social facts include democracy, the value of money and human rights.[24]

Different types of expertise are associated with each knowledge domain. In the land of brute and hybrid facts, science reigns,[25] while norm entrepreneurs operate in the field of social facts. Distinct and different political processes are associated with each set of actors. Scientific expertise thus has a widespread reputation for authority in domains of brute and hybrid facts.

Scientific expertise enjoys authority for both functional and historical reasons. Functionally, the social deployment of science and organized rigorous and systematic scientific-type thought (such as statistics) contributes to state control over domestic society through information and revenue generation.[26] Organized science and technology also contribute to modern wealth and power generation, and thus to national security and prosperity.[27] Historically, this social authority persists, despite widespread findings by the social studies of knowledge generation that the sociology of science often does not correspond to the norms of the scientific model, and that scientific claims are often co-produced in tandem with the needs of commercial and political patrons. Still, the political influence of science and scientific experts persists despite such academic challenges.[28]

[23] L. T. Tribe, C. Schelling and J. Voss, *When Values Conflict* (Cambridge, MA: Ballinger, 1976).

[24] A. Giddens, *The Constitution of Society* (Berkeley: University of California Press, 1984); J. Searle, *The Construction of Social Reality* (New York: Free Press, 1995).

[25] K. Knorr Cetina, 'Epistemic Cultures: Forms of Reason in Science', *History of Political Economy*, 23 (1991), 105–22; G. S. Drori, J. W. Meyer, F. O. Ramirez and E. Schofer, *Science in the Modern World Polity: Institutionalization and Globalization* (Stanford University Press, 2003); S. Maasen and P. Weingart (eds.), *Democratization of Expertise?* (Dordrecht: Springer, 2005); C. Camic, N. Gross and M. Lamong (eds.), *Social Knowledge in the Making* (University of Chicago Press, 2011).

[26] T. M. Porter, *The Rise of Statistical Thinking, 1820–1900* (Princeton University Press, 1986); I. Hacking, *The Taming of Chance* (Cambridge University Press, 1990).

[27] M. E. Mann, *The Sources of Social Power* (Cambridge University Press, 1993).

[28] W. E. Bijker, R. Bal and R. Hendriks (eds.), *The Paradox of Scientific Authority* (Cambridge, MA: MIT Press, 2009).

A number of distinctive features are associated with each of these domains of knowledge, including governance patterns and social mechanisms (or political dynamics), as is indicated in the following table.

Table 2.1 *Comparison of key features of epistemic and normative domains*[29]

Key features	Brute facts	Hybrid facts	Social facts
Primary actors	Epistemic communities		Social movements, norm entrepreneurs, transnational activist movements
Common political project	Yes		Yes
Causal beliefs	Shared		Disputed or absent
Shared principled beliefs	Yes		Yes
Shared truth tests	Yes		No
Boundaries between expert communities and decision makers	Relatively clear		Fuzzy
Internal homogeneity	Low		High
Means of changing the world/social mechanisms	Persuasion by facts and arguments Social learning		Persuasion and pressure by action and framing campaigning
Logic	Appropriateness and consequence		Appropriateness
Examples	Pollution control, macroeconomic coordination, nuclear strategy		Decolonization, apartheid, human rights, mercenaries, whaling, land mines, slavery, genocide, piracy
Governance pattern	Regulatory		Bans, moratoria, prohibition regimes
Social organization	Advisory panels, consultants		Advocacy networks, social movements

[29] Haas, 'Introduction: Epistemic Communities'; L. Dobusch and S. Quack, 'Epistemic Communities and Social Movements', *Max Planck Institut für Gesellschaftsforschung Discussion Paper 08/8* (2008), 10; M. K. Davis Cross, 'Rethinking Epistemic Communities Twenty Years Later', *Review of International Studies* (2012), 1–24.

In the brute and hybrid domain, epistemic communities provide authoritative expertise. They induce change in governance and behaviour through persuasion and patterns of social learning. Other actors become subject to their new causal advice through direct means of persuasion and through more indirect means by being subject to institutions created based on the new causal arguments, leading to broader patterns of convergent behaviour subject to the incentives and inducements generated by those institutions. Governance tends to be regulatory, based on deductive applications of scientific expertise in a particular domain. For instance, many environmental treaties apply a finely calibrated and differentiated set of commitments to different countries based on their different pollution profiles and the sensitivity of the ecosystems in question, such as the management of stratospheric ozone.

Social facts remain the domain of advocates and norm entrepreneurs.[30] Advocacy networks lack the internal socialized disciplinary beliefs that characterize epistemic communities. They operate more opportunistically through international networks of convenience around moments of political opportunity, sharing a common set of normative values, but without necessarily sharing any causal beliefs. Their political impact results from their efforts to deploy influence on a global and transnational scale. The governance outcomes of such pressure tends to lead to uniform bans and moratoria, based on their principled beliefs, rather than the more nuanced regulatory approach of epistemic communities.[31]

Law or international law as a field appears to be too abstract to fit the epistemic community mould.[32] Members do not fit the narrow definitions of an epistemic community and lack the broader social deference necessary to command influence. In addition, they lack the coherence of social beliefs and warrants for those beliefs held by scientists.[33] Instead, the influence of the legal community has been characterized as an

[30] M. Finnemore and K. Sikkink, 'International Norm Dynamics and Political Change', *International Organization*, 52 (1998), 887–917; M. Keck and K. Sikkink, *Activists Beyond Borders* (Ithaca, NY: Cornell University Press, 1998).

[31] E. A. Nadelmann, 'Global Prohibition Regimes', *International Organization*, 44 (1990), 479–526; W. Sandholtz and K. Stiles (eds.), *International Norms and Cycles of Change* (Oxford University Press, 2009).

[32] J. d'Aspremont (ed.), *Participants in the International Legal Systems* (London: Routledge, 2011); M. Noortmann, 'The International Law Association and Non-state Actors: Professional Network, Public Interest Group or Epistemic Community?' in J. d'Aspremont (ed.), *Participants in the International Legal Systems* (London Routledge, 2011), 233–47.

[33] Y. Dezalay and D. Sugarman (eds.), *Professional Competition and Professional Power* (London: Routledge, 1995).

interpretive community,[34] an invisible college[35] and argumentative practices.[36] Political science studies of international law tend to treat international law as an extension of political theory, and thus a class of normative and advocacy governance conducted in the zone of social facts.[37] In practice, individual lawyers may be part of epistemic communities or operate as norm entrepreneurs. In their systematic treatment of regulatory regimes, Braithwaite and Drahos conclude that 'really interesting lawyers'[38] operate as normative leaders and entrepreneurs or in conjunction with epistemic communities whose ideas they help to codify into legal commitments.

2.3 Epistemic communities[39]

2.3.1 Characteristics and collective learning

Epistemic communities are networks of knowledge-based communities with an authoritative claim to policy-relevant knowledge within their domain of expertise. They are the agents of constructivism in the domain of brute and hybrid facts. Their members share knowledge about the causation of social or physical phenomena in an area for which they have a reputation for competence, and a common set of normative beliefs about what actions will benefit human welfare. In particular, they are a group of professionals, often from a number of different disciplines, who share the following set of characteristics:[40]

(1) Shared principled beliefs which provide a value-based rationale for social action of the members of the community.

[34] I. Johnstone, 'Treaty Interpretation: The Authority of Interpretive Communities', *Michigan Journal of International Law*, 12 (1990), 371–419.

[35] O. Schachter, 'The Invisible College of International Lawyers', *Northwestern University Law Review*, 72 (1977), 217–26.

[36] M. Koskenniemi, 'The Politics of International Law', *European Journal of International Law*, 1 (1990), 4–32.

[37] C. Beitz, *Political Theory and International Relations* (Princeton University Press, 1979); T. Nardin, *Law, Morality and the Relations of States* (Princeton University Press, 1983).

[38] J. Braithwaite and P. Drahos, *Global Business Regulation* (Cambridge University Press, 2000), 502.

[39] This section is drawn from P. M. Haas, 'Epistemic Communities' in J. Krieger (ed.), *The Oxford Companion to International Relations* (2013), 351–9.

[40] P. M. Haas, 'Do Regimes Matter? Epistemic Communities and Mediterranean Pollution Control', *International Organization*, 43 (1989), 377–403; P. M. Haas, *Saving the Mediterranean: The Politics of International Environmental Cooperation* (New York: Columbia University Press, 1990); Haas, 'Introduction: Epistemic Communities'.

(2) Shared causal beliefs or professional judgements which provide analytic reasons and explanations of behaviour, and offer causal explanations for the multiple links between possible policy actions and desired outcomes.
(3) Common notions of validity which provide intersubjective, internally defined criteria for validating knowledge and allow community members to differentiate between warranted and unwarranted claims about states of the world and policies to change those states.
(4) A common policy enterprise consisting of a set of practices associated with a central set of problems which have to be tackled, presumably out of a conviction that human welfare will be enhanced as a consequence.

The interplay of these characteristics is vital for the social and political influence of epistemic communities. The internal consensus, according to intra-community standards, provides the glue for collective action amongst the individuals of the community. The validation of their claims, according to external social standards, provides the political legitimation for their continued involvement.[41] Peer review, non-political appointment based on merit to authoritative panels, publications and training provide some of the warrants for their authority. Their track record, which is publicly available because of the social norm of peer review and publications, provides an ongoing warrant for their reputation for expertise and impartiality.[42]

'Epistemic communities' is a concept applied by constructivist political science scholars to focus analytic attention on the process by which states formulate interests and reconcile differences of interest. Epistemic communities are a principal channel through which consensual knowledge about causal understandings is applied to international policy coordination and by which states may learn through processes of international cooperation.

John Ruggie introduced the term *episteme*, borrowed from Foucault, to describe the overarching perspective through which political relationships are visualized and understood.[43] Ruggie depicted epistemic communities as the social whole of beliefs at a particular moment, rather than

[41] P. M. Haas, 'When Does Power Listen to Truth? A Constructivist Approach to the Policy Process', *Journal of European Public Policy*, 11 (2004), 569–92.
[42] Noortmann, 'The International Law Association and Non-state Actors', at 239.
[43] J. G. Ruggie, 'International Responses to Technology', *International Organization*, 29 (1975), 557–83, at 569–70.

the more agentic view developed here. The idea of epistemic communities as agents started its journey in the winter 1992 issue of *International Organization* (*IO*), which concentrated on the actors responsible for articulating and aggregating knowledge-based understanding in the areas of security, environment and international political economy.[44] The *IO* issue developed the now-standard four-element definition of an epistemic community provided above.

By analysing epistemic communities, constructivist scholars gained leverage on understanding the processes of social construction and collective learning. Epistemic communities are associated with distinctive patterns of social change that involve persuasion and learning. Given the complexity of contemporary international relations and the uncertainty that this complexity creates, state interests are often unknown or incompletely specified. International relations then become a matter of applying embedded and institutionalized beliefs about the nature of problems and the appropriate means of collective response, rather than a process of resolving rationally formulated state preferences, as argued by many international relations theorists.[45] Changes in information processing are likely to follow well-publicized shocks or crises. Only at such times are decision makers likely to recognize major anomalies and pursue new policy patterns. During less revolutionary periods, these new doctrines or orthodoxies assume the status of taken-for-granted assumptions, which persist until called into question by external stimuli. Because of the disjointed equilibrium nature of policy change, an evolutionary focus on institutional learning[46] and path dependence may provide an appropriate model for understanding international recognition of and response to global change. Such an approach may provide a better understanding of factors which influence the introduction of new policy frames, collective understandings or doctrines, as well as illuminating mechanisms of lock-in and identifying those factors which may influence the degree of irreversibility of national and collective actions.

Epistemic communities aggregate and articulate knowledge in terms of state interests for decision makers and disseminate those beliefs internationally. They provide one of the major channels through which

[44] Haas, 'Introduction: Epistemic Communities'; P. M. Haas (ed.), *Knowledge, Power and International Policy Coordination* (Columbia: University of South Carolina Press, 1997).

[45] Katzenstein, Keohane and Krasner, 'International Organization and the Study of World Politics'.

[46] Siebenhüner, Chapter 7, this volume.

overarching regime principles, norms and rules are articulated for the international community and are disseminated internationally. The extent to which principles, norms and rules become more deeply diffused and embedded internationally depends on the political influence of epistemic community members: their ability to persuade others, their ability to consolidate bureaucratic influence in important institutional venues and their ability to retain and wield influence over time. State interests and decisions to deploy state power are thus identified subject to consensual knowledge.

The epistemic community literature is now nearly thirty years old. The concept was initially favourably received in international relations because it provided a means for focusing on the ideational component of politics and allowed for agency in theorizing about governance, decision making and policy making. Since its initial reception, analysts have developed clarifications, refined hypotheses, continued empirical work and provided empirical confirmation of the predicted social patterns associated with epistemic communities.

2.3.2 Reception

Initial critiques of the work on epistemic communities by political scientists called for a clearer theory of the state[47] and the role of domestic politics in mediating the reception of transnational epistemic communities.[48] The need to develop a clearer metric by which epistemic communities could be recognized and consensus within an epistemic community measured was also identified.

SSK literature critically regarded the degree of political autonomy enjoyed by epistemic communities. This literature also challenged the normative and consequentialist value of science-based arguments in general for public policy, questioning the political consequences of such ideas and emphasizing the potential implicit political bias in research programmes pursued by epistemic community members.[49] It

[47] H. Milner, 'International Theories of Cooperation among Nations', *World Politics*, 44 (1992), 466–96.

[48] T. Risse-Kappen, 'Ideas Do Not Float Freely: Transnational Coalitions, Domestic Structures, and the End of the Cold War', *International Organization*, 48 (1994), 185–214.

[49] K. Litfin, *Ozone Discourses: Science and Politics in Global Environmental Cooperation* (New York: Columbia University Press, 1994); K.T. Litfin, 'Framing Science: Precautionary Discourse and the Ozone Treaties', *Millennium: Journal of International Studies*, 24 (1995), 251–77; V. Walsh, *Global Institutions and Social Knowledge: Generating Research at the Scripps Institution and the Inter-American Tropical Tuna Commission, 1900s–1990s* (Cambridge, MA: MIT Press, 2004).

was feared that epistemic communities might be anti-democratic and anti-participatory by depoliticizing expertise and the consequences of expert-based advice.[50] Because epistemic communities are responsible for simplifying a complex and ambiguous policy environment, critics felt that analysis should focus on the resolution of contention within the knowledge space of epistemic communities rather than on the consensual beliefs of these communities. Similarly, because epistemic knowledge includes that which a community's members agree about and that which they disagree and remain uncertain about, critics called for closer attention to the extent that epistemic knowledge was contested within its own community.

Many of these critical points were acknowledged in the initial formulation of the epistemic community research programme, under the heading of the political nature of all policy debate. The epistemic community argument recognized that all policy advice reflects hidden assumptions and biases and has distributional effects, and thus is subject to normative scrutiny. However, the argument was also that epistemic communities ultimately provided *better substantive* advice than other modes of policy advice, because of the internal consensual processes, based on integrity and peer review,[51] by which they develop claims. These internal processes also result in advice that is more likely to be usable and applied in practice because it is politically untainted and is therefore more likely to 'work', in the political sense that it will be embraced by political authorities concerned about being impartial. Epistemic community advice is also more likely to be technically effective in the sense of obtaining the desired goals while balancing economic and technical trade-offs than negotiated approaches to policy making based on political compromise. Analytically, the epistemic community approach offered a causal pathway by which ideas came to inform political practices. This approach is superior to conventional approaches to the study of politics that are unable to provide credible explanations for how ideas influence politics or the conditions under which ideas are likely to be influential.

[50] S. Jasanoff, 'Science and Norms in International Environmental Regimes' in F. O. Hampson and J. Reppy (eds.), *Earthly Goods* (Ithaca, NY: Cornell University Press, 1996), 173–97; Maasen and Weingart (eds.), *Democratization of Expertise?*; Maasen and Weingart, 'What's New in Scientific Advice to Politics?'; S. Jasanoff, 'Climate Science: The World is its Jury' in Transparency International, *2010 Global Corruption Report: Climate Change* (London: Earthscan, 2011).

[51] Klabbers, Chapter 5, this volume.

As they are social collectivities, it is not always easy to identify the members of epistemic communities. Members may be identified through interviews, secondary literature (especially by journalists) and by cross-checking membership lists for international negotiations and consultations over time. Recurrent names are eligible candidates. Snow-ball techniques, in which prospective members identify others with whom they think they share beliefs, also serve to identify members of epistemic communities. The content and development of the consensual knowledge shared by epistemic community members can be ascertained through their publications and conducting open-ended interviews with them. Because epistemic communities are defined by their shared beliefs, the extent of tolerable contestation and consensus is a matter of community belief and is ascertained by the internal norms and practices of the epistemic community in question. The causal mechanisms by which they exercise influence – *learning* – can be understood by process-tracing, focused comparative case studies, counterfactuals and alternative hypothesis testing. More recent methodological advances in network analysis[52] and bibliometric studies offer fruitful techniques for identifying epistemic community members and depicting the connections between members of the community, although not for tracking their influence.

2.3.3 Refinements

A number of refinements and clarifications to the original research programme were undertaken, leading to a richer political understanding of the role of causal ideas in world politics. Haas,[53] Dunlop[54] and Antoniades[55] refined and clarified assumptions, including the following concepts and claims. States are key juridical actors and act wilfully. States are functionally differentiated and vary widely according to their state–society relations and their capacity to formulate and enforce public policies in technical domains. States operate in a complex policy

[52] C. Roth, S. Obiedkov and D. G. Kourie, 'Towards Concise Representation for Taxonomies of Epistemic Communities', *Lecture Notes in Computer Science*, 4923 (2008), 240–55.

[53] P. M. Haas, 'Epistemic Communities and Policy Knowledge' in *International Encyclopedia of Social and Behavioral Sciences* (New York: Elsevier, 2001), 11578–86.

[54] C. Dunlop, 'Epistemic Communities: A Reply to Toke', *Politics*, 20 (2000), 137–44.

[55] A. Antoniades, 'Epistemic Communities, Epistemes and the Construction of (World) Politics', *Global Society*, 17 (2003), 21–38.

environment and value information about this environment. Yet, knowledge is asymmetrically distributed within and between countries. Finally, while perceptions are socially constructed, political actors and social science experts are not subject to the same set of influences.[56]

Stronger hypotheses about the mechanisms, effects and variation of epistemic communities' influence were also developed. Epistemic communities are likely to be found in issue areas where scientific disciplines have been applied to policy making and in countries with well-established institutional capacities for administration, science and technology. Governments with such capacities are likely to value the technical skills which epistemic community members command. Moreover, such professionals would only enter governmental service when they believe that it will further their policy enterprise.

It has been hypothesized that crises or widely publicized shocks are probably necessary precipitants of international regime creation, but crises alone are insufficient to explain how or which collective responses are likely to develop. Epistemic communities subsequently help identify cause-and-effect relationships, elucidate interlinks between problems, define the consulting state's or organization's interests, and formulate policy. Their aggregate influence depends upon the extent to which their ideas become embedded in influential multilateral institutions more generally: powerful countries and international institutions, and possibly non-governmental organizations (NGOs), who will deploy their own influence to disseminate the ideas developed by an epistemic community. Overall, learning will occur in the policy system as new policy-relevant knowledge is identified and applied to a common problem.

The ideas generated by epistemic communities are likely to be received more warmly in rich democratic societies, where scientific capacity and the free flow of information are high. However, other countries may also be receptive to epistemic communities' ideas, but not as quickly. For instance, with regard to pollution control in the Mediterranean, the first adopters of epistemic communities and their beliefs were in Israel, Greece, France and the United Nations Environment Programme (UNEP), while later adopters included Algeria and Egypt.[57] Similarly, treaties developed with a strong contribution from epistemic communities may enter into force more rapidly than those developed through other political mechanisms, as the social

56 Haas and Haas, 'Pragmatic Constructivism'.

57 Haas, 'Do Regimes Matter?'; Haas, *Saving the Mediterranean*.

influence of epistemic community members will accelerate ratification in domestic legislative venues.[58]

Insights into when the ideas generated by epistemic communities are likely to be influential have been provided by the economic historian Paul David.[59] David points to the role of state capacity and the political economy of knowledge. Public acceptance of scientific expertise, and thus the external authority enjoyed by an epistemic community, is a function of the cost of research and a sign of the relevance of the research to the core mission of the sponsoring agency. Thus, in areas where the cost is relatively small and the relevance is far from the core mission of the sponsor, the independence of researchers and the epistemic community is greater and they are thus likely to be seen as more legitimate.

Multiple mechanisms of diffusion are possible through various international channels at different political scales, involving inducements, coercion, learning and persuasion, and market responses to price changes.[60] Epistemic communities remain a necessary component for learning within a broader pattern of policy diffusion. For instance, in stratospheric ozone protection the regulatory scheme arose from atmospheric chemists, but the new technologies to satisfy those regulations emerged through the interplay of multinational corporations (such as DuPont, ATOCHEM and ICI), international institutions (the Montreal Ozone Protocol's technical advisory panels and the Montreal Ozone Fund) and NGOs (most notably Greenpeace).

International organizations can play a role in popularizing and disseminating the ideas of epistemic communities. International organizations that are insulated from the influence of member states and enjoy bureaucratic resources (such as an adept executive head, adequate budgets and a professional staff recruited by merit) play a strong role in disseminating epistemic ideas.[61] They subsequently affect the practices of other international

[58] B. I. Spector and A. R. Korula, 'Problems of Ratifying International Environmental Agreements', *Global Environmental Change*, 3 (1993), 369–81.

[59] P. Dasgupta and P. A. David, 'Toward a New Economics of Science', *Research Policy*, 23 (1994), 487–521; P. A. David, 'Reputation and Agency in the Historical Emergence of the Institutions of "Open Science"', paper presented to the National Academy of Sciences Colloquium on the Economics of Science and Technology, held at the Beckman Center, UC Irvine, 20–21 October 1995.

[60] B. Simmons and Z. Elkins, 'On Waves, Clusters and Diffusion', *Annals of the American Academy of Political and Social Sciences*, 598 (2005), 33–51; B. Simmons, F. Dobbin and G. Garret, 'Introduction: The International Diffusion of Liberalism', *International Organization*, 60 (2006), 781–810.

[61] P. M. Haas and E. B. Haas, 'Learning to Learn: Improving International Governance', *Global Governance*, 1 (1995), 255–85; C. N. Murphy, *The United Nations Development Programme*

organizations, international regimes and state expectations, interests and practices.[62] However, the mechanisms of influence by which international organizations deploy epistemic ideas vary by target.[63]

2.3.4 *Applications*

Efforts to apply the epistemic communities' research programme have spanned a variety of topics, at times blurring the distinction between studying the role of expertise and experts' ideas.

Epistemic communities have been causally implicated in the formation and persistence of international regimes, including the nineteenth-century free trade regime.[64]

Without the presence of epistemic communities, negotiated outcomes remain possible, but will not involve learning, will be narrow in scope and will not lead to recursive learning processes by which states continue to pursue more comprehensive goals across other related international regimes and policy domains. More recently, epistemic community members have played a strong role in negotiating international environmental agreements. Hypotheses that epistemic communities cause distinctive patterns of epistemic collective action through social learning were confirmed by focused comparative case studies of a wide array of multilateral environmental regimes.[65] Members of the epistemic community

(Cambridge University Press, 2006); B. Siebenhuner, 'Learning in International Organizations in Global Environmental Governance', *Global Environmental Politics*, 8 (2008), 92–116; F. Biermann and B. Siebenhuner (eds.), *Managers of Global Change* (Cambridge, MA: MIT Press, 2009).

62 E. B. Haas, *When Knowledge is Power: Three Models of Change in International Organizations* (Berkeley: University of California Press, 1990); Haas and Haas, 'Learning to Learn'.

63 P. M. Haas, 'Lessons from Environmental Governance for Debt Forgiveness' in V. K. Aggarwal (ed.), *Sovereign Debt, Origins, Crises and Restructuring* (London: Royal Institute of International Affairs, 2003), 255–80.

64 R. Rothstein, 'Consensual Knowledge and International Collaboration', *International Organization*, 38 (1984), 733–62; J. Bhagwati, *Protectionism* (Cambridge, MA: MIT Press, 1989).

65 E. B. Weiss and H. K. Jacobson, *Engaging Countries: Strengthening Compliance with International Accords* (Cambridge, MA: MIT Press, 1998); S. Andresen, T. Skodvin, A. Underdal and J. Wettestad, *Science and Politics in International Environmental Regimes* (Manchester University Press, 2000); E. L. Miles, A. Underdal, S. Andresen, J. Wettestad, J. B. Skjærseth and E. M. Carlin (eds.), *Environmental Regime Effectiveness: Confronting Theory with Evidence* (Cambridge, MA: MIT Press, 2002); P. M. Haas, 'Epistemic Communities' in D. Bodansky, J. Brunnee and E. Hey (eds.), *Oxford Handbook of International Environmental Law* (Oxford University Press, 2007), 791–806; P. M. Haas, 'Environment: Pollution' in P. J. Simmons and C. De Jong Oudraat (eds.), *Managing a Globalized World* (Washington DC: Carnegie Foundation, 2001), 310–53.

who have dominated technical discussions in environmental regimes have subscribed to holistic ecological beliefs about the need for policy coordination subject to ecosystemic laws. They promote international environmental regimes which are grounded on policies offering coherent plans for the management of entire ecosystems, sensitive to interactions between environmental media (such as air and water), sources of pollution and contending uses of common property resources, rather than being limited to more traditional policies for managing discrete activities or physical resources spaces within fairly short-term time horizons. Epistemically informed collective action has a distinctively comprehensive form and is politically resilient, yielding patterns that are not associated with political dynamics involving any other sets of political actors. Moreover, epistemically informed treaties are more likely to be effective because the regulatory standards fit the behaviour of the socio-ecosystem being managed.

Further studies of international institutions refined the characteristics of formal international organizations that are likely to absorb the lessons of epistemic communities and to disseminate them. Design principles for international scientific panels were also identified.[66]

The EU has been a particularly ripe area for epistemic community studies. This is not surprising, given the relatively high socio-economic status of the countries involved and the multilevel governance structures that should be hospitable to epistemic community influences. To mention a few, epistemic communities have been associated with negotiated policies for drug policy,[67] monetary policy and the European Monetary Union (EMU),[68] environmental policy,[69] agricultural policy[70] and legal convergence.[71]

[66] Haas, 'When Does Power Listen to Truth?'; P. M. Haas and C. Stevens, 'Organized Science, Usable Knowledge and Multilateral Environmental Governance' in R. Lidskog and G. Sundqvist (eds.), *Governing the Air* (Cambridge, MA: MIT Press, 2011), 125–61.

[67] M. Elvins, *Anti-drugs Policy of the European Union: Transnational Decision-Making and the Politics of Expertise* (Basingstoke: Palgrave Macmillan, 2003).

[68] A. Verdun, 'The Role of the Delors Committee in the Creation of the EMU: An Epistemic Community?', *Journal of European Public Policy*, 6 (1999), 308–28.

[69] A. R. Zito, 'Epistemic Communities, Collective Entrepreneurship and European Integration', *Journal of European Public Policy*, 8 (2001), 585–603.

[70] W. D. Coleman and A. Perl, 'Institutionalized Policy Environments and Policy Network Analysis', *Political Studies*, 47 (1999), 691–709.

[71] F. van Waarden and M. Drahos, 'Courts and (Epistemic) Communities in the Convergence of Competition Models', *Journal of European Public Policy*, 9 (2002), 913–34.

The transnational diffusion of national policies and regulatory standards clearly bears the imprint of epistemic communities. Such studies include Keynesianism,[72] public health doctrines,[73] accounting standards,[74] legal doctrines and interpretations,[75] pension reform,[76] privatization,[77] human development,[78] and the Washington Consensus and macroeconomic responses to financial crises.[79]

National policy choice has been analysed in terms of epistemic community involvement, in particular their independence from broad political goals of the state and from domestic interest groups. Studies have looked at pension reforms in Sweden[80] and economic reform in Latin America.[81]

Epistemic communities have been subject to some conceptual stretching, including applications to diplomacy and appropriate state behaviour,[82] religious actors and conflict resolution,[83] and futurists.[84]

[72] J. K. Galbraith, 'How Keynes Came to America' in *Economics, Peace and Laughter* (Boston: Houghton Mifflin Company, 1971), 43–59; P. A. Hall (ed.), *The Political Power of Economic Ideas* (Princeton University Press, 1989).

[73] R. N. Cooper, 'International Cooperation in Public Health as a Prologue to Macroeconomic Cooperation' in R. N. Cooper, B. Eichengreen, C. R. Henning, G. Holtham, R. D. Putnam and C. R. Henning, *Can Nations Agree?: Issues in International Economic Cooperation* (Washington DC: Brookings Institution, 1989), 178–254.

[74] Dezalay and Sugarman (eds.), *Professional Competition and Professional Power*.

[75] Y. Dezalay and B. G. Garth, *Internationalization of Palace Wars* (University of Chicago Press, 2002); A.-M. Slaughter, *A New World Order* (Princeton University Press, 2004).

[76] M. Orenstein, *Privatizing Pensions: The Transnational Campaign for Social Security Reform* (Princeton University Press, 2008).

[77] B. Kogut and J. M. MacPherson, 'The Decision to Privatize: Economists and the Construction of Ideas and Policies' in B. A. Simmons, F. Dobbin and G. Garret (eds.), *The Global Diffusion of Markets and Democracy* (Cambridge University Press, 2008), 104–40.

[78] M. ul Haq, *Reflections on Human Development* (Oxford University Press, 1995).

[79] J. Williamson and S. Haggard, 'The Political Conditions for Economic Reform' in J. Williamson (ed.), *The Political Economy of Reform* (Washington DC: Institute for International Economics, 1994), 527–96; C. Gore, 'The Rise and Fall of the Washington Consensus as a Paradigm for Developing Countries', *World Development*, 28 (2000), 789–804.

[80] P. Marier, 'Empowering Epistemic Communities', *West European Politics*, 31 (2008), 513–33.

[81] K. Weyland, 'Theories of Policy Diffusion', *World Politics*, 57 (2005), 262–95; E. Dargent, 'Agents or Actors? Assessing the Autonomy of Economic Technocrats in Colombia and Peru', *Comparative Politics*, 43 (2011), 313–32.

[82] M. K. Davis Cross, *The European Diplomatic Corps* (Basingstoke: Palgrave Macmillan, 2007).

[83] N. A. Sandal, 'Religious Actors as Epistemic Communities in Conflict Transformation', *Review of International Studies*, 37 (2010), 929–49.

[84] R. Cinquegrani, 'Futurist Networks: Cases of Epistemic Communities?', *Futures*, 34 (2002), 779–83.

The ideational focus was absorbed into the broader constructivist research programme developed in international relations and comparative politics, which looked at the role of beliefs and ideas in shaping state interests and practices, with epistemic communities serving as one of the mechanisms by which new ideas are developed and circulated.[85] Whereas social construction occurs through multiple causal pathways, the causal knowledge provided by epistemic communities contributes analytically distinct outcomes of new and better environmental management that is robust and resilient.

2.3.5 Applying constructivism to different epistemological domains: epistemic and normative governance in environmental and human rights

The cases of environmental and human rights governance help to clarify the difference between patterns of epistemic and normative governance, with norm entrepreneurs playing an important role in the latter.

Multilateral environmental governance encompasses hundreds of treaties and dozens of international regimes. These governance arrangements fall into two broad classes: regulatory and prohibitionary. Environmental regulatory efforts – such as stratospheric ozone, the Mediterranean, and European acid rain – are cases with active involvement of epistemic communities.[86] In the absence of epistemic communities, environmental governance occurs through other means. Advocacy groups promote prohibitionary regimes such as whaling. More traditional state-based diplomacy yields patterns of regimes based on weak hortatory language, without commitment, such as the United Nations Framework Convention on Climate Change, or political compromise, such as the North Sea regime. Regulatory regimes occur through a process of learning as epistemic communities help draft treaties and persuade governments of the need for more effective governance based on their estimates of environmental sustainability. The institutions influenced by the epistemic communities – at the national and international levels – then help to diffuse those ideas, leading to broader

85 Katzenstein, Keohane and Krasner, 'International Organization and the Study of World Politics'.

86 Andresen, Chapter 6, this volume; Andresen et al., *Science and Politics in International Environmental Regimes*; Miles et al. (eds.), *Environmental Regime Effectiveness*; Haas, 'Epistemic Communities'.

patterns of environmental regulation within the specific governance area. Over time, a more diffuse and higher order form of social learning may occur, as decision makers become more accustomed to dealing with complexity and delegating to epistemic communities, thus leading to the recognition of systemic links and greater policy links between issues (such as trade and environment, or environment and security).

Conversely, human rights governance occurs through processes of political pressure deployed by advocacy coalitions based on normative justifications.[87] While human rights discourse has spread dramatically since the Second World War, the degree to which it has influenced government practice is modest at best. Comparative studies show that changes in practice largely occur before signing an international human rights treaty and in regions (such as Europe and North America) where norms preceded international law.[88] Case studies demonstrate that human rights ideas are adopted through the intervention of entrepreneurial individuals who use their institutional foundations to apply their ideas to governance. Sikkink's study, for example, shows how in Argentina, Portugal and Spain, changes in the administration of human rights law occurred via domestic political processes that required a change in policy, combined with the individual efforts by jurists to promote a human rights agenda outside and within the courts.[89]

These two cases illustrate the different patterns of governance operating in different epistemic domains. The human rights case illustrates how ideas in the social epistemic domain are promoted by norm entrepreneurs and are adopted and applied through more conventional political mechanisms of institutional power. The environment cases illustrate how epistemic communities, in the epistemic domain of brute and hybrid facts, persuade political leaders to pursue new policies based on a political process of persuasion and learning.

[87] T. Risse, S. C. Ropp and K. Sikkink (eds.), *The Power of Human Rights* (Cambridge University Press, 1999); H. P. Schmitz and K. Sikkink, 'Human Rights' in W. Carlsnaes, T. Risse and B. A. Simmons (eds.), *Handbook of International Relations* (London: Sage, 2002), 517–37; B. A. Simmons, *Mobilizing for Human Rights* (Cambridge University Press, 2009); K. Sikkink, *The Justice Cascade* (New York: Norton, 2011).

[88] E. M. Hafner-Burton and J. Ron, 'Seeing Double: Human Rights Impact through Qualitative and Quantitative Eyes', *World Politics*, 61 (2009), 360–401; J. R. Hollyer and P. Rosendorff, 'Why Do Authoritarian Regimes Sign the Convention against Torture?', *Quarterly Journal of Political Science*, 6 (2011), 275–327.

[89] Sikkink, *The Justice Cascade*.

2.4 Conclusion: research frontiers

More recent publications in the epistemic communities' research programme have examined the context in which epistemic communities arise and operate. Current work seeks to clarify the institutional factors that shape or amplify ideational consensus and dissemination, the factors that influence the creation of relatively impartial and usable scientific advice, and tries to separate the causal mechanisms of social learning from other causal mechanisms that drive collective action.

The epistemic community research programme during the past thirty years has generated significant insights into how ideas shape international regulatory regimes. The programme has thereby also contributed to the development of constructivism as a means of analysing how international actors make sense of the ambiguous and confusing world in which they operate. Yet, under-studied areas remain, and it is these areas that will be the focus of the remaining paragraphs of this chapter.

The social construction of catalysing crises remains under-theorized. While a crisis can easily be identified *ex post* as a catalyst of change, we do not have a strong understanding *ex ante* of how or why actors recognize that a set of events constitute a crisis.

More focus might also be devoted to explaining which epistemic community (or communities) will prevail and when. Most work has considered the situation where one epistemic community was superseded by another, following repudiation by events. Little attention has been paid to reconciling contending knowledge claimants.[90] While hypotheses have been raised about the factors likely to influence the attractiveness of a particular epistemic community and its ideas to decision makers at moments of crisis,[91] these are all grounded on fixed unitary state preferences. They do not account for differential pressures within states. The US decision to radically attack ozone depletion in 1985 in the face of steadfast opposition by top levels of the US administration

[90] J. Youde, 'The Development of a Counter-Epistemic Community: AIDS, South Africa, and International Regimes', *International Relations*, 19 (2005), 421–39.

[91] J. S. Odell, 'Understanding International Trade Policies: An Emerging Synthesis', *World Politics*, 43 (1990), 139–67; G. Garrett and B. Weingast, 'Ideas, Interests and Institutions: Constructing the European Community's Internal Market' in J. Goldstein and R. O. Keohane (eds.), *Ideas and Foreign Policy* (Ithaca, NY: Cornell University Press, 1993), 173–206; J. Goldstein, *Ideas, Interests and American Trade Policy* (Ithaca, NY: Cornell University Press, 1993); M. Kahler, 'Rationality in International Relations', *International Organization*, 52 (1998), 919–41.

is a powerful anomaly for such conventional hypotheses.[92] One could ask why environmental scientific experts have tended to prevail over economists in all environmental issues other than climate change, or how in the realm of economics the Chicago School and the Washington Consensus approaches have varied in their national uptake.

Other research frontiers include a closer study of anomalous cases of failed epistemic communities – such as desertification and whaling – as well as the larger scale dynamics by which social learning leads to understandings of world politics and interdependence, and identifies formation and reformation. A closer study of the international whaling regime would shed light on the conditions under which normative approaches prevail over regulatory approaches. A deeper concern is the ontological setting of the epistemic community's project and its claim to expertise. A major backlash to scientific authority is occurring in the USA, as a rhetorical move to unseat the authority of the experts responsible for promoting environmental regulation. After the IPCC and Al Gore were awarded the 2007 Nobel Prize, conservative political groups in the USA and the UK heightened their efforts to undermine the authority of climate science, but also of science as a source of authority more generally.[93] Walter Russell Mead speaks of a deeper generational shift in American attitudes towards a populist epistemology that replaces social deference with reliance on individual experience as a warrant for claims about managing complexity.[94]

92 Haas, 'Introduction: Epistemic Communities'.

93 N. Oreskes and E. M. Conway, *Merchants of Doubt* (New York: Bloomsbury, 2010); R. S. Bradley, *Global Warming and Political Intimidation* (Amherst: University of Massachusetts Press, 2011).

94 W. R. Mead, 'The Tea Party and American Foreign Policy: What Populism Means for Globalism', *Foreign Affairs*, 90 (2011), 28–44.

3

The politics of expertise: applying paradoxes of scientific expertise to international law

WOUTER G. WERNER

3.1 Introduction

Today, world politics has become the politics of international law as well. Increasingly, political decisions are framed and assessed in international legal terms, coalitions formed or broken up in the name of international law, and international courts and tribunals implicated in intense political disputes.[1] The legalization of world politics, in other words, has been accompanied by new forms of legalistic politics. As a consequence, international legal expertise has become a valuable currency for those engaged in the struggles for power and influence. Legal experts provide an increasingly relevant vocabulary to convince allies, to label enemies, to mobilize support and to win cases in court.

This chapter explores the role of international legal expertise in world politics. It does so by means of a comparison between the (political) role of scientific and technical experts on the one hand and the politics of international legal expertise on the other. The role of scientific experts has been studied quite extensively in sociological literature on the place of knowledge and information in (post-)modern societies. This chapter examines which lessons can be learned from studies on the role of scientific experts for a better understanding of the nature and function of international legal experts in global politics. It does so by exploring some underlying forces that have shaped the role and activities of experts, the paradoxes of expertise and the politics of expert knowledge and advice.

[1] See, for example, S. Nouwen and W. G. Werner, 'Doing Justice to the Political: The ICC in Uganda and Sudan', *European Journal of International Law*, 11 (2010), 941–65; M. Glasius, 'Expression of Justice or Political Trial? Discursive Battles in the Karadzic Case' (2012) (currently under review, on file with the author).

Section 3.2 of this chapter discusses three transformations in society that have contributed to the specific, sometimes paradoxical position of experts in decision making: the rise of knowledge society, changing conceptions of risk and the legalization of society. Section 3.3 focuses more specifically on the specific nature of international legal expertise. What makes it possible for someone to claim authority on the basis of international legal expertise? Section 3.4 explores the relevance for international law of two approaches that have sought to make sense of the impact of experts on international decision making: transnational advocacy networks and epistemic communities. It argues that the nature of legal knowledge makes it unavoidable that legal experts combine advocacy and epistemic community elements in their activities.

3.2 The paradox of scientific expert knowledge

This section discusses one of the main paradoxes of expert knowledge in contemporary societies: while legal and political decision making increasingly relies on expert knowledge to ground decision making and justify policies, the authority of experts to do exactly that has decreased. In order to understand this paradox of expert knowledge, it is necessary to delve deeper into some societal transformations that, at the same time, elevated and undermined expert knowledge.

3.2.1 Expansion and fragmentation of scientific knowledge

In 1973, the American sociologist Daniel Bell forecast the coming of a post-industrial or knowledge society in the USA, Western Europe, Japan and the USSR.[2] In contrast to industrial societies that are organized around machine technology, post-industrial societies are primarily organized around information and knowledge. These societies, Bell argues, are knowledge societies as their innovation depends largely on research and development – and in particular on *theoretical* knowledge – while more and

[2] D. Bell, *The Coming of Post-industrial Society: A Venture in Social Forecasting* (New York: Basic Books, 1973) (reissued with new introduction in 1976). Note that Bell deliberately used the term 'forecasting' and not 'predicting'. His aim was to sketch, on the basis of long-term trends in Western societies (especially the USA), a 'speculative construct . . . against which the sociological reality could be measured decades hence' (foreword in 1976 edition, at ix).

more of a country's gross national product is produced in the field of knowledge.[3] Although Bell's theory of post-industrial society has met with severe criticism,[4] the idea that we live in a knowledge society has become almost commonplace. Different scholars have used terms such as 'information society', 'informational society' or 'knowledge society' to indicate the crucial role of knowledge, both as a driving force for production and innovation and as a direct source of employment and income.[5] Moreover, governments and international organizations have employed the term 'information society' or 'knowledge society' to foster political aims, varying from opening up markets in Third World countries to the empowerment of disadvantaged groups around the globe.[6]

One of the characteristics of a knowledge society is the availability of an ever-growing stock of knowledge – a growth that went hand in hand with an immense specialization and fragmentation of knowledge. A telling example is the way in which the *Encyclopædia Britannica* has been put together from its earliest editions up to the mid-twentieth century. Whereas the first editions were drafted by one or two men who could master 'the whole of human knowledge', the 1967 edition involved 10,000 recognized experts.[7] The ever-growing stock of knowledge is also constantly reproduced, on the Internet, in journals, books, documentaries, etc., up to a point that 'the superstructure of society has by now become so immense that the majority of social actions are not production, but rather reproduction: in particular, the reproduction of knowledge itself'.[8]

Decision making in contemporary society relies heavily on the expanding and fragmented body of scientific knowledge. The reliance on scientific knowledge, however, is not only caused by the mere availability of

[3] *Ibid.*, at 212. Note that Bell prefers the term 'post-industrial society' over 'knowledge society' to describe the general trends in Western societies. Yet, he does argue that clearly, post-industrial societies are knowledge societies.

[4] For a useful overview of the critiques voiced against the theory of post-industrial society, see N. Stehr, *Knowledge Societies* (London: Sage, 1994), 52–63.

[5] S. Brint, 'Professionals and the "Knowledge Economy": Rethinking the Theory of Postindustrial Society', *Current Sociology*, 49 (2001), 101–32. For an overview, see Stehr, *Knowledge Societies*.

[6] For an overview, see S. Burch, 'The Information Society/The Knowledge Society', available at: http://vecam.org/article517.html.

[7] Bell, *The Coming of Post-industrial Society*, at 174, quoting the Prefatory Note to the 11th edn of the *Encyclopedia Britannica*.

[8] R. Grundmann and N. Stehr, *Experts: The Knowledge and Power of Expertise* (London: Routledge, 2011), at 7.

knowledge,[9] it is also related to the fact that the legal and political system has reached out to almost all aspects of society and has become more specialized and fragmented, roughly since the First World War. States have assumed unprecedented responsibilities for the well-being of their citizens and constantly aim to protect societies against risks such as global financial crises, food safety or ecological degradation. Often, these risks appear as almost virtual to the layperson: they cannot be detected by the ordinary human senses, but require the 'sensory organs of science (theories, experiments, measuring instruments) to become visible and interpretable as threats at all'.[10]

Scientific knowledge is thus indispensable for rational decision making, yet is difficult to access because of the abundance and fragmentation of that very same knowledge. This has spurred a demand for experts in decision making. Experts, then, can be described as persons located in-between the production and the application of knowledge, as 'mediators between producers of knowledge and users of knowledge; and thus, between those who create the capacity to take action and those whose task it is to act'.[11] Typical reasons for calling in experts include the establishment of an empirical basis for decision making, reducing complexity, distinguishing between reliable and unreliable knowledge, and justifying decision making by providing authoritative support.[12] However, as we will see below, it is exactly the capacity of experts to deliver unambiguous, legitimate knowledge that is increasingly called into question.

3.2.2 *The politics of expert knowledge*

While expert knowledge often forms the bedrock of legal and political decision making, this should not be read as a displacement of politics by expert knowledge *tout court*. Knowledge societies may even involve more politics than before *because* of the pivotal role of scientific experts. While experts are called in to reduce complexity and provide legitimacy

[9] See also the argument made by Drucker, who has argued that the emergence of knowledge society is also the result of the growing number of people with long-term higher education, who subsequently seek knowledge-based jobs. P. Drucker, *The Age of Discontinuity: Guidelines to Our Changing Society* (New York: Harper & Row, 1969).

[10] U. Beck, *Risk Society: Towards a New Modernity* (London: Sage, 2005), at 162.

[11] Grundmann and Stehr, *Experts*, at 40.

[12] Of course, for those opposing particular decisions, experts can also fulfil the opposite functions: providing doubt, showing that a problem is more complex than originally presented, redefining a situation, delegitimizing decisions. See also section 3.2.2.

by enabling well-informed decision making, in practice their answers are often partial, conditional and contested. Using experts in decision making may then yield opposite results: an increase in complexity, openly contested decisions and a struggle over alternative definitions of problem situations. Some even consider the loss of authority on the part of experts to be a characteristic of decision making in contemporary society. Beck, for example, has observed that 'the more science and technology permeate and transform life on a global scale the less expert knowledge is treated as a given'.[13] In a similar fashion, Limoges has argued that 'the involvement of scientists in public disputes has promoted the political polarization of controversies ... expert knowledge has been almost routinely deconstructed in the course of litigations' and 'expert interventions have tended to be seen as ritualistic or manipulative schemes, thus losing much of their credibility'.[14]

The distrust in expert input can partly be explained by the fact that scientific experts sometimes ally with specific commercial firms, interests groups and political parties. One of the most disturbing examples are the so-called 'merchants of doubt', a group of scientific experts with strong links to industry and conservative politicians who proved willing to cast doubt on results of scientific research in the areas of smoking tobacco, acid rain, the depletion of the ozone layer and global warming.[15] Another reason for this distrust is that science itself has become subject to intensive governmental control and to systems of management. The bureaucratization of scientific research went hand in hand with attempts to turn academia into instruments for the achievement of governmental and societal goals[16] – and thus to situate science in the midst of political debate. A third factor that helps to explain the decrease in the legitimacy of experts is the increasing realization that translating scientific knowledge into legal and political decision making is not a neutral enterprise, but involves a politics of framing and defining. The point of involving experts in decision making, after all, is not to find 'the truth' as such, but

[13] U. Beck, *World at Risk* (Cambridge: Polity Press, 2008), 6.

[14] C. Limoges, 'Expert Knowledge and Decision-Making in Controversy Contexts', *Public Understanding in Science*, 2 (1993), 417–26, at 417.

[15] N. Oreskes and E. Conway, *Merchants of Doubt: How a Handful of Scientists Obscured the Truth on Issues from Tobacco Smoke to Global Warming* (New York: Bloomsbury, 2010).

[16] Bell, *The Coming of Post-industrial Society*, xvii. For a recent critique on the instrumentalization of science, see R. Munch, *Akademischer Kapitalismus, Ueber die politische Oekonomie der Hochschulreform* (Berlin: Suhrkamp, 2011).

rather to establish a factual basis that makes it possible to take action and justify choices. The advice provided by experts is thus shaped by the selection of experts, the composition of expert groups, the questions posed to experts and the language they need to speak in order to be heard by those in power. In their turn, experts also engage more directly in politics of framing as they have to choose between competing definitions of a situation, different conceptualizations of a problem and varying options for dealing with the problem at hand. A number of chapters in this volume deal extensively with the politics of framing by experts. Gruszczynski, for example, studies how the design of the World Trade Organization's dispute settlement procedures affects the ways in which experts frame their knowledge, while Everson analyses the manner of framing expertise in the European system for financial supervision, leading to a technology of expertise.[17]

In addition, the political role of experts also results from more paradoxical or even dialectical developments within science and expertise itself. Experts nowadays operate in what Ulrich Beck has called a 'world risk society'.[18] In terms not unrelated to Bell's distinction between pre-industrial, industrial and post-industrial societies, Beck witnesses a transformation from 'early modernization' (industrial society) to late or reflexive modernization ('risk society'). This process of transformation, Beck argues, is primarily visible in the changing understanding of the concept of 'risk'. In modern societies, 'risk' was used as a means to calculate and master the future. Risk was one of the ways in which scientific knowledge enabled societies to master the world, to get dominion over nature and to regulate society. In late modernity, however, the conception of risks as calculable and positively linked to scientific progress has come under pressure. Increasingly, modern societies are confronted with threats that are not the result of an *under*production of scientific knowledge, but that result from an *over*production thereof. Society, in other words, is now also confronted with possible hazards and uncertainties that result from the process of modernization itself.[19] An

[17] Gruszcznyski, Chapter 11 and Everson, Chapter 15, both this volume.

[18] Beck, *Risk Society*; U. Beck, A. Giddens and S. Lash (eds.), *Reflexive Modernization: Politics, Tradition and Aesthetics in the Modern Social Order* (Stanford University Press, 1994); U. Beck *Ecological Politics in an Age of Risk* (Cambridge: Polity Press, 2002); U. Beck, *World Risk Society* (Cambridge: Polity Press, 1999).

[19] Hence the term 'reflexive' modernization. This term should not be equated with the connected term 'reflective'. Reflexive modernization indicates that modernization is increasingly confronted with its own products and thus increasingly becomes its own

example is what Ewald has called the 'two infinites of risk': the infinitely small-scale risks (biological, natural and food-related risks) and the infinitely large-scale risks (major technological risks or technological catastrophes).[20] In line with the development of such risks, Beck describes (world) risk society as: 'A phase of development of modern society in which the social, political, ecological and individual risks created by the momentum of innovation increasingly elude the control and protective institutions of industrial society.'[21] In this context, the involvement of experts in decision making may also have a self-perpetuating effect: the application of scientific knowledge *itself* to address issues brings about new problems, which can only be properly detected and addressed through the application of scientific knowledge.[22] In this process, it becomes increasingly clear that science and expert knowledge are not just neutral instruments used to address problems; they are ways of framing a problem and potential sources of new problems as well.

Beck identifies a second (and related) paradox of expert knowledge in risk society.[23] In early modernization, the growing impact of scientific knowledge was based on a specific division: internally, science applied methods of critique, scepticism and fallibilism, while externally, the products of scientific research generally functioned as socially binding formulations of truth. Increasingly, however, the belief in science as deliverer of truth has been accompanied by an awareness that scientific statements are subject to recall and radically contextual, while scientific experts increasingly publicly disagree. In other words, the methods of scepticism and fallibilism that characterized internal scientific discourse are now externalized, to the extent that expert knowledge is increasingly

topic. For a discussion of the term 'reflexivity', see Beck, Giddens and Lash, *Reflexive Modernization*.

20 F. Ewald, 'Two Infinities of Risk' in B. Massumi (ed.), *The Politics of Everyday Fear* (University of Minnesota Press, 1993), at 221–8.

21 U. Beck, 'The Reinvention of Politics: Towards a Theory of Reflexive Modernization' in Beck, Giddens and Lash (eds.), *Reflexive Modernization*, at 27. Beck's argument that incalculable risks escape the existing institutional framework has been (convincingly) challenged by Aradau and van Munster, who explore the different ways in which institutions make a radically uncertain future manageable. See C. Aradau and R. van Munster, *Politics of Catastrophe* (London: Routledge, 2011).

22 Grundmann and Stehr, *Experts*, at 99.

23 This paragraph is partly based on W.G. Werner, 'Responding to the Undesired: Responsibility, Risk-Management and Precaution', *Netherlands Yearbook of International Law*, 36 (2006), 39–63.

perceived as dependent on context and the particular ways in which a problem is framed. In Beck's formulation:

> reality has sublimated into *data* that are *produced*. Thus 'facts' – the former centrepieces of reality – are nothing but answers to questions that could just as well have been asked differently, products of rules for gathering and omitting. A different computer, a different specialist, a different institute – a different 'reality'. It would be a miracle if it did not already exist, a miracle and not science.[24]

Of course, the distrust in experts and scientific knowledge should not be exaggerated. Not all scientific knowledge is effectively contested all the time and there are examples where scientific experts have been able to reduce complexity and to provide legitimacy. Yet, Beck's analysis shows that the increasing importance of experts in decision making cannot be simply equated with their capacity to present binding definitions of truth, let alone with a replacement of politics by expertise. Rather, it highlights the politics of scientific expert knowledge; the way in which truth claims are used to pursue political aims.[25] A good illustration of the political use of scientifically validated truth claims is provided by Haas' analysis of 'epistemic communities' (see also the following section).[26] Epistemic communities harbour experts who share normative beliefs, causal beliefs and notions of validity in a common effort to affect policy.[27] Epistemic communities build on consensus among a *group of like-minded experts* to capture control over policy terrains, such as marine pollution or the depletion of the ozone layer.[28] Epistemic communities therefore utilize consensus among a group of experts to pursue political goals. This consensus, however, cannot be treated as a given – it may break down or can be challenged

[24] Beck, *Risk Society*, at 166, emphasis in original.

[25] For 'knowledge politics', see also R. Grundmann and N. Stehr, 'Social Control and Knowledge in Democratic Societies', *Science and Public Policy*, 30 (2003), 183–8.

[26] Haas, Chapter 2, this volume; P. M. Haas, 'Do Regimes Matter? Epistemic Communities and Mediterranean Pollution Control', *International Organization*, 43 (1989), 377–403; P. M. Haas, 'Introduction: Epistemic Communities and International Policy Coordination', *International Organization*, 46 (1992), 1–35; P. Haas and E. B. Haas, 'Learning to Learn: Improving International Governance', *Global Governance*, 1 (1995), 255–85.

[27] See Haas, 'Introduction: Epistemic Communities, at 3. See also the analysis of epistemic communities below.

[28] See Haas, 'Do Regimes Matter?', who discusses the role of scientists in Mediterranean pollution control. For the role of epistemic communities in ozone depletion, see P. M. Haas, 'Banning Chloroflurocarbons: Epistemic Community Efforts to Protect Stratospheric Ozone' in P. Haas (ed.), *Knowledge, Power and International Policy Coordination* (Columbia, SC: University of South Carolina Press, 1992), 187–225.

by alternative scientific insights, sometimes resulting in political truth struggles between epistemic communities.[29]

3.3 The paradoxes of legal expert knowledge

It is not possible to translate the findings of the previous section automatically to the realm of law. The nature and organization of scientific expert knowledge differs in many ways from the way in which knowledge is produced and transmitted in the legal profession. Having said that, it is possible to detect some structural similarities in the development of law and science in (post-)modern societies. In particular, both fields have undergone a simultaneous process of expansion and specialization, and in both fields experts have proven to be both indispensable and increasingly contested. In this section, I will sketch the trend towards juridification and fragmentation, with a specific focus on the international arena (section 3.3.1), discuss the politics of international legal expert knowledge (section 3.3.2) and examine two dominant models that help to explain the nature of legal expert knowledge (section 3.3.3).

3.3.1 Expansion and fragmentation of (international) law

The expansion of law first emerged within the realm of the sovereign state. According to Habermas, the juridification of Western societies took place in four subsequent phases: (1) the legalization of sovereign prerogatives and transformation of contractual relations in absolutism; (2) the constitutonalization of individual rights in the nineteenth century; (3) the expansion of participatory rights since the late nineteenth century; and (4) the legalization of social welfare rights in the twentieth century.[30] In line with Beck's theory of the risk society, one could add a fifth phase here, in which states and international organizations use legal regulation to protect citizens against incalculable, yet potentially catastrophic risks. The legalization of society went hand in hand with an increasing departmentalization of the legal system: new fields arose (e.g., administrative law) and already-established fields broke up in subfields.

[29] See Haas and Haas, 'Learning to Learn', at 261: 'In the absence of such a knowledge monopoly, competing epistemic communities seek to take over bureaucracies in order to promote their preferred knowledge scheme.'

[30] See the discussion of Habermas' views on law in M. Deflem (ed.), *Habermas, Modernity and Law* (London: Sage, 1996). The four phases discussed here are analysed in the introduction to the book by Deflem at 1–20.

The compartmentalization of law was also visible at universities, with ever more specialized chairs, journals, institutes, etc. The proliferation of fields and subfields in law meant that, increasingly, law was not just a profession but also a collection of specializations.[31] In addition to being a professional lawyer, one could now be a recognized legal expert in an unprecedented number of specialized fields.

The legalization of society extended to the international level as well. In the twentieth century, international law expanded in several directions: (a) geographically, with the inclusion of newly independent states as a result of the process of decolonization; (b) in terms of legal persons, with the incorporation of rights, powers and obligations for non-state actors such as international organizations, individuals or peoples; (c) substantively, with the regulation of areas such as human rights, the environment and criminal law; (d) *qua* impact on domestic legal orders; and (e) in terms of independent supervisory bodies that monitor compliance.[32] In the words of the International Law Commission's study group on fragmentation and expansion: 'It is difficult to imagine today a sphere of social activity that would not be subject to some type of international legal regulation.'[33]

However, the degree to which international society has become legalized varies from field to field and from region to region. In some areas, legalization takes the form of precisely formulated, legally binding norms, supervised and applied by independent organs.[34] In other areas, legalization takes the form of hortatory norms or relatively open norms that are not (or only partially) interpreted by independent third parties. Even in cases of incomplete legalization, however, the expansion of international law can have profound political implications. Take,

[31] Professions are here understood as 'a number of persons ... practicing a definite technique founded upon specialized training'. The formulation is ascribed by Haas to A.M. Carr-Saunders in Haas, 'Introduction: Epistemic Communities', at 19.

[32] See also W. Friedmann, *The Changing Structure of International Law* (London: Stevens & Sons, 1964), who argues that international law has expanded vertically and horizontally, and is complementing the law of coordination with a law of cooperation.

[33] Report of the Study Group of the International Law Commission, *Fragmentation of International Law: Difficulties Arising From the Diversification and Expansion of International Law*, A/CN.4/L.702, para. 4.

[34] I here borrow from Goldstein, Kahler, Keohane and Slaughter, who defined legalization of world politics in terms of: '(a) the degree to which rules are obligatory (b) the precision of those rules (c) the delegation of some functions of interpretation, monitoring, and implementation to a third party'. J. Goldstein, M. Kahler, R.O. Keohane and A. Slaughter, 'Introduction: Legalization and World Politics', *International Organization*, 54 (2000), 385–99, at 387.

for example, the development of the law of armed conflict, a field that has often been described as the 'vanishing point of the vanishing point of international law'.[35] By now, the law of armed conflict is codified in numerous treaties, which often contain some specific provisions. Moreover, provisions of the law of armed conflict are applied (and reinterpreted) by third parties, such as international criminal tribunals. Notwithstanding this development, many of its core provisions (e.g., those regarding proportionality or unnecessary suffering) remain relatively underdetermined, while their effectiveness largely depends on the willingness of warring parties to apply them. Still, the legalization in this field has affected the way in which powerful actors have used their military force in international relations. Kennedy, for example, has argued that the laws of armed conflict today provide a 'common vernacular' for participants in warfare, including humanitarian organizations, media and the army.[36] Since law and politics have become so closely intertwined, Kennedy argues, war has now become the continuation of law with the inclusion of other means as well. Anecdotal evidence of Kennedy's point can be found in the complaints by former North Atlantic Treaty Organization (NATO) Supreme Allied Commander, Europe, General Jones: 'It used to be a simple thing to fight a battle . . . In a perfect world, a general would get up and say, "Follow me, men", and everybody would say "Aye, sir" and run off. But that's not the world anymore . . . [now] you have to have a lawyer or a dozen. It's become very legalistic and very complex.'[37]

Just as domestic law simultaneously expanded and compartmentalized, the growth of international law came with increased specialization. Sub-regimes such as human rights, economic law, criminal law and environmental law emerged, each with their own imperatives, procedures, principles and vocabularies. In international legal discourse, the specialization of international law is generally discussed in terms of the threat (or lack thereof) to the unity of the international legal order as a

[35] 'If international law is, in some ways, at the vanishing point of law, the law of war is, perhaps even more conspicuously at the vanishing point of international law.' H. Lauterpacht, 'The Problem of the Revision of the Law of War', *British Yearbook of International Law*, 29 (1952), 360–82, at 382.

[36] D. Kennedy, *Of War and Law* (Princeton University Press, 2006).

[37] L. Wallwork Winik, 'A Marine's Toughest Mission', *Parade*, 19 January 2003 (quoting General James L. Jones, a former NATO commander, explaining how the legalistic nature of today's warfare has complicated the fight).

whole.[38] However, it is not my intention to add here to the already impressive body of literature on the effects of specialization on the unity of international law as such.[39] Instead, I focus here and in the next section on the relation between the compartmentalization of international law and the position of legal experts. Not surprisingly, the emergence of functional subfields in international law has made legal experts indispensable in (international) decision making, just like the fragmentation of scientific knowledge has spurred calls for scientific experts. Experts in specific (sub) fields of international law are typically called to provide legal bases for decision making, to define situations and to justify decision making by providing authoritative support. Legal experts themselves, however, are also increasingly dependent on experts from other disciplinary fields. The fragmentation of international law has created functional subfields where legal norms can often only be applied on the basis of scientific expert knowledge.[40] This has created a series of questions regarding the relation between legal rationality and scientific rationality, the possibilities and limits of translating scientific knowledge into legal forms, the desired composition of expert panels, etc. As several other chapters in this volume deal with these questions, I will not take them up further here.

3.3.2 *Paradoxes of international legal expertise*

As was noted above, scientific experts can be understood as mediators between the production of knowledge and the application of knowledge.[41] Of course, there is no absolute dividing line between the production and the

[38] See, for example, the report by the study group on fragmentation of the International Law Commission: 'New types of specialized law do not emerge accidentally but seek to respond to new technical and functional requirements . . . In order for the new law to be efficient, it often includes new types of treaty clauses or practices that may not be compatible with old general law or the law of some specialized branch. Very often new rules or regimes develop precisely in order to deviate from what was earlier provided by the general law. When such deviations become general and frequent, the unity of law suffers.' Report of the Study Group of the International Law Commission, *Fragmentation of International Law*, A/CN.4/L.702, at 15. Note that not all scholars argue that the unity of international law is endangered by the diversification of international law. However, the question whether fragmentation affects legal unity and coherence is the underlying question for almost all contributions to this topic.

[39] For a critical reading of general principles as guardians of the unity of international law, see the special issue of the *Netherlands Yearbook of International Law* (2010) on the application of the concept of necessity across international law.

[40] Lawrence, Chapter 9; Herwig, Chapter 10; Gruszczynski, Chapter 11; Everson, Chapter 15; Knio, Chapter 16; Schout and Sleifer, Chapter 17; and Busuioc, Chapter 18, all this volume.

[41] See section 3.2.1.

transmission of knowledge. Experts are not neutral mouthpieces of science – they select, interpret and frame available knowledge, and thus in a sense also constitute the knowledge they pass on. At the same time, scientific experts can only claim authority *qua* experts if they are able to present their results as not depending on their personal preferences or the political whims of their employers. Scientific experts, in other words, can only fulfil their function in politics if they are perceived as not being (completely) politicized. In the same fashion, the role of international legal experts in world politics depends on their capacity to present their advice as based on a system of rules that enjoy relative autonomy from politics. If it is not possible to identify rules separated from day-to-day politics, international legal advice becomes indistinguishable from other types of political advice and loses its own specific legitimizing function. Of course, it is still possible that those in power simply want legal experts to back up their decisions and find whatever legal ground to justify what has already been decided. A telling example is former US Secretary of State Madeleine Albright's answer when lawyers told her that bombing Serbia without a UN mandate would be illegal: 'get new lawyers'.[42] In such cases, however, it becomes virtually impossible to cash the legitimacy bonus of independent legal advice; the latter would then simply be taken for what it is – a twist of arguments to comfort those in power. Decision makers who seek legal advice thus need to navigate between the desire to obtain a legitimacy bonus that comes with independent legal advice and the wish to control the outcomes.[43]

The politics of legal advice thus rests on the idea of law as something out there, 'as a discrete entity, discernibly different from morals and politics'.[44] For Shklar, this idea constitutes the core of the 'internal professional ideology' of lawyers, which makes possible a specific type of politics – the politics of legalism.[45] One of the most radical examples

[42] As reported by M. Glennon, *The Limits of the Law, Prerogatives of Power* (Basingstoke: Palgrave Macmillan, 2001), at 178.

[43] This insight is drawn from Kirchheimer's analysis of political trials, where a similar tension is present. The more courts are perceived as being independent and impartial, the greater the legitimacy bonus for the political regime. However, the integrity of courts also confronts political leadership with a dilemma: 'Is the prestige advantage it draws from the validation of its claims by such agency worth the corresponding loss of direction in dealing with its foes?' O. Kirchheimer, *Political Justice: The Use of Legal Procedure for Political Ends* (Princeton University Press, 1961), at 26.

[44] J. Shklar, *Legalism, Law, Morals and Political Trials* (Cambridge, MA: Harvard University Press, 1984) (first edition published in 1964), at 9.

[45] *Ibid.*, at 16 (the term 'internal professional ideology' is attributed by Shklar to Max Weber).

of this way of thinking can be found in Kelsen's pure theory of law, which attempts to categorically separate legal science from morals, politics and empirical sciences.[46] For Kelsen, legal norms are the result of acts of will, as validated by higher norms. The interpretation of these norms by legal scientists, by contrast, are treated as acts of legal cognition; the *finding* of 'the possible meanings of the legal norm undergoing interpretation; and, then, to show their consequences, leaving it to the competent legal authorities to choose from among the various possible interpretations the one which they, for political reasons, consider to be preferable'.[47] Today, not many scholars will agree with Kelsen's reading of legal interpretation.[48] Still, his contested reading of the relation between the production of law and the interpretation of law captures an important aspect of the way in which law and legal experts operate. If legal experts were to present their advice as an arbitrary product of acts of will, they would have difficulties being heard as legal voices. Legal expertise has to be presented as a form of knowledge – despite the fact that it is widely acknowledged that this knowledge results from particular readings and constructions of law.

A case in point is the recently published *Tallinn Manual on the International Law Applicable to Cyber Warfare*.[49] The *Manual* was written at the invitation of the NATO Cooperative Cyber Defence Centre of Excellence by an international group of experts. The point of the *Manual*, according to its chair, was to provide answers to the thorny questions relating to the application of international law to cyberwar.[50] Not surprisingly, the *Manual* has a geographical bias (with experts coming basically from Western countries and with a particular reliance on NATO military manuals) and is unable to provide certainty on

[46] For an overview of the main points of Kelsen's pure theory, see H. Kelsen, *Pure Theory of Law* (Berkeley: University of California Press, 1967); H. Kelsen, *General Theory of Norms* (Oxford: Clarendon Press, 1991).

[47] H. Kelsen, *The Law of the United Nations: A Critical Analysis of Its Fundamental Problems* (London: Lawbook Exchange, 2000) (originally published in 1950, New York: Praeger), at xvi.

[48] For an insightful critique of Kelsen's theory of interpretation, see S. Paulson, 'Formalism, "Free Law", and the "Cognition" Quandary: Hans Kelsen's Approaches to Legal Interpretation', *University of Queensland Law Journal*, 27 (2008), 7–39.

[49] *Tallinn Manual on the International Law Applicable to Cyber Warfare* (Cambridge University Press, 2013). This example builds on O. Kessler and W. Werner, 'Expertise, Uncertainty and International Law', *Leiden Journal of International Law*, 26 (2013), 793–810.

[50] See, for example, the presentation by Michael Schmitt on the *Tallinn Manual*: 'CyCon 2012 | Michael Schmitt: Tallinn Manual', Part I, posted on YouTube: www.youtube.com/watch?v=wY3uEo-Itso (at 0:40).

several core issues of conflict and security law.[51] Nevertheless, the *Manual* takes great pains to emphasize that it is based on knowledge derived from an impressive list of sources and authorities, as listed at the very first pages of the text. Moreover, it claims that readers should trust the outcomes because of 'the professional knowledge, experience, and expertise of the Experts'.[52]

The increasing compartmentalization of law has further complicated the politics of international legal expertise. Different functional subfields of law contain different forms of expert knowledge, each organized around their own functional imperatives. This means that the politics of framing becomes even more crucial – not just the framing of political issues in the language of international law, but also the choice for a particular functional legal regime and the expert idiom that comes with it. As Koskenniemi has put it:

> the most important political conflicts in the international world are often legally articulated as conflicts of jurisdiction and applicable law . . . Political intervention is today often a politics of re-definition, that is to say, the strategic definition of a situation or a problem by reference to a technical idiom so as to open the door for applying the expertise related to that idiom, together with the attendant structural bias.[53]

3.3.3 International legal experts between advocacy and an invisible college

So far, two models have been dominant in explaining the political role of experts in international decision making: the model of transnational advocacy groups and the notion of epistemic communities. The first model primarily focuses on the way in which groups ally around values and principled ideas, while the second highlights attempts to influence policy by groups held together by shared knowledge beliefs and standards of validity.[54] The two models cannot always be easily applied to

[51] For an analysis, see Kessler and Werner, 'Expertise, Uncertainty and International Law'.

[52] *Tallinn Manual*, at 20, 22. The quote specifically refers to the trust we should have in the expert's judgement as to the customary status of legal rules and their application to non-international armed conflicts.

[53] M. Koskenniemi, 'The Politics of International Law – 20 Years Later', *European Journal of International Law*, 20 (2009), 7–19, at 10–11.

[54] The classical text on transnational advocacy networks is M. E. Keck and K. Sikkink, *Activists Beyond Borders: Advocacy Networks in International Politics* (Ithaca, NY: Cornell University Press, 1998). For epistemic communities, see Haas, 'Do Regimes

communities of international lawyers, nor are they able to capture the wide variety of different roles played by international legal experts. Still, the two models are worth discussing as they do reflect two constitutive aspects of legal expert knowledge discussed in the previous section. Namely, legal experts make their arguments based on normative assumptions about the nature and purpose of international law, and they select and frame issues in particular, often contested ways. At the same time, they can only make their claims *qua legal expert* if they base their arguments on criteria for validity that are accepted in a broader community of international lawyers. In Oscar Schachter's words, international legal experts are both advocates and members of an 'invisible college of international lawyers'.[55]

The model of *transnational advocacy networks* has been developed by Keck and Sikkink to make sense of the changing structure of international decision making. Alongside states, transnational pressure groups have managed to affect policy outcomes and transform the terms of political debates, especially in areas 'characterized by high value content and informational uncertainty', such as human rights or environmental protection.[56] Transnational advocacy networks are defined in terms of 'the centrality of values or principled ideas, the belief that individuals can make a difference, the creative use of information, and the employment ... of sophisticated political strategies'.[57] Transnational advocacy groups typically use four such political strategies: (1) information politics – the generation and framing of information; (2) symbolic politics – the use of catching symbols to further a cause; (3) leverage politics – allying with more powerful players in world politics; (4) accountability politics – confronting powerful players with policies and principles they adhered to earlier.[58] In light of the previous discussion on the fragmentation of international law, it is important to note that information politics involves the politics of framing: should an issue be treated as the concern of a broad constituency or as a technical matter for experts and, if so, which of the available technical-institutional idioms should be mobilized to further a cause?[59]

Matter?'; Haas, 'Introduction: Epistemic Communities'; Haas and Haas, 'Learning to Learn'; Haas, 'Banning Chloroflurocarbons'.

55 O. Schachter, 'The Invisible College of International Lawyers', *Northwestern University Law Review*, 72 (1977), 217–26.

56 Keck and Sikkink, *Activists Beyond Borders*, at 2. 57 *Ibid.*, at 16. 58 *Ibid.*

59 *Ibid.*, at 19.

Transnational advocacy networks bring together activists and are not necessarily dominated by (legal) experts. However, even for transnational advocacy networks, the use of legal expertise can be an important part of their political strategies. An example is the way in which non-governmental organizations (NGOs) have lobbied for an effective international criminal court – an institution that for good reasons has been characterized as a 'global civil society achievement'.[60] In 1995, hundreds of NGOs came together in the so-called 'Coalition for the International Criminal Court' (CICC) in a joint effort to affect policy outcomes and transform the terms of the debate. The NGOs used a mixture of political strategies, such as accountability politics (holding states to their promise of ending impunity), leverage politics and shaping the discourse in terms of the fair and equal administration of global justice.[61] An additional crucial factor contributing to the success of the NGOs was their legal expertise. As Struett notes, governments – especially from smaller and economically less well-off states – often asked NGOs for advice on proposals for the Court's Statute and took their opinions very seriously.[62] In other words, NGOs were able to be an effective lobbying force, partly because they were able to present their policy preferences in the expert language of international law.

The model of *epistemic communities* was already introduced in the previous section.[63] Epistemic communities are defined as groups of professionals sharing: '(1) a set of normative and principled beliefs, which provides a value-based rationale for social action . . . (2) causal beliefs derived from their analysis of practices . . . (3) notions of validity – that is intersubjective, internally defined criteria for weighing and assessing knowledge . . . (4) a common policy enterprise'.[64]

It is not easy to apply the model of epistemic communities to international legal experts. As epistemic communities require shared principled beliefs and a common effort to affect policy, they cannot be equated with disciplines or professions as a whole, such as the community of international law professionals.[65] Moreover, one can doubt whether more

[60] M. Glasius, *The International Criminal Court: A Global Civil Society Achievement* (Oxford: Routledge, 2005).

[61] For an analysis, see M. Struett, *The Politics of Constructing the International Criminal Court: NGOs, Discourse and Agency* (New York: Palgrave Macmillan, 2008).

[62] *Ibid.* [63] See section 3.3.2. [64] Haas, 'Introduction: Epistemic Communities', at 3.

[65] For an attempt to define the international law community as an epistemic community, see A. Olson, 'An Empire of Scholars: Transnational Lawyers and the Rule of *Opinio Juris*', *Perspectives on Political Science*, 29 (2000), 23–32. However, as Haas makes clear, epistemic communities are to be distinguished from professions as a whole, as not all

specific groups of international lawyers can count as epistemic communities at all, given the need for shared causal beliefs derived from methods and techniques accepted in the discipline or profession they practise.[66] While specific groups of international lawyers may share causal beliefs, these beliefs are not based on the application of *legal* methods, but rather on insights derived from other disciplines or from what members consider to be common sense. However, Haas himself argues that (international) lawyers cannot be epistemic communities for a different reason. Members of epistemic communities, he argues, have a capacity to learn and adapt: 'they subordinate their advocacy to the certified body of knowledge to which they subscribe . . . and are willing to jettison those beliefs when confronted with significant anomalies consistent with their pre-established truth tests'.[67] Lawyers, by contrast, would be 'mere advocates' who are unwilling to change their position when confronted with new insights obtained via accepted methods in the discipline.[68]

However, if the latter were true, international legal expertise itself would become highly problematic. Where legal arguments are regarded as nothing more than political preferences phrased as law, without any link to a certified body of knowledge and shared criteria for validity that could, at least potentially, make someone change her position, the legitimizing function of law and legal expertise would be at stake. This is one of the concerns voiced by Kennedy in the area of modern warfare. Participants in modern warfare, Kennedy argues, use international humanitarian law as the 'common vernacular' to make strategic arguments. However, a widely shared strategic attitude towards humanitarian law may eventually undermine its normative force.[69] If all parties concerned believe that legal arguments are produced merely to gain military or political advantage, debates on the legality or illegality of behaviour turn into a 'dialogue of the deaf . . . as we use the discourse more, we believe it less – at least when spoken by others'.[70] Taken to its extreme, this development would be self-defeating as eventually no additional legitimacy bonus could be gained from the use of legal arguments.

Legal argumentation, in other words, is only possible when participants assume that there are some criteria and a body of knowledge that can be used to validate or invalidate specific claims if they *also* act as

professionals within a profession share principled beliefs or interests. Haas, 'Introduction: Epistemic Communities', at 18.

[66] Haas, 'Introduction: Epistemic Communities', at 16.

[67] Haas and Haas, 'Learning to Learn'. [68] *Ibid.* [69] *Ibid.*, at 135. [70] *Ibid.*

members of Schachter's 'invisible college' and not just as advocates. Even if one were to accept that it is virtually impossible for international lawyers to form an epistemic community in the sense described by Haas, it is still possible to form coalitions of like-minded lawyers and influence policy on the basis of knowledge-based claims that go beyond mere advocacy. Where this possibility is ruled out *a priori*, the very existence of international *legal* expertise becomes impossible.

3.4 Conclusion

There are structural similarities between the paradoxes of scientific expert knowledge and the paradox of international legal expertise. In (post-)modern society, scientific experts have become indispensable as transmitters of an ever-growing and fragmenting body of knowledge. Legal and political decision making is often bound to rely on scientific insights that only experts can disclose and explain. At the same time, however, the authority of experts to deliver socially binding truth statements has come under strain, due to the exact same developments that made experts indispensable in legal and political decision making. As Beck has put it, today the methods of fallibilism and scepticism are applied to the outcomes of scientific research, to the effect that expert knowledge is seen as partial, contestable and socially constructed. Still, expert knowledge can only fulfil a separate function if it is seen as not wholly dependent on personal or political preferences, as something that gains validity on the basis of a shared set of scientific criteria. In a similar fashion, international legal expertise has become indispensable in many fields of international decision making. World politics is increasingly dependent on a body of international legal rules that has grown unprecedentedly and, at the same time, broke up into different functional subfields. This has made legal expertise both important and contestable. While legal experts are needed to disclose the requirements of international law, it is widely recognized that their advice is based on a particular way of framing and prioritizing issues; the more international law expands and fragments, the more room there is for such legalistic politics. The politics of international law, however, can only function as long as international legal expertise is seen as *also* stemming from sources that are independent of the political whims of one party or another. If international law is politics, it is a form of politics that is only possible if it is perceived as grounded in some shared criteria of validity – in some area beyond day-to-day politics as well.

4

Reflections on the different roles of expertise in regulatory policy making

LORNA SCHREFLER

4.1 Introduction

The role of experts and expert knowledge[1] in policy making in national and international settings has come to occupy a prominent position in academic and policy debates. The complex and increasingly transnational nature of policy problems, such as climate change and economic governance, has strengthened the demand for policy-relevant expertise. As a result, the use of expertise is considered one of the central pillars of the better/smart regulation systems.[2] This is reflected in the proliferation

[1] Following Boswell, expert knowledge, as used here, is defined very loosely as 'the knowledge produced by academic research' (C. Boswell, *The Political Uses of Expert Knowledge: Immigration Policy and Social Research* (Cambridge University Press, 2009), 23–4). As Boswell explains, this type of knowledge can be distinguished from other forms of expert input into policy making such as lay knowledge, on the basis of two-point criteria: (1) the method of knowledge production, i.e., the methodology used to produce the knowledge at stake should be explicit and in line with standards commonly accepted by the relevant expert community; and (2) the institutional setting of knowledge production, i.e., knowledge is produced in a locus that is detached from political considerations and debates, for example, in academic departments, independent think tanks and specialized research units within agencies or government departments. In what follows, the terms 'expertise' and 'expert knowledge' are used as synonyms.

[2] For further details, see R. Baldwin, 'Is Better Regulation Smarter Regulation?', *Public Law*, Autumn (2005), 485–511; European Commission, *European Governance: A White Paper* (COM, Brussels, 2001), 428 final; European Commission, *Better Regulation for Growth and Jobs in the European Union* (COM, Brussels, 2005), 97 final; R. W. Hahn and P. C. Tetlock, 'Has Economic Analysis Improved Regulatory Decisions?', *Journal of Economic Perspectives*, 22 (2008), 67–84; A. C. Meuwese, *Impact Assessment in EU Law-Making* (Alphen aan den Rijn: Kluwer Law International, 2008); S. N. Nutley, I. Walter and H. T. O. Davies, *Using Evidence: How Research Can Inform Public Services* (Bristol: Policy Press, 2007); C. M. Radaelli, 'The Political Consequences of Regulatory Impact Assessment', paper delivered at the *Governing the Regulatory State? Comparing Strategies and Instruments* conference (British Academy, London, 15 January 2009); I. Sanderson, 'Intelligent Policy Making for a Complex World: Pragmatism, Evidence, and Learning', *Political Studies*, 57 (2009), 699–719.

and adoption of specific tools and methods to produce, systematize and feed expertise into policy making.[3] The increased use of expertise is also connected to the administrative reform movements,[4] and in particular to the creation of new regulatory institutions with delegated powers and different degrees of independence from elected politicians, i.e., regulatory agencies.[5] As some of the contributions in this book clearly show, the role of expert input into policy making is particularly relevant for this type of organization, as very often the legitimacy of agencies and the justification for their existence are based on the assumption that they will use expert knowledge to perform their duties rather than political considerations.[6] This assumption on the role of expert knowledge is particularly strong for the so-called independent regulatory agencies (IRAs), such as central banks and utilities regulators at the national or

3 C. M. Radaelli, 'Diffusion without Convergence: How Political Context Shapes the Adoption of Regulatory Impact Assessment', *Journal of European Public Policy*, 12 (2005), 924–43; C. M. Radaelli, 'Whither Better Regulation for the Lisbon Agenda?', *Journal of European Public Policy*, 14 (2007), 190–207; Schout and Schleifer, Chapter 17, this volume.

4 European Commission, *European Governance*; European Commission, *Better Regulation*; OECD, *Regulatory Policies in OECD Countries: From Interventionism to Regulatory Governance* (Paris: OECD, 2002); G. Galli and J. Pelkmans (eds.), *Regulatory Reform and Competitiveness in Europe* (Cheltenham: Edward Elgar, 2000); C. M. Radaelli and A. C. Meuwese, 'Better Regulation in Europe: Between Management and Regulation', *Public Administration*, 87 (2009), 639–54.

5 Note that, as pointed out by Maggetti, 'not all agencies are regulatory agencies: some have only executive tasks; others are simply consultative organizations for policy-makers' (M. Maggetti, 'The Role of Independent Regulatory Agencies in Policy-Making: A Comparative Analysis', *Journal of European Public Policy*, 16 (2009), 450–70, at 450). Regulatory agencies instead have the power to issue binding rules affecting the policy areas falling within their competence and/or to monitor the implementation of those rules. These powers are conferred (with different degrees of formal independence) to the regulatory agency by elected politicians via specific laws or statutes. For further details, see Maggetti, 'The Role of Independent Regulatory Agencies in Policy-Making'. On the growing number of regulatory agencies, see G. Majone, *Regulating Europe* (London: Routledge, 1996); C. Pollitt, K. Bathgate, J. Caulfield, A. Smullen and C. Talbot, 'Agency Fever? Analysis of an International Policy Fashion', *Journal of Comparative Policy Analysis: Research and Practice*, 3 (2001), 271–90; F. Vibert, *The Rise of the Unelected: Democracy and the New Separation of Powers* (Cambridge University Press, 2007). I do not discuss here the complex issue of agency classification, as this would fall outside the scope of this chapter. Instead, the remarks that follow should be taken as a general reflection on regulatory policy making by institutions whose legitimacy is strongly linked to the use of expert knowledge.

6 European Commission, *Communication from the Commission: The Operating Framework for the European Regulatory Agencies* (COM, Brussels, 2002), 718 final; House of Lords, *UK Economic Regulators*, Volumes I (report) and II (evidence), HL Paper 189 I and II, First Report of Session 2006–2007 (Select Committee on Regulators, 13 November 2007); Majone, *Regulating Europe*; Vibert, *The Rise of the Unelected.*

supranational level,[7] which are portrayed as technical policy makers operating in isolation from political factors.[8] In their field of competence and for the policy areas falling within their mandate, IRAs are considered as central producers and users of policy-relevant knowledge. In-house expertise is often a core feature of their independence.[9]

Yet, the empirical question of how expert knowledge is actually *used* in regulatory policy making remains relatively untouched, with some notable exceptions.[10] As mentioned, it is assumed that expertise will play a fundamental role in these organizations.[11] However, this conclusion has been almost taken for granted without being adequately problematized.

Questions on the *gap between the production and use* of policy-relevant expertise were already raised three decades ago by Carol Weiss in her seminal work on knowledge utilization.[12] Several scholars[13] have followed

7 As explained by Thatcher, IRAs 'are formally separated from parent ministries and are not elected nor managed by elected officials'. M. Thatcher, 'Regulation after Delegation: Independent Regulatory Agencies in Europe', *Journal of European Public Policy*, 9 (2002), 954–72, at 956.

8 M. Maggetti, 'De Facto Independence after Delegation: A Fuzzy-Set Analysis', *Regulation and Governance*, 1 (2007), 271–94; M. C. Stephenson, 'Bureaucratic Decision Costs and Endogenous Agency Expertise', *Journal of Law, Economics & Organization*, 23 (2007), 469–98.

9 On this point, see the seminal contribution by K. Bawn, 'Political Control versus Expertise: Congressional Choices about Administrative Procedures', *American Political Science Review*, 89 (1995), 62–73.

10 See, for instance, T. O. McGarity, *Reinventing Rationality: The Role of Regulatory Analysis in the Federal Bureaucracy* (Cambridge University Press, 1991); R. D. Morgenstern, *Economic Analysis at EPA: Assessing Regulatory Impact* (Washington DC: Resources for the Future, 1997); E. T. Jennings and J. L. Hall, 'Evidence-Based Practice and the Use of Information in State Agency Decision-Making', *Journal of Public Administration Research and Theory*, 22 (2012), 245–66.

11 On this point, the following quote from the European Commission's operating framework for European Regulatory Agencies is rather telling: 'The independence of their technical and/or scientific assessments is, in fact, their real raison d'être. The main advantage of using the agencies is that their decisions are based on purely technical evaluations of very high quality and are not influenced by political or contingent considerations.' European Commission, *Communication from the Commission*, at 5.

12 C. H. Weiss, 'The Many Meanings of Research Utilization', *Public Administration Review*, 39 (1979), 426–31.

13 See, for instance, M. S. Feldman and J. G. March, 'Information in Organizations as Signal and Symbol', *Administrative Science Quarterly*, 26 (1981), 171–86; F. Heller (ed.), *The Use and Abuse of Social Science* (London: Sage, 1986); E. A. Lindquist, 'What Do Decision Models Tell Us about Information Use?', *Knowledge, Technology & Policy*, 1 (1988), 86–111; B. Wittrock, 'Social Knowledge and Public Policy: Eight Models of Interaction' in P. Wagner, C. H. Weiss, B. Wittrock and H. Wollmann (eds.), *Social Science and Modern States: National Experiences and Theoretical Crossroads* (Cambridge University Press, 1991), 333–54.

Weiss' insights to explore the path linking expert input to actual policy decisions.

This chapter aims to reflect on the different possible uses of expert input into regulatory policy making. I will focus in particular on the implications in terms of legitimacy that the different roles of expertise described in the knowledge utilization literature have for independent regulatory agencies. As will be explained below, expertise can be used in different ways by regulators: instrumentally, to identify the best solution to a given problem (instrumental/problem-solving approach); strategically, to support a pre-defined position; or even as a symbolic tool to strengthen the agency's reputation and legitimacy.

To address these issues, this chapter is structured as follows. Section 4.2 will provide a brief overview of the literature on knowledge utilization. Section 4.3 will introduce a possible classification of the different roles that expertise can play in regulatory policy making. Section 4.4 will reflect on the implications that the different roles of expert knowledge may have for independent regulators and the position of these organizations in contemporary policy making. Finally, section 4.5 will offer some concluding thoughts.

4.2 Insights from the knowledge utilization literature

There is still an underlying tendency in some policy-making circles to assume that if expert input is available at the right time and place and in the right format, it can be used to solve a given policy problem. This view is based on the (often criticized) rational view of the policy process.[14] As a result, this assumption ties discussions on the role of knowledge with questions of procedural design establishing how expertise should be produced and channelled at the right point in the policy-making process.[15] But what if the use of expertise in policy making also followed a different logic, one that cannot be fully governed by procedures? Perhaps a different perspective can shed light on the observation that policy-relevant knowledge is not always used by policy makers.

[14] On this point, see J. Hertin, J. Turnpenny, A. Jordan, M. Nilsson, D. Russel and B. Nykvist, 'Rationalising the Policy Mess? Ex Ante Policy Assessment and the Utilisation of Knowledge in the Policy Process', *Environment and Planning A*, 41 (2008), 1185–200.

[15] On this point, see Bawn, 'Political Control versus Expertise'.

As mentioned, the apparent contrast between the decoupling[16] of policy-relevant research and specific policy decisions on the one hand, and the increasing emphasis on the importance of expertise in policy making on the other hand, is not new to researchers. As the knowledge utilization literature of the late 1970s and 1980s had already highlighted, the separation finds its roots in different logics that are only loosely connected with a rational approach to policy making. Understanding the different usages of expertise in policy making and why they occur has become central, particularly today, as the traditional channels for feeding expert input into policies are changing and increasingly feature added layers of complexity. This last point is exemplified by the spreading of networks of experts into certain areas transcending national boundaries, such as human rights, Internet governance and climate change. In these cases, the chain linking expertise to a policy decision becomes even more difficult to reconstruct. Hence, it is worth going back to the different rationales that may guide the use of expertise by policy makers. It is to this question that we now turn.

According to Nathan Caplan's classical theory of the 'two communities', there exists a cultural gap in terms of values and ideologies between academics and politicians that severely hampers the transfer of knowledge between the two. In her seminal work,[17] Carol H. Weiss has suggested a possible explanation for the observed disconnection between researchers and policy makers by going beyond Caplan's 'two communities'.[18] Weiss has certainly acknowledged the existence of such a divide, which she partly attributes to researchers and the way they craft and sometimes miscommunicate expert knowledge to policy makers.[19] Her work also points to one of

[16] In this chapter, the term 'decoupling' is used to indicate the separation between the process of producing policy-relevant expertise and the process of policy making in individual cases. Decoupling can occur at different levels: when political principals commission research to experts, but do not use it when deciding on a given issue; and also within the same organization, when the production of expertise is not systematically linked to decisions, as described by Nils Brunsson in his distinction between action and talk in organizations. For further details, see N. Brunsson, *The Organization of Hypocrisy: Talk, Decisions and Actions in Organizations* (Chichester: John Wiley & Sons, 1989).

[17] Weiss, 'The Many Meanings'.

[18] N. Caplan, 'The Two-Communities Theory and Knowledge Utilization', *American Behavioral Scientist*, 22 (1979), 459–70.

[19] Classical examples of miscommunication are: research that is too theoretical to be used in policy making; limited user-friendliness in the presentation of relevant findings; lack of clarity on the methodology followed by the researcher and the link between findings and the policy problem under examination. On the 'communication sins' of researchers,

the main weaknesses of the 'two communities' theory: it only sheds light on one segment of the whole picture, that is, the dichotomy between the use and non-use of expertise.

The use of knowledge is not a monolithic concept corresponding to a linear transfer of research findings into policy making. As has been extensively demonstrated by Weiss, expert knowledge can play several functions in policy making. In fact, Weiss identified six types of possible knowledge usages besides the general role of contributing to the 'intellectual pursuit of a society'.[20] The first type is: (1) the knowledge-driven model that mimics the approach adopted by the natural sciences, where research discloses some option/answer and ideally policy will follow this initial input. Weiss has stressed that this type of usage rarely occurs among policy makers. Conversely, the remaining five models easily find their place in the daily practice of policy making: (2) the problem-solving model, where researchers produce knowledge to solve a given policy question; (3) the interactive model, where social scientists and other actors pool resources to feed research into the policy process; (4) the political model, where research is used by policy makers as ammunition to advocate a predetermined position; (5) the tactical model, where research is used by policy makers 'for purposes that have little relation to the substance of the research',[21] such as gaining legitimacy towards external actors; and finally (6) the enlightenment model, in which research has a long-term impact on the way decision makers interpret the world and the challenges facing them.

Following Weiss' initial intuition, several authors have developed their own classification of the different uses of knowledge, and one can identify several commonalities between these categorizations by looking at the rationale underpinning each type of use. Although they occur in different contexts, very often knowledge usages correspond to one of the following logics: instrumental/problem solving; strategic; and finally a symbolic logic, where knowledge is used to conform to certain expectations. The last approach is often referred to as the 'logic of appropriateness'.[22] These three logics are the foundations of the classification explained below, which is based on Boswell's comprehensive

see Weiss, 'The Many Meanings'; and C. E. Lindblom, 'Who Needs What Social Research for Policy Making?', *Science Communication*, 7 (1986), 345–66.

[20] Weiss, 'The Many Meanings', at 429–30. [21] *Ibid.*, at 429.

[22] On this concept, see J. G. March and J. P. Olsen, *Rediscovering Institutions: The Organizational Basis of Politics* (New York: Free Press, 1989).

synthesis of previous attempts to describe and categorize existing uses of expertise.[23] The next section briefly describes these three usages.

4.3 The different uses of expertise in policy making

Accordingly, a regulatory agency can essentially choose between three possible uses of expert knowledge: instrumental, strategic and symbolic. While the instrumental and symbolic uses each have only one rationale (problem solving and enhancing legitimacy, respectively), the strategic use can play two different functions: advocating a pre-defined policy position or providing arguments to expand the power of the agency.

The instrumental use of expert knowledge corresponds to the problem-solving approach portrayed in rational accounts of the policy process[24] and is commonly presented in normative debates on evidence-based policy making as 'the' correct way to use expertise.[25] This instrumental usage can be chosen to tackle specific policy issues in the short term, but also to cope with future problems by accumulating relevant expertise.[26]

Expert knowledge can also be subject to strategic usages to advocate a preferred policy position either in front of stakeholders or vis-à-vis political principals. Schout and Sleifer in this volume mention a classical case of strategic use of knowledge when they refer to European Commission impact assessments being drafted at a late stage of policy making to justify/substantiate a decision that has already been taken.[27] Another example could be when data or assumptions in an economic analysis are carefully selected to present a certain picture of reality, often exploiting the informational asymmetries between agents (in this case, the experts within the

[23] While I essentially follow Boswell's classification of knowledge usages, I use a slightly different labelling for the various usages of expertise. C. Boswell, 'The Legitimizing Function of Expert Knowledge in the Administration', unpublished manuscript (2006); Boswell, *The Political Uses of Expert Knowledge*.

[24] See, for instance, E. Albæk, 'Between Knowledge and Power: Utilization of Social Science in Public Policy Making', *Policy Sciences*, 28 (1995), 79–100; Caplan, 'The Two-Communities Theory and Knowledge Utilization'; D. Torgerson, 'Between Knowledge and Politics: Three Faces of Policy Analysis', *Policy Sciences*, 19 (1986), 33–59.

[25] See, for example, European Commission, *European Governance*; European Commission, *Better Regulation*; House of Lords, *UK Economic Regulators*; OECD, *Regulatory Policies in OECD Countries*.

[26] On this point, see Weiss, 'The Many Meanings'; L. Schrefler, 'The Usage of Scientific Knowledge by Independent Regulatory Agencies', *Governance*, 23 (2010), 309–30.

[27] Schout and Schleifer, Chapter 17, this volume.

agency) and principals.[28] Strategic uses of knowledge to expand the regulatory agency's powers occur, for instance, when the agency produces a report that shows how intervention in an area not fully covered by its current mandate would be beneficial. This could help the regulator in convincing its political principals to review/extend the agency's mandate.

Finally, symbolic usages of expertise occur when produced knowledge is decoupled from policy decisions[29] and used, among other things, to signal that the organization has sufficient expertise or conforms to external expectations.[30] In this case, the use of knowledge follows the logic of appropriateness[31] and is often driven by the organization's need to establish its reputation as a credible player in the policy arena or to tactically manage expectations in the absence of actual intervention on a given issue. A classical example of symbolic usage would be the case of an agency that produces literature reviews and other studies that do not respond to the actual informational needs of the organization, but still communicate to the outside world that something is being done on an issue.[32] The difference between this approach and the instrumental and strategic expert knowledge usages lies in the fact that the latter are always connected to a specific policy decision, while symbolic uses are generally decoupled from decisions.[33]

Of course, an agency can also choose not to use the relevant expert knowledge for several reasons. First, research findings could damage a preferred policy option which was chosen on other grounds, or the decision adopted is the only viable one in political terms at a given point in time.[34]

[28] For instance, the agency can have privileged access to data that its political principals have no time or capacity to process. Without oversight mechanisms, the agency could use this information selectively to support a certain course of action.

[29] On the decoupling between talk and action within an organization, see Brunsson, *The Organization of Hypocrisy*; Boswell, 'The Legitimizing Function of Expert Knowledge in the Administration'; Boswell, *The Political Uses of Expert Knowledge*.

[30] P. J. Di Maggio and W. Powell, 'The Iron Cage Revisited: Institutional Isomorphism and Collective Rationality in Organizational Fields', *American Sociological Review*, 48 (1983), 147–60.

[31] For an extensive discussion of the mechanisms underpinning this logic, see E. Goffman, *The Presentation of Self in Everyday Life* (New York: Doubleday Anchor Books, 1959).

[32] This can occur, for instance, in relation to politically or economically sensitive policy questions, when the right conditions to take a decision are not present. If the agency cannot afford (in terms of reputation) to keep silent on the issue, a symbolic production of general research on the topic can be a good strategy.

[33] On decoupling, see above, note 16.

[34] It is worth reminding that I am describing knowledge utilization from the perspective of the regulatory agency and not from the perspective of its political principal(s) when they

Another possibility is that an agency is simply bound by the electoral commitments of the principal and thus expert knowledge, although available, does not really play a role in the agency's policy decisions. This particular case would signal that there is a discrepancy between the formal and the real independence of the agency from its political principals.[35] Finally, a third explanation could be that pre-existing approaches to tackle and decide on a given policy issue are so entrenched in an agency that expertise does not really make a difference when decisions are taken, particularly when these decisions trigger only small incremental changes in existing policies.[36]

Against this backdrop, it becomes worth exploring under which conditions an agency is more likely to opt for a certain usage of knowledge or will refrain from using available expertise. Unfortunately, empirical testing remains rather limited in this strand of research, as it is relatively difficult to operationalize and measure expert knowledge utilization variables and, more broadly, to distinguish the influence of expertise from other factors affecting policy decisions. This point is possibly one of the main explanations for the gradual decrease in the number of publications on the topic after the productive initial phase.[37] I have suggested elsewhere[38] a set of hypotheses based on different combinations of the level of conflict surrounding a policy problem and the availability of accumulated knowledge that could explain when different uses of knowledge by an independent regulatory agency are likely to occur. These were tested empirically[39] on the basis of a set of case studies on the use of economic expertise in individual regulatory decisions taken by

have to make policy decisions based on the expertise provided by the agency. As explained above, in the case of IRAs, an agency is normally the main decision maker for the areas covered by its legal mandate. Hence, the agency is also in a position to decide not to use its own expertise for one of the reasons described here.

35 In other words, although formally independent, the agency will systematically take into account the preferences of its political principals, even when these preferences conflict with available evidence/expertise. On the question of formal versus de facto autonomy of independent regulators, see Everson, Chapter 15, this volume.

36 P. A. Hall, 'Policy Paradigms, Social Learning and the State: The Case of Economic Policy-Making in Britain', *Comparative Politics*, 25 (1993), 275–96.

37 The main exceptions are the following: Jennings and Hall, 'Evidence-Based Practice and the Use of Information in State Agency Decision-Making'; C. M. Radaelli, 'The Role of Knowledge in the Policy Process', *Journal of European Public Policy*, 2 (1995), 159–83; C. M. Radaelli and B. Dente, 'Evaluation Strategies and Analysis of the Policy Process', *Evaluation*, 2 (1996), 51–66; C. H. Weiss, 'The Interface Between Evaluation and Public Policy', *Evaluation*, 5 (1999), 468–86.

38 Schrefler, 'The Usage of Scientific Knowledge by Independent Regulatory Agencies'.

39 L. Schrefler, *Economic Knowledge in Regulation: The Use of Expertise by Independent Agencies* (Colchester: ECPR Press, 2013).

the Office of Communications (Ofcom), the UK independent regulator for electronic communications. While describing these empirical findings would fall outside the scope of this chapter, it is important to note that the occurrence of the different expert knowledge usages illustrated in this section (albeit with different degrees) is confirmed by the case studies I performed on Ofcom.

Other similar analyses on the use of expertise and evidence-based policy-making tools by regulators (with different degrees of independence from political principals) show similar results. For instance, when reviewing the use of economic analysis by the US Environmental Protection Agency, Morgenstern described a series of episodes featuring the various uses of expertise depicted above, ranging from an instrumental use (e.g., the 1991 rule on permissible levels of lead in drinking water) to a non-use of relevant expert knowledge (e.g., the revision of the worker protection standard for agricultural pesticides).[40] In its 2001 and 2004 reviews of impact assessment practice in the UK, the National Audit Office found that the evidence provided during the *ex ante* appraisal of a proposal is often used strategically and crafted at a late stage to support a pre-defined position.[41] Nilsson et al. performed 37 case studies on the use of various policy assessment tools in the European Commission, Germany, the UK and Sweden for policy areas such as climate change, transport and pharmaceutical services regulation. While their research questions only addressed the role of expertise in policy making indirectly, their findings indicate the rather frequent occurrence of strategic and non-use of expert knowledge.[42] More recently, Dunlop et al. reviewed 49 regulatory cases from the European Union (EU) and the UK. While they also reported the strategic and the non-use of expertise, they observed an increase in the instrumental use of expertise

40 Morgenstern, *Economic Analysis at EPA*, at 205–32 and 303–32.

41 National Audit Office, *Better Regulation: Making Good Use of Regulatory Impact Assessments*, HC 329 session 2001–02 (London, 2001), available at: www.nao.org.uk/wp-content/uploads/2001/11/0102329.pdf; and National Audit Office, *Evaluation of Regulatory Impact Assessments Compendium Report 2003–04: Report by the Comptroller and Auditor General*, HC 358 session 2003–2004 (London, 2004), available at: www.nao.org.uk/wp-content/uploads/2004/03/0304358.pdf.

42 According to the authors, one of the main drivers of this phenomenon is the fact that the usage of policy assessment tools was not fully institutionalized in the jurisdictions under examination. For further details, see M. Nilsson, A. Jordan, J. Turnpenny, J. Hertin, B. Nykvist and D. Russel, 'The Use and Non-use of Policy Appraisal Tools in Public Policy Making: An Analysis of Three European Countries and the European Union', *Policy Sciences*, 41 (2008), 335–55.

in comparison with previous studies. This shift towards more frequent instrumental uses of expertise under certain circumstances also emerged in my analysis of a selection of regulatory decisions in the telecommunications sector by Ofcom.[43] Such a trend seems to be driven by some specific conditions, some of which were also stressed by Jennings and Hall in their review of the use of information in state agency policy making in the USA.[44] Specifically, I found that due to a series of procedural (the statutory duty to perform regulatory impact assessments coupled with judicial review on the merits), institutional (e.g., the presence of scrutiny by other bodies like a court of auditors) and organizational features (a strong in-house research capacity), the prevalent use of expertise is of the instrumental type. Yet, symbolic and strategic uses of expert knowledge remain complementary and politically expedient strategies in some cases.

Another point that emerges clearly from empirical research on knowledge utilization[45] is the inherently adversarial nature of regulatory policy making in many sectors, where any policy decision quickly turns into a zero-sum game with winners and losers.[46] This feature of regulatory policy making, in turn, seems to significantly affect the environment in which experts have to produce and use policy-relevant expertise. In other words, it seems as if the very nature of policy making reduces the number of instances where the ideal conditions for an instrumental or

[43] Schrefler, *Economic Knowledge in Regulation.*

[44] Jennings and Hall, 'Evidence-Based Practice and the Use of Information in State Agency Decision-Making'.

[45] E.g., Morgenstern, *Economic Analysis at EPA*; Schrefler, *Economic Knowledge in Regulation.*

[46] As extensively discussed in the literature (e.g., Majone, *Regulating Europe*; Maggetti, 'De Facto Independence after Delegation'), the shift towards regulatory policies is a common feature of modern states and is a consequence of the retreat of the state from sectors such as electricity, telecommunications and so on. As clearly illustrated by F. Gilardi, 'Policy Credibility and Delegation to Independent Regulatory Agencies: A Comparative Empirical Analysis', *Journal of European Public Policy*, 9 (2002), 873–93, at 873: 'the state retreats from sectors . . . where it used to be highly interventionist, but, on the other hand, it reregulates the now-liberalized markets with less intrusive instruments. This implies a shift in the very functions of the state, notably from stabilization and redistribution to regulation'. Another major consequence of this shift is that those bearing the costs of reregulation (e.g.., the firms that own or manage the infrastructure and other facilities to provide those services) are normally very clearly identifiable, while beneficiaries (most often, citizens enjoying the benefits of increased competition and choice on the market) are less visible. As the costs of each rule are often unevenly spread among a limited number of market players competing with one another, this naturally leads to policy conflict.

problem-solving use of expert knowledge are present, unless certain arrangements are put in place, as discussed in the next section. In general, the presence of specific procedures such as the obligation to consult stakeholders and perform *ex ante* impact assessments can limit the strategic use of knowledge and foster the instrumental use of knowledge. Conversely, they are only loosely connected to the symbolic use of expertise, where knowledge is produced to gain or enhance legitimacy rather than to inform a policy decision.

4.4 Implications of the role of expertise for regulatory policy making

While the empirical findings discussed above are often based on case studies and cannot be easily generalized, they still shed some light on certain features of modern (independent) regulatory agencies that it is worth discussing further.

The finding that under certain procedural and institutional conditions the prevalent use of expert knowledge is instrumental (i.e., problem solving) contradicts the most fervent critics of rational accounts of the policy process who portray an instrumental use of expert knowledge as extremely rare, if not a sort of technocratic utopia. In a way, the expectations that procedures, if correctly implemented, can indeed create the right incentives for channelling relevant expertise into policy making are partially vindicated.[47] In this sense, the emphasis on evidence-based policy making and tools such as public consultation and regulatory impact assessment has positively changed the culture and practice of policy making.[48] However, it has also reinforced the myth of 'the rational decision maker' and opened new avenues for questioning the legitimacy

[47] Note the conditionality of the statement: the 'if' acquires a significant weight when an agency is not adequately staffed to produce or correctly use knowledge (on this point, see Jennings and Hall, 'Evidence-Based Practice and the Use of Information in State Agency Decision-Making') or if there is no system to control whether these procedures for the transparent and accountable use of knowledge are actually complied with and do not become a tick-the-box exercise. On this point, see, for instance, A. Alemanno, 'The Better Regulation Initiative at the Judicial Gate: A Trojan Horse within the Commission's Walls or the Way Forward?', *European Law Journal*, 15 (2009), 382–401.

[48] C. M. Radaelli, L. Allio, A. Renda and L. Schrefler, *How to Learn from the International Experience: Impact Assessment in The Netherlands*, Report prepared for the Dutch government (Exeter: Regulatory Reform Group, 2010); A. Renda, *Law and Economics in the RIA World* (Cambridge: Intersentia, 2011).

of regulators when they do not or cannot conform to this ideal vision. As mentioned above, the level of conflict that surrounds many policy decisions can limit the number of instances where the ideal conditions for an instrumental or problem-solving use of knowledge are present. In regulatory policies, which are often characterized by dispersed benefits and concentrated costs,[49] conflict is always around the corner. The zero-sum nature of policy debates puts independent regulators in a delicate position, where an increasing number of conflicting demands, often backed by contrasting sources of expertise, have to be managed. At times, an instrumental use of expertise, even when intentionally sought by the agency, may not be a viable option. In other instances, however, a regulatory agency may deliberately follow a different logic and opt for symbolic or strategic usages, or even for a non-use of expert knowledge.

What can then be concluded on the legitimacy of independent regulators? On the one hand, the claim put forward in the beginning of this chapter that these organizations were created and are legitimate because they use expert knowledge instrumentally and not politically is somewhat incorrect. The days of the independent regulator shielded from political influence[50] are long gone. However, the presence of the political component in the policy making activities of independent agencies does not necessarily imply that the image of the politically insulated regulator is wrong. Rather, the complexity of current policy problems and the reality of policy making indicate that this image is in need of some serious rethinking. At least, we should acknowledge that the legitimacy of regulatory agencies is not solely grounded on a neutral or impartial use of expertise. In fact, the last point is not surprising if it is accepted that independent regulators operate in a policy environment that is eminently but not exclusively technical. To survive in a (at least partially) political environment, regulators have to deploy usages of expert knowledge that deviate from the instrumental type.

Rather than anomalies, these different usages of expert knowledge appear as a natural feature of the policy process and can at times be beneficial, damaging or simply the only possible path for a regulator. While it is difficult to deny that an instrumental usage of expertise is

[49] On this point, see M. Olson, *The Logic of Collective Action* (Cambridge, MA: Harvard University Press, 1965).

[50] See G. Majone, 'From the Positive to the Regulatory State: Causes and Consequences of Changes in the Mode of Governance', *Journal of Public Policy*, 17 (1997), 139–67; and Vibert, *The Rise of the Unelected*.

the 'ideal' one, it may not always be appropriate. For example, building a reputation can be vital for an organization, and symbolic usages of expert knowledge have become a crucial step to achieve this goal. This was shown, for instance, by Boswell in her recent case study on the creation of a research group by the German Federal Office for Migration and Refugees.[51]

In fact, alternative uses of expertise can positively complement an instrumental use, for instance, in terms of legitimacy. These alternative uses become 'wrong' (i.e., not effective) when they are prevalent and create a distorted approach to the use of evidence in policy making; for instance, when an organization systematically ignores existing research because it goes against the wishes of its political principals.

4.4.1 Expert versus political decision making?

The traditional dichotomy between neutral or bureaucratic and political decision making has increasingly fewer supporters. Arguably, it cannot be upheld. Regulatory policy making is better depicted as a continuum ranging from 'government by experts' to 'government by politicians'. In this context, there is no such thing as a neutral policy appraisal. Nor is it, consequently, realistic to conceive that a purely technical use of power exists.

It is also difficult to imagine that organizations, such as independent regulatory agencies, will not make use of the regulatory and policy-making powers they have received at the time of delegation. In some instances the use of delegated powers may imply venturing into more 'political' territory, depending on the nature of the policy problem at stake. In other words, we have to accept that a portion of regulatory policy making is political.[52] However, claiming that policy making is inevitably politicized and that this undermines the rationale for having independent regulators in the first place would be incorrect. Very often, independent regulators possess and are developing a wealth of expertise that is crucial for modern policy making. I concur with Vibert[53] that having an independent but accountable locus for policy making contributes to the success and equilibrium of today's regulatory states.

[51] Boswell, *The Political Uses of Expert Knowledge.*

[52] On this, see also H. E. Meier, 'Independent Regulatory Bodies and Impossible Jobs: The Failure of German Broadcasting Regulation', *Public Administration*, 86 (2008), 133–48, at 131.

[53] *Ibid.*

At the same time, we can also state that the often-feared scenario of unaccountable regulatory experts running out of control can and has been avoided. To be sure, concerns in this respect remain. Yet, for all types of political and institutional settings, there are effective procedural and organizational steps to counter the risk of a runaway bureaucracy. These will be discussed in the next section.

4.4.2 *Fostering an instrumental use of expert knowledge*

In procedural terms, the statutory duty to widely consult and to 'give reasons' through impact assessment is a valid approach. When coupled with the incentive provided by judicial review, these procedures can lead to a system where analytical rigour, transparency and accountability are preserved. Some authors[54] have claimed that impact assessments and evidence-based policy making cannot really be effective unless their content is subject to judicial review. Otherwise, these tools risk becoming box-ticking exercises that fulfil a correct function in procedural terms, but may produce evidence that has little bearing on the final decision. In the context of the different uses of expertise presented above, one could, for instance, imagine that judicial review on the merits can only allow a non-usage of expert knowledge when an agency is dealing with high-level policy issues. In those cases, it is potentially easier to disregard available expertise, particularly when current circumstances do not open a window of opportunity[55] for a certain course of action. However, in cases where policy goals are agreed upon and the agency has to decide on the best approach to implement them, disregarding available expert knowledge could be easily challenged in court and would thus be a dangerous strategy in terms of legitimacy. Judicial review on the merits can also limit strategic uses of expert knowledge to support a pre-defined policy solution, unless this strategic approach is carefully hidden in the choice of assumptions or the interpretation of information within, for example, an economic model, or departures from evidence-based solutions are explicitly and transparently justified by the regulator. Symbolic usages of expertise to strengthen the legitimacy and reputation of an

[54] Alemanno, 'The Better Regulation Initiative at the Judicial Gate'; G. Majone, 'Foundations of Risk Regulation: Science, Decision-Making, Policy Learning and Institutional Reform', *European Journal of Risk Regulation*, 1 (2010), 5–19.

[55] On this concept, see J. W. Kingdon, *Agendas, Alternatives, and Public Policies*, 2nd edn (New York: Longman, 1995).

agency are normally independent from decisions.[56] Hence, they are not affected by judicial review. Accordingly, they can only be influenced by monitoring how an agency allocates and uses resources devoted to the production and use of expertise throughout the policy cycle.

It is worth adding that in the case of independent regulatory agencies exercising delegated powers, judicial review on the merits directly contributes to the legitimacy of these organizations and their decisions. The possibility of having a decision overturned by a court provides an incentive for the regulator to use expert knowledge instrumentally: the reputational costs of being accused of making poor decisions are high. Policy makers should, however, strive to find solutions that deliver the benefits of review on the merits without falling into the traps of adversarial legalism,[57] where judicial review is tactically used by regulatees to delay the regulatory process. In any event, these judicial procedures are not sufficient to keep the use of knowledge on an instrumental path if an agency is not adequately staffed in terms of the expertise and resources needed to implement such procedures. In the long run, a competent agency with a strong reputation (hence the importance of symbolic usages of knowledge) can generate a positive set of incentives for regulatees and can also push regulated parties to use expert knowledge more instrumentally.

Although the balance between these three elements (procedural requirements, incentives and capacity) may vary depending on the policy area and the national/institutional context, all three are equally important. Actually, they are essential in order to build and consolidate trust in the regulatory system.

4.4.3 Balancing the autonomy and accountability of regulatory agencies

Finally, the knowledge utilization perspective allows us to revisit traditional research questions on the balance between the autonomy and accountability of agencies from the inside, showing how an agency builds

56 As explained above, symbolic uses of knowledge work as mechanisms to signal the competence of the agency and reinforce its public image and are thus decoupled from specific policy decisions.

57 R. Kagan, 'Should Europe Worry about Adversarial Legalism?', *Oxford Journal of Legal Studies*, 17 (1997), 165–84; R. D. Kelemen and E. C. Sibbitt, 'The Globalization of American Law', *International Organization*, 58 (2004), 103–36; and R. D. Kelemen and E. C. Sibbitt, 'Lex Americana? A Response to Levi-Faur', *International Organization*, 59 (2005), 463–72.

(internally, via organizational processes) the basis of its autonomy and reputation. This is particularly relevant if traditional post-delegation questions, such as how an independent regulator interacts with its principals and its policy environment, are studied.

Several years ago, Cornelius Kerwin concluded his review of rule making in the USA by noting that we need to add a theory of negotiation to the theory of delegation.[58] He argued that delegation is a foundational act that establishes a contract between elected politicians and independent regulatory agencies. But independent regulators and their principals keep re-defining the substance of the delegation contract in daily interactions, when individual rules are created. The implementation of delegation contracts thus appears as a constant evolution and negotiation of who does what in relation to specific episodes of rule making.

Negotiation between the agency and the other actors in a policy arena occurs via the implementation of specific procedures and processes, including those to channel expertise in policy making. Procedures, such as impact assessments and consultations, are thus constantly re-defined by different constellations of actors involved in rule making. These procedures do not necessarily bias policy decisions in one direction or the other: they are somewhat malleable. In this connection, it can be argued that some of the bold statements made by delegation theorists about cost–benefit analysis requirements, such as 'stack the deck' devices designed to steer the regulatory process in a certain direction (e.g., favouring particular stakeholders or policy solutions), need to be re-examined in light of what individual case studies of rule making tell us.[59] Overall, procedures are more likely to ensure that the agency remains accountable. They could also potentially reinforce its autonomy if the agency can use them as a proof that it has acted correctly, even in terms of knowledge usage.[60]

In turn, these comments raise a new set of research questions for scholars studying individual regulatory agencies: is the regulator well equipped in terms of resources and powers to survive and act effectively in its policy context? Given the growing complexity of policy problems

[58] C. M. Kerwin, *Rulemaking: How Government Agencies Write Law and Make Policy*, 3rd edn (Washington DC: CQ Press, 2003).

[59] On this point, see also A. C. Dunlop, M. Maggetti, C. M. Radaelli and D. Russel, 'The Many Uses of Regulatory Impact Assessment: A Meta-Analysis of EU and UK Cases', *Regulation and Governance*, 6 (2012), 23–45.

[60] On this point, see M. Maor, 'A Scientific Standard and an Agency's Legal Independence: Which of These Reputation Protection Mechanisms is Less Susceptible to Political Moves?', *Public Administration*, 85 (2007), 961–78.

and the interdependence of policy decisions, do (independent) regulators need more or less in-house expertise? And can and should expertise provide an answer to intractable and highly uncertain and risky policy issues? Some of these questions, and particularly the last one, are not completely new. Yet, a balanced and pragmatic[61] answer has to be found.

4.5 Conclusions

This chapter has highlighted how the tenets of the knowledge utilization literature in political science allow us to look behind widespread and often implicitly normative assumptions on the role of expert knowledge in modern policy-making processes. As regards linear/rational representations of the policy process, which are commonly associated with evidence-based policy-making initiatives, empirical testing of the use of expert knowledge indicates that the ideal conditions to foster an instrumental use of knowledge are not always present in modern policy processes. But there are solutions to create a climate that is conducive to an instrumental use of expert knowledge or to at least ensure that it is distinguishable from other types of usages. In this light, expertise and, more importantly, its production and use are legitimate (and contribute to the agency's legitimacy) if they are embedded in a specific procedural, organizational and incentive-based context. It is on these three aspects that political principals should concentrate when they delegate and monitor the usage of regulatory powers.

The above considerations are particularly relevant for agencies and non-elected bureaucracies such as the European Commission and national independent regulators, as it is often assumed that one of the justifications for delegating power to such organizations lies in the fact that they will use expertise to make decisions. But if this assumption is only referring to a rational problem-solving usage of expert knowledge, reality risks falling short of expectations, and yet another legitimacy problem may occur (inside administrations, when civil servants lose interest for tools such as impact assessment because 'things do not work that way', and outside if stakeholders perceive that decisions are not linked to evidence or are a mere box-ticking exercise for the regulator).

The knowledge utilization literature and, particularly, reflections on the symbolic role that expertise can play, also provide a new angle to look at questions on the measurement of de facto agency autonomy, which is

[61] Sanderson, 'Intelligent Policy Making for a Complex World'.

often grounded in reputational variables.[62] In this context, instrumental/problem-solving uses of expertise can sometimes be usefully complemented by symbolic uses of knowledge to signal that a given organization possesses the necessary expertise in-house and is a credible player in the policy arena. As explained in this chapter, symbolic uses do not replace actual policy making, but remain a viable solution in some instances.

Finally, these remarks bring us back to the main topic of this book: the role of experts. Although the position of experts with regulatory powers is not entirely comparable to that of their counterparts in academia, think tanks and other non-governmental epistemic communities, the different uses of knowledge described above can be relevant for experts inside and outside a regulatory agency. In fact, it is fair to conclude that experts who provide evidence to inform policy decisions have to constantly find the right equilibrium to avoid falling into the opposite traps of the 'scientification of policies' and the 'politicization of science'. In other words, the use of expertise in policy making needs to be transparent and balanced in its dealing with values and core beliefs,[63] which inevitably bring about a political dimension in policy debates. Only when this equilibrium is found are the relevance and, ultimately, the legitimacy of expert input in policy making preserved.

[62] M. Busuioc, D. Curtin and M. Groenleer, 'Agency Growth between Autonomy and Accountability: The European Police Office as "Living Institution"', *Journal of European Public Policy*, 18 (2011), 848–67; A. Wonka and B. Rittberger, 'Perspective on EU Governance: An Empirical Assessment of the Political Attitudes of EU Agency Professionals', *Journal of European Public Policy*, 18 (2011), 888–908.

[63] On this point, see, for instance, P. Sabatier and H. Jenkins-Smith (eds.), *Policy Change and Learning: An Advocacy Coalition Approach* (Boulder, CO: Westview Press, 1993).

5

The virtues of expertise

JAN KLABBERS

5.1 Introduction

Whether engaged as advisors, as decision makers or as gate-keepers between advice and decision, experts and their expertise meet with ambivalent responses in everyday life. Expert advice is often ignored: people smoke, drink, lead sedentary lives and eat industrially produced food. They have unprotected sex, listen to loud music on their headphones and may ignore traffic lights, and do all this not in order to be obstinate, but because somehow they feel confident that in their individual case, smoking will not lead to cancer, loud music will not contribute to loss of hearing and unprotected sex will not lead to sexually transmitted diseases or pregnancy.

Yet, a cough prompts a visit to the doctor, pregnancy involves buying books on 'what to expect when you're expecting', and when people want to lose weight they see a dietician, hire a personal trainer or watch *Oprah*. This is done because deep down inside, people realize that they cannot know everything and may well be in need of expert advice, especially in a world characterized by uncertainty and risk.[1] Hence, expertise is caught between two impulses: expert knowledge is considered necessary but rarely decisive, if only because even if the experts say alcohol is bad for you, there is nonetheless a political trade-off to be made.

This dual impulse owes much to the realization that while experts may get it right, they can also get it wrong. It may be the case that expert knowledge is wrongly presented or represented: research indicating a possible correlation between eating peanut butter and cancer quickly becomes: 'Peanut-butter causes Cancer!' Expert knowledge is also, typically, single-minded, non-holistic and isolated knowledge: it may well

[1] For a useful overview of the convoluted relationship between risk and law, see J. Steele, *Risks and Legal Theory* (Oxford: Hart Publishing, 2004).

be that eating eggs is bad for one's cholesterol level, but nonetheless has a positive overall health effect. The latter is more difficult to establish, though, and often follows the former – by that time, the earlier expert knowledge has already been transmitted.

Expert knowledge is also, often enough, localized knowledge. Pregnant women in Finland are advised not to eat ginger during pregnancy; it is difficult to imagine that the same advice goes out to pregnant women in India, Thailand or China. Likewise, in some cultures it is customary to enjoy a glass of wine with dinner and, typically, medical experts in those cultures do not consider this to be problematic. Yet, in more austere cultures, even the consumption of a single unit of alcohol will be frowned upon. Clearly then, expert knowledge may owe much to time and place. It may not be universally valid, but may be influenced by the culture in which it is embedded, and if that is the case, the truth-claim of the expert knowledge is compromised.

Expert knowledge is often generalized knowledge that, so it is hoped or feared, does not apply in concrete cases. Granted, it may be the case that smoking generally causes cancer, but that does not mean that my smoking will give me cancer. It may be the case that if we work out enough, we will lose weight, but sadly it does not mean that this will also apply to me.

5.2 Politics and expertise

The general ambivalence concerning expert knowledge has carried over to discussions on politics and expertise: leaving decisions to politicians makes for easier accountability mechanisms, but risks uninformed decision making, while upgrading the role of experts may result in better informed decisions, but without any accountability for unpopular decisions, unfair decisions or decisions that turn out to be mistaken.[2]

Hence, there is a tendency to isolate expert knowledge from political influence.[3] Directors of central banks are deemed not to be subject to political directives, as are the various economic and financial advisory institutions. Likewise, supreme court judges may be appointed for life to

[2] See also generally M. A. Hajer, *Authoritative Governance: Policy-Making in the Age of Mediatization* (Oxford University Press, 2009), at 165.

[3] To some extent, this tension between politics and expertise influences public law. For a fine exercise in comparative public law with this in mind, see T. Koopmans, *Courts and Political Institutions: A Comparative View* (Cambridge University Press, 2003).

protect them from political influences, and the directors of food safety agencies or drug safety agencies are often appointed on the basis of their scientific merits.

Yet, expertise is never completely trusted. While directors of central banks and other economic bodies may be constitutionally independent, it will be rare to find any among them without political affiliation. Often, the heads of such bodies and leading civil servants tend to belong to mainstream political parties. And while Supreme Court Justices in the USA are appointed for life, their appointments involve highly politicized Senate hearings, a process from which not all candidates emerge undamaged. Indeed, being embedded in political life is useful to some extent, if only to help guarantee the legitimacy of policy making.

This ambivalence is replicated at the international level. Possibly the most clear-cut example is to be found in the EU, where expertise-based decision making is closely scrutinized by political bodies ('watchdog committees'), while simultaneously the risk of all-too-politicized decision making is hemmed in by involving expert bodies under the infamous label of 'comitology'.[4]

But elsewhere too, expert knowledge is involved in policy planning and decision making.[5] The Executive Board of the World Health Organization (WHO), for example, consists of individuals (representing Member States) who are technically qualified in the field of health. Financial institutions, such as the World Bank and the International Monetary Fund, employ many people trained in finance and economics, and many of their Executive Directors will have similar backgrounds. The ambivalent relationship between politics and expertise is nicely symbolized in the Intergovernmental Panel on Climate Change (IPCC). It was established by two political bodies (the United Nations (UN) Environment Programme and the World Meteorological Organization), has an impressive number of Member States (194) and calls itself an intergovernmental body, yet its work is carried out by independent scientific experts.[6] The scientific reports are ultimately subject to approval

[4] See P. Nedergaard, *European Union Administration: Legitimacy and Efficiency* (Leiden: Martinus Nijhoff, 2006). See also Everson, Chapter 15 and and Busuioc, Chapter 18, this volume.

[5] Note that expertise is also seen as a source of legitimate authority in global governance. See generally D. D. Avant, M. Finnemore and S. K. Sell (eds.), *Who Governs the Globe?* (Cambridge University Press, 2010).

[6] This information is culled from its website: see www.ipcc.ch/organization/organization.shtml; Siebenhüner, Chapter 7, this volume.

by government representatives: the science needs political ratification. And to further illustrate its embeddedness in politics, its work is often taken as biased. Environmental conservatives think the IPCC's prescriptions go too far, while conservationists think they do not go far enough.

In some cases, experts are even given a relatively free hand in standard-setting and decision making, especially on supposedly technical topics. The setting of environmental standards is often left to the International Organization for Standardization. Food standards are the province of the Codex Alimentarius Commission, whereas fisheries standards may be developed under auspices of regional fisheries organizations, such as the Inter-American Tropical Tuna Commission.[7] Financial institutions set their own standards and use highly sophisticated indicators to measure whether governments live up to these standards.[8] In turn, these institutions themselves are subject to credit rating by nominally independent agencies, such as Moody's or the curiously but appropriately named Standard & Poor's.[9]

In short, global governance suggests a constant oscillation between politics and technocracy,[10] between decision makers and experts, sometimes embodied in one and the same institution, sometimes given shape in a complex set of checks and balances. In part, this stems from the very same ambivalence towards the possible role of expertise: necessary, but not sufficient.[11] And both, in turn, arise from the difficulty of assuming responsibility. Decision makers are reluctant to assume responsibility for political decisions and would like to offload some of it to experts, yet they are also aware that responsibility for decision making eventually has to rest with them – that is why they are elected or appointed and that is what justifies their position to begin with. Hence, experts need to be involved, but subjected to some form of political control.

[7] Some of its standards were recently given probative value by a WTO panel deciding *United States – Tuna II (Mexico)*, WT/DS381/R, 15 September 2011.

[8] For a fine recent discussion, see G. A. Sarfaty, *Values in Translation: Human Rights and the Culture of the World Bank* (Stanford University Press, 2012).

[9] This applies, for example, to the Nordic Investment Bank. See www.nib.int/about_nib/rating.

[10] As an observation, this is hardly novel. See already R. Howse, 'From Politics to Technocracy and Back Again: The Fate of the Multilateral Trading System', *American Journal of International Law*, 96 (2002), 94–117; M. Koskenniemi, 'The Fate of Public International Law: Between Technique and Politics', *Modern Law Review*, 70 (2007), 1–30.

[11] One might of course cleverly quip that the reverse applies to politics: sufficient, but not necessary.

5.3 Accountability mechanisms: the oscillation between politics and expertise

This oscillation between expertise and politics informs much of the design of modern bureaucracy, both domestically and internationally, and potentially it may result in an infinite regression. Political decision makers appoint experts, yet experts cannot be trusted to take all perspectives into account and thus need to be subjected to either political scrutiny or a different, higher level of scrutiny by experts. This scrutiny, in turn, may result in an additional layer of political decision making, which should take available expertise into account, leading to another layer of experts. Different types of activities may be subjected to different groups of scrutinizers (whether expert or political) and different constituencies may demand different, sometimes even conflicting, forms of accountability.[12] The result is not only an endless list of bodies (expert and political) involved in decision making, but also a complex set of accountability arrangements. This complexity is perhaps particularly visible in international financial institutions, where the variety of decision-making levels is accompanied by a variety of accountability mechanisms. Financial institutions are, on a broad level, subjected to control by their Member States. Their activities are also increasingly subject to internal control in the form of compliance mechanisms, offices of internal oversight and other auditing mechanisms. Moreover, as noted above, their creditworthiness is subject to control by credit-rating agencies, while the organizations themselves control the activities of those Member States that use their operational services and apply for loans. In addition, the individual projects for which loans are granted will have technical features subject to control by technical experts: the building of a dam is not entrusted to economic expertise alone, but also involves engineering expertise. And, often enough, various social forms of control are built in as well: a financial project will be subjected to human rights, gender equality and environmental scrutiny, for which the organization typically employs different experts. In addition, a role is played by civil society and various official or self-appointed watchdogs, ranging from human rights non-governmental organizations (NGOs) to NGOs specialized more broadly in accountability, with a leading example being the

[12] As Grant and Keohane have observed, it may make a difference whether the financial institutions are held to account by their Member States or by the poor and dispossessed. See R. W. Grant and R. O. Keohane, 'Accountability and Abuses of Power in World Politics', *American Political Science Review*, 99 (2005), 29–43.

Global Accountability Project of One World Trust, a UK-based NGO.[13] Typically, such entities boast specialist expertise but also have a political agenda, thus entangling politics and expertise once more.

In the UK, such a complex set of accountability arrangements has been characterized as an 'audit society'.[14] The same label may well come to apply globally, even if a 'global audit society' is probably not a desirable state of affairs. Such a society is based, in essence, on a total lack of trust, and as such is unsustainable. Moreover, it is difficult to reconcile with democratic concerns. Democracy, at least in its liberal manifestation, is to some extent a trust-based system: the electorate entrusts the making of public policy to its elected representatives.[15] If and when the representatives make a mess, do not live up to their responsibilities or abuse the trust placed in them, they can be replaced, at least as long as the system works in the way people expect it to work.[16] In short, a global audit society may well be almost inevitable, but does not appear particularly desirable, precisely because it sidelines democracy and trust.[17]

How then can the further increase of accountability mechanisms be curtailed? They all create and nurture their own level of distrust in those whose activities they oversee and therewith stifle creativity. They render responsibility or accountability opaque and are subject to the problem that where many hands cooperate, it is difficult to tell who did what[18] and, more importantly perhaps, do little to solve recognized problems. How, in other words, can an acceptable level of 'intelligent accountability', as the British philosopher Onora O'Neill once put it, be achieved where the baby does not disappear down the same drain as the bathwater?[19]

13 See M. Blagescu, L. de Las Casas and R. Lloyd, *Pathways to Accountability: The GAP Framework* (London: One World Trust, 2005).

14 See M. Power, *The Audit Society: Rituals of Verification* (Oxford University Press, 1997).

15 Article 67 of the Dutch Constitution, for example, provides that Members of Parliament (MPs) are to vote without consulting their constituencies (*zonder last*): MPs are to make up their own minds.

16 This was, arguably, the problem with the 2000 US elections, which required intervention by the Supreme Court.

17 Especially as accountability is often conceptualized in terms of control and punishment, instead of socialization and learning. But see Blagescu, De Las Casas and Lloyd, *Pathways to Accountability*. For a more theoretically informed discussion, see A. Ebrahim and E. Weisband (eds.), *Global Accountabilities: Participation, Pluralism, and Public Ethics* (Cambridge University Press, 2007).

18 See generally M. Bovens, *The Quest for Responsibility* (Cambridge University Press, 1998).

19 See O. O'Neill, *A Question of Trust* (Cambridge University Press, 2002).

The domestic solution often resorted to is simply to put a stop to further levels of scrutiny. Typically, for instance, court systems have limited levels, often three in number: local courts, courts of appeal and supreme courts. It is not that supreme courts always do the right thing or are even trusted to always do the right thing. Instead, the limitation relates to the sound intuition that one has to stop somewhere: otherwise, scrutiny (in this case of judgements) may result in an infinite regression. In short, someone at some point in time has to be given the power to have the final say, and there is little to be gained by postponing this moment indefinitely. Should a supreme court get it wrong, politics can pass legislation to correct things.

Something similar is visible in international judicial mechanisms of some sophistication, although there are typically one or two levels. The EU has two courts – not counting the specialized civil service court – to allow for the possibility that the first instance court (the General Court) gets it wrong. Much the same applies to the World Trade Organization (WTO) dispute settlement system, with its panels and Appellate Body. The International Criminal Tribunal for the Former Yugoslavia has an appeals chamber, as does the International Criminal Tribunal for Rwanda; the European Court of Human Rights (ECtHR) works in chambers, but can have cases considered or reconsidered by its Grand Chamber, while the International Criminal Court (ICC) has an Appeals Division. What needs to be taken into account is that some of these courts in effect function as additional layers to domestic courts, even if not, strictly, as appellate courts. Relevant examples are the Court of Justice of the European Union, with its preliminary reference procedure, and the ECtHR, which, according to one observer, 'has essentially become Europe's constitutional court of last resort'.[20]

There might be alternative possibilities in order to prevent the emergence of a global audit society, and one of those resides in the Aristotelian tradition of virtue ethics. In this tradition, what matters is not so much the existence of external standards and accountability mechanisms, but whether actors' behaviour displays virtuous character traits. For Aristotle,[21] the virtues were indispensable for leading a happy, flourishing life (*eudaimonia*), and since a flourishing life involved a life

[20] See D. J. Bederrman, *Globalization and International Law* (New York: Palgrave Macmillan, 2008), at 176.

[21] See Aristotle, *Ethics*. I have used the edition published by Penguin (New York) in 1976, based on the 1953 translation by Thomson as revised by Tredennick.

lived in public, in relations with others (men being a political animal, after all), the virtues were eminently suitable for public life. Working in a distinct Aristotelian mould, Hannah Arendt added the thought that all of us, regardless of our station in life, owe a certain responsibility to the world at large: we need to take care of our common world.[22] It would seem to follow that to the extent that we operate in public, in different roles, different virtues may legitimately be expected from us.

This may not be the case when we act in private or in professions that lack a public element. It is an open question whether one can legitimately expect the plumber to do his plumbing with charity or with empathy or temperance, or legitimately expect the waiter to divide the food among the hungry and thus act justly, although we can expect people to abide by any rules relating to the exercise of their profession.

Things are clearer with those engaged in some kind of public task: people working in healthcare and education, priests and ministers, lawyers, police officers, etc.[23] Here, the public nature of their tasks implies a special responsibility for public affairs, and the public may legitimately expect that its officials (broadly defined) behave in a virtuous manner. This connection to virtue is not solely dependent on the legal status of the entity concerned: education or healthcare may have been privatized to some extent but still perform public functions.[24] Hence, healthcare professionals and teachers may be expected to behave in a manner concordant with their roles, whether they teach or practise medicine at a private university or at a community college or hospital. Citizens too may be expected to perform virtuously in their capacity as citizens, to the extent that being a citizen implies a public function: for example, the task to vote carefully rather than 'with one's feet', or to act with empathy and be honest about one's private interests at public hearings.

When it comes to global governance, public functions are entrusted to diverse groups of people. Here, special tasks may be distinguished for

[22] This is a general theme running through much of Arendt's work in political theory. See, e.g., H. Arendt, *The Human Condition* (University of Chicago Press, 1958). For a general discussion, see J. Klabbers, 'Possible Islands of Predictability: The Legal Thought of Hannah Arendt', *Leiden Journal of International Law*, 20 (2007), 1–23.

[23] This follows J. Oakley and D. Cockley, *Virtue Ethics and Professional Roles* (Cambridge University Press, 2001).

[24] John Dewey already pointed out that the public sector is not a static given: tasks that were once private (e.g., education) have by and large become public, whereas walks of life that were once deemed public (religion) have by and large come to be regarded as private. See J. Dewey, *The Public and its Problems* (Athens, OH: Ohio University Press, 1954 [1927]).

statesmen, but also for the directors-general of international organizations, those working for transboundary civil society organizations (Greenpeace, Amnesty International, etc.), the directors of international financial institutions and those entrusted with advisory or decision-making functions due to their expertise.[25]

5.4 The deontological reflex versus virtue ethics

It is tempting to give in to the kneejerk deontological reflex and devise ethical codes for experts, a set of rules that would apply to experts, whether they render advice, participate as decision makers or act as gate-keepers between expert knowledge and political decision making. But doing so would miss the point that codes of ethics or conduct come with inherent limitations – limitations that apply to all sets of rules. For one thing, by relying on language, rules tend to be both over-inclusive and under-inclusive: they capture acts we might not want them to capture and they fail to capture some of the acts we might want to capture.[26]

Therefore, rules need to come with exceptions: there are very few absolute rules and, to the extent such rules exist, they may often be characterized as 'idiot rules'.[27] Most rules will come – and will have to come – with exceptions, but this renders them vulnerable to further interpretation, perhaps even manipulation: someone will need to decide when to apply the rule and when to apply the exception, and on what basis. This need for interpretation, in turn, suggests that rules never get to apply themselves: rules always need someone to apply them. This 'someone' may be a judge, but is often likely to be an administrative officer, the customs official at the airport or the soldier on the battlefield. Since it is somehow not fair to place the burden of making the hardest interpretative decisions on people 'on the ground', this may lead to attempts to make the rules as detailed and sophisticated as possible: witness the 'elements of crime' detailing what constitutes a

[25] This is not meant to be an exhaustive enumeration.

[26] On this, the *locus classicus* is F. Schauer, *Playing by the Rules: A Philosophical Examination of Rule-Based Decision-Making in Law and in Life* (Oxford: Clarendon Press, 1991).

[27] This is how Franck characterized Article 51 of the UN Charter, only allowing for self-defence 'if an armed attack occurs'. The rule cannot mean what it says and cannot say what it means. See T. M. Franck, *The Power of Legitimacy among Nations* (Oxford University Press, 1990).

war crime before the ICC or the hefty handbooks published on humanitarian law.[28]

For these reasons, then, not too much may be expected from a 'code of ethics' for experts and expert bodies. Instead of focusing primarily on desirable behaviour, it might be more appropriate to concentrate on the individuals engaged in that behaviour: what type of person is it to whom we can entrust expert tasks? What kind of character traits should such a person ideally possess and display?

To some extent, an insistence on moral character is generally shared. This is why the rules governing international courts specify that international judges be individuals 'of high moral character', as the Statute of the International Court of Justice (ICJ) puts it.[29] Likewise, but in far greater detail, the code of conduct for UN special rapporteurs specifies that such persons should work on the basis of 'truthfulness, loyalty and independence' and shall uphold 'the highest standards of efficiency, competence and integrity, meaning, in particular, though not exclusively, probity, impartiality, equity, honesty and good faith'.[30] Clearly, the drafters of these rules shared the idea that the character – the virtues displayed – of people in positions of public responsibility is relevant, and most would intuitively agree that people who habitually cheat and lie would make bad judges, bad special rapporteurs and, more generally, might not be fit to carry public responsibility of any kind.

By the same token, it is not uncommon for political leaders to be evaluated not just on the basis of their achievements, but also on the basis of their character. This applies most prominently perhaps to Secretaries-General of the UN and other high-ranking international officials, whose function by definition cannot be scaled down to include a *raison d'état* and who for that reason are often judged on their ethics.[31]

[28] See, e.g., T. D. Gill and D. Fleck (eds.), *The Handbook of the International Law of Military Operations* (Oxford University Press, 2010), which offers a useful overview of the applicable law in some 600 pages and condenses it to some 50 pages of 'black letter manual'.

[29] See Article 2 of the ICJ Statute. The same term is used in Article 21 of the European Convention on Human Rights. Article 36(3) of the ICC Statute also uses this phrase and adds that judges should be persons of 'impartiality and integrity'.

[30] See Human Rights Council, Resolution 5/2 (2007), *Code of Conduct for Special Procedures Mandates-Holders of the Human Rights Council*, Article 3(d) and (e).

[31] This is a clear underlying theme in, for example, Power's biography of Sergio Vieira de Mello. See S. Power, *Chasing the Flame: One Man's Fight to Save the World* (London: Penguin, 2008). For a more systematic ethical evaluation of Dag Hammarskjöld, see M. Fröhlich, *Political Ethics and the United Nations: Dag Hammarskjöld as Secretary-General* (London: Routledge, 2008); Kofi Annan's biographer remarks that while Annan

5.5 Virtue ethics and universality

It is perhaps useful to point out that an insistence on virtue ethics is not all that vulnerable to criticisms relating to a lack of universality. Such criticism is often lodged whenever values enter the discussion: to build a world based on respect for human rights, for example, would presuppose that people by and large share the same values. Yet, so the critique goes, even if people generally consider torture to be a bad thing, there are bound to be strong local differences as to what constitutes torture. Or even if people cherish freedom of expression, there are bound to be strong local differences as to where to draw the line between acceptable freedom of speech and unacceptable incitement to hatred or demonstrations of political opinions.[32] Hence, talk about human rights often becomes mired in charges of disrespect for local particularities, Asian values, etc. and not unjustifiably so.

It may be the case, as Sir Isaiah Berlin, one of the leading representatives of liberal pluralism, once said, that many people across the globe actually hold quite similar values.[33] If Berlin is right, then the claims concerning value-based imperialism are somewhat overdone. More importantly, though, there is a fundamental difference between values ('torture is a bad thing', 'abortion is acceptable') and virtues. This difference becomes visible when one asks whether proponents of abortion would morally accept abortion in the case of a woman who, on reflection, decided that instead of having a baby, she'd rather have a dog or who undergoes an abortion just to upset the child's father, or in order to make an appearance on a TV reality show to earn lots of money. Many of those who find abortion acceptable would nonetheless shudder at abortion without a good reason. Likewise, many who might find torture acceptable under some circumstances (for example, the ticking time

may have made mistakes, nonetheless 'all his decisions were made with honesty, moral grounding, loyalty to the universal spirit of the United Nations, and a deep aversion to bloodshed'. S. Meisler, *Kofi Annan: A Man of Peace in a World of War* (Hoboken, NJ: Wiley, 2007), at 278.

32 One of the *loci classici* is J. H. H. Weiler, 'Fundamental Rights and Fundamental Boundaries: On the Conflict of Standards and Values in the Protection of Human Rights in the European Legal Space', as reproduced in J. H. H. Weiler, *The Constitution of Europe* (Cambridge University Press, 1999), 102–29.

33 He did so when being interviewed by the sociologist Steven Lukes: 'A great many believe, roughly speaking, the same sort of thing. More people in more countries at more times accept more common values than is often believed.' See S. Lukes, 'Isaiah Berlin in Conversation with Steven Lukes', *Salgismundi*, 120 (1998), 52–134, at 119. Lukes himself makes much the same point in S. Lukes, *Moral Relativism* (London: Profile, 2008).

bomb scenario) would hesitate to approve of acts of torture committed out of sheer cruelty, or committed as entertainment, or because it is Wednesday.

Values are like political opinions: one can hold them and one can shed them. Indeed, they can be shed so easily that Arendt once spoke of the 'bargain sale of values' (*Ausverkauf der Werte*)[34] when discussing the position of her fellow Germans upon the emergence of the Nazi regime: while telling on your neighbours had been 'not done', during the Nazi era it became a practice in which people happily engaged. Values became commodified and therewith something to be traded; the very term 'value', closely linked as it is to exchange-value, suggests as much.

In more general terms, philosophers have claimed that deontological approaches to ethics fail to make a distinction between reasons for acting and motives for acting, or, put differently, ignore the psychological element inherent in acting ethically.[35] An ethical command may be a reason to act, but need not find its cause in the desire to act ethically. By contrast, virtue ethics approaches aim to integrate reasons and motives, as the man who acts honestly without a desire to do so (say, by chance) is not quite as virtuous as one would hope him to be. Hence, to act virtuously implies the desire to do so, at least to some extent.[36]

The claim that values or virtues need to be universal is less crucial to the success of virtue ethics, largely for two reasons. The first is generic: while different people hold different values, people tend to be far more unanimous about what constitutes virtue. Put differently, while it is no doubt true that virtue ethics in the West goes back to Aristotle, there is much that people raised in non-Western traditions will recognize. This point has been made with respect to Confucianism[37] and might in all probability just as

[34] See H. Arendt, 'The Crisis in Culture: Its Social and its Political Significance' in H. Arendt, *Between Past and Future: Eight Exercises in Political Thought* (London: Penguin, 1977), 197–226, at 204.

[35] See M. Stocker, 'Die schizophrenie moderner ethischer theorien' in K. P. Rippe and P. Schaber (eds.), *Tugendethik* (Stuttgart: Reclam, 1998), 19–41. This is a translation of an article first published in English as 'The Schizophrenia of Modern Ethical Theories', *Journal of Philosophy*, 73 (1976), 453–66 (trans. M. Sandhop).

[36] The precise extent of the relevance of the intention to act virtuously is subject to some debate among virtue ethicists. See, e.g., J. Driver, *Uneasy Virtue* (Cambridge University Press, 2001); N. E. Snow, *Virtue as Social Intelligence: An Empirically Grounded Theory* (London: Routledge, 2010), and J. Annas, *Intelligent Virtue* (Oxford University Press, 2011).

[37] See, e.g., M. Hamburger, 'Aristotle and Confucius: A Comparison', *Journal of the History of Ideas*, 20 (1959), 236–49.

easily extend to other traditions (Buddhism, the Japanese tradition, etc.). Thus, there are not many cultures, real or imagined, where injustice, dishonesty, lack of empathy, etc. will be praised. In fact, if anything, it might be possible to suggest that Western culture has become the least virtuous, given its emphasis on competition, individualism, selfishness, making money and markets.[38]

Second, and much more relevant for present purposes, virtue ethics, as operationalized through the intermediary of professional roles, does not demand the universal acceptance of the virtues. All it demands is that there is a modicum of agreement on what can legitimately be expected from people engaged in public tasks. What kind of character traits would we expect the directors-general of international organizations to display? What kind of character traits are fitting for the individuals tasked with guaranteeing financial stability in the world, such as central bankers? Surely, few would suggest that central bankers should aim for personal enrichment or should favour their national interests over the interest of the world at large, and few would suggest that the Secretary-General of the UN should, ideally, be a lying, conniving, back-stabbing individual.[39]

5.6 Experts and virtues

What virtues then can be expected from experts? A first point to clarify relates to the role played by experts: sometimes their role is purely advisory, sometimes it involves decision making and sometimes they may be positioned between advisors and decision makers. A common trait nonetheless is that the expert is appointed rather than elected in a public position[40] and, typically, he or she is appointed (ostensibly, at any rate) on the basis of his or her expertise. Hence, I will treat 'experts' as a single category, regardless of whether their role includes decision-making powers, gate-keeping tasks or not.

[38] For a recent critique, see M. Sandel, *What Money Can't Buy: The Moral Limits of Markets* (London: Allen Lane, 2012).

[39] I have very briefly discussed some of the desirable virtues of secretaries-general in J. Klabbers, 'Controlling International Organizations: A Virtue Ethics Approach', *Helsinki Review of Global Governance*, 2 (2011), 49–51. A monograph on the topic (working title 'Controlling International Organizations: Between Function and Virtue') is forthcoming.

[40] This calls for a nuance, of course, in that some appointment procedures leave a choice between a handful of candidates who can therefore be said to be elected. The point though is that their election is not the result of mass politics.

A second point to clarify is that the virtues discussed below do not amount to an exhaustive list – or, more accurately, that I do not regard the list as closed. It might well be possible to identify additional virtues or flesh out some virtues in greater detail and distinguish them from similar virtues. For instance, I refrain from discussing a virtue such as loyalty in any specific manner, as it is to some extent covered by some of the virtues that are discussed. Nonetheless, it would be possible to think of loyalty in separate terms and attach it, for instance, to the institution whom the expert is meant to serve.[41]

In what follows, I single out honesty, temperance, humility, fortitude, empathy, sympathy and justice as virtues – loosely derived from Aristotle – that may have some application when it comes to evaluating the work of experts engaged in the exercise of global governance. These virtues as such are not specific to experts: they may, by and large, also be expected from others engaged in global governance. What is specific, however, is the way the virtues attach to professional roles. In other words, while one would hope that honesty is a character trait of the expert and secretary-general alike, it may be the case that honesty demands different acts from people in different functions.

A first character trait one may legitimately expect from the expert is *honesty*. An obvious element thereof is that experts should not falsify information, invent data or take other short-cuts so as to achieve results they may deem desirable but which have little to do with proper research or expertise. Obvious though this may sound, it is decidedly troubling that the newspapers have recently featured numerous stories about expert malpractice. In 2011 alone, several incidents graced the headlines of European newspapers, suggesting that experts are not always as honest as one would hope. In Finland, a man was caught for having pretended to be a medical doctor without having the required training (he claimed to have obtained his medical training in the former USSR, thus playing with the plausible proposition that records may not have been reliable); in the Netherlands, a psychology professor and a professor of medicine were discovered to have invented data;[42] and in Germany, a leading politician and member of the government was found

[41] For such a conceptualization (albeit in a different context), see L. D. Terry, *Leadership of Public Bureaucracies: The Administrator as Conservator*, 2nd edn (Armonk, NY: Sharpe, 2003).

[42] At the time of writing, investigations in the Netherlands concerning a second psychology professor are pending.

to have plagiarized his doctoral thesis. While the latter was not appointed because of his special expertise, nonetheless his fraudulently acquired doctor's title will have served him nicely.

The honesty demanded of experts is not honesty at all costs. The responsible expert may, on occasion, be allowed a 'white lie', provided there are good reasons for doing so. Clearly, the food safety expert who claims that a product is completely safe while knowing that this is not the case is not acting virtuously. Nonetheless, there are circumstances where the 'white lie' may come in. Premature honesty, for instance, may give rise to massive panic. It may also be the case that a product is risky in large doses, but harmless when consumed in small doses; the expert's advice may well take this into account. Just as the teacher cannot tell her unintelligent student that he is 'plain stupid' and the doctor cannot tell her terminal patient bluntly that he will be dead in six weeks, so too the food safety expert should take into account how honest messages can be received: honesty here commingles with empathy.

The same applies, *mutatis mutandis*, to other experts, in particular those working in disciplines where the degree of certainty is less high and where predictions can easily become self-fulfilling prophecies. The financial expert, for example, may not want to cause a meltdown of the global financial system by making dire predictions that then end up coming true due to the panic he created. Likewise, the legal expert cannot make blunt and possibly unfounded accusations,[43] and needs to be careful in delimiting his or her mandate: off-the-cuff comments not based on his or her expertise should not be presented as expertise-based and legal experts (for example, in the guise of UN special rapporteurs) should resist the temptation to speak out on topics that are not, or only tangentially, related to their mandate.

Obviously, there is a grey area here, and in particular UN special rapporteurs will have a hard time avoiding all political discussion, as their work is typically embedded in a highly political –and politicized – context. Nonetheless, it would seem that intentionally stretching the

[43] The ICJ actually hinted at this in the 1999 *Cumuraswamy* opinion, when it suggested that the UN Special Rapporteur on the Independence of the Judiciary did not have licence to shoot off his mouth. See *Difference Relating to Immunity from Legal Process of a Special Rapporteur of the Commission of Human Rights*, Advisory Opinion [1999] ICJ Reports 62. The Court's final words were as follows: 'it need hardly be said that all agents of the United Nations, in whatever official capacity they act, must take care not to exceed the scope of their functions, and should so comport themselves as to avoid claims against the United Nations'.

mandate in order to include topics not normally included (and therewith perhaps satisfy a personal agenda)[44] is a questionable practice, whereas bringing new developments under the mandate is not.[45]

A closely related virtue one may expect from experts is *temperance.* Experts should resist the temptation to take impulsive action and approve proposals just because of possibly existing political momentum, and should resist the temptation to 'push the envelope'. This is especially relevant as expert knowledge and responsibility are typically compartmentalized: even if the expert is convinced that there is a causal link between A and B when studied in isolation, there may nonetheless be factors C and D that would intervene and complicate matters in real life. Ignoring this possibility by being overzealous is not to be recommended.

One would also quite legitimately expect experts to possess at least a minimum amount of *humility*, especially if the experts are professional scientists. Experts should thus realize that rarely, if ever, has the final word about any topic been said, and even generally accepted truths can be discovered to be less than truthful as scientific revolutions occur and scientific evolution continues.[46] Hence, the expert priding himself on possessing an eternal truth may well turn out to be mistaken (or the truth might end up showing a few relevant nuances) and therefore should be careful not to push his 'truth' in the face of competing claims.[47] Instead, competing truth claims should be taken seriously, investigated and scrutinized. This applies quite obviously to such topics as climate change, where

44 It has been remarked, in a similar vein, that the most dangerous US Secretary of State of late has been Henry Kissinger, in particular because, having been an academic, he was inclined to mould the world to fit his theories. Sadly, I do not recall the source of the remark.

45 Thus, one might frown if a Special Rapporteur on, say, torture would use his mandate to report on activities that are not considered to be torture (even if one would agree that the activity concerned might well be atrocious). However, one might applaud the Special Rapporteur on extra-judicial killings who would draw attention to the use of drones, resulting in extra-judicial killings. On UN human right rapporteurs, see Subedi, Chapter 12, this volume.

46 See generally T. S. Kuhn, *The Structure of Scientific Revolutions*, 2nd edn (University of Chicago Press, 1970).

47 There is also a vital distinction between factual truth and political truth. Yet, the boundary might not always be easy to draw and may often be coloured by the practical impossibility of escaping the use of non-evaluative language ('Is the US action in Iraq invasion or liberation?'). On this, see H. Arendt, 'Truth and Politics' in Arendt, *Between Past and Future*, 227–64; and F. V. Kratochwil, *Rules, Norms, and Decisions: On the Conditions of Practical and Legal Reasoning in International Relations and Domestic Affairs* (Cambridge University Press, 1989).

scientists seem to quibble about the precise effects, such as the magnitude of rising sea levels.

The same applies, *a fortiori* perhaps, to expert knowledge stemming from the social sciences, where rigorous proof of cause and effect is less plausible, and where the object of study (humanity) might intervene so as to distort any earlier – and at the time valid – truth claims and predictions. Experts addressing issues such as population growth, housing and settlements or education can never be too sure of their knowledge, and the same applies to economic advisors. In the face of scientific uncertainty, one might as well err on the side of humility. By the same token, religious certainties, no matter how strongly felt, should not be allowed to masquerade as scientific truths, although it would be plausible to argue for inclusion of religious representation in discussions among stakeholders.[48]

Then again, some *fortitude* may also be seen as a virtue.[49] The expert who is honestly convinced that a certain proposal will lead to disaster should speak up and make sure she is heard, even in the face of strong opposition. One can sympathize with the legal advisor who resigns rather than giving popular but bad advice, or the food safety expert who dissents, perhaps even abdicates, rather than assuming responsibility for a defective product. This element of fortitude is also generally recognized in the phenomenon of the 'whistleblower'.

One would also legitimately expect one's experts to be able to *empathize* with others and *sympathize* with their plight. The brilliant econometrist who cares only about models without being able to assess (let alone care about) the possible real-life consequences for people of flesh and blood might not be the best policy advisor. In a sense, this is an obvious requirement: with many expert positions, it would be decidedly odd if empathy would be entirely absent. Few would think that a human

[48] Again, there might be a grey area, but if individuals are appointed on the basis of expert knowledge (rather than religious affiliation), they should not let their religion get in the way of their expertise. *Mutatis mutandis*, the same applies to political or moral convictions. While none of this can be entirely de-activated, at least the individuals concerned should take care not to let their non-scientific opinions overshadow anything else: this is precisely where humility comes in. Merely having the conviction that teenage sex will lead to Sodom and Gomorrah does not, after all, an expert make.

[49] Aristotle developed the doctrine of the 'mean': too much of something is not good, but too little is not good either. While the idea may well be unworkable, there is little merit in thinking in terms of absolutes. For a critical review of the doctrine of the mean, see B. Williams, *Ethics and the Limits of Philosophy* (Cambridge, MA: Harvard University Press, 1985).

rights rapporteur or gender advisor without empathy would make a good rapporteur/advisor. And in more technical fields too, much of the work is directed towards human well-being, so one would expect the experts (be they engaged in food safety, airline safety or environmental engineering) to possess at least a modicum of empathy. Although there is something to be said for keeping a cool head, the head should not be so cool as to be cold.

While Aristotle probably never thought of *charity* as a virtue, Aquinas introduced it as one of the religious virtues (together with faith and hope).[50] The religious affiliation has been shed, however, and one might legitimately expect experts to be charitable persons even without divine inspiration. What this means in concrete settings is not easy to specify, although in some cases it might involve, say, a refugee officer being sympathetic towards someone who may not be very articulate in discussing her plight[51] and give her the benefit of the doubt. It might involve a judge allowing equity to mitigate the worst effects of an otherwise standard legal solution.[52]

For Aristotle, *justice* was the overarching virtue: it qualified as one of the virtues in its own right and worked as the aggregate of other virtues. Be that as it may, it is important that experts and also their bodies do not lose sight of justice in their work. Thus, economists advising solutions leading to great wealth disparities within vulnerable societies should, perhaps, think again. Medical advisors confronted with a pandemic and a shortage of vaccinations may need to think of a just distribution of available vaccinations, while individuals representing the pharmaceutical industry should, in such circumstances, resist the temptation to be overly secretive about patents or reluctant to accept licensing.[53]

[50] See St Thomas Aquinas, *Treatise on the Virtues*. I have used the edition published by Notre Dame University Press in 1984, based on translation by J. A. Oesterle.

[51] See K. Bergtora Sandvik, 'On the Social Life of International Organisations: Framing Accountability in Refugee Resettlement' in J. Wouters, E. Brems, S. Smis and P. Schmitt (eds.), *Accountability for Human Rights Violations by International Organisations* (Antwerp: Intersentia, 2010), 287–307 on how refugee law demands an articulate subject.

[52] What I have in mind here (although the context is not identical) is something similar to how the ICJ and arbitral panels on occasion have incorporated equitable considerations in maritime delimitation cases.

[53] In this sense, the long-standing debate about the Trade-Related Aspects of Intellectual Property Rights (TRIPS) Agreement and HIV/AIDS is as much a debate about virtue ethics as it is a legal quagmire. Indeed, while legally the right answer would be elusive, the virtue ethicist would have some inkling as to what to do. For a discussion of the convoluted and fragmented legal framework and the various options for legally framing the issue, see

5.7 Conclusions

To advocate the virtues is one thing, but it is quite another to discuss how to implement them in practice. A first question might inquire into the acquisition of virtues. For Aristotle, it was clear that people would need to be educated into the virtues, and he singled out family and school as sites for education, but also legislation. The latter is echoed by some conservative thinkers, aiming to educate people into sexual modesty by means of legislation.[54] Such an approach is based on a misconception or, at best, a long-term strategy, as it risks falling into the same trap as much deontological thinking by ignoring the distinction between reasons and motives to act: the person who acts virtuously because that is what the law demands may not be truly virtuous.

Of greater practical relevance then is that education offers space for the virtues. Indeed, one might claim that this is essential for the coexistence of seven billion people on planet earth. With the virtues come such useful social skills as respect while others are speaking, toleration of other people's thoughts and accepting the wishes of a majority as relevant. As it is, education may well have become too focused on teaching skills that are of direct economic use (mathematics and economics, and technological skills to foster technological innovation), with the liberal arts losing out.[55] Moreover, much education has become geared towards doing well at exams and being highly competitive, not just among pupils but also among schools and even, stimulated by the Organisation for Economic Co-operation and Development's PISA programme, among states.[56]

A second relevant question is how to give effect to the virtues in appointment procedures. Whenever experts are appointed, a number of formal characteristics are emphasized, including the right education and the right experience. In addition, a number of political factors may

A. Fischer-Lescano and G. Teubner, *Regime-Kollisionen: Zur Fragmentierung des Globalen Rechts* (Frankfurt am Main: Suhrkamp, 2006).

54 See R. P. George, *Making Men Moral: Civil Liberties and Public Morality* (Oxford: Clarendon Press, 1993); somewhat less preoccupied with sexuality is D. F. Brosnan, 'Virtue Ethics in a Perfectionist Theory of Law and Justice', *Cardozo Law Review*, 11 (1989/90), 335–426.

55 The point is elegantly made by M. Nussbaum, *Not for Profit: Why Democracy Needs the Humanities* (Princeton University Press, 2010).

56 See A. von Bogdandy and M. Goldmann, 'The Exercise of International Public Authority through National Policy Assessment: The OECD's PISA Policy as a Paradigm for a New International Standard Instrument', *International Organizations Law Review*, 5 (2008), 241–98.

be considered so as to ensure a decent geographical spread and gender balance. Surely, it should not be too difficult to also start to consider virtue as a relevant characteristic, and while there is no objective measure for virtue, often enough people will be known in their peer communities as more or less virtuous.

In conclusion, it would seem that emphasis on virtue ethics may well assist the management of modern complex societies, and global governance is no exception. First, there are situations where rules (i.e., deontological standards) are insufficient, contradictory or too open-ended to provide much guidance. Here, a focus on the virtues of the expert (as displayed in their actions or inactions) may well be helpful. Second, it provides an additional evaluative vocabulary: even if virtue ethics do not immediately tell us what to do in quite the same way as rules can, nonetheless it sometimes transpires afterwards that the action taken (even the action taken in accordance with existing and relatively clear rules) was not felicitous – and virtue ethics may help explain why.

Above all, virtue ethics is useful because it helps to remind us that our common world is our common responsibility. Politics, whether local or global, is not only about 'who gets what, when and how', as it has come to be defined, but is also about taking care of our common world. Doing so entails not just that we follow rules (although it does that too), but also that we act in a virtuous manner by taking responsibility. Paradoxically, this is the aspect so often forgotten amid all the talk about responsibility, accountability and attributability: whoever gets to decide on political action and whoever gets to advise on political action need to be people who will take responsibility for our common world. A world where this does not happen is a world where decision makers and advisors can hide behind rules and are forever able to 'pass the buck': to another committee, another layer of decision makers or another expert body. Governance is, ultimately, the work of humans, not of bloodless and faceless institutions, and we can legitimately expect those humans to behave in a humane fashion, as exemplified by the virtues.

PART II

Expert involvement in international decision making in the environmental sphere

6

The role of scientific expertise in multilateral environmental agreements: influence and effectiveness

STEINAR ANDRESEN

6.1 Introduction

The focus of this chapter is on the role of scientific expertise in multilateral environmental agreements (MEAs). The involvement of scientific expertise in MEAs has been institutionalized through the establishment of specific scientific bodies, which may indicate that scientific advice is more adhered to within these regimes than in cases where no such institutionalization exists.[1] Examples and findings on how scientific expertise interacts with policy making will be drawn primarily from studies involving the following five international regimes: the international whaling regime,[2] the climate regime,[3] the ozone regime,[4] the North Sea environmental

[1] A. Gupta, S. Andresen, B. Siebenhuner and F. Biermann, 'Science Networks' in F. Biermann and P. Pattberg (eds.), *Global Environmental Governance Reconsidered* (Cambridge, MA: MIT Press, 2012), 69–95.

[2] S. Andresen, 'The Effectiveness of the International Whaling Commission' in D. Victor, K. Raustiala and E. Skolnikoff (eds.), *The Implementation and Effectiveness of International Commitments: Theory and Practice* (Cambridge, MA: MIT Press, 1998), 431–75; S. Andresen, 'The International Whaling Regime' in S. Andresen, T. Skodvin, J. Wettestad and A. Underdal (eds.), *Science and Politics in International Environmental Regimes: Between Integrity and Involvement* (Manchester University Press, 2000), 35–70; S. Andresen and T. Skodvin, 'Non-state Influence in the International Whaling Commission' in M. M. Betsill and E. Corell (eds.), *NGO Diplomacy: The Influence of Nongovernmental Organizations in International Environmental Negotiations* (Cambridge, MA: MIT Press, 2008), 119–49.

[3] T. Skodvin, 'The Intergovernmental Panel on Climate Change' in Andresen et al. (eds.), *Science and Politics*, 146–81; S. Andresen and E. L. Boasson, 'International Climate Cooperation: Clear Recommendations, Weak Commitments' in S. Andresen, E. L. Boasson and G. Hønneland (eds.), *International Environmental Agreements: An Introduction* (London: Routledge, 2012), 49–67.

[4] T. Skodvin, 'The Ozone Regime' in Andresen et al. (eds.), *Science and Politics*, 122–46; J. B. Skjærseth, 'North Sea Pollution Control: One Problem, Different Solutions' in Andresen et al. (eds.), *International Environmental Agreements*, 83–97.

regime[5] and the regime for reducing long-range air pollution in Europe.[6] A few observations will also be linked to the biodiversity regime.[7] As these are all rather long-standing comprehensive regimes with several components, they provide a fairly broad overview of the state of the art regarding the involvement of scientific expertise in MEAs. However, in a strict methodological sense the findings cannot be generalized to other regimes on the basis of what is but a fairly modest sample, compared to the vast universe of MEAs. In relation to these case studies, the chapter builds on findings from Underdal,[8] Andresen et al.,[9] Andresen and Skjærseth[10] and Andresen et al.[11]

The scientific bodies associated with the five regimes mentioned above were set up either before the political component of the regime was established or shortly thereafter. These bodies are usually composed of scientific experts from most or all of the Member States of the regime; some may include independent scientists who do not represent any of the Member States. Although they differ significantly, in general, these international scientific or expert bodies are considered to be both more representative and more legitimate than national-level scientific advisory bodies.[12]

Scientific expertise essentially serves to provide 'early warning' about environmental problems and may provide guidance on what to do in order to alleviate or solve a problem.[13] At the international level, the

[5] J. Wettestad, 'Dealing with Land-Based Marine Pollution in the North-East Atlantic: The Paris Convention and the North Sea' in Andresen et al. (eds.), *Science and Politics*, 70–95; J. B. Skjærseth, 'International Ozone Cooperation: Effective International Cooperation' in Andresen, Boasson and Hønneland (eds.), *International Environmental Agreements*, 38–49.

[6] J. Wettestad, 'The ECE Convention on Long-Range Transboundary Air Pollution: From Common Cuts to Critical Loads' in Andresen et al. (eds.), *Science and Politics*, 95–122; J. Wettestad, 'Reducing Long-Range Transport of Air Pollutants in Europe' in Andresen, Boasson and Hønneland (eds.), *International Environmental Agreements*, 23–38.

[7] K. Rosendal and P. J. Schei, 'Convention on Biological Diversity: From National Conservation to Global Responsibility' in Andresen et al. (eds.), *International Environmental Agreements*, 119–34.

[8] A. Underdal, 'The Politics of Science in International Resource Management: A Summary' in S. Andresen and W. Østreng (eds.), *International Resource Management* (London: Belhaven Press, 1989), 253–69.

[9] Andresen et al. (eds.), *Science and Politics*.

[10] S. Andresen and J. B. Skjærseth, 'Science and Technology' in D. Bodansky, J. Brunnée and E. Hey (eds.), *The Oxford Handbook of International Environmental Law* (Oxford University Press, 2007), 182–205.

[11] Andresen, Boasson and Hønneland (eds.), *International Environmental Agreements*.

[12] Andresen and Skjærseth, 'Science and Technology'.

[13] A. Underdal, 'Science and Politics: The Anatomy of an Uneasy Partnership' in Andresen et al. (eds.), *Science and Politics*, 1–22.

search for knowledge that scientific experts represent typically takes place among knowledge producers who function within or are associated with the specific international regime – such as the Intergovernmental Panel on Climate Change (IPCC).[14] In these regimes, scientific advice usually has a 'positive' impact on addressing the problem at hand, to the extent that such advice is heeded.

This last point is the focus of this chapter: how can scientific expertise contribute to enhance the *effectiveness* of international environmental policies? To answer this question, we need to know the extent to which scientific expertise is able to *influence* decision makers. This chapter suggests that the nature of the problem and the problem-solving capacity of a regime are functions that can help to explain the effectiveness of a regime, and that scientific expertise plays a role in determining these functions.

To address these questions, first the five regimes covered are introduced briefly. Subsequently, the concept of regime effectiveness and the general role that scientific expertise plays for regime effectiveness are outlined. This is followed by an empirical analysis of the role played by scientific expertise within the five regimes studied, with a discussion of the factors that explain the influence and significance of scientific expertise. The chapter ends with some brief conclusions.

6.2 The five regimes: a snapshot of the regimes covered

The International Convention for the Regulation of Whaling (ICRW) was adopted in 1946; two years later, the International Whaling Commission (IWC) was established, originally with fifteen and at present counting 89 members. This is a global convention open to all states, irrespective of their material whaling interests. The goal of the Convention is to establish regulations for purposes of conservation and utilization of large whales. Article V(2) of the Convention explicitly states that regulations adopted by the IWC shall be based on scientific findings; to that end, the Scientific Committee was established in 1951. Since its establishment, the IWC has experienced significant changes. Initially, it was completely dominated by states with whaling interests, which resulted in the commercial depletion of the large whale species. In the late 1960s and 1970s, management of whaling activities gradually became more sustainable. Then, in the mid-1980s, the IWC turned into a 'protectionist club' and

[14] Siebenhüner, Chapter 7, this volume.

commercial whaling was prohibited. Since the mid-1990s, the influence of the pro-whaling forces has increased again.[15] Assessments as to whether the whaling regime is an effective regime vary considerably.

The Convention on Long-Range Transboundary Air Pollution (LRTAP) is a regional instrument adopted within the United Nations Economic Commission for Europe in 1979 and currently has 51 parties. Although its geographical focus is on Europe, both the USA and Canada are also parties. Its objective is to protect human beings and the environment against air pollution, and to limit and, as far as possible, reduce and prevent such pollution, including long-range air pollution.[16] The first substance-specific protocol, on sulphur, was signed in 1985; five other substance-specific protocols were added before the integrated multi-pollutant Gothenburg Protocol was signed in 1999, thereby establishing a very elaborate institutional framework. A comprehensive scientific apparatus involving various bodies has evolved over time to provide advice to the decision makers, and considerable improvements have been achieved in terms of pollution abatement.[17]

The IPCC was established in 1988, four years prior to the adoption and six years prior to the entering into force of the *United Nations Framework Convention on Climate Change* (UNFCCC). The Convention now counts over 190 parties. The goal of the Convention is to stabilize greenhouse gas (GHG) concentrations in the atmosphere at a level that would prevent dangerous anthropogenic interference with the climate system.[18] In 1997 the *Kyoto Protocol* was adopted, finally entering into force in 2005. The IPCC provides scientific advice for the decision-making process under the UNFCCC and the Kyoto Protocol by means of its Assessment Reports, published in 1990, 1995, 2001 and 2007, with a fifth report in preparation for final publication in the autumn of 2014.[19] Since the publication of its first report, the Commission has maintained that GHG emissions must be sharply reduced, but emissions have continued to rise steeply at the global level. Despite considerable advances in knowledge about and understanding of this issue, the overall effectiveness of the climate regime, in terms of

[15] Andresen and Skodvin, 'Non-state Influence in the International Whaling Commission'.

[16] O. S. Stokke and Ø. Thommessen (eds.), *Yearbook of International Co-operation on Environment and Development* (London: Earthscan, 2002).

[17] Wettestad, 'Reducing Long-Range Transport of Air Pollutants in Europe', 23–38.

[18] Stokke and Thommessen (eds.), *Yearbook of International Co-operation on Environment and Development.*

[19] Parts of the report have been released as of the autumn of 2013: see IPCC Media Center, http://ipcc.ch/activities/activities.shtml.

problem solving, has been assessed as very modest.[20] Currently, intense negotiations are under way on the future institutional architecture of the climate regime.

The Vienna Convention for the Protection of the Ozone Layer, another global MEA, was adopted in 1985, and its *Montreal Protocol* in 1987. The Convention and the Protocol entered into force in 1988 and 1989, respectively. Participation in the regime is now virtually universal. The objective of the ozone regime is to protect health and the environment against adverse effects resulting from human activities likely to modify the ozone layer. Various amendments, strengthening the commitments of the parties, have been added over time. Importantly, a fund to assist developing countries in meeting their obligations was established in 1990. The regime has underlined the need for scientific cooperation.[21] Scientific panels, established to assist decision makers, have published four-yearly comprehensive assessment reports about the depletion of ozone.[22] The ozone regime is widely recognized as very effective.[23]

The North Sea pollution control regime is quite complex and has developed considerably since its first component, the *Oslo Convention for the Prevention of Marine Pollution Dumping from Ships and Aircraft* (hereinafter 'the Oslo Convention'), was adopted in 1972. Two years later, the *Paris Convention for the Prevention of Marine Pollution from Land-Based Sources* (hereinafter 'the Paris Convention') was drafted. Scientific working groups were set up to monitor pollution levels, but scientific progress was slow and uncertainty was high. Progress remained limited until well into the 1980s, when a new institution, the *North Sea Conference*, was established, which provided new political energy. Scientific efforts were also strengthened by way of the establishment of various working groups and a precautionary approach emerged. While all states bordering the North-East Atlantic Ocean (including the North Sea) and the European Union (EU) participated in the processes of the Oslo and Paris Conventions, the North Sea Conference process was initiated by the eight North Sea states. In 1992 the two conventions were merged into the *Oslo–Paris Convention for the Protection of the Marine Environment of the North-East Atlantic* (OSPAR). The EU, through

20 Andresen and Boasson, 'International Climate Cooperation'.

21 Stokke and Thommessen (eds.), *Yearbook of International Co-operation on Environment and Development*.

22 See http://esrl.noaa.gov/csd/assessments/ozone.

23 Skjærseth, 'International Ozone Cooperation'.

relevant directives, has become an increasingly important actor in this regime, and the North Sea Conference approach has now been abandoned. The effectiveness of this regime seems somewhat mixed, but has clearly improved over time.[24]

6.3 Determining effectiveness and the role of scientific expertise

6.3.1 Defining and explaining effectiveness: a brief overview

The study of effectiveness of international environmental regimes has been a well-established subfield within the broader study of regimes since the early 1990s.[25] A consensus has gradually evolved whereby effectiveness is conceived in terms of *outputs*, *outcomes* and *impacts*. *Outputs* consist of the rules, regulations and programmes flowing from the regime, and are essentially indicators of the potential effectiveness of the regime. This is usually the indicator that international jurists focus on, given that normally effectiveness is higher when there are strict and comprehensive rules and regulations addressing the problem at stake. However, whether this is really the case should be assessed by investigating what is happening on the ground, and this is where the other indicators come in. *Outcomes* are the behavioural changes of key target groups resulting from the regime, whereas *impacts* concern the extent to which the problem in question is actually solved by the regime in the environment at stake. It has also been suggested that a 'softer' indicator of effectiveness, that is, agenda-setting, may be used as a precondition for subsequent effectiveness.[26] Needless to say, there are severe methodological challenges concerning causality associated with determining outcome and impact, but we will not dwell on them in this chapter.[27]

[24] Skjærseth, 'North Sea Pollution Control'.

[25] E. Miles, A. Underdal, S. Andresen, J. Wettestad and E. Carlin, *Environmental Regime Effectiveness: Confronting Theory with Evidence* (Cambridge, MA: MIT Press, 2002); O. Young, L. King and H. Schröder (eds.), *Institutions and Environmental Change: Principal Findings, Applications and Research Frontiers* (Cambridge, MA: MIT Press, 2008).

[26] S. Andresen, 'The Effectiveness of UN Environmental Institutions', *International Environmental Agreements: Politics, Law and Economics*, 7 (2007), 317–36.

[27] J. Hovi, D. Sprintz and A. Underdal, 'Regime Effectiveness and the Oslo-Potsdam Solution: A Rejoinder to Oran Young', *Global Environmental Politics*, 3 (2003), 105–7; O. Young, 'Determining Regime Effectiveness: A Commentary to the Oslo-Potsdam Solution', *Global Environmental Politics*, 3 (2003), 97–104; S. Andresen, 'International Regime Effectiveness' in R. Falkner (ed.), *Handbook of Global Climate Change and Environmental Policy* (Oxford: Wiley-Blackwell, 2013), 304–19.

Due to these methodological challenges – not the least because of the significant 'distance' between expert advice and action on the ground as well as the influence of a host of other factors – in this chapter we focus mostly on the less-demanding indicators of agenda-setting and outputs. Nonetheless, the outcome indicator will also be used to some extent.

One way to explain effectiveness is to approach the question from the perspectives of the *nature of the problem* and the *problem-solving capacity* of the relevant regime.[28] As to the nature of the problem, the basic idea is that some problems are intellectually and politically less complicated and more 'benign' than others, and are thus easier to solve or deal with than more 'malign' problems. The ozone and the climate problems illustrate this distinction, with the former representing a far more benign problem than the latter. This distinction provides an important explanatory factor for the higher effectiveness of the ozone regime as compared to the climate regime. As to problem-solving capacity, the underlying reasoning is that some problems are addressed more effectively because they are tackled with greater political and institutional skill and energy. This function is conceived of as a combination of the power, leadership and institutional set-up of the regime. If, for example, powerful actors are pushers, we may expect higher effectiveness from the regime in question. Similarly, the more prominent and skilful the leadership is, the higher the chances of a more effective regime.

These perspectives are analytical devices, which means that in practice there will be links and overlaps between them. Over time, for example, strong problem-solving capacity can reduce the malignancy of the problem. This insight is pertinent for analysts and decision makers, as it implies that malignancy can be reduced through deliberate institutional design. The political challenge then becomes to mobilize relevant actors to support collective action in pursuit of an effective solution. The intellectual challenge is to identify and diagnose the problem, and to identify effective response measures – and this is where various types of scientific expertise come in. Natural scientists typically diagnose problems, while social scientists offer advice on institutional design. So how does scientific expertise fit into this overall analytical perspective? This question is addressed in the next section.

[28] Miles et al., *Environmental Regime Effectiveness*; Gupta, Chapter 8, this volume.

6.3.2 *The role of scientific expertise and knowledge*

At the interface between the political and intellectual (scientific) dimensions lies the task of transforming knowledge into premises for decision making. The main question to be addressed here is how scientific knowledge can be utilized so as to enhance the effectiveness of the regimes at hand. There has been much debate concerning the fruitfulness of separating the 'scientific' from the 'political' sphere, and discussion of the links between science and knowledge.[29] These are important debates with no easy answers. However, our point of departure here is simple. In line with the rationalist tradition, it is assumed that knowledge about the environment is a necessary but not sufficient condition for designing effective international institutions.

In environmental regimes, science can be regarded as representing a 'neutral' input on behalf of the resource or environment in question. This is, indeed, a simplified assumption. But reflect for a moment on the state of the art in the *absence* of science. Without fairly good knowledge about the environment and the natural resources in question, management will tend to be based either on luck or exclusively on economic and political priorities. The depletion of the number of large whales in Antarctic waters has shown with devastating clarity what can happen when science is weak and disputed, and short-term economic interests dominate.[30] However, even in the face of strong scientific warnings, fish stocks are constantly being depleted and the level of GHG emissions continues to rise. Why is good scientific knowledge alone not sufficient for effective management? Because various legitimate political factors will usually be more decisive for the actual conduct of management.

Scientific expertise plays a role in determining the nature of the problem as well as the strength of the problem-solving capacity of a regime. The extent to which we know about the problem can indicate how intellectually 'malign' or 'benign' the problem is. Similarly, the way we design the science–policy interface may make a difference in terms of the ability of the regime to solve the problem. As to the role of science in determining the nature of the problem, the simple assumption here

[29] T. S. Kuhn, *The Structure of Scientific Revolution*, 2nd edn (University of Chicago Press, 1970); P. M. Haas, 'When Does Power Listen to Truth? A Constructivist Approach to the Policy Process', *Journal of European Public Policy*, 11 (2004), 569–92; Gupta et al., 'Science Networks'.

[30] See T. Schweder, 'Distortion of Uncertainty in Science: Antarctic Fin Whales in the 1950s', *Journal of International Wildlife, Law and Policy*, 3 (2000), 73–92.

is that, all other things being equal, the better and the more consensual our knowledge is, the higher the chances of increased regime effectiveness.

Concerning the role of scientific expertise in relation to the problem-solving capacity of a regime, our initial assumption in the mid-1990s was that achieving a *balance* between *autonomy* and *involvement* would be the best way to organize scientific input.[31] Autonomy is needed to ensure that the scientific input is not tilted by influence from political and economic stakeholders. And involvement is needed to ensure that the scientific experts recognize the needs of decision makers and present scientific results that can be utilized in practice. This assumption proved somewhat simplistic when confronted with political realities through the case studies.[32]

Scientific expertise and knowledge have generally made only a modest difference for the effectiveness of the five regimes considered in this chapter. Environmental management is ultimately a political question where powerful economic actors are usually involved, and we find few, if any, examples where science (and the environment) 'wins' when there are powerful counterforces within 'malign' regimes. The effectiveness of a regime is largely determined by the political will and/or the ability of parties to collectively address the problems identified. Still, scientific expertise has proven particularly important in creating awareness about environmental problems and it can provide incentives that may trigger political processes for dealing with emerging problems. Under some conditions, it may also make a difference when subsequent decisions are taken, as highlighted below.

The main units of analysis then are the relevant scientific bodies within or associated with the regimes and their political or management components; for instance, for studying the whaling regime, the focus is on the Scientific Committee and the management body, the IWC. What has been recommended by the Scientific Committee in terms of catch and management, and to what extent have these recommendations been followed by the IWC? This approach provides us with an indication of the influence of scientific expertise on the policies adopted, although a host of other factors may also make a difference. Scientific bodies can never be truly impartial: we know that they may be 'infected' by policy and other non-scientific concerns. This has been a key characteristic

31 Andresen et al. (eds.), *Science and Politics*.

32 *Ibid.*; Andresen and Skjærseth, 'Science and Technology'.

during much of the history of, for example, the whaling regime. However, remedies have been introduced to reduce the problem of 'infected' science, and recently provided advice has been much more consensual and precise.[33] This positive trend also characterizes the development in the other relevant scientific bodies studied here, although there are variations. As will also be shown below, even consensual and precise scientific findings do not necessarily impact on practice.

6.4 The role of scientific expertise in international environmental regimes

To what extent is scientific expertise a major input for decision makers in the regimes studied? The answer to this question can provide an indication of whether decision makers find the scientific advice relevant – but that does not necessarily mean that they will decide to follow this advice. Rather, it means that decision makers under certain circumstances may see scientific expertise, among other factors, as a relevant and necessary input for decision making. Analysing the extent to which expert advice is well received provides us the basis for the subsequent discussion on the potential influence of scientific expertise on decision making within the regimes studied here.

6.4.1 Scientific expertise is crucial for initial agenda-setting, but help is usually needed

In a traditional sequential approach to the development of MEAs, the first step of agenda-setting is followed by negotiations, before the parties start the process of implementation. Some scholars have argued that this is an overly simplistic approach to studying the highly dynamic processes of international environmental treaty making today.[34] This observation is supported by the current situation in the climate regime, where agenda-setting, negotiations and implementation have been taking place simultaneously.

However, what we will consider here is the *initial* agenda-setting: the necessary framing phase prior to the start of formal negotiations. Scientific expertise played a crucial role in such agenda-setting in all five regimes

[33] Andresen and Skodvin, 'Non-state Influence in the International Whaling Commission'.

[34] R. Mitchell, 'Problem Structure, Institutional Design and the Relative Effectiveness of International Environmental Agreements', *Global Environmental Politics*, 6 (2006), 72–89.

studied. Had it not been for scientific expert input, the collective environmental challenges to be dealt with by these regimes would not have been identified – or they would have surfaced much later. For instance, the problem of global warming was first noted by US scientists in the late 1950s, although it remained primarily within the sphere of international scientific expert bodies for more than twenty years before the United Nations Environment Programme (UNEP), some green non-governmental organizations (NGOs), activist policy makers and activist scientists simplified and expanded the problem, adding political spin to the issue in the 1980s.[35] This development paved the way for the establishment of the IPCC, as well as the process towards the adoption of the UNFCCC. In contrast, the lack of scientific agreement on the status of whale stocks hampered progress in the IWC for a long time.[36] Interestingly, states are rarely involved in the initial agenda-setting process: the agenda-setters are often groups composed of non-state actors, often qualifying as epistemic communities.[37] Although the significance of scientific advice usually wanes somewhat in the subsequent process of negotiation and implementation when political and economic considerations loom large, the role of scientific experts as 'whistleblowers' is crucial. On the other hand, due to their traditional 'ivory-tower' position, scientific experts usually need some help from other actors to amplify and simplify their messages in order to capture the attention of decision makers.

6.4.2 *Scientific research is generally recognized as a major supplier of relevant knowledge*

In all the regimes examined here, decision makers have turned to science for problem identification and diagnosis, and, as noted, all five regimes incorporate scientific bodies. However, one key global regime – the biodiversity regime – until recently lacked a scientific body, and that may be *one* reason, if not necessarily the most important one, for the low effectiveness of this regime. It was not until 2010, after years of negotiations, that more than ninety states agreed to establish an Intergovernmental Science–Policy Platform on Biodiversity and Ecosystem Services (IPBES).

[35] S. Andresen and S. Agrawala, 'Leaders, Pushers, and Laggards in the Making of the Climate Regime', *Global Environmental Change*, 12 (2002), 41–51.
[36] Andresen, 'The International Whaling Regime'.
[37] P. M. Haas, 'Introduction: Epistemic Communities and International Policy Coordination', *International Organization*, 46 (1992), 1–35; Haas, Chapter 2, this volume.

The purpose of this platform is to generate knowledge and capacity building in order to better protect biodiversity.[38]

It seems reasonable to assume that the existence of scientific expert bodies at least increases the possibility for more effective management of the environment and resources at hand. There is also a tendency towards greater formalization of the links between decision-making bodies and the scientific community as regimes 'mature'. As mentioned above, while it took a few years before the Scientific Committee was established within the oldest of these regimes, the whaling regime, in all the more recent regimes, scientific/technical bodies were set up concomitantly with – or even before – the establishment of international political bodies. Tendencies towards broadening the range of scientific inputs requested can also be observed. First, the participation of natural scientists has expanded in scope, and economic expertise is included to an increasing extent. The IPCC, the most comprehensive scientific expert body in our sample here, also includes social science and legal experts. Second, measures have been taken to achieve greater participation from scientists and other experts from the South, thereby heightening the legitimacy of the bodies involved.[39]

6.4.3 *'Consensual scientific knowledge' is rarely disputed over time*

In the early stages of negotiations when the scientific basis may be disputed and weak, uncertainty and knowledge gaps are often exploited for tactical purposes to serve perceived national interests in international negotiations. Progress has often been hampered by one or more parties demanding more conclusive evidence, or by competing interpretations of available information. A typical example is the position of the UK in the early phase of both the acid rain regime and the North Sea regime. The UK claimed that science was uncertain and that therefore no action was needed. Similarly, the Netherlands exploited the uncertainty and disagreement in the early days of the IWC Scientific Committee to cater for its commercial whaling interests.[40] In both the North Sea and the acid rain regimes, these political conflicts have lessened considerably over time and strong measures have been adopted. One contributing

[38] Rosendal and Schei, 'Convention on Biological Diversity'.
[39] Andresen and Boasson, 'International Climate Cooperation'.
[40] Schweder, 'Distortion of Uncertainty in Science'.

reason for this change may be that there is no longer conflict over the science involved in these areas.[41] Data on these cases show that most governments are reluctant to dispute openly the factual conclusions that a clear majority of competent scientific experts consider state-of-the-art knowledge. The scientific underpinning is particularly strong – and consensual – in the acid rain and ozone regimes.

Moves to exploit uncertainty or favour biased interpretations are common, but open and explicit challenges are rare. For example, when in 2001 US President George W. Bush rejected the Kyoto Protocol, he first claimed that the science was uncertain and expressed doubts as to whether any problem existed. However, it did not take long before he changed his position[42] – still rejecting the Kyoto Protocol, but acknowledging the climate change problem. The only major exception to this evolving pattern is the IWC, where the majority has repeatedly rejected scientific advice. For example, the Scientific Committee concluded in 1991 that a modest Norwegian catch of North Atlantic minke whales did not represent a threat to this population. This finding was set aside by the IWC and the majority still opposes the Norwegian catch, even though it is endorsed by the Scientific Committee. This situation is primarily due to the deep conflict over values, a topic we will return to below.

6.4.4 *More and improved scientific information – more advanced MEAs?*

Studies of the development of MEAs have suggested that there have been considerable advances over time.[43] In the 1970s (first-generation agreements) when the process started, the parties typically acknowledged the problem and agreed to take some kind of unspecified action. These were the typical framework conventions adopted for four out of the five regimes studied here, the exception being the ICRW, which modelled the IWC on international fisheries organizations. The next stage, typical of the 1980s (second-generation agreements), was the adoption of uniform targets and timetables for specific commitments. Although experiences with this approach have varied considerably, this stage represents progress compared to the first-generation agreements in that it enabled

[41] Skjærseth, 'North Sea Pollution Control', 83–97; Wettestad, 'Reducing Long-Range Transport of Air Pollutants in Europe'.
[42] Andresen and Skjærseth, 'Science and Technology'.
[43] Andresen et al. (eds.), *Science and Politics*.

the parties to the relevant regime to measure progress – or the lack thereof. However, this approach with uniform targets and timetables for all parties ran counter to the growing calls in the 1990s for cost-effectiveness, as well as fairness and justice between developing and developed countries in global agreements. These two stages paved the way for the third and current generation of MEAs, which are characterized by differentiated obligations.

This brief account indicates that there has been considerable progress in terms of the approach to environmental treaty making – an important point in a period where 'doom and gloom' often dominate discussions concerning international environmental issues. The key question here, however, is whether scientific expert advice and scientific institutions can take any credit for this development. That question is not easy to answer, but it seems that these steps have been taken, at least in part, in response to scientific evidence and advances in some of the regimes studied. The typical initial pattern is one where new evidence about environmental damage or resource depletion leads, first, to increased attention to the problem and requests for further study and, at a later stage, to some substantive measures designed to alleviate the problem –which by no means suggests that scientific evidence is a *sufficient* condition for collective action or that policy responses are typically *derived* from scientific expert-based knowledge. Take, for example, the observation that policy makers usually apply round numbers like 30, 50 or 70 per cent reductions – rarely does the need to reduce emissions by, say, 23.5 per cent surface in negotiations. When a key policy maker was asked why a 50 per cent target was adopted for the North Sea regime in the late 1980s, he answered that 10 per cent seemed too modest and 90 per cent seemed too ambitious, whereas 50 per cent seemed like a good middle-of-the-road target. This indicates that the general direction of scientific advice may often be more important than highly specific points of advice. Only in a few instances, in the later periods of the ozone negotiations and the LRTAP regime, can the regulations adopted be seen as coming close to the specific scientific advice provided. One reason was probably that better and more consensual scientific expertise had been developed by then. This was the case especially within the LRTAP regime, where sophisticated models had been designed – to a large extent independently of the control of the parties – by, for example, the International Institute of Applied Systems Analysis (IIASA).[44] However, even in these cases, it would be an

[44] Wettestad, 'Reducing Long-Range Transport of Air Pollutants in Europe'.

exaggeration to claim that regulations were in any strict sense derived from scientific inputs. The *substance* of the responses seems to have been based primarily on politics, not scientific expertise.

6.4.5 *Conclusive evidence is not always a necessary condition for collective action*

Based on the case studies referred to in this chapter, the 'normal' pattern is that a broad consensus among competent scientific experts about the nature and ramifications of a problem tends to facilitate problem solving. However, substantive measures may sometimes be agreed even in the absence of conclusive evidence as to the amount of environmental damage. A case in point was the decision of the 1987 North Sea Conference to adopt very stringent and ambitious targets to reduce pollution, even though the scientific message was far from conclusive. The precautionary principle served to justify this shift on the part of the decision makers. However, two points should be noted in this specific connection. First, this was a period characterized by strong environmental attention among the public of Western Europe: green policies meant more votes and so voters became highly instrumental to the adoption of ambitious environmental goals. Second, the adoption of ambitious policies did not necessarily translate into their (costly) implementation.[45] It has also happened, but even more rarely, that the regulatory body has moved substantially *beyond* the recommendations made by its scientific expert advisory body. The best-known example is perhaps the 1982 IWC decision to ban commercial whaling even though the Scientific Committee found no reason to go so far. The decision was taken against the backdrop of a strong global anti-whaling movement, spearheaded by the USA and Greenpeace. These two examples from the 1980s might seem to indicate a development towards a more precautionary approach, as the ozone regime has also shown a similar trend over time. Of the five cases studied here, however, the climate regime and the biodiversity regime did not follow suit, so we can hardly say that there is a general trend to move beyond scientific expert input. In practice, the development of a regime is heavily dependent on the nature of the problem at hand. In benign issue areas, such as the ozone regime, the costs of adopting a precautionary approach are low. This is not so when it

[45] Skjærseth, 'North Sea Pollution Control'.

comes to malign issue areas, such as climate change, even if it is in these areas that precautionary policies are most urgently needed.

6.4.6 *Autonomy and involvement serve different functions*

As noted above, our original assumption[46] that a balance should be struck between scientific expert involvement and autonomy proved overly simplistic. Involvement and autonomy seem to serve different functions at different stages of the science–policy nexus. Autonomy is necessary for *producing* 'good' science, whereas *involvement* is essential for *transforming* science into policy-relevant scientific expert input. The climate regime and the acid rain regime exemplify this approach, as both have specifically designed forums to deal with these two questions. In the acid rain regime, it is the Working Group on Strategies that serves this function of transformation. In the climate regime, the scientific summaries prepared for policy makers may be subjected to hard political negotiations that bear the imprint of influence from policy makers.[47] Perhaps even more important, autonomy and involvement may serve different functions for different parties. This finding applies in particular to global regimes and to the relationship between developed and developing countries. For developed countries, especially in Western Europe and North America, the autonomy of scientific expertise is a core value that is seen to boost its credibility. From the perspective of the South, 'autonomous' scientific expertise is often perceived as science done by the North – and often *for* the North. The more marginal the role of developing countries in the development of scientific expertise, the more critical they tend to be towards 'autonomous' scientific expertise. This situation has prompted an increase in the number of scientists from developing countries, for example, in the IPCC. This development in turn offers an important lesson for the parties to the Biodiversity Convention given that they are in the process of setting up a similar scientific body. The 'design' lesson is that involvement and some political control over the scientific process is required in order to secure the *legitimacy* of scientific expertise in global regimes, in particular from the perspective of the South.[48]

[46] See Andresen et al. (eds.), *Science and Politics*.
[47] Andresen and Boasson, 'International Climate Cooperation'.
[48] D. Bodansky, 'Legitimacy' in Bodansky, Brunnée and Hey (eds.), *The Oxford Handbook of International Environmental Law*, 704–27.

6.5 Explaining various degrees of influence of scientific expertise on decision making

What is the 'distance' between scientific expert advice and collective action decision making? We need to address this question in order to determine the role of scientific expertise in relation to regime effectiveness. There are, however, many possible other explanatory factors that complicate the determination of causality. We should therefore address the question by examining the general characteristics associated with the problems at hand (problem structure), which may have an impact on the extent to which scientific expertise influences decision making.[49] The general characteristics of environmental problems may be conceived as follows:

- consensual knowledge versus controversial and uncertain conclusions;
- feasible cure (technology) available versus no cure available;
- more 'neutral' issues versus strong values involved;
- strong 'pushers' versus strong 'laggards';
- problems developing rapidly and surprisingly versus slowly and as expected;
- low political conflict versus high political conflict.

Only the first point listed above refers specifically to the role of scientific expertise. The others refer to the characteristics of the problems to be addressed, which may be determinative of the impact that scientific expertise has on the regime in question.

The characteristics listed on the left-hand side of each of the six opposites given above make a problem more benign and, arguably, increase the chance that scientific expert advice will be followed; the elements on the right-hand side render a problem more malign, arguably decreasing the chance that scientific expert advice will be followed. According to this line of reasoning, the likely impact of scientific expert input depends not only on the quality and organization of scientific expertise but also (and perhaps more so) on how the other characteristics play out for a given problem.

From our cases, if the scientific expertise involved is relatively consensual, this increases the chances that scientific expertise will have an impact on or will influence decision makers. Such an impact of

[49] See Underdal, 'The Politics of Science in International Resource Management'; Andresen and Skjærseth, 'Science and Technology'.

consensual expertise is clearly seen in the acid rain regime, the North Sea regime and the ozone regime: the science involved had initially been both uncertain and controversial, but gradually became more consensual and scientific influence increased correspondingly. Further, it should be noted that, over time, the two regional and relatively homogeneous regimes (the North Sea and the acid rain regimes) have also been characterized by relatively low political conflicts and the (partial) availability of feasible technological solutions. All three of the above-mentioned regimes have also had fairly strong pushers at critical crossroads. Relevant examples are Germany in the regional acid rain regime and the USA in the ozone regime. In the ozone regime, the link to other benign factors is central: the availability of feasible technical solutions and the presence of low political conflicts. In such situations, scientific expert input interacts with other 'benign' factors that seem to foster the influence of science. Still, these are all examples of rather high-effectiveness regimes where scientific expertise has played a part, although it probably does not constitute the main explanatory factor for the effectiveness of the regime.

Based on our cases, it can be concluded that scientific consensus alone is not sufficient to ensure the impact of scientific expertise on decision makers: other factors are also at play. This is demonstrated in three of the regimes studied here – biodiversity, climate change and whaling. Although the formal scientific underpinning has been weak in the biodiversity regime, there has never been much scientific controversy over the fact that biodiversity is disappearing at an alarming rate. The simple problem is that most parties do little to alleviate the problem. No doubt, a major reason is that this regime faces an extraordinarily 'malign' problem, perhaps even more difficult than the climate change problem. Deep political conflicts, not least over access and benefit sharing, often overshadow the need for conservation. The problem is also characterized by low visibility, laggard actors and a lack of feasible technological cures. By most standards, this is a low-effectiveness regime and scientific expertise has played only a modest role.[50]

Another global regime characterized by deep political conflicts is the climate regime. In line with the dimensions listed above, it has most of the characteristics of a politically 'malign' problem. Although the regime is characterized by as much scientific consensus as it is probably possible to achieve on such a complex issue, scientific warnings have not been heeded. Our findings also show that a fairly good balance between

[50] Rosendal and Schei, 'Convention on Biological Diversity'.

involvement and autonomy has been achieved, but that has not helped much either. It is widely acknowledged that the Kyoto Protocol, for all its political and institutional merits, will have little actual effect on climate change. Seen from this vantage point, the effectiveness of this regime is low and scientific expertise has not contributed much to enhance its effectiveness. Between 2005 and 2008, a surge in public interest occurred in relation to climate-change issues, probably triggered by what seemed to be the actualization of the problem, with hurricanes, melting glaciers and polar bears searching for ice.[51] The high prestige enjoyed by the IPCC was also demonstrated when it (together with Al Gore) was awarded the Nobel Peace Prize in 2007. Thus, when science interacts positively with other forces, again we see that it seems to open a window of opportunity for more political action – as at the thirteenth conference of the parties in Bali. But this environmental enthusiasm was effectively 'killed' by the financial and economic crisis that hit the world with full force in the autumn of 2008. The 'climate-gate' episode in 2009 did not help to boost the influence of scientific experts in the climate change regime either.[52] These events remind us of the significance of (negative) external factors beyond the control of scientific experts and policy makers.

As to the whaling regime, the third phase (1980–95) in its history stands out as particularly interesting from a science–policy interface perspective. Following the implementation of the moratorium in 1986, there was a strong surge in the conduct of innovative scientific research.[53] Although a scientific consensus emerged that cautious whaling could be conducted, this was repeatedly rejected by the majority in the IWC. The explanation is fairly straightforward: this is the only case in our sample that has been characterized by deep-going conflict over *basic values*. Scientific expertise can produce information on the state of a stock or an ecosystem and can provide factual inputs for determining sustainable levels of harvest, but there is no way that scientific experts can resolve the issue of whether it is morally right or wrong to utilize a particular species for purposes of consumption or gain. Introducing a 'rational' element represented by science has limited effect when the bargaining really concerns values and not numbers. To complicate matters further, some analysts claim that the

[51] Andresen and Boasson, 'International Climate Cooperation'.

[52] For further information, see the review of the IPCC by the InterAcademy Council of the IPCC, at http://reviewipcc.interacademycouncil.net.

[53] Andresen, 'The International Whaling Regime'.

whaling regime scores low on effectiveness.[54] By contrast, others conclude that it is a highly effective regime because after years of depletion, the IWC finally managed to protect large whales – one of the rare examples of a truly precautionary approach.[55] This debate illustrates the difficulty of evaluating the effectiveness of regimes and that there is no universal consensus that management should be based on scientific expertise.

6.6 Conclusions

This chapter has discussed the role of scientific expertise and under what conditions such expertise can influence decision makers and enhance the effectiveness of certain international environmental regimes. A first observation is that scientific expertise represents an important decision premise for decision makers in these regimes. All the five regimes examined here now have scientific bodies as part of their institutional set-up, with a tendency towards greater utilization of scientific research and a broadening of the scope of scientific expert input. As regimes mature, governments are less inclined to explicitly dispute scientific 'consensual knowledge'. And when scientific experts issue warnings, some kind of collective action normally follows by decision makers. However, we find no uniform pattern in political responses to scientific expert advice. Sometimes conclusive scientific evidence is not a prerequisite for undertaking collective action; instead, policy makers may decide to take precautionary measures. Generally, scientific expertise is most important in the agenda-setting phase, and gradually declines in significance as politics and governments take control over the relevant decision-making processes, notably in regimes facing 'malign' political problems.

A second main observation is that scientific expertise usually has only a moderate influence on decisions taken and on regime effectiveness – unless scientific expert advice interacts with other 'benign' factors associated with the features of the problem at hand. When there are deep political conflicts, including conflicts over value judgements, scientific expertise has scant room for influence. Thus, we see that the substance of the response is determined essentially by politics, not by scientific expertise.

54 Andresen, 'The Effectiveness of the International Whaling Commission'.

55 S. Holt, 'Whale Mining, Whale Saving', *Marine Policy*, 9 (1985), 92–114.

The two final observations strike a more positive note. According to our data, considerable progress has been made within some of the regimes (ozone, the North Sea and acid rain) and scientific expertise has played a role in this progress. These three regimes, particularly the two regional ones, are not well known outside the realm of the negotiators involved and a small research community. Both decision makers in general and the public at large remain unaware of the progress made in important international environmental agreements dealing with issues involving the protection of the atmosphere and the oceans. Too many decision makers, as well as the public at large, continue to believe that there has been little or no progress in international environmental politics – which is simply not true. This links up with the last observation: the massive focus on climate change. The observations I have offered here have been rather sober as regards both the role of scientific expertise and the effectiveness of the climate regime. However, knowledge about climate change is now widespread among the public in the Organisation for Economic Co-operation and Development (OECD) region as well as in many key developing countries, such as the emerging economies. The important cognitive message sent by the IPCC has clearly made a huge difference here. Moreover, much is being done to address climate change at the national level – and, importantly, at the level of industries and consumers. We should also bear in mind that this is a long-term and incredibly complex problem, so it may be premature or unfair to dismiss the climate regime as ineffective at this stage. Moreover, after natural science experts, the time has come for social science experts to come up with innovative suggestions for institutional design – not least in order to break the political deadlock during negotiations, where natural science experts can play only a limited role.

7

Changing demands at the science–policy interface: organizational learning in the IPCC

BERND SIEBENHÜNER

7.1 Introduction

Most observers consider the Intergovernmental Panel on Climate Change (IPCC) to be a prime example of an effective institution at the science–policy interface in the field of climate policy. As a high-level body of experts, the IPCC has attained significant recognition both in policy domains and with the general public. The Nobel Peace Prize awarded in 2007 provides a most obvious indication of its success. However, this recognition was followed by an intensive debate about its reliability in 2010 under the label 'climate-gate'.[1] Despite the critical debate that took place, it remains a fact that over a period of more than two decades, the IPCC has developed significantly and has undergone numerous processes of learning and change. As an international scientific assessment process, it pioneered the development of forms of international science–policy interaction, especially by way of its governmental approval mechanism. It was the first process of its kind that explicitly acknowledged the political dimension of expert assessments by including governments in the final phases of the drafting of, and attaining agreement on, the texts of its reports. It has provided a model for other assessment processes and served as a blueprint for the Intergovernmental Platform for Biodiversity and Ecosystem Services (IPBES). By engaging up to 1,500 scientists as authors of its assessment reports, it can be seen as an epistemic community as proposed by Haas,[2] even though some caveats are due as regards the extent of consensus on what would be appropriate solutions.

Notwithstanding its achievements, the IPCC's influence on the political realm has been questioned and it has been suggested that the body is

[1] See section 7.3.5, below.

[2] P. M. Haas, 'Introduction: Epistemic Communities and International Policy Coordination', *International Organization*, 46 (1992), 1–35.

not as effective as it could be in furthering international political decision making.[3] Some maintain that the IPCC's advice is too focused on scientific credibility rather than on the political impact of its advice. In the view of these critics, this one-sided focus explains the lack of progress in international climate politics.[4] Others argue that the structure of the climate problem is hostile to any form of scientific intervention, which implies that, no matter how well organized it is, the IPCC is doomed to be largely irrelevant politically.[5] This chapter presents a middle line between these two positions by focusing on the different demands of the political processes and the responses by the IPCC over time.

The overall objective of this chapter is to analyse when and why the IPCC has learned to be better prepared to provide effective policy advice and whether it was influential in the decision-making process under the conditions of changing negotiation dynamics. Therefore, in section 7.2 the chapter first develops a short conceptual framework for analysing the learning processes of the IPCC. In section 7.3 the internal learning processes of the IPCC will be studied in order to discern the impact of the IPCC assessment process on climate change decision making in its different phases. Finally, after briefly summarising the findings of the previous sections, conclusions will be drawn about the role of experts in decision making and the importance of learning processes.

7.2 Conceptualizing organizational learning and policy impact at the science–policy interface

7.2.1 Conceptualizing learning

Processes of social learning have been studied under various labels within different social science disciplines.[6] To qualify as 'social', learning

[3] B. Siebenhüner, 'How Do Scientific Assessments Learn? Conceptual Framework and Case Study of the IPCC', *Science & Policy*, 5 (2002), 411–20; P. M. Haas, 'When Does Power Listen to Truth? A Constructivist Approach to the Policy Process', *Journal of European Public Policy*, 11 (2004), 569–92.

[4] U. E. Simonis, 'The IPCC and Climate Politics: Small Potatoes', *Environmentalist*, 29 (2009), 330–2.

[5] M. Hulme, *Why We Disagree About Climate Change: Understanding Controversy, Inaction and Opportunity* (Cambridge University Press, 2009).

[6] A. Bandura, *Social Learning Theory* (Englewood Cliffs, NJ: Prentice Hall, 1977); D. Gale, 'What Have We Learned from Social Learning?', *European Economic Review*, 40 (1996), 617–28; C. Pahl-Wostl, M. Craps, A. Dewulf, E. Mostert, D. Tabara and T. Tallieu, 'Social Learning and Water Resources Management', *Ecology and Society*, 12 (2007), 5, available

processes have to refer to a level that exceeds the realm of individual decision making. What all approaches also have in common is the need to conceptualize the link between individual behaviour and collective processes, and the need to indicate what counts as learning as opposed to non-reflective evolutionary processes.

In this chapter, the focus will be on organizational learning processes as special forms of social learning. Studies in organizational learning help us to understand the dynamics as well as the drivers and the hindrances of learning processes within organizations. Concepts of organizational learning – also referred to as 'the learning organization' – have been developed in management studies to describe processes of organizational change that take place at a collective level.[7] In this body of literature the distinction between individual and collective action is crucial – in particular for the choice of the appropriate theoretical and analytical approach. It is commonly assumed that organizations exist on the basis of collective action. While most studies in this field address business organizations, the concept of organizational learning has also been applied to other forms and types of organization, such as public authorities or social networks.[8]

7.2.1.1 Definition of learning

Organizational learning encompasses a dimension of change in values, norms and beliefs that transcends the sphere of explicit cognitive knowledge. Therefore, simple training of cognitive skills or technological improvements might be helpful, but will hardly suffice to tackle the tacit dimensions of commonly shared values, norms and general convictions. In order to be able to conceptualize organizational learning processes of collective actors, such as the IPCC, a broad but precise

at: www.ecologyandsociety.org/vol12/iss2/art5; M. S. Reed, A. C. Evely, G. Cundill, L. Fazey, J. Glass, A. Laing, J. Newig, B. Parrish, C. Prell, C. Raymond and L. C. Stringer, 'What is Social Learning?', *Ecology and Society*, 15 (2010): 4, available at: www.ecologyandsociety.org/vol15/iss4/resp1.

[7] For prominent studies in the field, see L. Argote, *Organizational Learning. Creating, Retaining, and Transferring Knowledge* (Boston, MA: Kluwer, 1999); C. Argyris and D. A. Schön, *Organizational Learning II. Theory, Method, and Practice* (Reading, MA: Addison-Wesley, 1996); J. Denton, *Organisational Learning and Effectiveness* (London: Routledge, 1998); P. Senge, *The Fifth Discipline: The Art and Practice of the Learning Organization* (New York: Doubleday, 1990).

[8] J. LaPalombra, 'Power and Politics in Organizations: Public and Private Sector Comparisons' in M. Dierkes, A. Berthoin Antal, J. Child and I. Nonaka (eds.), *Handbook of Organizational Learning and Knowledge* (Oxford University Press, 2001), 557–81.

definition of learning is required, one that enables empirical research on a diversity of actors and their individual dynamics.[9]

In the conceptual model of organizational learning, collective actors are addressed from an organizational perspective. Actors in this collective sense are citizen groups, interest groups, business corporations, governments, non-governmental organizations (NGOs) or actor networks. However, the distinction between the individual and collective levels is particularly tricky when it comes to learning concepts. Although the notion of 'organizational learning' implies that it is more than the mere sum of individual learning by the members of an organization, organizational learning is dependent on individuals, their learning and their behavioural changes. In this line of thought, organizational learning can be seen as changes in the procedures, structures, shared beliefs and knowledge of an organization that are constituted by contributions from individuals on the basis of the division of labour and attribution of responsibilities within the organization, that is, the structural framework of internal relations. This assumption does not imply a complete analogy between all forms of organizations; it merely maintains that learning by and in these collective actors can be more than mere individual learning because of an existing structural framework of internal relationships between the members of the collective entity. If organizational learning is to be enhanced, it is these structures and relations that need to change.[10]

Thus, organizational learning is understood as a process in which collective actors acquire knowledge and/or values that lead to a change in their behaviour in a certain direction. Behavioural change is the noticeable result of the cognitive change on the side of the individuals involved, which is a necessary element of a learning process.

7.2.1.2 Forms of learning

In the various models of organizational learning, different types and levels of learning have been distinguished. With regard to the definition

[9] E. Parson and W. C. Clark, 'Sustainable Development as Social Learning: Theoretical Perspectives and Practical Challenges for the Design of a Research Program' in L. H. Gunderson, C. S. Holling and S. S. Light (eds.), *Barriers and Bridges to the Renewal of Ecosystems and Institutions* (New York: Columbia University Press, 1995), 428–60.

[10] B. Siebenhüner, 'The Role of Social Learning on the Road to Sustainability' in J. N. Rosenau, E. U. von Weizsäcker and U. Petschow (eds.), *Governance and Sustainability* (Sheffield: Greenleaf, 2005), 86–99.

of 'learning' employed in this study, further specification is needed in order to identify an empirically meaningful notion of learning that can be applied to social actors. In their seminal study, Argyris and Schön distinguished different types of learning.[11] The fundamental criteria for their classification is how far the underlying 'theory in use', that is, the often unconsciously and tacitly used set of values and causal beliefs that the members of an organization share, has changed during the learning process. The basic level of learning is framed as single-loop learning. It is the simplest form of learning and it addresses the adaptation of new knowledge to existing frameworks of objectives and causal beliefs. Based on a simple feedback loop between given expectations and the real outcomes of a process, this instrumental type of learning allows for error correction and leads to an adjustment of results that deviate from the pre-existing expectations. According to Argyris and Schön, an advanced form of learning, referred to as double-loop learning, includes the underlying theory in use within the learning process. Thus, there will be two feedback loops: an instrumental one of error correction and a more fundamental one that connects the former to changes in the general framework of beliefs, norms and objectives.[12]

The adoption of Argyris and Schön's framework for empirical studies confronts researchers with the task of discerning the scope of the involvement of the theory in use in the learning process, which is particularly difficult given the tacit nature of this form of knowledge and the broad definition of the concept of theory in use. Therefore, Fiol and Lyles proposed a more clear-cut theoretical approach that conceptualizes learning as opposed to adaptation.[13] In their conceptualization, learning comprises 'the development of insights, knowledge, and associations between past actions, the effectiveness of those actions, and future actions', whereas adaptation refers to the 'ability to make incremental adjustments as a result of environmental changes, goal structure changes, or other changes'.[14]

Based on Fiol and Lyles' approach, this chapter distinguishes between adaptation and reflection as two forms of learning that lead to changes in behavioural patterns, with 'reflection' referring to Fiol and Lyles'

[11] Argyris and Schön, *Organizational Learning II.* [12] *Ibid.*

[13] C. M. Fiol and M. A. Lyles, 'Organizational Learning', *Academy of Management Review*, 10 (1985), 803–13.

[14] *Ibid.*, at 811. A similar distinction between learning and adaptation was made in E. B. Haas, 'Collective Learning: Some Theoretical Speculations' in P. E. Tetlock (ed.), *Learning in US and Soviet Foreign Policy* (Boulder, CO: Westview Press, 1991).

conceptualization of learning. The nature of the behavioural changes associated with each form of learning differs due to their distinct impact on underlying knowledge structures and related belief systems. In the case of adaptation, changes in behaviour are induced by external processes that do not engage the cognitive framework of the organization and its members. In other words, adaptation comprises error correction, but does not engage the fundamental knowledge and belief systems behind the form of behaviour at stake. By contrast, reflection induces change in the prevalent knowledge structure, including the prevalent cognitive frame. Reflection thus engages higher-level processes involving cognitive and behavioural changes.

7.2.2 Conceptualizing policy impact

What is to be learned in a scientific assessment process such as the one conducted by the IPCC, which can be viewed as an intermediary body between science and the international policy process? The IPCC provides information to the negotiation bodies of international climate politics and thereby potentially influences policy outcomes. As such, this intergovernmental body has been designed to reduce scientific uncertainties and, thereby, support decision-making processes.

Research within the Global Environmental Assessment (GEA) Project developed an understanding of when and how scientific assessments are able to affect political decision making.[15] It was found that such assessments have the most influence when they are salient to potential users, credible in terms of scientific standards and legitimate in terms of the way in which the assessment is designed.[16] Thus, the following three criteria indicate the direction for learning:

- Saliency: learning in an assessment process or by its participants takes place when the process or its products are well known to participants in a certain area of policy making and these participants perceive the assessment as relevant to them and their decision-making situations.

[15] For further information, see www.hks.harvard.edu/gea.

[16] W. C. Clark and N. M. Dickson, 'The Global Environmental Assessment Project: Learning from Efforts to Link Science and Policy in an Interdependent World', *Acclimations*, 8 (1999), 6–7; R. B. Mitchell, W. C. Clark, F. Alcock and D. Cash (eds.), *Global Environmental Assessments: Information, Institutions, and Influence* (Cambridge, MA: MIT Press, 2006).

- Credibility: an assessment process or its participants learn to become more credible when the facts, causal beliefs and options developed in the assessment are increasingly regarded as 'true' or, at least, worth using instead of other, competing information by other actors.
- Legitimacy: learning in an assessment process takes place when it is increasingly able to convince others that the goals pursued in the assessment correspond to those that the recipients would have kept in mind had they conducted the assessment.

Assessments that are able to advance in establishing a balance between these criteria can be expected to help the policy process. They are likely to provide decision makers with relevant knowledge on the actual and future causes and consequences of climate change as well as on possible solutions, their consequences and repercussions.

7.3 Organizational learning of the IPCC

The IPCC was established in 1988 as a scientific advisory body to the United Nations Environment Programme (UNEP) and the World Meteorological Organization (WMO) in order to provide scientific knowledge for the negotiation processes in international climate politics. It was designed as an intergovernmental organization whose members are scientific experts, but it also involves governmental participation in the process of approving the major conclusions reached. Since its beginning, it has produced four major assessment reports (published in 1990, 1995, 2001 and 2007) and is to finalize a fifth report in 2014. In addition, it published a considerable number of special reports and technical papers, as well as supporting materials such as guidelines and documentary materials. Over the years, it has undergone several changes with regard to its internal structures and procedures.

Here, the IPCC will be analysed in a chronological order in terms of its predominant learning processes that target the generation of policy-relevant knowledge and its political impact on the negotiation process. These learning processes will be classified in relation to the predominant forms of learning that were presented above, that is, adaptation and reflection.[17]

[17] This case study is based on an analysis of written documents and on personal and telephone interviews with experts in the field. First findings were documented in Siebenhüner, 'How Do Scientific Assessments Learn?'

7.3.1 The First Assessment and Supplementary Reports (1988–92)

When the IPCC was founded in 1988, it exhibited a unique and innovative structure and design. Its precursor in the international arena, the Advisory Group on Greenhouse Gases (AGGG), established in 1986, consisted of a handful of scientists almost exclusively from Northern industrialized countries.[18] By contrast, the IPCC introduced an intergovernmental approval mechanism open to governments from all over the world. The centrepiece of this mechanism was the involvement of numerous governments in the formulation of the questions to be addressed in the assessment process and in the approval of the final reports.[19]

When studying the first phase of the IPCC in the light of the typology of learning, the set-up of the IPCC – with its unique organizational structure – seems to qualify as a form of reflection. It resulted in significantly different forms and institutionalizations than previous attempts to design the science–policy interface in the climate area by way of the AGGG. The IPCC provided a new and advanced way to facilitate science–policy communication by ensuring saliency and credibility, which clearly affected the underlying cognitive frames and strategies in the assessment. The government's ownership of the whole process and the final documents led to a significant increase in saliency when compared with the loosely connected AGGG assessment process.[20] Credibility was ensured through the design of the IPCC as a scientific expert body, with political decision makers not being involved as authors of the report's main text. Even the First Assessment Report was subject to a review procedure that was deemed to ensure high scientific standards. In addition, the legitimacy of the process was increased, as compared to the AGGG process, by the inclusion of scientists from all parts of the world – even though scientists from developing countries were highly under-represented in the preparation of the First Assessment Report.

The finalization of the First Assessment Report in 1990 provided the opportunity to consider the experiences of the IPCC processes themselves and what could be learned for future assessments. This process

18 S. Agrawala, 'Early Science–Policy Interaction in Climate Change: Lessons from the Advisory Group on Greenhouse Gases', *Global Environmental Change*, 9 (1999), 157–69.

19 B. Bolin, 'Science and Policy Making', *Ambio*, 23 (1994), 25–9.

20 S. Agrawala, 'Context and Early Origins of the Intergovernmental Panel on Climate Change', *Climatic Change*, 39 (1998), 605–20.

took place in the form of discussions in the IPCC Bureau and its plenary sessions, but no formal document on the outcomes of this learning process emerged from these discussions. One of the main lessons learned by the participants in the first assessment was the political nature of the IPCC process, which was new to most of the participating scientific experts. They had to adapt to the fact that the agenda of the assessment was mostly set by political needs and that scientific outcomes would also be challenged by political decision makers. As a result, major discussions emerged about the possibilities of scientific work under political pressures and significant scepticism was expressed by some of the experts involved. Nevertheless, acknowledging the political function of the whole endeavour, a supplementary report was prepared by IPCC scientists that, together with the First Assessment Report, turned out to be highly influential on the negotiations of and final agreement on the UN Framework Convention on Climate Change (UNFCCC) in 1992.[21]

The findings presented in the First Assessment Report demonstrated the urgency and the relevance of the problem of climate change to the international community. However, the assessment also acknowledged that numerous uncertainties regarding the actual human influence on climate change remained, and pointed to questions regarding the reliability of the model predictions and the causal relationships in the global climate system.[22] Policy makers nevertheless took the findings significantly more seriously than those of previous assessments.

The learning processes in the later period of the First Assessment Report fit the adaptive mode of learning and did not lead to fundamental changes of the underlying assumptions and norms on how to conduct the assessment. The changes in regard to the saliency, credibility or legitimacy of the assessment process remained limited, since the general design of the assessment process was left untouched.

7.3.2 The Second Assessment Report (1992–5)

The Second Assessment Report was completed in 1995. It integrated the results of the flourishing area of climate research in the early 1990s. The

[21] S. Agrawala, 'Structural and Process History of the Intergovernmental Panel on Climate Change', *Climatic Change*, 39 (1998), 621–42; B. Bolin, 'Next Step for Climate-Change Analysis', *Nature*, 368 (1994), 94.

[22] Intergovernmental Panel on Climate Change (IPCC), *Climate Change. The IPCC Scientific Assessment* (Cambridge University Press, 1990).

emergence of the IPCC and the signing of the UNFCCC gave a boost to the entire field of atmospheric and climate research, in particular in the natural sciences. Governments were increasingly willing to fund this type of research. New institutes were founded and novel global circulation models were developed or older ones significantly improved. While the climate change problem itself had gained significant awareness among governments, NGOs and business actors, the awareness of significant uncertainties and knowledge gaps spurred the scientific debate and research. The main objective of this body of research was to reduce the uncertainties and to find clear evidence for the human causation of climate change.

After the experience in the ozone negotiations, scientific experts as well as political actors hoped to advance international negotiations through the provision of scientifically sound evidence. In ozone policy, the emergence of scientific evidence for the damaging effects of chlorofluorocarbon (CFCs) to the ozone layer fostered the efforts of the international community to negotiate an international treaty and to phase out CFCs.[23] In contrast, in the field of climate change, no similar evidence could be established, causal chains turned out to be much more complex and indirect in the global climate system, and research into the issue had not yet matured. However, the fact that policy makers felt the need to negotiate a second legally binding international climate change instrument, the Kyoto Protocol, can also be perceived as a fundamental achievement of the Second Assessment Report. The Kyoto Protocol was signed in 1997, two years after the publication of the Second Assessment Report.

During the preparation of the Second Assessment Report, one crucial incidence of learning took place. At its sixth session, the IPCC Panel established a special Task Force on the IPCC Structure. It reported to the eighth plenary session of the IPCC in 1992. Its purpose, on the one hand, was to bring the IPCC in line with the institutional requirements of the UNFCCC, which introduced several new bodies, such as the Conference of the Parties and two Subsidiary Bodies. On the other hand, the Task Force was asked to outline the Working Group structure for the preparation of the Second Assessment Report and to suggest ways to allow for the

[23] P. Canan and N. Reichman, *Ozone Connections. Expert Networks in Global Environmental Governance* (Sheffield: Greenleaf, 2002); K. T. Litfin, *Ozone Discourses: Science and Politics in Global Environmental Cooperation* (New York: Columbia University Press, 1994).

participation of NGOs in the IPCC process, a demand that was expressed by several environmental NGOs. The Task Force was open to all the members of the IPCC, including government representatives, authors and the Bureau members. The Task Force prepared a report that led to the adoption of a four-page-long document about new rules of procedure of the IPCC.[24]

The core of these new rules dealt with the specific and highly sophisticated type of review procedure that was imposed to ensure scientific quality and credibility to both the scientific and the political community. Whereas in the first assessment no precise formal rules on the review process had been available and each chapter had been reviewed by two or three experts and government officials simultaneously, during the second assessment this process became much more refined. Now, the review process took place in two subsequent rounds: first by scientific experts and second by governmental officials.

The acknowledgement of the role of NGOs and industry in the preparation of the assessment was an important step towards increasing the legitimacy of IPCC assessments. However, their actual impact on the assessment process remained limited, given that they were allowed to submit advice, but not to vote in the plenary sessions. Moreover, the inclusion of these groups did not result from a thorough reflection on the assessment process and its political functions, but from political pressure exerted by these groups. The additional formalization of the peer-review process as expressed in the document prepared by the special Task Force aimed at increasing credibility, but the suggestions implied few significant changes to the processes already in place. Nevertheless, these minor changes in the review process led to a tremendous increase in the number of reviews that each author had to take into account.[25]

The report of the Task Force and the resulting decisions by the plenary responded to critical comments from governments, whereas only a few criticisms from the scientific community were addressed both in the report and during the revision of the rules of procedure. By addressing governmental concerns, the report thus promoted saliency to political decision makers. Nevertheless, the Task Force can be seen as a first

[24] Intergovernmental Panel on Climate Change (IPCC), *Draft Report of the Ninth Session of the Intergovernmental Panel on Climate Change, IPCC-X/Doc. 2* (Geneva: IPCC Secretariat, 1994).

[25] InterAcademy Council, *Climate Change Assessments. Review of the Processes and Procedures of the IPCC* (Amsterdam: InterAcademy Council, 2010).

institutionalized effort to consider the experiences of the first period of the IPCC's existence and it was fairly successful in promoting changes in its procedures. Moreover, the fact that the Task Force was open to all members of the IPCC provided a high degree of legitimacy to its outcome. In terms of a learning typology, these learning efforts can be characterized as adaptation, considering that the changes were rather reactive and complied with external criticisms. However, there was no fundamental change in the underlying assumptions.

7.3.3 The Third Assessment Report (1995–2001)

A somewhat different approach was taken to facilitate learning from the process for the Second Assessment and to feed the results into the design of the process for the preparation of the Third Assessment Report, starting in 1996. At that time, the first chairman of the IPCC was about to step down and his successor had just been elected. During a one-year transition period, they worked together closely to ensure continuity and to allow for the transfer of knowledge.

The new chairman started out by considering how the structure of the IPCC might be improved. Instead of establishing a specific task force, he took it upon himself to prepare a White Paper addressing a number of key questions and suggesting a new structure as well as procedural improvements for the Third Assessment Report.[26] The draft White Paper was based on critical articles in the scientific literature, government statements and a number of workshops on specific substantial matters, such as mitigation technologies, regional projections of impacts and uncertainty.[27] The chairman received over ninety responses from governments, NGOs and scientific experts, which he considered in the final decision paper on the design of the process for the preparation of the Third Assessment Report, which was then adopted by the plenary session. Altogether, this iterative process took a little over a year and it was a larger effort than the design of the process for the Second Assessment when measured in terms of the number of comments considered and iterative rounds.

[26] Intergovernmental Panel on Climate Change, *Draft Report of the Twelfth Session of the IPCC Bureau, BUR-XIII/Doc. 2* (Geneva: IPCC Secretariat, 1997).

[27] R. Moss, 'Ready for IPCC-2001: Innovation and Change in Plans for the IPCC Third Assessment Report', *Climatic Change*, 45 (2000), 459–68.

One of the main challenges for the design of the preparation process for the Third Assessment Report was how to deal with the criticisms raised in the so-called 'Chapter 8 debate'.[28] In the aftermath of the release of the Second Assessment Report, a number of US-based scientists backed by the Global Climate Coalition (GCC) launched a massive attack against the final version of Chapter 8 of Working Group I. Chapter 8 concluded that 'the balance of evidence suggests a discernible human influence on global climate'.[29] The accusations were published in widely read newspapers such as the *Wall Street Journal* and were serious. They charged that the lead authors of the chapter had changed the text of the final version after it had already been officially approved by the Working Group plenary. They thereby claimed that the chapter authors had violated the IPCC's rules of procedure and the fundamental standards of peer review. However, the accused authors and the leaders of the IPCC process successfully proved that these accusations were wrong and no IPCC Member State joined in the criticism.[30] Yet, the debate brought some deficits to the surface that had to be addressed in future assessments, such as the need for clarification about which parts in the main text have to be revised on the basis of changes in the summary for policy makers.

Awareness of these deficits led the IPCC leaders to introduce further institutional innovations in the process for the preparation of the Third Assessment. The incoming chairman in his White Paper suggested the introduction of so-called 'review-editors', whose function would be to oversee the review process to ensure that authors appropriately dealt with the comments from the expert and government reviewers.[31]

[28] An extensive analysis of the Chapter 8 debate can be found in M. Lahsen, 'The Detection and Attribution of Conspiracies: The Controversy over Chapter 8' in G. E. Marcus (ed.), *Paranoia within Reason: A Casebook on Conspiracy as Explanation* (University of Chicago Press, 1998), 111–36. An in-depth study of the arguments concerning peer review put forward in this discussion is included in P. N. Edwards and S. H. Schneider, 'Self-governance and Peer Review in Science-for-Policy: The Case of the IPCC Second Assessment Report' in C. Miller and P. N. Edwards (eds.), *Changing the Atmosphere: Expert Knowledge and Environmental Governance* (Cambridge, MA: MIT Press, 2001), 219–46.

[29] J. Houghton, L. G. Meira Filho, B. A. Callandar, N. Harris, A. Kattenberg and K. Maskell (eds.), *Climate Change 1995. The Science of Climate Change. Contribution of Working Group I to the Second Assessment Report of the Intergovernmental Panel on Climate Change* (Cambridge University Press, 1996), at 4.

[30] Edwards and Schneider, 'Self-governance and Peer Review in Science-for-Policy'.

[31] Intergovernmental Panel on Climate Change, *Draft Report of the Twelfth Session of the IPCC Bureau*, at 9f.

Because sceptics were afraid of delays in the timing of the Assessment, the number of review editors was limited to two per chapter. Review editors were invited to the author meetings in order to witness the processes and to provide timely comments and suggestions. No serious delays occurred due to the introduction of review editors, although they had to work under intense time pressures. Even so, not all authors regarded the introduction of review editors as an improvement of the process, since not all of the review editors were similarly diligent in fulfilling their job – a task that required reading and consideration of the various versions of the draft chapters and of up to 200 comments.

The introduction of review editors demonstrated a considerable degree of reconsideration of the ongoing processes and can be regarded as more than a single-loop learning process because it significantly exceeded the framework of previous IPCC processes. These changes were accompanied by a shift in the general perception of the IPCC process. This shift emerged from the fact that IPCC scientific experts were confronted with legal arguments about their scientific statements and the procedures that led to them. This debate resulted in the realization that the form of scientific discourse that scientific experts were used to was not appropriate under circumstances in which they encountered procedural arguments from lawyers. These arguments could not be dealt with on the basis of scientific discourse grounded on a common notion of truth and credibility. The IPCC experts thus had to reflect on the conditions of legal discourse, which resulted in more precise formulations of the rules of procedure and in procedural innovations. The IPCC thus had to incorporate a new rationale that originated in the political realm. Nevertheless, the outcome of this reconsideration process was the introduction of further refinement of the scientific procedures that increased the credibility of IPCC findings at the expense of further bureaucratization and extension of the assessment process. In so doing, the saliency of the assessment was put under jeopardy because the assessment process was extended and the IPCC had even more problems in delivering timely and policy-relevant information. In retrospect, this reconsideration process helped to protect the IPCC against legal claims and to increase its policy impact, since criticism on legal grounds was now much more difficult to raise. However, these changes had little influence on legitimacy issues as they did not lead to changes in the goals pursued in the assessment process, which remained to produce information about climate change grounded in the natural sciences.

With regard to the political saliency, the Third Assessment Report exhibited another reflection process. Since the launch of the IPCC, the topic of uncertainties was intensely debated among the participating scientific experts and authors, who used different approaches to estimate and document uncertainties. Many of them even refused to provide any estimation on uncertainties, based on their scientific ethos to focus exclusively on reliable and certain research findings. Several researchers had to be convinced that the policy-oriented approach of the IPCC urgently required these estimations in order to advise decision makers about specific risks – even when no or little scientific certainty was available. In order to enable the IPCC to improve its advice to decision makers and to achieve more consistency in the use of language regarding uncertainty, Moss and Schneider developed a guidance paper that was sent to all Working Groups during the third assessment process.[32] They introduced a qualitative framework to describe 'states of knowledge' and suggested a numerical scale of the various degrees of confidence. The objective was to allow the authors to make their partly inevitably subjective estimations more transparent and understandable for policy makers and to increase the overall consistency of the report.

While most authors adhered to this framework, one group of lead authors from Working Group I refused to do so. Instead of using the suggested scale with intervals of five percentiles (5 per cent, 10 per cent . . . 95 per cent confidence), they employed numbers of a third or 99 per cent likelihood, thereby avoiding the exact description of uncertainties by referring to the assumptions of various models and leaving policy makers without clear guidance on how to evaluate the related risks. After lengthy discussions among the authors and following a request from governments, the authors partly revised the chapter. Therefore, minor inconsistencies can also be found in the Third Assessment Report, although the general treatment of uncertainties is significantly more reflective, consistent and clear than in previous reports.

The central findings of the Third Assessment Report demonstrated the increased urgency of political action against climate change. The report presented matured simulation results with severely increased

[32] R. Moss and S. Schneider, 'Uncertainties in the IPCC TAR: Recommendations to Lead Authors for More Consistent Assessment and Reporting' in K. Tanaka (ed.), *IPCC Supporting Material, Guidance Papers on the Cross Cutting Issues of the Third Assessment Report of the IPCC* (Cambridge University Press, 2000), 33–51.

estimates of temperature and sea level rise until the year 2100. In addition, first evidence for climate change was documented in the report. Changes in the migration of species, rising mean temperatures on a global scale and over-proportionally increased numbers and costs of extreme weather events alerted many policy makers. After publication, little criticism was voiced publicly. Most of the science-based criticisms were integrated in the process and, together with the sophisticated procedures of the IPCC, this enhanced the credibility and legitimacy of the process.

As regards policy impact, the Third Assessment Report was discussed critically. In 2001, the US administration decided to withdraw from the Kyoto Protocol and caused significant troubles in the international negotiation process. The publication of the report was unable to motivate the US government to refrain from this step. Nevertheless, an inquiry from the US administration to the US Academy of Science asking whether the IPCC process was legitimate and delivered credible results brought new support for the IPCC, even though it did not result in further political processes of the US government in support of the climate regime. However, the remaining signatory states of the Kyoto Protocol continued their efforts to implement the accord and finally succeeded in reaching the necessary number of signatory states for its entry into force. In 2005, the Kyoto Protocol became legally binding and the novel policy instruments foreseen in the Protocol, such as clearly defined GHG reduction obligations for developed and economy-in-transition states, Emissions Trading and the Clean Development Mechanism, have subsequently been implemented. These results can in part also be credited to the Third Assessment Report that helped to reduce uncertainties in particular with regard to the current and future impacts of climate change.

7.3.4 The Fourth Assessment Report (2001–7)

While still concerned with the process of completing the Third Assessment Report, in early 2001 the IPCC Bureau was already reflecting on the past assessment process and developed ideas about future steps. As in the Third Assessment, the chairman prepared a so-called 'Issues Paper on the Future Work Program of the IPCC' and submitted it to the Bureau for discussion.[33] Comments were sought from the vice-chairs,

[33] R. Watson, *Future Work Program of the IPCC* (Paris: Mimeo, 2001).

the co-chairs, the lead authors and the governments, but not from individuals or organizations external to the IPCC.

The chairman of the IPCC, who had initiated this process, was not allowed to conclude it. His strong and outspoken position motivated his critics to convince a majority of governments to elect another chair. Thus, a new chair from a developing country headed the process. As it turned out, in most respects he continued to follow the path set out by his predecessor. In particular, the elaborate review mechanism was maintained. Nevertheless, in 2001 the IPCC Bureau found that the preparation of the next report would take more time, since research output was expected to be slower and more time-consuming than for previous reports. The Bureau decided not to publish the next report before 2007.

This Fourth Assessment Report presented a number of new scientific findings. First, these related to new modelling results. Latest simulations showed an even stronger increase in global mean temperature and more severe damaging impacts than had been mentioned in the Third Assessment Report. Second, insights into the actual impacts of climate change and the mature data about ongoing changes in ecosystems and the climate system led scientists to pay more attention to issues of adaptation and vulnerability to climate change in specific world regions. The report of Working Group III on mitigation strategies, however, has been regarded as the weakest part of the assessment,[34] given the moderate guidance that it provides for policy makers. It merely lists policy options and summarizes findings from the literature on the potential effects of these options. Given the acknowledged political nature of this type of assessment, the lack of policy recommendations or advice in the report can also be regarded as a political weakness, in particular if the need for the guideline to be policy-relevant, but not policy-prescriptive, is taken into consideration.[35]

Where the report and its presentation proved to be most effective was in the field of communication and raising media attention. As Grundmann and Krishnamurthy showed, the media coverage on climate change issues and the findings of the IPCC's Fourth Assessment Report increased immensely in 2007 in the UK, the USA, Germany and France.[36] Following the publication of the Stern

[34] Simonis, 'The IPCC and Climate Politics'.

[35] See R. Pielke, 'Science and Politics: Accepting a Dysfunctional Union', *Harvard International Review*, 30 (2008), 36–41.

[36] R. Grundmann and R. Krishnamurthy, 'The Discourse of Climate Change: A Corpus-Based Approach', *Critical Approaches to Discourse Analysis across Disciplines*, 4 (2010), 113–33.

Review,[37] the IPCC managed to play the media game most successfully by sticking closely to confidentiality rules up to the final publication date and by creating events around the publication of each part of the assessment.

Even though this new communication strategy was a tremendous jump in public awareness raising and recognition for the IPCC, the learning process can be characterized as a single-loop process and can therefore be categorized as adaptive. The IPCC became better and more effective at its political moves and thereby increased its *saliency*, in particular vis-à-vis the public media.

The political impact of the report found its acknowledgement in the Nobel Peace Prize awarded to the IPCC and its main authors in 2007. The IPCC shared the prize with Al Gore 'for their efforts to build up and disseminate greater knowledge about man-made climate change, and to lay the foundations for the measures that are needed to counteract such change'.[38] This award underscored the actual political impact of the IPCC, beyond the reflection of IPCC findings in the negotiation processes. Despite high expectations by many observers, the negotiations at the December 2007 Conference of the Parties (COP) in Bali came up with limited results. The COP could only agree upon a negotiation road map (the Bali Road Map) towards a new protocol rather than on a new binding agreement following the Kyoto Protocol from 2012 onwards.

7.3.5 Climate-gate and the Fifth Assessment Report (2008–14)

In the early phase of preparing for the Fifth Assessment Report, the IPCC faced a series of harsh criticisms, creating a moment of crisis and leading to subsequent revision of the report and its procedures. Politicized under the term 'climate-gate', a private email correspondence between IPCC authors was leaked to the media. It concerned dramatizing interpretations of specific data series. The campaign was obviously launched by climate sceptics, but nevertheless created some damage to the reputation and credibility of the IPCC. Subsequently, a number of errors in the Fourth Assessment Review became obvious and the IPCC had to apologize for them. The most debated mistake refers to a

[37] N. Stern, *The Economics of Climate Change: The Stern Review* (Cambridge University Press, 2007).

[38] O. D. Mjøs, speech given by the Chairman of the Norwegian Nobel Committee, available at: www.nobelprize.org/nobel_prizes/peace/laureates/2007/presentation-speech.html.

statement on the meltdown of the Himalayan glaciers during the first half of this century. It relied on a weak and unchallenged database, but made its way into the final report. This flaw was particularly delicate since it could be connected to a business interest of the research institute that the IPCC chair happened to lead. Similar errors also occurred in other chapters of the report.

To review these accusations and incidents, the United Nations established an international committee to review the IPCC's structures and procedures and to submit recommendations for its future development. The committee developed a list of balanced recommendations on how to revise the IPCC processes.[39] The most important suggestions include, first, the introduction of formal arrangements to limit conflicts of interests for the IPCC chair and the co-chairs of the individual Working Groups. Second, the committee developed a number of precise improvements regarding increased transparency in the selection of authors, better tests of data sources and more refined treatment of uncertainties.

Following these recommendations, the IPCC established a Task Group on Procedures to advance revisions of the IPCC process. In most parts, it followed the recommendations regarding the actual processes and the preparation of decisions by the IPCC plenary. However, the Task Group was more reluctant with regard to the implementation of recommendations concerning the modernization of the IPCC management and its executive levels. In general, the resulting changes supported the general concept and set-up of the IPCC, and tried to find pathways for further improvements rather than radical change.[40] In essence, the changes introduced therefore qualify as adaptive learning. Qualitative change in saliency or credibility has not been recommended by the InterAcademy Council (IAC) review, nor has it been implemented by the IPCC itself. The revisions largely aimed at restoring the damaged credibility and legitimacy of the IPCC processes.

7.4 Conclusions

By way of both modes of learning, the IPCC improved its procedures to accommodate political claims questioning its legitimacy while maintaining and even strengthening its scientific standards towards credibility. In

[39] InterAcademy Council, *Climate Change Assessments.*
[40] Intergovernmental Panel on Climate Change, *Report of the 34th Session of the IPCC, IPCC-XXXIV/Doc. 1* (Geneva: IPCC Secretariat, 2011).

addition, most of the scientific experts participating in the IPCC process learned to orient the assessment process towards the needs of the policy-making process, ensuring saliency. Nevertheless, the balance in particular between credibility and saliency is a delicate one, influencing the extent to which the IPCC process can have an impact on policy making. On the one hand, many scientists had and still have difficulties with the political aspects of the IPCC process, especially the government approval mechanism. On the other hand, many negotiators feel challenged by the scientific contents of the reports and the political implications. In particular, many of them remain critical about the policy options contained in the assessment reports, since they see them as too strong an influence on the political process.

In terms of the study of organizational learning processes in entire policy fields, it remains difficult to evaluate the contribution of the IPCC process to political decision making in the domestic and international realms. The magnitude of the influences and sources of relevant knowledge does not enable the tracing of individual decisions to one particular cause or one particular insight provided by a social actor. However, the sequence of the published results of the IPCC assessments and the steps in the international negotiation process show a pattern that may warrant assuming a certain causal influence. This finding relates in particular to the adoption of the UNFCCC and the Kyoto Protocol. Analysis of the IPCC also allows for conclusions to be drawn regarding the overall learning process in international climate policy. The IPCC seems to be a crucial actor in this process, the strength of which is derived from the credible and legitimate provision of policy-relevant knowledge and the reduction or clarification of uncertainties.

The IPCC exhibited different modes of organizational learning processes. The incidences of reflective learning can be observed in two critical events where fundamental reconsiderations of former practices and cognitive frames took place. These moments of crisis in the beginning of the work of the IPCC and during the Chapter 8 debate required radically new ways of (re)thinking and action to address the problems and external criticisms raised. This finding resonates well with insights from organizational learning, where crises have been described as key triggers for reflective learning processes in general.[41] The other IPCC

[41] L. Kim, 'Crisis Construction and Organizational Learning: Capability Building in Catching Up at Hyundai Motor', *Organization Science*, 9 (1998), 506–21; I. Nonaka, 'A Dynamic Theory of Organizational Knowledge Generation', *Organization Science*, 5 (1994), 14–37.

learning processes discussed fall into the category of adaptive learning with incremental changes and adaptations in the cognitive frames and stepwise improvements of procedures. Both types of learning processes demonstrate the IPCC's ability to change and monitor its procedures and outcomes, as well as to safeguard basic political influence. Three main elements underscore this ability.[42]

First, learning was promoted by the existence of a small and well-connected group of scientific experts in the Bureau that coordinates the work of the IPCC. This group was able to exchange knowledge and new insights rather quickly, had considerable authority in the preparation of the assessment reports and was selected according to scientific as well as political criteria set by government officials. Moreover, their commitment to learning and solving the climate change problem greatly assisted the overall learning processes of the IPCC.

Second, the communication structures in the IPCC allowed for a broad diffusion of new expert knowledge. The inclusion of most relevant scientific experts enabled the IPCC to gather the most up-to-date scientific expertise, and its sequential process has proven to be effective in synthesizing this knowledge. However, there is room for improving the formal communication structures relevant to the internal interaction between the working groups. In particular, cross-disciplinary communication and exchange can be improved since the separation of the Working Groups along disciplinary domains precludes the emergence of common integrative frameworks, as in the Millennium Ecosystem Assessment (2005).[43] External communication with the negotiating bodies and the general public was also not entirely optimal when viewed from a learning perspective. In particular, dialogue with the general public was scant in the preparation of the four IPCC reports. Communication remained in a one-way mode where scientific experts tried to explain their findings to the public. The procedures were ill-suited for fostering a more open dialogue to include so-called lay knowledge or the general concerns, thoughts and attitudes of the public in different parts of the world that might trigger significant learning processes within the IPCC.

Third, the IPCC established functional mechanisms for its learning and improvement. The organization of the sophisticated review process

[42] Siebenhüner, 'How Do Scientific Assessments Learn?'.

[43] Millennium Ecosystem Assessment, *Ecosystems and Human Well-Being: Synthesis* (Washington DC: Island Press, 2005).

offered manifold opportunities to reflect and reassess substantial findings and procedures. Moreover, each new assessment started with a reconsideration of the assessment process and led to changes of the procedures and the emergence of well-elaborated cross-cutting guidance papers. This procedure ensured a continuous improvement process with learning elements.

Despite these characteristics and capabilities, the IPCC can be criticized from a structural point of view. Haas maintained that its set-up as an intergovernmental process kept the IPCC scientific expert process on a 'tight leash' held by governments.[44] He assumed that the highly complex approval mechanism of the IPCC hampers the political leverage of the assessment products. Thus, future revisions of the IPCC process might consider offering more leeway to scientific experts and introducing more cross-disciplinary structures, while not compromising too much on the achieved saliency and legitimacy of the process. Hence, further learning processes for the IPCC should be on its agenda.

In this regard, the experts in the IPCC serve as external experts to political decision-making processes who are, at best, able to deliver advice to international negotiators and national governments. However, the strong emphasis on ensuring credibility in particular within the scientific and the related political expert community limits the immediate saliency to political decision-making contexts and also provides a challenge to the perceived legitimacy of the assessment processes. Nevertheless, the IPCC has been more advanced in particular in improving its legitimacy and saliency when compared to almost all other international assessment processes. However, the IPCC's experts are not able to take politically relevant decisions by themselves or to directly influence the negotiation outcomes.

[44] Haas, 'When Does Power Listen to Truth?'.

8

Global scientific assessments and environmental resource governance: towards a science–policy interface ladder

JOYEETA GUPTA

8.1 Introduction

In the past, international environmental governance processes and legal cooperation focused on harmonizing existing state practice rather than creating new governance solutions, including innovative treaties. This approach had a high compliance pull as those treaties, to some degree, reflected existing state practice. This historical *incremental model* of law making contrasts heavily with the current *structural model*,[1] where problems are seen as more complicated, and scientific examinations of the problems and their solutions provide an array of options to governmental and non-governmental policy makers. This array of options leads to the creation of *new* policy choices, which may or may not have been rooted in the culture of the countries concerned, and the compliance pull of these options is no longer self-evident. Furthermore, there is competition between countries to upload policy options on to the global arena as this will reduce the costs of implementing their own policies. These new types of problems call for closer science–policy interface in order to improve treaty design.

Joyeeta Gupta has worked on this project as part of the EU FP7 Project on REDD Alert (Reducing Emissions from Deforestation and Degradation through Alternative Landuses in Rainforests of the Tropics). Many thanks to the critical and constructive comments of Professor Bernd Siebenhüner and Dr Aarti Gupta, and to those participating at the International Research Seminar 'Irrelevant, Advisors or Decision Makers? The Role of Experts in International Decision Making', Organized by the Erasmus School of Law and the International Institute of Social Studies, 24–25 June 2011, and to Andrea Brock for helping me to finalize this chapter.

[1] See J. Gupta, 'Industrial Transformation and International Law' in X. Olsthoorn and A. Wieczorek (eds.), *Sciences for Industrial Transformation: Views from Different Disciplines* (Dordrecht: Springer, 2006), 53–74.

An examination of the global resource and environmental arena reveals that the science–policy interface is structured differently in different issue areas. Since this book aims, *inter alia*, to understand how the science–policy interface is structured at the global level, this chapter focuses on the following questions. What are the different types of science–policy interface in different environmental issue areas? Can one derive a pattern from these interfaces?

Based on a literature review, case studies and observation/experience,[2] I first present a brief theoretical and methodological framework, then four case studies and a comparative analysis of these case studies, and thereafter inductively develop a 'science–policy interface ladder', before making suggestions for further research and drawing some conclusions.

8.2 Theoretical approaches and methodological framework

8.2.1 Theoretical approaches to science–policy interfaces

There is considerable literature on whether and how scientific expertise influences policy processes. This literature examines the role of scientific expertise in international policy processes from the perspective of different schools of thought. While rationalist and cognitive schools argue that experts have a major role in influencing international treaties and lead to convergent state policy, realists and neo-realists, at the other extreme end, deny any independent influence of science – scientific expertise being influential only when it happens to be in line with the interests of the most powerful countries. The early realist literature focuses on the gap between the scientific culture and the policy culture, which makes communication difficult.[3] Within the framework of these two cultures, policy makers often accept those scientific recommendations that are in the public interest[4] and match their own policy interests,

[2] I have participated in the Intergovernmental Panel on Climate Change (IPCC), the Millennium Ecosystem Assessment (MA), the Global Environmental Outlook (GEO) and the pre-discussions on the Intergovernmental Platform on Biodiversity and Ecosystem Services (IPBES).

[3] N. Caplan, 'The Two-Communities Theory and Knowledge Utilization', *American Behavioral Scientist*, 22 (1979), 459–70; R. F. Rich, 'Knowledge Creation, Diffusion, and Utilization', *Science Communication*, 12 (1991), 319–37; cf. E. J. Woodhouse and D. A. Nieusma, 'Democratic Expertise: Integrating Knowledge, Power, and Participation' in M. Hisschemöller, J. Ravetz, R. Hoppe and W. Dunn (eds.), *Knowledge, Power and Participation* (New Brunswick, NJ: Transaction, 2001), 73–96.

[4] Rousseau, cited in D. Held, *Models of Democracy* (Stanford University Press, 1987).

intuition or knowledge base (the concept of half-knowledge and public choice theories).[5]

However, some argue further that this 'two-cultures-approach' is too simplistic, that expert knowledge does not move freely, and that scientific expertise and expert knowledge are co-produced.[6] Such co-production can be formulated in terms of understanding the interface between senders and receivers of expert knowledge. It has been shown that the receptivity of receivers depends on awareness perceptions (the definition of a problem and need for change), association perceptions (the benefits of using expert knowledge and learning), acquisition perceptions (connections between senders and receivers) and application perceptions (adoption and implementation of expert knowledge).[7] Others argue that boundary organizations – organizations that connect science and policy by virtue of being located in between these two arenas – play a critical role in linking scientific experts with the policy community.[8] Still others regard the term 'boundary organization' as too static and favour the notion of hybrid management organizations, which engage in hybridization, deconstruction, boundary work and cross-domain orchestration.[9] To some extent, this approach incorporates the idea that scientific expertise is not necessarily neutral or objective, but socially constructed, and that it has its own inherent value biases and biases of focus, which, when translated into policies, can lead to winners and losers.[10]

[5] R. F. Rich, *The Knowledge Cycle* (Beverly Hills, CA: Sage, 1981); P. F. Lazarsfeld, 'Introduction' in P. F. Lazarsfeld, W. H. Sewell and H. L. Wilensky (eds.), *The Uses of Sociology* (New York: Basic Books, 1967), 1–22; B. Marin, 'What is "Half-Knowledge" Sufficient for and When? Theoretical Comment on Policymakers Uses of Social Science', *Knowledge: Creation, Diffusion, Utilization*, 3 (1981), 43–60; C. E. Lindblom and D. K. Cohen, *Usable Knowledge* (New Haven: Yale University Press, 1979).

[6] R. Lidskog and G. Sundqvist, 'The Role of Science in Environmental Regimes: The Case of LRTAP', *European Journal of International Relations*, 8 (2002), 77–101.

[7] N. Bressers, 'Co-Creating Innovation: A Systemic Learning Evaluation of Knowledge and Innovation Programmes', PhD thesis, Erasmus University Rotterdam (2011).

[8] T. F. Gieryn, 'Boundaries of Science' in S. Jasanoff, G. E. Markle, J. C. Petersen and T. Pinch (eds.), *Handbook of Science and Technology Studies* (Cambridge, MA: MIT Press, 1995), 393–443; T. F. Gieryn, *Cultural Boundaries of Science: Credibility on the Line* (University of Chicago Press, 1999); D. H. Guston, 'Boundary Organizations in Environmental Policy and Science: An Introduction', *Science, Technology & Human Values*, 26 (2001), 399–408.

[9] C. Miller, 'Hybrid Management: Boundary Organizations, Science Policy, and Environmental Governance in the Climate Regime', *Science, Technology & Human Values*, 26 (2001), 478–500.

[10] J. Gupta, *The Climate Change Convention and Developing Countries: From Conflict to Consensus?* (Dordrecht: Kluwer Academic Publishers, 1997); J. Gupta, 'Effectiveness of Air

However, throughout history, there has always been a populist anti-science reaction that regards science as elitist and serving its own goals and those of its stakeholders.[11] In reaction to the need to get the public on board, Shiva and Bandyopadhyay[12] refer to the concept of public interest science – science that is driven by what social actors see as important (such as the equity impacts of science). Others use the concept of post-normal science, which calls for engaging and interacting with stakeholders to help in understanding a problem and taking appropriate action – especially where the science is uncertain and the political stakes are high.[13] Still others refer to the notion of civic science – science that incorporates the views of citizens and/or stakeholders[14] – which often advocates participatory integrated assessments. Lastly, there is literature analysing Global Environmental Assessments (GEAs) and their impact on policy.[15] However, lacking is work on patterns of science–policy interface, which is the focus of this chapter.

8.2.2 *Methodological framework to analysing the case studies*

In order to assess patterns of science–policy interface, I use a four-step approach.

First, I examine the *nature of the problem*[16] in terms of the following three elements:

(1) Is the problem primarily a global problem or is the global nature of the problem disputed? While some may argue that the scale of a problem may be objectively determined, the key argument here is

Pollution Treaties: The Role of Knowledge, Power and Participation' in Hisschemöller et al. (eds.), *Knowledge, Power and Participation*, 145–74; L. Levidow and C. Marris, 'Science and Governance in Europe: Lessons from the Case of Agricultural Biotechnology', *Science and Public Policy*, 28 (2001), 345–60.

11 Haas, Chapter 2, this volume.

12 V. Shiva and J. Bandyopadhyay, 'Environmental Conflicts and Public Interest Science', *Economic and Political Weekly*, 21 (1986), 84–90.

13 J. Ravetz, 'What is Post-normal Science?', *Futures*, 31 (1999), 647–53; S. O. Funtowicz and J. R. Ravetz, 'Three Types of Risk Assessment and the Emergence of Post-normal Science' in S. Krimsky and D. Golding (eds.), *Social Theories of Risk* (London: Praeger, 1992), 251–74.

14 K. Bäckstrand, 'Civic Science for Sustainability: Reframing the Role of Experts, Policy-Makers and Citizens in Environmental Governance', *Global Environmental Politics*, 3 (2003), 24–41.

15 R. B. Mitchell, W. C. Clark, D. W. Cash and N. M. Dickson (eds.), *Global Environmental Assessments: Information and Influence* (Cambridge, MA: MIT Press, 2006).

16 On the nature of the problem, see also Andresen, Chapter 6, this volume.

that the level of a problem is socially or politically constructed for a number of reasons.[17]

(2) Is the problem a wicked or simple problem (malign/benign)? A wicked problem is a scientifically complex problem with poor alignments between costs and benefits.[18]

(3) Is the problem a structured problem? A structured problem is one where consensus exists on the science underlying the problem and the values according to which responsibilities and rights are to be allocated amongst actors.[19]

Second, I examine the *nature of the governance process*. Is this process centralized and structured with clear rules of membership, participation and procedure? Or, rather, is it decentralized, diffused and network-like? Is it a regime[20] where substantive rules and regulations governing state behaviour emerge from negotiations that take place in one location and lead to collective learning, convergent state policies[21] and state practice that is in accordance with the policy adopted?[22] Although much has been written on shifts in governance patterns – shifts in forums[23] and forms[24] – this chapter does not examine these aspects.

[17] J. Gupta, 'Global Change: Analysing Scale and Scaling in Environmental Governance' in O. R. Young, H. Schroeder and L. A. King (eds.), *Institutions and Environmental Change: Principal Findings, Applications, and Research Frontiers* (Cambridge, MA: MIT Press, 2008), 225–58.

[18] W. P. Cunningham and M. A. Cunningham, *Principles of Environmental Science: Inquiry and Applications* (Boston, MA: McGraw-Hill, 2002).

[19] M. Hisschemöller, *De democratie van problemen. De relatie tussen de inhoud van beleidsproblemen en methoden van politieke besluitvorming* (Free University Amsterdam, 1993).

[20] S. D. Krasner, 'Structural Causes and Regime Consequences: Regimes as Intervening Variables', *International Organization*, 36 (1982), 185–205, at 186.

[21] P. M. Haas, 'Do Regimes Matter? Epistemic Communities and Mediterranean Pollution Control', *International Organization*, 43 (1989), 377–403, at 377.

[22] V. Rittberger, 'Research on International Regimes in Germany: The Adaptive Internalization of an American Political Science Concept' in V. Rittberger and P. Mayer (eds.), *Regime Theory and International Relations* (Oxford: Clarendon Press, 1993), 3–22, at 11.

[23] See, e.g., K. van Kersbergen and F. van Waarden, *Shifts in Governance: Problems of Legitimacy and Accountability* (The Hague: Netherlands Organization for Scientific Research, 2001).

[24] E. Hey, 'The Climate Change Regime: An Enviro-Economic Problem and International Administrative Law in the Making', *International Environmental Agreements: Politics, Law and Economics*, 1 (2001), 75–100; B. Kingsbury, N. Krisch and R. B. Stewart, 'The Emergence of Global Administrative Law', *Law and Contemporary Problems*, 68 (2005), 15–61; N. Krisch, 'The Pluralism of Global Administrative Law', *European Journal of International Law*, 17 (2006), 247–78.

Third, I look at the *nature of the organization of scientific expertise.*[25] Is it organized? Is there a systematic, continuous assessment process? Is there a sort of ad hoc summary process of the available science? Does the science include a participatory process? How exclusive is the information covered in the assessment? Does it map complexity?

Fourth, I look at the *nature of the science–policy interface* and examine how it is structured. This is done by examining whether the scientific framing requires specific outputs and links to (treaty) negotiation bodies, and the role of science within the specific negotiation bodies and their treaties and/or other policy documents.

8.3 Case studies

This section examines science–policy interfaces in four areas: the environment in general, climate change, forests and water. Although climate change, forests and water are all environmental issues, the four areas are dealt with in four parallel governance processes at the global level. The United Nations Environment Programme (UNEP) leads on many environmental issues, the Food and Agriculture Organization (FAO) leads on forest governance, climate change came under the governance purview of the United Nations General Assembly (UNGA), and water, which is perceived more as a cross-cutting issue, is dealt with by many United Nations (UN) agencies. The scientific arrangements are also distinct in each field. Furthermore, all these issues are related to many others (agriculture, industry, economy, health and so on) and cannot be compartmentalized in any ideal manner. At the same time, institutional integration of the different policy dimensions (developmental, economic, environmental and social issues) and the different issue areas (climate change, forests, water and other environmental issues) would engender extreme complexity and make the problems at stake unmanageable.

8.3.1 Environmental governance in general and environmental science

Different environmental issues are dealt with as global (the depletion of the ozone layer, biodiversity) or as contested global issues (desertification and land degradation). Some are seen as relatively simple, for example, the depletion of the ozone layer with a large degree of consensus on science

[25] On the organization of science, see also Haas, Chapter 2, this volume.

and values, while some are seen as far more contentious, such as biodiversity and waste. Accordingly, most global environmental problems are wicked and many are moderately structured in terms of science.

Global governance on environmental issues can be traced back to the first UN Conference on the Human Environment (1972), which led to the establishment of UNEP. UNEP has a Governing Council/Global Ministerial Environment Forum, a Committee of Permanent Representatives, seven divisions and six regional offices. It is the nerve centre for environmental work at the global level and has initiated treaty negotiations to deal with many environmental problems (e.g., biodiversity, wetlands and species, and waste movement). However, it was not considered strategically placed enough to initiate the climate change treaty negotiations or seen as the key body to discuss forests. Important policy developments at UN level include the World Charter for Nature (1982), the World Commission on Environment and Development (1987), the United Nations Conference on Environment and Development (1992), the Rio Declaration (1992), the World Summit on Sustainable Development (2002) and the 2012 summit Rio+20 (2012).[26] Since almost all development processes have environmental impacts, most UN agencies also work on issues having environmental dimensions. The proliferation of environmental initiatives has led the UNGA to establish the UN Environmental Management Group (UN EMG) in 1999[27] to promote agency-wide coordination on environmental issues. It includes forty-five programmes, organs and specialized agencies of the UN system, as well as secretariats of multilateral environmental agreements. In 2008, UNEP initiated a consultative process on reforming global environmental governance. Governance of environmental issues is relatively structured in that UNEP is the natural centre of gravity for environmental issues and the secretariat of the UN EMG is located at UNEP in Geneva. However, there is a tendency to take an issue-by-issue approach, leading to what many see as a fragmented, but legitimate, governance process. In 2012, following the Rio+20 meeting, UNGA decided to strengthen the role of UNEP 'as the leading global environmental authority that sets the global environmental agenda'.

[26] UN, Report of the United Nations Conference on Sustainable Development, A/CONF.216/16, Rio de Janeiro (2012). Available at: www.uncsd2012.org/content/documents/814UNCSD%20REPORT%20final%20revs.pdf.

[27] UNEP, Governing Council of the United Nations Environment Programme Global Ministerial Environment Forum, eighth special session (2004), UNEP/GCSS.VIII/8: 35; UNGA, Report of the Secretary-General on Environment and Human Settlements: Declaration and Programme of Action on a Culture of Peace (1999), A/RES/53/242.

Organizations and treaty negotiations have preceded comprehensive efforts towards scientific assessments in most cases. However, following a decision of its Governing Council in 1995, UNEP has been publishing the Global Environment Outlook (GEO), which is based on a participatory process to facilitate science–policy interface. Five GEOs have been produced thus far. GEOs are less structured and formal than the Intergovernmental Panel on Climate Change (IPCC) Assessment Reports, but are published regularly. In addition, the Millennium Ecosystem Project, initiated by the UN Secretary-General in 2001, assessed science in relation to four treaties on biological diversity, desertification, wetlands and migratory species in 2005. An UNGA resolution of 2011 notes UNEP's Governing Council's decision to set up the Intergovernmental Platform on Biodiversity and Ecosystem Services (IPBES) and requests a plenary to discuss the modalities of such a group.[28] Follow-up activities have been initiated since. Furthermore, Diversitas – a network of scientists who collaborate under the Earth System Science Project – prepared a science plan in 2002 to guide scientific experts in doing research on biodiversity related issues. Diversitas has signed a Memorandum of Understanding with the Convention on Biological Diversity (CBD), and the CBD has also provided an *ex officio* member to the scientific steering committee of Diversitas since 2005. Some other treaties have their own collaborative processes with scientific expert bodies. For example, when scientists discovered the problem of the depletion of the ozone layer, UNEP organized a conference in 1977, leading to the establishment of the Coordinating Committee on the Ozone Layer. The Committee consisted of experts who were responsible for assessing the state of the science on the issue, which preceded the decision to negotiate a treaty on the subject. Following the entry into force of the Ozone Depletion Treaty, Advisory Panels on Science, Environment and Technology and Economics were established to help the parties. The Convention to Combat Desertification (1994) has its own Committee on Science and Technology, but as there has been no real communication between the scientific expert community and the Committee, the regime has faced major knowledge gaps.[29]

[28] UNGA, Report of the Governing Council of the United Nations Environment Programme on its eleventh special session (2011) A/RES/65/162; A. Larigauderie and H. A. Mooney, 'The Intergovernmental Science-Policy Platform on Biodiversity and Ecosystem Services: Moving a Step Closer to an IPCC-like Mechanism for Biodiversity', *Current Opinion in Environmental Sustainability*, 2 (2010), 9–14.

[29] S. Bauer and L. C. Stringer, 'The Role of Science in the Global Governance of Desertification', *Journal of Environment & Development*, 18 (2009), 248–67; A. Grainger, 'The Role of Science in Implementing International Environmental Agreements: The Case of Desertification', *Land Degradation & Development*, 20 (2009), 410–30; M. Long Martello, 'Expert Advice and

Some see the focus of the desertification regime on civil knowledge rather than science, and the regime's reliance on Chapter 12 – on combating desertification – of Agenda 21, the document setting policy initiatives adopted at the Rio Conference in 1992, as a critical problem in structuring links with the available expert knowledge. The Institutional Dimension of Global Environmental Change of the International Human Dimensions Programme and its successor, the Earth System Governance Project, have prepared their science plans to structure and guide scientific research in the area of environmental management.[30]

As the word 'environment' covers a number of issue areas, there are different scientific and policy processes being undertaken. In the early days, the science processes were linked to specific treaty processes; in recent decades, the GEO takes a more comprehensive approach and feeds information into UNEP's decision-making processes.

8.3.2 Climate change

The global nature of climate change is undisputed in the scientific literature,[31] political declarations[32] and treaty documents.[33] Although initially only the need for climate change mitigation was defined as 'global' in the UNFCCC,[34] the necessity of dealing with adaptation at a global level has now also been agreed upon. However, the problem is wicked in that it is scientifically complex and there is poor alignment between the costs and the benefits. Since scientific expertise is well organized within the IPCC, which received the Nobel Peace Prize in 2007, the climate regime is moderately structured in

Desertification Policy: Past Experience and Current Challenges', *Global Environmental Politics*, 4 (2004), 85–106; A. Tal and J. A. Cohen, 'Bringing "Top-Down" to "Bottom-Up": A New Role for Environmental Legislation in Combating Desertification', *Harvard Environmental Law Review*, 31 (2007), 163–217; C. Toulmin, 'If You Want to Get a Job Done, You Need the Right Tools: Next Steps for the UN Convention to Combat Desertification', *International Institute for Environment and Development* (IIED), 2006.

30 F. Biermann, M. Betsill, J. Gupta, N. Kanie, L. Lebel, D. Liverman, H. Schroeder, B. Siebenhüner and R. Zondervan, 'Earth System Governance: A Research Framework', *International Environmental Agreements: Politics, Law and Economics*, 10 (2010), 277–98.

31 IPCC-3, *Climate Change: The IPCC Scientific Assessment. Report prepared for Intergovernmental Panel on Climate Change by Working Group I* (1990).

32 See e.g., the Noordwijk Declaration on Climate Change: Conference Report (1989).

33 United Nations Framework Convention on Climate Change (New York), 9 May 1992, in force 24 March 1994, 31 I.L.M. 1992, 822.

34 D. Bodansky, 'The United Nations Framework Convention on Climate Change: A Commentary', *Yale Journal of International Law*, 18 (1993), 451–558.

terms of the science, but not in terms of the values underlying the regime.[35] Scientific expertise is occasionally questioned for specific mistakes (e.g., the climate-gate controversy) and some errors in the IPCC reports.[36] Nevertheless, the bulk of the scientific expertise/expert assessment remains sound, although improvements are possible,[37] and authoritative, as governments continue to support the process. Nevertheless, the underlying values remain contested. Debates in the political arena are about free-rider problems and how the common but differentiated responsibilities and respective capabilities principle should be interpreted.[38]

Climate change is governed primarily from within the UNFCCC regime. Although many UN agencies work on climate change, they have observer status within the UNFCCC, align their policies to UNFCCC outcomes (e.g., to the UNFCCC work on Reducing Emissions from Deforestation and Degradation (REDD)) and only rarely compete with it (e.g., the Global Environment Facility (GEF) seeks to implement decisions of its governing assembly and council, which are not always compatible with the decisions of the Conference of the Parties (COP) to the UNFCCC).[39] Outside the climate regime, various international agreements on climate change exist, but are not explicitly linked to the UNFCCC regime (e.g., the Global Methane Initiative). The USA is engaged in a number of these initiatives and has claimed on its own website that these initiatives are in line with the UNFCCC. Some scholars refer to climate governance as fragmented[40] or as a regime complex, arguing that different actors in the regime have their own mechanisms.[41] However, I would argue that the climate change regime is one of the most centralized regimes in international environmental governance. All relevant

35 See also Siebenhüner, Chapter 7, this volume.

36 IAC, *Climate Change Assessments: Review of the Processes and Procedures of the IPCC* (2010).

37 *Ibid.*

38 J. Gupta and N. van der Grijp (eds.), *Mainstreaming Climate Change in Development Cooperation: Theory, Practice and Implications for the European Union* (Cambridge University Press, 2010).

39 J. Gupta, 'The Global Environment Facility in its North-South Context' in P. H. G. Stephens, J. Barry and A. Dobson (eds.), *Contemporary Environmental Politics: From Margins to Mainstream* (London: Routledge, 2006), 231–53; M. J. Mace, 'Funding for Adaptation to Climate Change: UNFCCC and GEF Developments since COP-7', *Review of European Community & International Environmental Law*, 14 (2005), 225–46.

40 F. Biermann, P. Pattberg, H. van Asselt and F. Zelli, 'The Fragmentation of Global Governance Architectures: A Framework for Analysis', *Global Environmental Politics*, 9 (2009), 14–40.

41 R. O. Keohane and D. G. Victor, *The Regime Complex for Climate Change*, Discussion Paper 10/33, Harvard Project on International Climate Agreements (2010).

international bodies, including the World Bank (WB), have observer status in the UNFCCC negotiation process and actively contribute to the implementation of the climate regime. This manner of proceeding has led to converging state policies, national reports and actual implementation.

Following recognition of the seriousness of the climate problem at the first World Climate Change Conference in 1979, the World Meteorological Organization (WMO), the International Council of Scientific Unions (ICSU) and UNEP established the Advisory Group on Greenhouse Gases (AGGG) in 1985 as a forum for climate scientists to reach consensus. In 1988, the WMO and UNEP established the IPCC to systematically assess (every five years) the state of the art of global climate science, the impacts of climate change and response strategies to it, and to undertake special reports, thereby mapping complexity. Endorsed by the UNGA, the IPCC has near-universal state membership. In terms of organization, it has a plenary meeting of state representatives, an IPCC bureau, three working groups, one task force and an army of volunteers who form the scientific team. The IPCC has an intergovernmental and scientific character, and conducts a complex assessment process based on peer-reviewed literature. Assessment reports result from an extensive writing process in which both government officials and experts participate.[42] The process of assessment is continuous, but it tends to be exclusive and elitist in nature.

In its preamble, the UNFCCC states that its goal is 'science-based policymaking'. It has established a permanent Subsidiary Body on Scientific and Technological Advice (SBSTA), which provides a direct link to the work produced by the IPCC. All parties are members of SBSTA and it is considered to be a good 'broker' between the scientific and policy communities.[43] It provides a venue for governments and non-governmental organizations to discuss the advice provided, and has been an active co-producer of expert knowledge, going beyond its mandate and allowing discussions about different models and theories, as well as competing values and systems. In addition, the IPCC also issues statements to the COP and the COP makes requests back to the IPCC.

8.3.3 Forest governance and forest science

Over the last sixty years, it has been debated whether forests are a national or a global issue. Arguments in favour of globalizing forest management have

[42] See Siebenhüner, Chapter 7, this volume.

[43] N. Oreskes, 'The Scientific Consensus on Climate Change', *Science*, 306 (2004), 1686.

been substantive – forests are the lungs of the earth and they serve as major carbon repositories and habitats for biodiversity. In consequence, global forest management is needed in order to regulate globalized trade in timber and forest products, and to generate resources to protect forests. One argument against globalizing forests is based on the reluctance of states to allow external actors to determine domestic land-use patterns which may impact national income. Others maintain that globalization is incompatible with decentralization and stakeholder participation in forest management.[44] As discussions in the climate arena now once more focus on the carbon content of forests, there is a return to consensus for dealing with forests at the global level. This development requires that developed countries be willing to raise the money to finance forest maintenance in the developing world in return for cheap carbon reduction units. Forest issues appear to be simple, but once unpacked in terms of social aspects, such as property rights,[45] or in terms of ecosystem services, forests become a very complex problem with an unequal distribution of costs and benefits. It thus qualifies as another wicked problem, and although the science is fairly uncontroversial, the values remain contentious, making the problem moderately structured in terms of science, but not in relation to the values underlying the regime.

Forest governance is highly fragmented, with a series of legally binding treaties dealing with specific forest functions.[46] So far, no comprehensive treaty dealing directly with the issue of forests and their multiple ecosystem services has been concluded. Many policy initiatives involve not just the secretariats to treaties addressing specific forest functions, but also international bodies (the FAO, the UN Development Programme (UNDP), UNEP, the WB, the GEF and the UN Forum on Forests) and hybrid

[44] J. Gupta, R. Matthews, P. Meyfroidt, C. Haug, O. Kuik and N. van der Grijp, 'The Future of Forests' in J. Gupta, N. van der Grijp and O. Kuik (eds.), *Climate Change, Forests and REDD: Lessons for Institutional Design* (London: Routledge, 2012), 229–58; D. Humphreys, *Logjam: Deforestation and the Crisis of Global Governance* (London: Earthscan, 2006).

[45] D. Barry and R. Meinzen-Dick, 'The Invisible Map: Community Tenure Rights' in *Proceedings of the 12th Biennial Conference of the International Association for the Study of Commons*, Cheltenham, 14–18 July 2008.

[46] For example, on species (Convention on the International Trade in Endangered Species CITES, 1973; Convention on International Trade in Endangered Species of Wild Fauna and Flora, 1973); on heritage (World Heritage Convention, 1975); on wetlands (Ramsar Convention on Wetlands of International Importance, 1973/75); on trade in tropical timber (International Tropical Timber Agreement, 1983); on indigenous peoples (ILO Conventions No. 107/169, 1957/1989); on biodiversity (Convention on Biological Diversity, 1992); and on climate change (UNFCCC, 1992).

public-private bodies such as the Forest Stewardship Council. These initiatives cover forest principles (e.g., the Forest Principles adopted at the 1992 UN Conference on Environment and Development), strategies (e.g., the FAO Strategic Plan for Forest 2007 and the 2002 WB Forest Strategy), and programmes (e.g., the Intergovernmental Forum on Forests (IFF)'s 'non-legally binding instrument on all types of forests' and 'multi-year programme of work', and the 2007 GEF Operational Programme on Forest Ecosystems). Forest governance tends to focus more on forest exploitation and liberalization than on conservation,[47] and is likely to focus on carbon conservation and trade rather than ecosystem services in the future, as debates on REDD reveal. In recent years, REDD has served as a mechanism to scale up forests as a global issue. Still, the forest arena remains an arena of diffuse governance and overlapping treaties with different goals, both dispersed and ad hoc.[48]

Forest science is published in both forest-specific as well as multi-disciplinary journals. There are very few attempts to actually assess forest science in a comprehensive manner. The Global Forest Resources Assessment (GFRA) is an effort of the FAO to collect data based on a questionnaire from its Member States. It covers the extent of forest resources and their contribution to the carbon cycle, forest health, forest biodiversity and productive, protective and socio-economic functions of forests, and it provides some indications of the legal, policy and institutional framework on forests. The organizational framework includes expert networks of national correspondents, an informal advisory group and expert consultations. To the extent that forests are closely linked with biodiversity and ecosystem services and climate change, the Millennium Ecosystem Assessment (MA) (see section 8.3.4 below) and the IPCC are also relevant. A key challenge here is the issue of drawing boundaries. When are a bunch of bushes or trees a forest? Should the focus simply lie on the trees or on forests as a habitat not only for animals, but also for humans, including indigenous peoples? Should forests be regarded in terms of the complete array of ecosystem services they provide or in terms of specific ecosystem services? Although scientific information is generated, structured, continuous and exclusive in nature, it is not a comprehensive assessment of peer-reviewed literature, nor is there a central body that governs forests.

[47] G. J. Nagtzaam, *The International Tropical Timber Organization and Conservationist Forest Norms: A Bridge Too Far?* (Victoria: Monash University, 2008), available at: http://works.bepress.com/gerry_nagtzaam/1.

[48] Humphreys, *Logjam: Deforestation and the Crisis of Global Governance.*

8.3.4 *Water governance and water science*

Water has historically been treated as a local or regional issue, and subsequently as a river basin issue, and used to be seen more as a resource than as an environmental issue. There is recent debate about whether water should be treated as a global issue because of the global nature of the hydrological cycle, the cumulative effects of water management issues, the impacts of global change on local water governance, and the inability of local and national actors to address their water problems alone, as some driving factors operate at the global level.[49] But most see water as a national security issue or as a transboundary issue. There is no consensus on the global nature of water or the water problem, or what global water goals should be. Water is used by all sectors and ecosystems. Certain water uses have low economic returns, while others have high returns. The nature of water problems differs from country to country. As the problem is difficult to assess, there is also limited consensus on global water norms. For example, the 1997 UN Watercourses Convention has not yet entered into force, which raises the issue whether global consensus exists on what is the core of the Watercourses Convention – the principles of equitable utilization and no harm.[50] In a similar vein, the UN General Assembly adopted a resolution on the Human Right to Water and Sanitation in July 2010,[51] but only 122 of the 193 Member States voted for it. Accordingly, the problem is both wicked and unstructured.

Water governance has a long history.[52] Currently, three parallel water governance processes exist: a bottom-up legal process at the bilateral and basin level over the last several hundred years, a top-down policy process promoted by water engineers and policy makers over the last sixty years (the Stockholm Conference of 1972, the Mar Del Plata Conference of 1977, the Water and Sanitation Decade of the 1980s, the Dublin Conference of 1992, Agenda 21 of 1992, the Millennium Development Goals of 2000 and the World Summit on Sustainable Development of 2002) and the large-scale process of social engagement in water management at the global level (World Water Forums, World Water Council,

[49] C. Pahl-Wostl, J. Gupta and D. Petry, 'Governance and the Global Water System: A Theoretical Exploration', *Global Governance*, 14 (2008), 419–35.

[50] J. Dellapenna and J. Gupta, 'The Evolving Legal Framework for Global Water Governance', *Global Governance*, 14 (2008), 437–53.

[51] UNGA, 'The Human Right to Water and Sanitation' (2010), A/RES/64/292.

[52] J. Dellapenna and J. Gupta, (eds.), *The Evolution of the Law and Politics of Water* (Dordrecht: Springer, 2009).

social movements and non-state actors). Unlike UNEP for environmental issues, there is no natural home for dealing with water-related issues at the UN level. Several UN agencies and hybrid bodies, such as the World Commission on Dams, the World Water Council and the World Water Forum, work on water. Remarkably, the World Commission on Dams is contested in terms of its legitimacy, as it was not democratically established within the UN systems,[53] and the World Water Forums are seen as talking shops that do not lead to legally binding decisions.[54] The need for a coherent strategy led to the establishment of a coordinating body, UN Water, in September 2003. It now includes about thirty UN agencies and many partners, but it is not comprehensive since it does not include all the relevant UN bodies. It aims to promote coherence and coordination of water policy within the UN, but its limited resources and authority impede its ability to steer UN policy.[55] Water governance thus remains diffuse and competitive, with gaps and overlaps.

Given water governance's deep cultural roots, scientific expertise has only relatively recently started to play a role in it, initially with the development of the 'hydraulic paradigm', where engineers were proactively promoting dams and subsequently through the establishment of water specific scientific communities. Water science is published in water journals (e.g., *Water Resources Research*, *Water Policy*, *Journal of Water Law* and *Urban Water Journal*). However, most water papers cover Northern interests and concerns, even if the focus is on the South.[56] Scientific experts and stakeholders meet at the annual Stockholm Water Week and the regular World Water Forums. The dispersed scientific expert communities may explain why mapping complexity in, for example, the Integrated Water Resource Management concept remains limited.[57] In 2000, a World Water

[53] W. Scheumann, 'How Global Norms for Large Dams Reach Decision-Makers' in W. Scheumann, S. Neubert and M. Kipping (eds.), *Water Politics and Development Cooperation: Local Power Plays and Global Governance* (Dordrecht: Springer, 2008), 55–80; K. Dingwerth, 'The Democratic Legitimacy of Public-Private Rule Making: What Can We Learn from the World Commission on Dams?', *Global Governance*, 11 (2004), 65–83.

[54] P. H. Gleick and J. Lane, 'Large International Water Meetings: Time for a Reappraisal', *Water International*, 30 (2005), 410–14.

[55] T. Baumgartner and C. Pahl-Wostl, 'UN Water and its Role in Global Water Governance', *Ecology and Society*, 18(3) (2010), 3; S. Schubert and J. Gupta, 'Can Coordination Mechanisms Address Global Governance Challenges?', *Ecology and Society*, 18(2) (2013), 22.

[56] P. van der Zaag, J. Gupta and P. Darvis, 'Urgent Water Problems are Not Sufficiently Researched', *Hydrology and Earth System Sciences*, 13 (2009), 905–12.

[57] K. Conca, *Governing Water: Contentious Transnational Politics and Global Institution Building* (Cambridge, MA: MIT Press, 2005).

Assessment Programme was established. In its triennial World Water Development Report (WWDR), the state of the world's water has been reviewed and policy advice provided. These reports are less structured than IPCC reports, depend on inputs from UN Water members and are not systematic assessments of the scientific literature. UN Water is closely linked to the World Water Assessment Programme. However, as mentioned above, UN Water itself has limited authority to coordinate and steer water strategy and policy, and to promote legally binding decisions; nor is it the nerve centre for water work in the UN, although it is increasingly moving centre-stage.

8.4 Comparative assessment

I now turn to compare the cases discussed in the previous section. First, in terms of the *problem*, the cumulative impacts of the problems make all of the problems studied global problems requiring global cooperation, at least in the area of assessing scientific research. However, states and non-state actors have diverse reasons for wishing to scale up a problem or not to the international level. While depletion of the ozone layer and climate change mitigation have been unconditionally accepted as global problems; adaptation, desertification, forests and water are often not seen as such.

Global	Global nature contested
Ozone layer	*Climate change adaptation*
Climate change mitigation	*Desertification*
	Forests
	Water

Furthermore, most issues studied are wicked in that they are complex, with varying actors bearing costs, risks and benefits. Moreover, the degree to which there is consensus on the science and values in a system differs from case to case, and to some extent also depends on whether the global community has a common problem definition (see Table 8.1).

Second, climate *governance* is centralized in the UNFCCC regime, with other instruments addressing climate change mostly in line with the commitments of the UNFCCC. The forest regime consists of regime complexes focusing on different forest functions, but there is no comprehensive and focused regime on forests as such. Environmental

Table 8.1 *Problems classified as structured or unstructured*

	Consensus on science	No consensus on science
Consensus on values	Structured problem *Depletion of the ozone layer*	Moderately structured (values)
No consensus on values	Moderately structured (science) *Climate change* *Forest (REDD: 2008–12)*	Unstructured problem *Water* *Environment*

Table 8.2 *Table of governance*

	Legally binding			
	Yes		No	
	Comprehensive	Fragmented	Comprehensive	Fragmented
Global	*Climate change (FCCC)*	*Forest* *Environment*		*Water*
Regional	*Transboundary river basin treaties*			

governance is also fragmented and the global water regime is highly diffuse, with very limited legally binding commitments (see Table 8.2).

Third, *scientific expertise* in the climate change regime is highly centralized, formalized and regulated, with its legal basis in an UNGA resolution[58] and 194 Member States focused on assessing existing peer-reviewed science. Water science is less formalized, although it is coordinated by UN Water; forest assessments focus on collating responses to questionnaires, and other environmental assessments depend either on the specific environmental issue area or are a general assessment such as the GEO (see Table 8.3).

Furthermore, *science–policy interfaces* in the different regimes can be differentiated using a two-by-two matrix (see Table 8.4).

The comparative analysis reveals that the IPCC provides the most structured science–policy interface; however, this does not make it devoid of

[58] UNGA, 'Protection of Global Climate for Present and Future Generations of Mankind' (1988), A/RES/43/53.

Table 8.3 *Table of science assessments in different issue areas*

Issue area	Scientific expert assessment	Nature
Environment	*GEO*	Formal, structured and regular, based on consultative process and reviews
	MA	Established by UN Secretary-General, one-time assessment with rigorous scientific method
	IPBES	Noted and supported by the UNGA, still in design stage
Climate change	*IPCC*	Endorsed by the UNGA, formal, structured, regular, intergovernmental and scientific, based on extensive review of published literature and three rounds of peer review
Forest	*GFRA*	Formal and regular, based on completed questionnaires from national experts
Water	*World Water Assessment Programme*	Formal, structured and regular, more policy experience than systematic assessment of science

Table 8.4 *Nature of science–policy interfaces*

		Governance	
		Structured, centralized	Diffuse
Science	Comprehensive, structured, centralized, formal assessment	IPCC, (IPBES), MA	GEO
	Less comprehensive and formal assessment	GFRA	WWDR

weaknesses. IPCC scientific expertise is dominated by Northern natural scientific experts, with references mostly to elite peer-reviewed Northern, English-language literature. Although it covers peer-reviewed papers on the results of participatory integrated assessments, it is not itself open to ideas of participatory integrated assessment, civic science, public interest science or even post-normal science. This may affect its saliency, credibility and legitimacy in the long term.[59] The design process of the IPBES is trying to deal with some of these challenges for biodiversity and ecosystem-related science.[60] All the other existing bodies are becoming more structured and formal over time.

8.5 Towards a science–policy interface ladder

Based on the above understanding of science–policy interfaces in different regimes, I have chosen to represent the patterns emerging in the form of a 'science–policy interface ladder' (see Figure 8.1). In doing so, I contend that the ladder is also relevant for assessing other types of expert–policy interfaces at the global level that have emerged in this volume. For example, human rights rapporteurs, as experts, report on the state of human rights in a country, and states, as policy makers, must try and respond to these reports.[61] Arguably, a parallel can be drawn here with states responding to reports that assess the state of the environment. The description of the ladder will be followed by an analysis of its implications for further research on the science–policy interfaces in environmental resources governance.

8.5.1 The ladder elaborated

At the top of the ladder is a highly formal, centralized, continuous, structured process of science–policy interface which includes participatory integrated assessment including indigenous knowledge. Such a type of civic science may increase the compliance pull of decisions. A potential example of this is the new IPBES.[62] At the next level, the more formal peer-reviewed science assessments, which dominate the work of the IPCC, are found.

[59] Bäckstrand, 'Civic Science for Sustainability'.

[60] A. Kumar Duraiappah and D. Rogers, 'The Intergovernmental Platform on Biodiversity and Ecosystem Services: Opportunities for the Social Sciences', *Innovation: The European Journal of Social Science Research*, 24 (2011), 217–24.

[61] Subedi, Chapter 12, Handmaker and Mora, Chapter 13 and Scholten and Terlouw, Chapter 14, all this volume.

[62] T. Koetz, K.N. Farrell and P. Bridgewater, 'Building Better Science–Policy Interfaces for International Environmental Governance: Assessing Potential within the Intergovernmental Platform for Biodiversity and Ecosystem Services', *International Environmental Agreements: Politics, Law and Economics*, 12 (2012), 1–21.

Below the IPCC I locate the highly formal, centralized, one-time, semi-structured processes of science–policy interfaces. This includes the MA-UNEP/CBD interface. This is followed by the formal, centralized, one-time, semi-structured processes of science–policy interfaces, including the AGGG-climate negotiations link. Thereafter, the less formal, centralized, continuous, but one-person expert teams (e.g., the human rights (HR) rapporteurs) that advise national governments as part of the international human rights regime can be situated.[63] The less formal, centralized, continuous and less structured assessment process with a less structured science–policy link, such as the GEO–UNEP/environmental issues link, are located one step below. At the next rung of the ladder is the GFRA–FAO and the WWDR–UN Water interface. Finally, at the bottom of the ladder, there is a less formal, diffuse process of science in a completely diffuse governance world, for example, biofuels.

One could argue that civic science does not play a very important role in practice – but perhaps in the future there will be a role for participatory integrated assessments at the top of the ladder, as hoped for in the IPBES assessments. The non-existence of any centralized assessment and the non-existence of any centralized governance process would be at the bottom of the ladder.

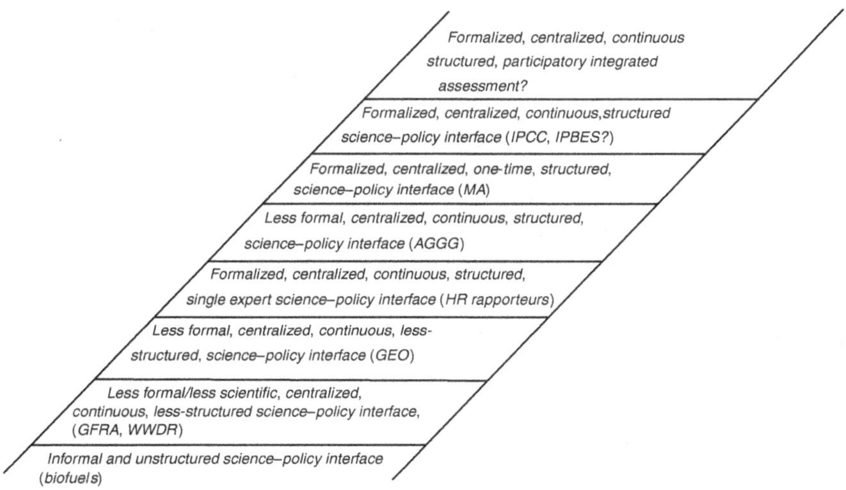

Figure 8.1 Ladder of global science–policy interface

[63] Subedi, Chapter 12, this volume.

8.6 Conclusions: implications of the ladder

In choosing the metaphor of a ladder, I have chosen for an implicit hierarchy in the science–policy interface. I now turn to some of the implications of this ladder.

First, clearly, the higher up the ladder one is located, the more institutionalized the science–policy interface is, although it may not necessarily lead to the best results.

Second, one would expect that the higher up the ladder a specific issue is: (a) the greater the degree of consensus one can expect between scientific experts and policy makers in terms of mapping complexity; (b) the greater the input and output legitimacy; and (c) the greater the interactions with civil society (including indigenous peoples) in generating scientific results. Conversely, the lower down the ladder an issue area is located, the more questions emerge regarding complexity mapping, input and output legitimacy, and whether the actors within these diffuse governance processes will not just pick and choose the science that serves their needs. These are hypotheses, which need further testing. However, one could provide some anecdotal evidence for a greater degree of consensus. For example, the 2°C target included in the Copenhagen Accord of 2009 can be related to the 2007 report of the IPCC, which is located high up in the ladder;[64] similarly, the 2007 Bali Plan of Action[65] explicitly referred to the IPCC report. At the bottom of the ladder, there is the little or non-coordinated biofuel science leading to ad hoc governance processes which can be characterized as misgovernance.[66] A research implication of this ladder is the following question: is such a hierarchy too simplistic and can it be empirically validated?

Third, the metaphor suggests that one can climb up and down the ladder. Anecdotal evidence shows that in the climate change regime climbing up seems to be possible. Institutionalized science in the climate change arena has moved up from the AGGG to the IPCC-UNFCCC process. While the AGGG was established by UN agencies, the IPCC and the UNFCCC were endorsed by the UNGA, the highest UN body. In the

[64] IPCC-1. *Climate Change 2007: The Physical Science Basis. Contribution of Working Group 1 to the Fourth Assessment Report of the Intergovernmental Panel on Climate Change* (2007).

[65] UNFCCC, Bali Plan of Action: Report of the Conference of the Parties on its thirteenth session, held in Bali from 3 to 15 December 2007 (2007) FCCC/CP/2007/6/Add.1.

[66] M. Bastos Lima and J. Gupta, 'The Policy Context of Biofuels: A Case of Non-governance at the Global Level?', *Global Environmental Politics*, 13 (2013), 46–64.

biodiversity regime, there is a movement from the MA to the IPBES, from a decision of the Secretary-General to the UNGA. A research implication is: can one assume upward mobility of science–policy interfaces in the future? At the same time, the increased institutionalization of scientific expertise does not imply a movement up the ladder – institutionalization has many gradations and forms.

Fourth, normally one starts at the bottom of the ladder and climbs up, or at the top and descends down. Empirical evidence shows that some issues leapfrog to a particular rung. For example, the AGGG was at the fifth rung of the ladder. The research questions that flow from this are: why do some issues emerge at a specific rung? Is this due to the decadal evolution of policies? Is it because of the nature of the problem – whether it is structured in terms of science or values? Andresen (Chapter 6, this volume) argues that in the 1970s, policies were less structured; in the 1980s, global policies were characterized by targets and timetables, and in the 1990s, the notion of common but differentiated responsibilities became more important.[67] Along similar lines, one could argue that the forest and water issues have been on the international agenda at least since the end of the Second World War and although scientific communities have played a role here, there was much less experience with structuring science. The need to structure scientific expert input in these policy arenas generally has come very much as an after-thought. Yet, by the time climate change emerged on the political arena in the 1990s, there was already experience from the regime on Long-Range Transboundary Air Pollution and the Montreal Protocol, and it was a natural evolution to move in the direction of structured scientific expert input, right from the start. This does not, however, explain the lack of structured scientific expert input in the biofuel field. Nor does it explain the fact that water scientific expert input has only recently been structured to some extent. However, the lack of structured scientific input in these problem areas might be related to the question whether an issue is uncontroversially global. A hypothesis might, then, be that the relative perceived scale of the problem may lead to prioritizing a structured assessment process for it at the international level. Thus, if countries perceive an issue to be of global importance and are willing to govern it at the global level, this implies a decline in actual sovereignty in that field and that they will also be willing to make resources available to deal with it, but only if there is consensus on the scientific facts relevant for the

[67] Andresen, Chapter 6, this volume.

regime. Indeed, climate change has been accepted as a global issue, but forests and water are more contested. If I am right, the uncontroversial global nature of a problem is likely to be an explanatory factor for the existence of a structured science–policy interface.

However, the degree to which a problem is wicked and unstructured may influence the effectiveness of the science–policy interface. And this brings us to the last proposition that may emerge from such a ladder construct. A ladder may suggest that the higher up an institutionalization process is, the more likely it is that the science–policy interface has output legitimacy and is effective. One could argue that if the science, the policy process and their relationship are structured and participatory, this should, by definition, lead to science-based policies with a high compliance pull. One expects that such a highly structured system will allow for the co-production of knowledge. At the bottom of the ladder, the science and policy processes are diffuse, and policy makers may pick and choose the scientific results they want. The lack of participatory processes may imply that the policy may not be easy to implement. However, whether this is so requires empirical testing. It may be that here the degree of wickedness and structure, and the issue of whose perception counts in shaping global politics, influence in determining whether a science–policy interface process is effective or not.

This chapter set out to address two questions based on four simple case studies: what are the different ways in which scientific expert input is organized for different environmental issue areas? Do different patterns of science–policy structure emerge? It is argued here that there are many different ways in which the science–policy interface is organized and that these can be represented in terms of a science–policy interface ladder. Furthermore, the ladder raises a number of hypotheses which can be tested in future research regarding environmental issues. Moreover, it may also be of wider relevance if conceived as depicting the manner in which the expert–policy interface is structured in general, a point which can also be tested by future research.

PART III

Experts in the World Trade Organization and risk regulation

9

The structural logic of expert participation in WTO decision-making processes

JESSICA LAWRENCE

9.1 Introduction

Many scholars of international trade law – including a few of the contributors to this volume – have discussed the question of whether expert participation enhances the legitimacy of the decision-making processes of the World Trade Organization (WTO).[1] When posed to those who study and work in the field of international trade law, the answers to this question generally come in the form of 'yes, but . . .'. Experts – whether in the field of trade, economics, the natural sciences or other disciplines – seem to enhance the legitimacy of decision making, *but* the process of including experts can be biased. Experts may enhance the legitimacy of decision making, *but* only when they come from a broad range of fields. Experts can enhance the legitimacy of decision making, *but* only when their recommendations are properly assessed and incorporated by regulating bodies and dispute settlement processes. In other words, experts and the scientific or technical modes of thought they represent are legitimacy-enhancing, but they may be compromised by bias, political manipulation or oversight.

If, on the other hand, we look to the vast literature critiquing the role of science and expert opinion in politics, the answers to this question are very different.[2] For these scholars, experts do not enhance the legitimacy of decision making because they reproduce the status quo. Experts do not enhance the legitimacy of decision making because they imply

[1] See, e.g., D.C. Esty, 'Good Governance at the World Trade Organization: Building a Foundation of Administrative Law', *Journal of International Economic Law*, 10 (2007), 509–27; J. Pauwelyn, 'The Use of Experts in WTO Dispute Settlement', *International and Comparative Law Quarterly*, 51 (2002), 325–64; C.A. Thomas, 'Of Facts and Phantoms: Economics, Epistemic Legitimacy, and WTO Dispute Settlement', *Journal of International Economic Law*, 14 (2011), 295–328.

[2] See below, section 9.4.

neutrality and consensus where there is really contestation and choice. Experts do not enhance the legitimacy of decision making because they replace democratic politics with technical reasoning. Or, to oversimplify, according to these critiques, experts do not enhance the legitimacy of decision making because their vocabulary and epistemology hide the fact that their contributions are also suffused with politics and value judgements.

Effectively, the answer to the question turns on our understanding of the concept of legitimacy.[3] For the WTO and its community of trade policy specialists, that understanding equates legitimacy – of decisions, rules and domestic trade policies – with conformity to the logics of law, economy and science.[4] Indeed, the system of governance at the WTO – both in terms of its founding documents and the trade policy professionals who apply them – *is* a system of expert knowledge.

Given this picture of the WTO and its expert community, it seems understandable that the organization would seek to enhance its legitimacy by attempting to conform more precisely with these underlying narratives of law, economy and science. The idealized process of (expert) decision making at the WTO then begins to look something like a mathematical equation: given a certain set of background facts (defined and measured by experts), what mix of trade law and dispute settlement will best contribute to achieving the outcomes sought by the organization?

This chapter's primary contention is that because the WTO's underlying normative structure is founded on the privileging of expert knowledge, asking whether and to what extent expert participation in decision-making processes is legitimacy-enhancing is a structural question, not a marginal one. While different individuals and types of experts can be added to and subtracted from the picture in order to make the WTO procedure more efficient or better suited to a particular need, the system is now and will

[3] A great number of political and legal scholars have devoted their considerable energies to creating a definition – working, absolute or otherwise – of 'legitimacy'. These debates are far beyond the scope of this contribution. Suffice it to say that from the perspective of this chapter, it is in all likelihood impossible to provide any definition of legitimacy that is not itself radically contingent. Fortunately, we are spared the theoretical gymnastics here by looking obliquely: not at normative legitimacy, but only at how perceptions of legitimacy are reflected in the explicit statements and practice of the WTO and the community of trade law specialists.

[4] See Esty, 'Good Governance at the World Trade Organization'; A. Orford, 'Trade, Human Rights and the Economy of Sacrifice' in A. Orford (ed.), *International Law and its Others* (Cambridge University Press, 2006), 156–96; Thomas, 'Of Facts and Phantoms'.

remain fundamentally the domain of experts – legal, economic, scientific or otherwise.

Examining the WTO in the context of Michel Foucault's discussion of biopolitics serves to illuminate this argument.[5] Biopolitics, in short, is the efficient management and optimization of the population, conceived as a scientific and political problem, at the aggregate level. Reading the WTO as a technique of biopolitical governmentality provides a coherent framework for understanding its practice and its insistence on the necessity of expert knowledge. As a biopolitical mechanism, the WTO's objective is to maximize the aggregate wealth and human capital of its members by means of statistically and technologically informed interventions. Within this biopolitical logic, it cannot help but rely on experts to obtain and interpret the vast amount of data, risk analyses, deductions and predictions on which its decisions must be based in order to be legitimate. Because it is an instance of biopolitical government, it cannot help but define its legitimacy by reference to expert opinion.

This chapter proceeds as follows. First, section 9.2 argues that legitimacy in WTO decision-making processes is not *enhanced by*, but rather is *defined as* the conformity of decisions with the logics of law, science and economy, as represented by expert contributions. Section 9.3 then turns to the notions of biopolitics and governmentality. After explaining Foucault's development of the concept, it presents a narrative of the WTO as a technique of biopolitical regulation. This reading, it argues, makes clear that the prominent role of experts in the WTO is a structural feature of the organization, and explains how and why it must define legitimacy as conformity with expert opinion.

Section 9.4 then turns to the scholarly debate over whether expert participation in the WTO is a good or bad thing for legitimacy. After a brief discussion of both internal and external critiques, it concludes that the WTO's definition of legitimacy precludes any 'solution' to the 'problems' identified by either set of critiques. On the one hand, proposals that seek to perfect the system of expert participation – for example, by scrubbing the selection process of bias or expanding the range of consulted disciplines – can help to make the system run better.

[5] See M. Foucault, *The History of Sexuality, Vol. 1: The Will to Knowledge* (trans. R. Hurley) (New York: Random House, 1978); M. Foucault, *Society Must Be Defended: Lectures at the College de France 1975–1976* (trans. D. Macey) (London: Allen Lane, 2003); M. Foucault, *The Birth of Biopolitics: Lectures at the College de France 1978–1979* (trans. G. Burschell) (Basingstoke: Palgrave Macmillan, 2008).

Even on their own terms, however, these proposals can never entirely eliminate the necessity of choice. On the other hand, proposals that challenge the enlightenment narratives of scientification, universalism and bureaucracy, and argue instead on behalf of values, situated knowledge and democracy can help us to see the ways in which politics are present in every choice made by experts. However, because the WTO's normative foundations rest on the narratives these latter proposals criticize, it would be difficult, and perhaps impossible, to 'reform' the WTO in a way that could eliminate the problems they identify. Section 9.5 concludes.

9.2 Legitimacy and expert knowledge at the WTO

Reliance on scientific expertise has become a standard practice at the WTO.[6] Panels can appoint individuals or groups of experts to assist them in decision making. Parties to disputes employ experts to support their positions. The WTO Secretariat employs experts on its support staff. WTO committees consult experts in making recommendations.[7] Panels receive *amicus* briefs detailing expert contributions to disputes. And conformity with scientific norms is an explicit criterion of compliance with a number of WTO obligations. Under the Agreement on Technical Barriers to Trade (hereinafter 'the TBT Agreement'), for example, technical regulations must not be more trade restrictive than is 'necessary' to achieve legitimate goals (e.g., protection of human health, animal or plant life or health, or environmental protection), and necessity is evaluated in terms of scientific and technical evidence.[8] The General Agreement on Tariffs and Trade (GATT) provides exceptions to its trade disciplines for measures that are 'necessary' to protect human animal or plant life or health, or that 'relate' to the conservation of natural resources – with 'necessity' again measured in terms of scientific demonstrability.[9] And the Agreement on Sanitary and Phytosanitary Measures (hereinafter 'the SPS Agreement')

[6] See, e.g., Pauwelyn, 'The Use of Experts in WTO Dispute Settlement' (discussing the increasing reliance on experts by the WTO dispute settlement bodies, Member States, and *amici curiae*).

[7] For an excellent discussion of the role of committees and their experts in WTO governance, see A. Lang and J. Scott, 'The Hidden World of WTO Governance', *European Journal of International Law*, 20 (2009), 575–614.

[8] TBT Agreement, Article 2.2. [9] GATT, Article XX.

defines scientific criteria for assessing the permissibility of health and safety regulations.[10]

These scientific experts are additional to a system that *is already* run by experts. Even without the inclusion of biologists, chemists or civil engineers into the process, WTO-style regulation is regulation on the basis of economic theory and law, by economists and trade lawyers. Economists are experts on the functioning of the international and domestic monetary, business and financial systems. And lawyers – like environmental scientists, doctors and geneticists – are also experts in their fields, a privileged group that understands, interprets and enforces a certain set of background norms using language and reasoning that is not immediately comprehensible to outsiders.[11]

These trade policy specialists make up 'a network of professionals with recognized expertise and competence in a particular domain and an authoritative claim to policy-relevant knowledge within that domain or issue-area'.[12] They share a particular set of beliefs, principles, goals and methods, including a common conception of international trade as a social good and a means of promoting development, and a commitment to economic analysis. Though these experts can and do differ – for example, over the degree to which social and environmental issues should be taken into account in trade law, the effect of preferential trade agreements on the international system or the weight that should be given to distributional concerns – they generally view and discuss problems using a shared vocabulary, invoking similar logics and using the same analytical procedures to reach their conclusions.

For WTO scholars, this suffusion of the process with expert knowledge is generally seen as a win-win situation, helping to increase both

[10] SPS Agreement, Articles 2.2, 5.1 and 5.7.

[11] This is often the case when lawyers speak of 'experts' as scientists or technicians outside of the legal field. But such an understanding overlooks the ways in which law itself is a highly technical discipline with its own vocabularies, practices and normative commitments, and that expert knowledge is necessary to understand the modes of operation of any of its subfields. See Gruszczynski, Chapter 11, this volume.

[12] P. M. Haas, 'Introduction: Epistemic Communities and International Policy Coordination', *International Organization*, 46 (1992), 1–35, at 2–3 (defining 'epistemic community'). A number of trade scholars describe international trade specialists as an epistemic community. See, e.g., J. E. Alvarez, 'The WTO as Linkage Machine', *American Journal of International Law*, 96 (2002), 146–58, at 148; R. Howse, 'From Politics to Technocracy – and Back Again: The Fate of the Multilateral Trading Regime', *American Journal of International Law*, 96 (2002), 94–117, at 98; G. Shaffer, M. Ratton Sanchez and B. Rosenberg, 'The Trials of Winning at the WTO: What Lies Behind Brazil's Success', *Cornell International Law Journal*, 41 (2008), 383–502, at 389.

input and output legitimacy.[13] Input legitimacy focuses on the means of decision making. It is defined as conformity with certain procedural conditions of decision-making processes that assure democratic participation and accountability. Decisions have input legitimacy if they are made in accordance with certain ideal formal procedures governing how laws, rules or decisions are made: impartiality, consistency, stability and transparency.[14] Output legitimacy, by contrast, focuses on the ends of decision making. It is a measure of the capacity to solve collective problems according to a particular normative standard. A decision's output legitimacy is therefore determined by its impact, results and effectiveness in promoting the values of the regulated community.[15]

As is the case with many international organizations, input legitimacy has sometimes been seen as problematic for the WTO. Ernst-Ulrich Petersmann noted that the WTO lacks 'traditional sources of democratic input-legitimacy', such as 'respect for human rights' and 'democratic and parliamentary decision-making'.[16] Joost Pauwelyn, too, commented that 'many countries and people, and in particular the poor and vulnerable, feel left behind or locked *outside* the WTO . . . In this sense, the WTO suffers, first and foremost, from a lack of popular support, loyalty, or input legitimacy'.[17] In view of these problems, recommendations for improving input legitimacy have included expanding the links between the WTO and other international regimes (i.e., environment or human rights), making the WTO more representative by including more developing country interests in the list of commitments (i.e., the 'Doha Development Round') and increasing the transparency of the organization and the room for NGOs and other groups to participate. Other scholars, however, have suggested that the best remedy may be enhancing the role played by experts in WTO decision-making processes.[18]

[13] See F. W. Scharpf, *Governing in Europe: Effective and Democratic?* (Oxford University Press, 1999), at 2 (distinguishing 'two dimensions of democratic self-determination, input-oriented authenticity (*government by the people*) and output-oriented effectiveness (*government for the people*)').

[14] *Ibid.* [15] *Ibid.*

[16] E.-U. Petersmann, 'Addressing Institutional Challenges to the WTO in the New Millennium: A Longer-Term Perspective', *Journal of International Economic Law*, 8 (2005), 647–65, at 651.

[17] J. Pauwelyn, 'The Sutherland Report: A Missed Opportunity for Genuine Debate on Trade, Globalization and Reforming the WTO', *Journal of International Economic Law*, 8 (2005), 329–46, at 336, emphasis in original.

[18] See, e.g., T. Christoforou, 'Settlement of Science-Based Trade Disputes in the WTO: A Critical Review of the Developing Case Law in the Face of Scientific Uncertainty', *NYU Environmental Law Journal*, 8 (2000), 622–49; Esty, 'Good Governance at the World

In the eyes of most WTO analysts, expert knowledge – economic, legal and scientific – contributes in several ways to input legitimacy.[19] They argue that the participation of experts in decision making de-politicizes these processes, giving them the appearance of greater neutrality and impartiality. Where it is made explicit, expert input increases transparency, as all parties can view and review the expert knowledge incorporated into decisions. Expert participation ensures that decision makers have the necessary empirical information to adequately assess the complex questions presented to them. And including more types of experts means greater representativeness in terms of interests and constituents, all of which helps to address the problems identified by Petersmann and Pauwelyn.[20] In sum, according to this view, expert participation enhances input legitimacy because expert input is impartial, transparent, well informed and representative: well-designed expert governance is the *definition* of legitimate governance.

The WTO has also attracted criticism with respect to its output legitimacy. Petersmann has pointed out that the WTO lacks 'traditional sources' of output legitimacy, such as 'promotion of general consumer welfare rather than producer interests' and 'consumer-driven competition rather than producer-driven border discrimination and other market distortions'.[21] The WTO has also struggled more generally with the accusation that the outcome of its decision-making processes is unfairly skewed in favour of economic growth at the expense of social and environmental concerns.[22] It has, however, made significant gains in trade liberalization, which members and the public alike see as contributing to the general welfare, and which further the normative ends of the organization.[23]

Trade Organization'; Thomas, 'Of Facts and Phantoms'; D. Winickoff, S. Jasanoff, L. Busch, R. Grove-White and B. Wynne, 'Adjudicating the GM Food Wars: Science, Risk, and Democracy in World Trade Law', *Yale Journal of International Law*, 30 (2005), 81–123; Herwig, Chapter 10, this volume.

19 *Ibid.*

20 Of course, increasing the value placed on expert opinion means decreasing the value assigned to non-scientific popular preferences and demands. But as these demands are already represented through the arguments of the parties (not to mention during the negotiation rounds that periodically update the founding texts), more expert participation is generally seen as increasing, rather than decreasing, input legitimacy. F. Scharpf, 'Interdependence and Democratic Legitimation', MPIfG Working Paper 98/2 (Cologne: Max Planck Institute for the Study of Societies, 1998), at 11.

21 Petersmann, 'Addressing Institutional Challenges to the WTO', at 651.

22 The protests in Seattle in 1999 are a prime example of this.

23 Although, as Joost Pauwelyn notes, the output legitimacy of the WTO is currently imperilled by the lack of further rounds of trade liberalization. Pauwelyn, 'The Sutherland Report', at 336.

In response to these critiques, a number of commentators contend that expert participation in WTO decision-making processes enhances its output legitimacy.[24] They argue that the appeal to expert opinion ensures that the community of WTO constituents (including members, trade experts, businesses and non-governmental organizations (NGOs)) can trust that the dispute settlement system is acting on a rational and verifiable, non-political basis. Panel and Appellate Body decisions become more acceptable to the Member States when the reports make reference to the 'universal' logics of science and economy. The WTO's endorsement of multinational standards, such as the Codex Alimentarius, furthers the harmonization of national regulations, leading to more 'universality', which in turn feeds back to enhance the legitimacy of WTO recommendations. Expert participation leads to decisions that are made on the basis of 'best practices, empirical necessity, good sense, or consensus values'[25] – and who could object to that? In short, expert participation enhances output legitimacy because expert contributions are rational, based on consensus values and therefore widely accepted: well-designed expert governance is the *definition* of output legitimacy.

In sum, the majority of WTO scholars seem to agree that by making decisions more rational, better informed and more broadly representative, the participation of legal, economic, scientific and technical experts increases both input and output legitimacy. This stance is entirely in keeping with the regulatory narrative of the WTO. Legitimate national trade measures are distinguished from illegitimate trade-restrictive measures by assessing their compliance with 'neutral' standards of economic and scientific logic. The primary concern is with preventing countries from circumventing their (legitimate) trade commitments for (illegitimate) political reasons. Whether a rule conforms with scientific and economic theory is essentially a proxy for whether it is a 'legitimate' trade rule. Thus, expert knowledge is a 'neutral' or 'scientific' check on potentially illegitimate 'political' rule making by Member States.[26]

[24] See, e.g., Thomas, 'Of Facts and Phantoms'; Winickoff et al., 'Adjudicating the GM Food Wars'.

[25] D. Kennedy, 'Challenging Expert Rule: The Politics of Global Governance', *Sydney Law Review*, 27 (2005), 5–28, at 11.

[26] For more on the opposition between science and politics, see Klabbers, Chapter 5, this volume; Howse, 'From Politics to Technocracy – and Back Again'; M. Koskenniemi, 'The Fate of Public International Law: Between Technique and Politics', *Modern Law Review*, 70 (2007), 1–30.

In the context of the WTO, expert knowledge is more than just an assurance of legitimacy – it is the *definition* of legitimacy. Conformity with scientific and economic theory – majority or minority, so long as it is evidence-based – means that rules and rulings are deemed fair, non-political and legitimate. Expert participation, coupled with the original consent of the states to the logic of the system, make up the underlying justification of the law's normative force. And it is the role of experts – legal, economic or scientific – to discover and interpret these background norms that structure the activity of the WTO.

9.3 The WTO, biopolitics and governmentality

The previous section argued that well-designed expert participation in decision-making processes is synonymous with legitimacy at the WTO. But what explains the privileged position of expert participation? By what mechanism has expert participation become a structural requirement of the system as currently defined? In order to understand the equation of experts with legitimacy, it helps to place the WTO in the context of Michel Foucault's work on biopolitics and governmentality.[27]

9.3.1 What is biopolitics?

In the last chapter of *The History of Sexuality, Vol. 1*, Michel Foucault describes a 'very profound transformation of [the] mechanisms of power' that takes place in the second half of the eighteenth century.[28] The essence of this shift, which marks the 'threshold of biological modernity',[29] is a reorientation in which the 'right of the sword' – the right to put to death – is complemented by a new form of power: the power to manage life. Whereas sovereignty was previously exercised via the ruler's power to seize things, bodies and ultimately the lives of subjects, this new type of authority is 'a power that exerts a positive influence on life, that endeavours to administer, optimize, and multiply

[27] The object of this section is not to argue that Foucault's notion of biopolitics is the only possible way of understanding the role that experts play at the WTO, or even necessarily the best one. Rather, its limited goal is to use Foucault's description to tease out certain features of the WTO governance system and make it easier to see them as part of an integrated structural logic.

[28] Foucault, *The History of Sexuality, Vol. 1*, at 136; see also Foucault, *Society Must Be Defended*, at 239–64.

[29] Foucault, *The History of Sexuality, Vol. 1*, at 143.

it, subjecting it to precise controls and comprehensive regulations'.[30] The power to mete out death or to refrain from doing so – the crude forms of old sovereignty – become less important than the power to manage all aspects of life, internal and external, from cradle to grave. Unlike the old sovereign regime, this new form of power does not aim to regulate by force, but rather by 'invest[ing] life through and through'.[31]

This new power to manage life takes on two basic forms, which make up 'the two poles around which the organization of power over life was deployed'.[32] The first, which focuses on the control and maintenance of the individual body, is what Foucault calls *disciplinary power*. This micro-power treats the body as a machine and seeks to encourage its integration into systems of control via 'the *disciplines:* an *anatomo-politics* of the human body'.[33]

The second, which focused on the control and maintenance of the population as a whole, is what Foucault referred to as *biopolitics*:

> focused on the species body, the body imbued with the mechanics of life and serving as the basis of the biological processes: propagation, births and mortality, the level of health, life expectancy and longevity, with all the conditions that can cause these to vary. Their supervision was effected through an entire series of interventions and *regulatory controls: a biopolitics of the population.*[34]

Biopolitical governance focuses on a specific set of phenomena, employs distinct methods and operates on a different scale than traditional or disciplinary power. The objects of its attention are the overall health, wealth and efficiency of the population. This includes, most directly, demographic phenomena such as the birth rate and mortality rate,[35] the prevalence of illnesses and accidents,[36] and the regulation of 'charitable institutions . . . insurance, individual and collective savings, safety measures, and so on'.[37] It also includes a focus on the natural and physical environments in which the population lives, and other factors that contribute to aggregate welfare and efficiency.[38]

In order to regulate these phenomena effectively, biopolitical governance employs scientific and technical methodologies. Populations are managed by means of 'demography, the evaluation of the relationship

[30] *Ibid.*, at 137. [31] *Ibid.*, at 139. [32] *Ibid.* [33] *Ibid.* [34] *Ibid.* [35] *Ibid.*, at 243.
[36] *Ibid.* [37] *Ibid.*, at 244.
[38] *Ibid.*, at 245. This includes, for example, 'the direct effects of the geographical, climatic, or hydrographic environment: the problem, for instance, of swamps, and of epidemics linked to the existence of swamps throughout the first half of the nineteenth century'.

between resources and inhabitants, the constructing of tables analyzing wealth and its circulation'.[39] There is an emphasis on statistics, forecasts and calculability. The goal is the *optimization* of society: 'distributing the living in the domain of value and utility'.[40]

These biopolitical techniques deal with collective phenomena that 'become pertinent only at the mass level': biopolitical governance does not aim to control the individual *per se*, but the population as a whole.[41] It implies 'complex systems of coordination and centralization'[42] and operates with a view to the long-term, focusing on 'serial phenomena' rather than unique events.[43] Biopolitics, in short, is the efficient management and optimization of the population, conceived as a scientific and political problem, at the aggregate level.

In a later series of lectures, Foucault expanded on this concept, arguing that biopolitics is the managing principle behind liberal governmentality.[44] This governmentality, which dates from the middle of the eighteenth century, employs a particular political rationality (systematized knowledge complex) and a particular political technology (the practices and institutions through which those knowledge complexes are brought to bear on populations) to achieve biopolitical ends.

The rationality of liberal governmentality consists of two inter-related concepts: the 'self-limitation' of government action and 'the question of truth'.[45] Self-limitation, which is imposed as a result of transactions between the governed and the governing, implies that government should be generally limited, that this limitation is a de facto and necessary component of attaining its objectives, and establishes a dividing line between what is to be done and what should not be done.[46] As Foucault put it: 'The whole question of critical governmental reason will turn on how not to govern too much.'[47] Proper government practice is that which is not 'excessive'. And whether or not an action is 'excessive' is determined with reference to the question of truth, which in this governmental order means the principles of political economy: the study of how to obtain 'the simultaneous, correlative, and suitably adjusted growth of population on the one hand, and means of subsistence on the other'.[48] Political economy identifies truth in the form of 'laws' of nature

[39] Foucault, *The History of Sexuality, Vol. 1*, at 140.

[40] M. Ojakangas, 'Impossible Dialogue on Bio-power: Agamben and Foucault', *Foucault Studies*, 2 (2005), 5–28, at 6.

[41] Foucault, *Society Must Be Defended*, at 246. [42] *Ibid.*, at 250. [43] *Ibid.*, at 246.

[44] See Foucault, *The Birth of Biopolitics*. [45] *Ibid.*, at 17. [46] *Ibid.*, at 11–12.

[47] *Ibid.*, at 13. [48] *Ibid.*, at 14.

(e.g., people will move to where wages are highest) and explains that government practice can meet its objectives only by respecting these laws of nature.[49] Accordingly, governmental actions are 'legitimate' if their effect is to advance political economic objectives.

Political economy reflects on governmental practices themselves and it does not question them to determine whether or not they are legitimate in terms of right. It considers them in terms of their effects rather than their origins, not by asking, for example, what authorizes a sovereign to raise taxes, but by asking, quite simply: what will happen if, at a given moment, we raise a tax on a particular category of persons or a particular category of goods? What matters is not whether this is legitimate in terms of law, but what its effects are and whether they are negative. It is then that the tax in question will be said to be illegitimate or, at any rate, to have no raison d'être.[50]

Success (effectiveness) in promoting political-economic objectives (the maximization of wealth and human capital), measured in terms of conformity with the laws of nature (economy, science), is the metric of good government. A legitimate government is therefore a government that employs 'experts whose task is to tell the government what in truth the natural mechanisms are of what it is manipulating'.[51]

9.3.2 *The WTO as a biopolitical organization*

It is easy to see biopolitical governmentality operating through the WTO. The rationality of the international economic regime is the management of economic processes, on the basis of scientifically derived economic theory, for the purpose of optimizing the efficient conduct of international trade and thereby increasing the welfare of populations. This rationality understands facilitating trade as directly linked with other measures of global social well-being. As the preamble to the 1994 Agreement Establishing the WTO puts it:

> The *Parties* to this Agreement ... *Recogniz[e]* that their relations in the field of trade and economic endeavour should be conducted with a view to raising standards of living, ensuring full employment and a large and steadily growing volume of real income and effective demand, and expanding the production of and trade in goods and services, while allowing for the optimal use of the world's resources in accordance with the objective of sustainable development, seeking both to protect and

[49] *Ibid.*, at 16. [50] *Ibid.*, at 15. [51] *Ibid.*, at 17.

> preserve the environment and to enhance the means for doing so in a manner consistent with their respective needs and concerns at different levels of economic development.

The WTO's regulatory techniques are scientific, managerial and appeal to universal reason. As Anne Orford writes in the context of the SPS Agreement:

> These trade agreements ... require that political decisions that affect market integration must be based on scientific method, assessment and management. All the language of the agreements is about privileging rationality. Indeed, for those supporting the form of these agreements, it is the focus on reason and science that is the contribution of these agreements to democratic politics . . . The logic of the Agreement is that a Member State may not regulate in the name of constraining the activities of the market unless those measures can be justified according to scientific evidence and risk assessment.[52]

Unlike a traditional sovereign, the WTO has no prisons, no power to take life or liberty. Nor does it exercise disciplinary power: the authority to intervene directly to manage on an individual basis the lives of the billions of citizens that are subject, via their respective governments, to its obligations. Instead, the WTO can be read as a tactic of biopolitical governance: a 'table' at which experts come together to order and manage the economic health of populations, optimize the distribution of human and capital resources, and scientifically determine the efficiency and rationality – and therefore the legitimacy – of domestic trade rules. It assesses the world according to a calculus of utility, benefit and aggregate welfare, and reproduces this metric through a series of institutional practices (dispute settlement mechanisms) and rewards (the benefits of membership). In doing so, it acts as a node in the broader political economic field, exercising power by means of epistemological privilege and defining legitimacy as the pursuit of biopolitical ends by biopolitical means.

The WTO reproduces the logic of biopolitical governmentality, managing processes in accordance with economic and scientific 'truth' in order to optimize the welfare of populations. It employs statistical, scientific and economic logic to regularize the international trading system. It operates at the aggregate scale by means of a complex and highly centralized system of coordination. And its legitimacy is assessed in biopolitical terms: on the basis of a political rationality that defines value neutrality,

52 Orford, 'Trade, Human Rights and the Economy of Sacrifice', at 171–2.

economic growth and the maximization of aggregate welfare as the ends of government.

9.3.3 *Expert rule as a structural feature*

Because of its focus on truth and optimization, biopolitical governmentality is heavily reliant on expert knowledge. Where maximizing economic wealth and human and environmental capital are the goals of the system, it makes perfect sense to consult experts as to the best way to achieve that maximization. Experts define the regime of truth: they tell us what the world looks like, identify and quantify relevant variables, provide statistical measurements and risk analyses, and solve the equations that indicate the path towards increasing the aggregate level of well-being. The biopolitical truths experts identify are, in turn, the limiting principles of governance – rule makers that exceed the limits suggested by experts act illegitimately because they act ignorantly or irrationally. Experts are not an *addition* to this biopolitical system – they *define* the system.

In the system of WTO governance, the ideal outcomes of decision-making processes (by committees, dispute settlement bodies or other organs) are the product of the economic, legal and scientific logics they aggregate. Legal, economic and scientific experts decide what is true and what is not; what meets systemic requirements and what does not; which facts are important and which are not; and how the facts should be interpreted in light of the truths that they have identified. Deviations from this structure – caused, for example, by political influence, bias or poor design – decrease the legitimacy of decisions.

Expert participation is thus a defining structural feature of biopolitical governmentality. Reading the WTO through this lens emphasizes the structural logic of expert participation in WTO decision-making processes. As a site of biopolitical governance, the WTO's goal is to increase the welfare of Member State populations by means of rational economic, legal and scientific management. Experts define this terrain and, in so doing, define the limits of legitimate governance.

9.4 Critiques of the role of experts

Given the deep structural significance of experts in the WTO context, it is hardly surprising that the vast majority of commentators – as described in section 9.2 – believe that well-designed expert participation works to enhance the input and output legitimacy of the WTO dispute settlement process. Despite the general faith in the power and propriety of expertise, however, some have criticized the role and process of expert participation in governance in general, and at the WTO in particular. These critiques generally come in two forms: internal critiques that highlight instances where the use of experts has or could become 'compromised' by politics; and external critiques that question the appropriateness of expert involvement more broadly.

9.4.1 Internal critiques

Given that many of those who comment on the WTO are members of the broader epistemic community of trade experts, it is perhaps unsurprising that even those most critical of expert involvement address the question from a thoroughly internal perspective. Where experts are perceived as being problematic, these problems are caused by their insufficient embodiment of scientific ideals, or the WTO dispute settlement system's failure to properly understand and incorporate their advice. Common critiques include such observations as the following:

- Expert selection processes can be biased, leading to the skewing of expert input.[53]
- The results of studies can be biased, as researchers prefer their in-house models or incorporate their own political commitments.[54]
- Developing countries are sometimes unable to appoint their own experts due to financial and technical constraints, which leads to a bias in favour of developed country positions.[55]
- Experts may fail to take account of a sufficiently broad range of variables or come from too narrow a range of fields, leading to an insufficient factual basis for decision making.[56]

[53] See, e.g., Gruszczynski, Chapter 11, this volume.

[54] See, e.g., Esty, 'Good Governance at the World Trade Organization'.

[55] See, e.g., M. Kostecki, *Intellectual Property and Economic Development: What Technical Assistance to Redress the Balance in Favour of Developing Nations?* (Geneva: International Centre for Trade and Economic Development, 2006).

[56] See, e.g., S. Charnovitz, 'The Supervision of Health and Biosafety Regulation by World Trade Rules', *Tulane Environmental Law Journal*, 13 (2000), 271–302; Thomas, 'Of Facts and Phantoms'; Herwig, Chapter 10 and Gruszczynski, Chapter 11, both this volume.

- Because of their lack of training and expertise in particular disciplines, WTO dispute settlement bodies often fail to adequately assess and incorporate scientific contributions.[57]

Essentially, these problems come down to the complaint that the use of expertise is not sufficiently scientific. The solutions to these problems involve cleansing these expert contributions of biases, reforming expert committees such that a greater variety of scientific perspectives are taken into account, providing financial and other support to developing countries so that they can hire their own experts, adding additional types of experts so that more factors can be taken account of, training WTO dispute settlement bodies so that they can make better use of scientific expertise and so on. In short, where politics and bias rear their heads, the answer is more expertise. Enhancing input and output legitimacy, as argued in section 9.2, is still a matter of making the system more 'expert'.

However, while the proposed tweaks would undoubtedly contribute to the good order of the system, they are fundamentally incapable of producing a solution to the problem they identify. Some form of bias will always be present in any system that makes choices. No matter which experts are included, there will necessarily be others that do not make the cut, raising the possibility of partiality. Some form of disciplinary or complexity-based limit will always need to be imposed, leaving expert contributions open to criticism on the grounds of incompleteness or lack of breadth. Panellists will never be sufficiently expert themselves to obviate the need to use their 'own judgement', and the well-recognized contestability of scientific evidence will always require them to make some choice among competing hypotheses.[58] In effect, so long as anything remains excluded from the calculations, there will always be some irreducible residual of irrationality or unscientific choice remnant in the

[57] See, e.g., A. O. Sykes, 'Domestic Regulation, Sovereignty, and Scientific Evidence Requirements: A Pessimistic View', *Chicago Journal of International* Law, 3 (2002), 353–68; Thomas, 'Of Facts and Phantoms'; V. R. Walker, 'Keeping the WTO from Becoming the "World Trans-science Organization": Scientific Uncertainty, Science Policy, and Factfinding in the Growth Hormones Dispute', *Cornell International Law Journal*, 31 (1998), 251–320; Gruszczynski, Chapter 11, this volume.

[58] A beautiful example of the unappeasable quest for additional expertise can be found in a recent article by C. A. Thomas, who laments the lack of adequate economic expertise in the WTO by noting that 'in nine disputes involving significant economic evidence and arguments, only five of the 27 panelists had PhDs in economics, and only a handful of others had undergraduate or masters level degrees in economics'. Thomas, 'Of Facts and Phantoms', at 313.

system. Like Borges' map of the empire, expert contributions will never be entirely sufficient until they coincide point for point with the world.[59]

If the conditions for legitimacy are based on the absence of bias and politics and the precision and completeness of expert testimony, they are destined to never be fully met. Tweaking the system by adding new experts, cleansing the selection process of bias and ensuring the impartiality of evidence cannot make the system perfectly legitimate – just more efficient.

9.4.2 *External critiques*

In addition to the internal critiques described above, there are also a number of external critiques of scientific expertise that focus more broadly on the value of science as a technique of government. The questions they identify are not new: for as long as there has been scientific governance, there have been critiques of its premises. The narratives that make it possible to see science as a check on politics and expert participation as legitimacy-enhancing have been identified and challenged by a wide range of legal and political scholars. These scholars have pointed out the ways in which the scientific ideal brings with it a particular set of epistemological and ontological claims that define the ways that society should be understood and evaluated. This section will examine three representative examples of external critiques and their alternative conceptions of legitimacy.

To begin with, there is the question of science and values. Our ideas about whose knowledge counts and which knowledge is valuable are tied up with the long-standing enlightenment ideal of scientification. This ideal privileges rational, context-independent, systematized knowledge over irrational, situated or value-laden knowledge. It is an ideal that believes in the possibility of truth and the possibility of right answers.

There have been a number of challenges to this paradigm over the last century. Feminists have pointed out the ways in which masculinity is taken as the baseline or 'control group' against which deviations are measured, and have explored the ways in which patriarchy is reproduced

[59] J. L. Borges, 'On Exactitude in Science' in *Collected Fictions* (trans. A. Hurley) (London: Allen Lane, 1999), at 325: 'In that empire, the Art of Cartography attained such Perfection that the map of a single Province occupied the entirety of a City, and the map of the Empire, the entirety of a Province. In time, those Unconscionable Maps no longer satisfied, and the Cartographers Guilds struck a Map of the Empire whose size was that of the Empire, and which coincided point for point with it. The following Generations . . . saw that that vast Map was Useless.'

in scientific procedure.[60] Scholars of Actor–Network Theory like Michel Callon and Bruno Latour have pointed out the gaps and confirmation biases that operate within the isolated world of scientific thinking.[61] A whole range of scholars have challenged the orthodoxy of the rational, positing an 'emotional turn' in the social sciences and arguing on behalf of situated knowledge.[62] And a growing movement has advocated a return to Aristotelian value ethics as an alternative to the dominance of utilitarian and Kantian thought.[63]

Second, there is the privileging of universal truth and consensus. According to the dominant narrative, science is presumed legitimate because it is universal, while politics is potentially illegitimate because it is particular. Science is objective; politics is subjective. The most legitimate forms of governance are those that are based on universal ideals, and that means those that are founded on the bedrock of scientific, economic, legal and liberal logics. But this narrative, too, has been challenged. Partiality and contestation are part and parcel of democratic governance. Legitimacy is not just a matter of a Habermasian search for communicative consensus, but can also be a matter of belief that the system will allow participants to challenge those rules with which they disagree. Chantal Mouffe's work on agonism, for example, has a lot to say about the value of disagreement and dissent in political life, and the importance of recognizing every decision as contested, partial and excluding.[64]

Finally, there is the question of the role of bureaucracy and the displacement of democracy by scientific government. Administration by experts – whether economic, legal or scientific – is increasingly the norm in modern societies. Bureaucratic/administrative/executive mechanisms have been gaining the upper hand over their legislative counterparts in domestic and international systems. The WTO is a particularly dramatic example of this, especially given the deadlock of its mechanism

[60] See, e.g., H. E. Longino, 'Can There Be a Feminist Science?', *Hypatia*, 2 (1987), 51–64.

[61] See, e.g., M. Callon, *Acting in an Uncertain World: An Essay on Technical Democracy* (trans. Graham Burchell) (Cambridge, MA: MIT Press, 2009); B. Latour, *Science in Action: How to Follow Scientists and Engineers through Society* (Cambridge, MA: Harvard University Press, 1988).

[62] See, e.g., L. Bondi, J. Davidson, and M. Smith, 'Introduction: Geography's "Emotional Turn"' in J. Davidson, L. Bondi and M. Smith (eds.), *Emotional Geographies* (Aldershot: Ashgate, 2005), 1–16; N. Mai and R. King, 'Love, Sexuality and Migration: Mapping the Issue(s)', *Mobilities*, 4 (2009), 295–307.

[63] See Klabbers, Chapter 5, this volume.

[64] C. Mouffe, *The Democratic Paradox* (London: Verso, 2009).

for democratic revision.[65] Max Weber connected the rise of bureaucracy with the growth of modern capitalism and the concomitant drive toward specialization and complexity, pointing out that governance by de-contextualized expert knowledge was the perfect form of government for a capitalist society that insists on calculability and quantification.[66]

But this 'legitimacy through technocracy' runs against an alternative story of 'legitimacy through democracy'. It was in this sense that Hannah Arendt expressed her concerns about the bureaucratic state: that the desire for 'scientifically-determined outcomes' in social policy is intrinsically interwoven with the decline of the public sphere of rational–critical debate – the 'rule by nobody' rather than the rule by autonomous democratic subjects.[67] And it is in this sense that David Kennedy laments the marginalization of opportunities for engaged political contestation and calls for a remaking of the possibilities of global political life.[68]

Science and values, universalism and dissent, bureaucracy and democracy – these are all old debates with long and pedigreed histories, and scholars of law and politics continue to refine their understandings of the way these questions relate to our ability to govern ourselves. The WTO, however, has certainly gone down the road of the scientific, the universal and the technocratic. This is not to say that trade specialists are unaware of these external critiques. In fact, several of them have been taken up at the margins, resulting, for example, in calls to accommodate non-scientific positions in dispute settlement proceedings,[69] to create a parliamentary body within the WTO,[70] to allow for the importance of context by deferring to national legislatures[71] and a general admonition

65 The recent demise of the Doha round is proof enough of this point; See also C. Barfield, *Free Trade, Sovereignty, Democracy: The Future of the World Trade Organization* (Washington DC: AEI Press, 2001), at 1.

66 M. Weber, *Wirtschaft und Gesellschaft* (1922), reprinted in W. G. Runciman (ed.) and Eric Matthews (trans.), *Weber: Selections in Translation* (Cambridge University Press, 1978), 341, at 350–1.

67 H. Arendt, *The Human Condition* (University of Chicago Press, 1958), at 40.

68 See also Kennedy, 'Challenging Expert Rule'.

69 See, e.g., Winickoff et al. 'Adjudicating the GM Food Wars'.

70 See, e.g., G. Shaffer, 'Parliamentary Oversight of WTO Rule-Making: The Political, Normative, and Practical Contexts', *Journal of International Economic Law*, 7 (2004), 629–54.

71 See, e.g., J. Bohanes, 'Risk Regulation in WTO Law: A Procedure-Based Approach to the Precautionary Principle', *Columbia Journal of Transnational Law*, 40 (2002), 323–90; D. Wirth, 'The Role of Science in the Uruguay Round and NAFTA Trade Disciplines', *Cornell International Law Journal*, 27 (1994), 817–60.

to keep in mind the 'dangers of managerialism'.[72] While accepting the value of certain of these external critiques, however, the WTO remains unable to make more than a nod to their implications.

The WTO's inability to engage with the external critiques in a meaningful way makes sense given that conformity with economic, legal and scientific norms is the basis of the WTO's normative force. To the extent that we read the WTO according to the logic of biopolitical governance, experts do not just 'contribute' to the system – they *are* the system. Values and emotions, partiality and irrationality, situated knowledge and particularity remain excluded from the ideal picture. To the extent that reliance on scientific and expert opinion is a structural feature of the WTO, any movement toward a more political, more partial and more emotional regime will *decrease* rather than increase its legitimacy. Because they challenge the narratives of science, universalism and bureaucracy that are so deeply entrenched in the system of international economic law, these external critiques cannot easily or unequivocally be incorporated into the existing WTO framework.

Though expert participation in WTO decision-making processes has been criticized from both internal and external perspectives, as this section shows, the WTO will be unable to fully respond to any of these concerns. It is not possible to correct the irrational 'problems' of the system by making it more scientific, as some remainder will inevitably remain outside of the reach of the quantifiable, reproducing the original problems at a new threshold. And with respect to the external critiques, it is not possible to abandon the reliance on expert knowledge at the WTO without abandoning the organization's underlying normative basis, and consequently its legitimacy.

Reading the WTO through the lens of biopolitical governance makes clear the way in which expert participation is a structural feature of WTO decision-making processes. Because of the fundamental relationship between biopolitical management, expertise and legitimacy, it is predictable that critiques of WTO decision making would take the form of calls for additional expertise. Criticisms that deviate from the logic of biopolitical governance will find it difficult to make their case, as they represent not merely practical but also foundational challenges to the order.

[72] See, e.g., Lang and Scott, 'The Hidden World of WTO Governance'; Thomas, 'Of Facts and Phantoms, at 324–5.

9.5 Conclusion

This contribution has discussed the question of whether, and to what extent, expert participation in WTO decision-making processes can be viewed as legitimacy-enhancing. Because the WTO is founded on the basis of a biopolitical logic that privileges scientification, consensus and technocratic processes over irrationality, situated knowledge and democracy, critiques that go beyond merely reforming the process of expert participation to challenge the role of expert knowledge more generally attack the normative commitments of the organization as a whole. Viewing the WTO through the lens of Foucauldian biopolitics and governmentality explains the fundamental nature of this connection. Insofar as the WTO is a technique of biopolitical governmentality, it is structurally committed to the principles of expert rule. Its legitimacy is a matter of hewing as closely as possible to the truth and limits that those experts identify.

This does not mean that it is impossible to challenge the regime of expert governance or that it is an inevitable feature of modern life. However, it does mean that when we think about the role of experts in the WTO, we must do so from a broad structural perspective. Experts are not something that can be 'added to' or 'subtracted from' the WTO in order to tweak its input or output legitimacy. Instead, their many visible and invisible contributions, interpretations and organizing logics are the fabric from which the organization is cut. We must think more critically about what this means in terms of our ability to participate in the system that governs us, and ultimately how it affects our ability to organize our political lives in accordance with our desires and normative aspirations.

10

Health risks, experts and decision making within the SPS Agreement and the Codex Alimentarius

ALEXIA HERWIG

10.1 Introduction

The World Trade Organization (WTO) Agreement on the Application of Sanitary and Phytosanitary Measures (hereinafter 'the SPS Agreement') provides rules for risk regulation by WTO members. These rules give experts an important role in risk regulation. WTO members and the panels and the Appellate Body (AB) need expert advice to determine whether the regulation of a WTO member has a sufficient basis in science.

Article 1.1 of the SPS Agreement[1] applies to the so-called 'SPS measures'. These measures are national laws, decrees, regulations, requirements and procedures that protect against a specific set of enumerated human, animal and plant health risks.[2] As this chapter shows, framing risk in this manner makes it difficult to accommodate the multidimensional nature of risk and results in the circle of relevant experts being drawn unduly narrowly.

The key obligations enshrined in the SPS Agreement are the following. SPS measures have to be based on international standards[3] or be maintained with sufficient scientific evidence unless the state of the evidence can be characterized as insufficient in the sense of Article 5.7.[4] The Annex identifies the Codex Alimentarius Commission (CAC) as the relevant food standard-setter. Article 5.1 specifies the obligation to maintain measures with sufficient scientific evidence. It calls on WTO members to base their measures on risk assessment. The AB has repeatedly held that a risk assessment has to focus specifically on the risk from exposure as targeted by the measure in

[1] All articles referred to in this chapter refer to the SPS Agreement, unless otherwise indicated.

[2] SPS Agreement, Annex A1.The definition also gives illustrations pertaining to kinds of risk regulatory issues covered, such as end-product criteria or production processes.

[3] SPS Agreement, Article 3. [4] *Ibid.*, Articles 2.2, 5.1 and 5.7.

question.[5] If experts consider it impossible to assess the risk or new suggestive evidence calls into doubt a prior risk assessment, a WTO member may consider the evidence to be insufficient and regulate on the basis of available pertinent information.[6] If the experts consider that the risk can be assessed and that such assessment is not called into doubt by alternative forms of indirect expert assessment, a WTO member is not entitled to rely on the more conservative assumptions about risk based on the less validated evidence. Accordingly, in the SPS Agreement, expert advice plays a crucial role in the threshold question of whether regulatory intervention is permitted.

In panel proceedings, the panel asks the input of the disputing parties in the selection of the experts, but ultimately takes the decision on which experts to select.[7] For instance, in *EC-Biotech*, the panel consulted fewer experts than requested by the European Community (EC) and their expertise was primarily technical and related to natural sciences. Commentators have criticized the important role the SPS Agreement provides for experts in policy making on risk. Peel disagrees with the use of science as the principal normative yardstick to the exclusion of non-scientific factors for evaluating consistency.[8] Scientists must make value choices on how to frame risk or approach uncertainty, and science, she submits, provides a limited basis for socially acceptable predictions.[9] For

[5] AB Report, *European Communities–Measures Concerning Meat and Meat Products (Hormones)*, WT/DS/26/AB/R, WT/DS/48/AB/R, adopted 13 February 1998, para. 200 (hereinafter *EC–Hormones*); Panel Report, *EC–Hormones (US)*, WT/DS26/R, adopted 13 February 1998, para. 8.257; *EC–Hormones (Canada)*, WT/DS48/R, adopted 13 February 1998, para. 8.260; AB Report, *Japan–Measures Affecting the Importation of Apples*, WT/DS245/AB/R, adopted 26 November 2003, para. 202 (hereinafter *Japan–Apples*); Panel Report, *Japan–Apples*, WT/DS245/R, adopted 26 November 2003, para. 8.271; Panel Report, *Australia–Measures Affecting Importation of Salmon*, WT/DS18/R, adopted 6 November 1998, para. 8.74 (hereinafter *Australia–Salmon*).

[6] SPS Agreement, Article 5.7; and AB Report, *Canada – Continued Suspension of Obligations in the EC–Hormones Dispute*, WT/DS321/AB/R, adopted 14 November 2008, para. 703; AB Report, *United States–Continued Suspension of Obligations in the EC–Hormones Dispute*, WT/DS320/AB/R, adopted 14 November 2008, para. 703; (both AB reports hereinafter *US/Canada–Continued Suspension*).

[7] For a study of the practice of expert consultation in international tribunals, see C. Foster, *Science and the Precautionary Principle in International Courts and Tribunals: Expert Evidence, Burden of Proof and Finality* (Cambridge University Press, 2011).

[8] J. Peel, 'Risk Regulation under the WTO/SPS Agreement: Science as an International Normative Yardstick', New York University School of Law Jean Monnet Working Paper, New York, 02/04 (2004), available at: http://centers.law.nyu.edu/jeanmonnet/archive/papers/04/040201.pdf, at 95–7; and J. Peel, *Science and Risk Regulation in International Law* (Cambridge University Press, 2010), at 7–8

[9] Peel, *Science and Risk Regulation*, at 6.

this reason, she considers it important to democratize science in order to deal with the influence of values and to make the expertise generated more consistent with public views.[10] Foster agrees that the SPS Agreement downplays the political aspects of risk. She suggests that the stage of *risk assessment*, focusing typically on mortality and morbidity, needs to be supplemented with a stage of *risk evaluation*, focusing on a qualitative appraisal of risk.[11] Foster's critique is that risk needs to be framed more broadly than the typical focus of experts in the natural sciences to take account of the complete regulatory risk.

The impact on life and health from risks within the scope of the SPS Agreement is one aspect relevant to citizens in their capacity as moral agents, and thus to justice, but is not the only normative or justice-related factor that should be taken into account. For example, the fact that a risk affects people who cannot choose or have difficulty avoiding the risk (e.g., children or the poor), that it results in early death of a large number of people or that it is an under-researched risk are also relevant issues. This chapter develops the view that the rational empirical basis of an SPS policy ought to be judged not only according to the epistemological standards of health experts, but also on the basis of the normative characteristics of the complete regulatory risk. Where a risk presents multiple aspects of justice, the policy maker should be entitled to introduce margins of safety in addition to what the technical health experts deem strictly necessary. These problems of justice may require consulting experts from different scientific domains than those customarily involved in health policy making, such as economists, marketing experts or psychologists, in order to establish a sound factual basis for normative judgement. In contrast, where a health risk presents fewer additional problems of justice, the policy maker should defer to the health expert's assessment of the risk. Note that I am not arguing for a democratization of science, which is vulnerable to several objections: expertise is based on exclusion via falsification, while democracy is based on the inclusion of all relevant views or preferences. Clearly, however, there is a need to reject some public views as unpersuasive and this cannot simply be done by voting because it would be absurd to vote on the correctness of empirical facts. One would need a criterion of validity across scientific

[10] *Ibid.*, at 10, 337–75.

[11] C. Foster, 'Public Opinion and the Interpretation of the World Trade Organisation's Agreement on Sanitary and Phytosanitary Measures', *Journal of International Economic Law*, 11 (2008), 427–58.

domains and between attempts to establish empirical facts and expressions of preference or normative judgement – I suspect there is none. Furthermore, any proposal to democratize science in an international setting ought to come up with a convincing conceptualization of the *demos* and of a decision rule, which has kept political philosophers busy for some time. The mere fact that outside interests are affected by national SPS measures is not *per se* enough to warrant their inclusion in nation-state decision making if national citizenship is morally significant from the perspective of democracy. But unless we know we have the right procedure for risk regulation from the perspective of democracy, inclusion of public views may not enhance democracy much. Foster's critique fails to explain what weight the stage of risk evaluation should have in the risk policy-making process and which aspects are legitimate to take account of in risk evaluation. This chapter seeks to fill the gaps by addressing when and what type of expert involvement is likely to be regarded as legitimate in SPS decision making.

The next section develops a normative framework, based on discourse theory and the concept of equality, which can be used to assess the legitimacy of expert involvement in SPS decision making. Section 10.3, based on this normative framework, analyses how the SPS Agreement and the CAC frame risk, and the type of expertise WTO members may or must provide in support of their risk regulations. It will also be ascertained whether, besides the epistemological standards of good science, political judgement, related to justice aspects of risk, matters in establishing the sufficiency of evidence. Section 10.3 thereby evaluates whether the involvement of experts in decision making foreseen by the SPS Agreement conforms with the normative framework and highlights whether the SPS Agreement and the CAC treat experts as decision makers, advisors or as irrelevant.

10.2 The legitimacy of expert involvement in policy making

Experts can simplify complex reality by providing a model of causal relationships, an interpretative framework (scientific theories) and a methodology for arbitrating between competing truth claims. An expert thus is not understood as someone with the ability to re-tell a passive observation (like the witness at trial), but as someone competent to take active, purposeful steps to generate new observations and analyse them so as to make a particular observation generalizable. As there is no vantage point of perfect information from which to judge whether individuals in fact possess the relevant analytical skills, indirect and procedural standards are typically relied upon to qualify someone as an expert. If the standards are met, the person in question is deemed to be an expert and the resulting evidence is deemed to be expert evidence.

I suggest that expert involvement in policy making legitimizes the resulting policies. In theories of deliberative democracy, law is legitimated through its connection to norms generated through open, participatory, consensus-geared discourses.[12] For instance, in Habermas' conceptualization of an ideal speech situation,[13] because decisions need to be taken by consensus, the speaker is forced to consider the concerns of the other participants and must advance deontological propositions (equal accountability). Based on Habermas' discourse theory, it is easy to see why experts can support discourse-generated legitimacy. Experts' involvement helps to establish the credibility of the factual basis of normative propositions and to prevent policy makers from lying or from advancing purely selfish propositions hidden behind factually false scenarios.[14] Experts help clarify why a proposed policy is in the general interest. They support the input legitimacy of policy-making processes by furthering equal accountability to all participants and the output legitimacy of policies by showing their contribution to the general interest.

While expert involvement in policy making promotes deontological accountability, it invariably fails in making policy makers fully accountable to each individual, because expert advice expresses collective assessments with selective framings of risk. In the food safety context, experts are typically specialized in disciplines such as toxicology, microbiology or genetics and thus focus on mortality and/or morbidity. However, a food safety risk can also present further problems of justice which these experts do not account for in their framing of risk. Examples of such problems include psychological suffering of patients and relatives, the distribution of risk across the population or chosen versus involuntary risks.

To go beyond a particular framing of risk and assess the *broader factual context* of all justice-related aspects of a risk, it is essential to involve the

[12] J. Habermas, *Between Facts and Norms: Contributions to a Discourse Theory of Law and Democracy* (Cambridge, MA: MIT Press, 1996), at 107, 110.

[13] J. Habermas, 'Discourse Ethics: Notes on a Program of Philosophical Justification' in J. Habermas, C. Lenhardt and S. Weber Nicholsen (eds.), *Moral Consciousness and Communicative Action* (Cambridge, MA: MIT Press, 1990), 43–115, at 86.

[14] The fact that expertise can even become manipulated and experts corrupted does not distract from the legitimacy-enhancing function of experts, because these dangers can be reduced through regulation of experts or ethical standards, as Jan Klabbers proposes in Chapter 5, this volume.

input of experts from various fields in policy making. Ultimately, only policy makers and citizens can assess what is normatively significant from the perspective of justice by using discursive reasoning. If discursive reasoning and expert evidence of the type evaluating normative concerns suggest that a risk possibly raises aspects of justice beyond morbidity or mortality, policy makers should be entitled to take additional precautions even if health experts do not consider them in their evaluations. For the purposes of the SPS Agreement and the CAC, this means that expert advice must also encompass the normative quality of risks with evidentiary support from experts in all the relevant fields.

Policy makers involved in setting SPS measures should base their risk policies most closely on the evidence of health experts when a risk is largely one-dimensional from the perspective of justice (i.e., there is only a health risk and it is largely self-imposed). Where a risk presents multidimensional aspects of justice, policy makers should be able to set policies based on the health risk in the broader factual context.

10.3 Experts, the framing of risk, the SPS Agreement and the CAC

Based on the framework developed above, this section analyses the role that the SPS Agreement assigns to experts in national risk policy-making processes and the role experts play in setting international food safety standards.

10.3.1 The SPS Agreement

There are, arguably, five ways in which considerations related to the above-devised *broader factual context* can enter directly into the SPS Agreement: (i) through the definition of risk assessment by setting the quantum of proof; (ii) through the framing of risk; (iii) in the assessment of whether or not scientific evidence is sufficient (to establish a risk and justify the risk control measure); (iv) in the choice of the appropriate level of protection; and (v) in the choice of risk control measures.

10.3.1.1 Risk assessment and the quantum of proof

The SPS Agreement defines risk assessment as follows:

> The evaluation of the likelihood of entry, establishment or spread of a pest or disease within the territory of an importing Member according to the sanitary or phytosanitary measures which might be applied, and of

> the associated potential biological and economic consequences; or the evaluation of the potential for adverse effects on human or animal health arising from the presence of additives, contaminants, toxins or disease-causing organisms in food, beverages or feedstuffs.[15]

The SPS Agreement thus distinguishes between two types of risk assessments, depending on the source of exposure. In the case of food and feedstuffs, an assessment concerns 'the evaluation of the *potential* for adverse effects on human or animal health arising from the presence of additives, contaminants, toxins or disease-causing organisms in food, beverages or feedstuffs'.[16] In the case of exposure to pests, animal or plant diseases, disease-carrying or disease-causing organisms, an assessment must identify the *likelihood* of risk to human, animal or plant health.[17] Furthermore, WTO members are allowed to prevent or limit other, non-health-related damage from pests in their territory.[18] In this case WTO members are also to assess the *likelihood* of risk. The AB confirmed that the two types of risk assessment require different thresholds for the establishment of the existence of any risk: potential denotes possibility, while likelihood denotes a higher threshold of probability.[19]

Both types of risk assessment relate to measures for protecting, amongst other things, human health. The immediate consequences (death or illness) of such risks are therefore comparable. However, depending on the source of exposure, either the possibility or likelihood of a risk needs to be established. It could be argued that to show the *possibility* of a risk, a WTO member need only establish that a human health hazard could exist at a given exposure for a single individual, but not how likely it is to affect a population. To show the *likelihood* of a risk, a WTO member needs to establish how many individuals are affected by a hazard at a given level of exposure. In natural sciences, such probability is ideally established through direct experiments under controlled conditions whose results are repeatable. This type of assessment enjoys the highest degree of epistemological validation. A new theoretical model suggesting a hazard is theoretically possible cannot be considered to show the likelihood of risk because it cannot demonstrate that the risk actually exists and is likely to materialize.

For food-borne risks, a lower standard is established. WTO members enjoy greater discretion as to which expert evidence of different

15 SPS Agreement, Annex A4. 16 *Ibid.*, Annex A4, emphasis added.
17 *Ibid.*, Annex A1 and A4. 18 *Ibid.*, Annex A1(d).
19 AB Report, *EC–Hormones*, para. 184.

epistemological validation they rely on to show consistency of their measure with Article 5.1: they may use expert opinions establishing the likelihood or possibility of risk. When national policy makers use this discretion, their decision on whether the state of evidence regarding risk warrants regulatory intervention can indirectly be influenced by what is at stake normatively, ie, in terms of justice.

Within their discretion, they may be influenced by experts from disciplines other than natural sciences. However, the SPS Agreement requires the national policy maker neither to make the normative assessment explicit nor to provide expert evidence supporting the assessment of what justice considerations may be at stake besides health risks. The normative framework developed above implies that a decision to accept less or more natural science expert proof must correspond with the normative severity of the risk in all its complexity, and any justice-related problems other than health risk must be supported with expert evidence as well. For food-borne risks, the risk assessment prescribed by the SPS Agreement is therefore insufficient to guarantee the legitimacy of the policy-making processes by giving too much unstructured discretion to the policy maker.

For animal-borne, plant-borne and pest-borne risks, expert evidence establishing the possibility of risk does not constitute a sufficient risk assessment under the SPS Agreement. Such evidence cannot be used by the national policy maker to meet the key obligation of Article 5.1. As illustrated below, here the risk is framed more broadly to include elements from the broader factual context relevant for justice. As a result, national policy makers also have to provide expert evidence from the non-natural sciences, but the evidence must establish the likelihood of risk. The policy maker's ability to respond to the normative quality of the risk (broadly defined) is reduced under Article 5.1 because the quantum of proof is set at a high level. This combination of a broader framing of risk with a high quantum of proof does not allow a decision for regulation to be based on a merely possible, but highly significant, justice-related impact in one domain (e.g., distribution of risk). This entails that normative considerations alone will not suffice to meet the requirements of Article 5.1.[20]

[20] Note that a WTO member would probably succeed in showing that scientific evidence on the health effects is insufficient to allow the performance of a risk assessment and thus adopt a provisional measure on the basis of Article 5.7. However, the obligations of Article 5.7 are different from those of Article 5.1. Under Article 5.7, the measure must be provisional and revised regularly against information from international standardization organizations.

I fail to see what difference the sources of exposure to risk (food versus animal, plant or pest) should make to the normative quality of the entire category of risks. Why does the fact that the exposure is via food allow a lower quantum of proof without the need for further explanation by the policy maker? This choice seems arbitrary from the point of view of justice.

10.3.1.2 Framing of risk

The manner in which risk is framed based on the two sources of exposure has further consequences. For animal-borne, plant-borne and pest-borne risks, the risk assessment requires the inclusion of associated biological and economic consequences in the risk assessment. Article 5.3 further specifies that members shall take into account loss of production or sales arising from diseases and pests, the cost of eradication and the relative cost-effectiveness of alternative risk control measures in assessing economic consequences. This provision prescribes what members minimally must assess, but it does not preclude assessing other issues as long as they can be considered biological or economic consequences. It should thus be possible to include matters of distributive justice in the risk assessment.

In contrast, for food-borne risks, the risk assessment is defined as the evaluation of adverse effects on human health. In addition to mortality and morbidity, which are typically considered by scientific experts, mental health-related effects are also health effects. However, circumstances related to the broader factual context, such as the income-dependent distribution of the risk across the population or the costs of risk control measures, would not be part of the applicable risk assessment because they do not concern adverse effects on human health. Food-borne risk is narrowly framed as a health risk. Animal-borne, plant-borne and pest-borne risks are broadly framed as health risks with economic and biological consequences and, in the case of pest-borne risks, any other damage.

Does the framing of food-borne risks in terms of health effects preclude a WTO member from considering the broader factual context as an essential part of risk assessment? The answer to this question is important for determining the ability of WTO members to rely on the broader factual context as a justification for characterizing the state of evidence as insufficient in the sense of Article 5.7 and, on this basis, to justify provisional measures.

According to an interpretation *in dubio mitius*, the omission of elements related to the broader factual context entails that WTO members have discretion as to whether to require these elements to be considered in the risk assessment. According to an *a contrario* interpretation, the omission of the term 'economic and biological consequences' for food-borne risk assessment means that evidence on anything other than health effects is not essential to the risk assessment. This latter interpretation would imply that a national policy maker cannot claim that an assessment of food-borne health risk is insufficient because it has failed to consider the broader factual context of the risk.

As an international treaty, the SPS Agreement must be interpreted in accordance with Articles 31 and 32 of the Vienna Convention on the Law of Treaties (VCLT). Pursuant to the VCLT, the interpreter must consider the context of the provision to be interpreted and the aim of the treaty alongside the textual meaning of the provision. Textually, it is clear that health effects do not include matters of social and distributive justice, economics and so forth. Similarly, neither the SPS provisions of a general nature nor the purpose of the SPS Agreement as enshrined in the preamble refer to anything like 'matters other than health risk'. This suggests that a national policy maker is not entitled to consider an assessment of the broader factual context as a requirement for a food-borne risk assessment. If this interpretation is correct, the framing of food-borne risks is inconsistent with the normative framework developed above, in that it precludes consideration of the broader factual context of risk.

10.3.1.3 Determining whether scientific evidence is sufficient to assess risk

Article 5.1 provides the obligation to base measures on risk assessment. It is a specification of the obligation contained in Article 2.2 to provide continuous, sufficient scientific support for SPS measures. The question that arises is whether compliance with Article 5.1 is the only way to meet the obligation of Article 2.2. Does the notion of sufficient scientific evidence coincide with the definition of a risk assessment? If the preceding question is answered in the affirmative, the definition of risk assessment is also determinative of which kinds of experts are to play a role in risk policy making in terms of Article 2.2 and importantly Article 5.7.

Article 5.7 allows a member to adopt provisional measures if scientific evidence is insufficient; however, it does not state for which purpose scientific evidence has to be insufficient. In the *Japan–Apples* case, the

AB decided that 'insufficient' refers to a state of the evidence that does not allow the performance of a risk assessment.[21] By including this reference to risk assessment, the decision in *Japan–Apples* makes the definition of a risk assessment applicable to the notion of sufficient/insufficient scientific evidence. As argued in section 10.3.1.2 above, the definition of food-borne risk assessment excludes non-health-related elements from being an essential requirement for a risk assessment. Therefore, the national policy maker cannot argue that the state of scientific evidence is insufficient because assessment of the broader factual context is lacking and thus cannot justify SPS measures based on Article 5.7 on this ground.

Imagine there is an assessment of health risks from exposure to a food product by the CAC, which assesses there to be no health risks, but this assessment does not consider the broader factual context. There is another assessment of lesser epistemological quality of the effects on health and of the broader factual context suggesting a significant risk to health. The second assessment of the health risk is not, however, sufficiently robust to cast doubt on the epistemological validity of the CAC's health risk assessment. The effect of the framing of food safety risks is that a WTO member cannot adopt a provisional SPS measure because the absence of an assessment of the broader factual context alone does not show that the state of scientific evidence is insufficient to allow the performance of a risk assessment. However, if this hypothetical situation had concerned animal-borne, plant-borne and pest-borne risks, a WTO member at least could have shown the insufficiency of the scientific evidence for an SPS risk assessment on the grounds that it fails to assess economic and biological consequences.

Based on the normative framework, it would be legitimate to adjust the quantum of proof required for health-related risks in view of the seriousness of the normative quality of a risk. In other words, it is legitimate for the policy maker to introduce extra margins of safety in addition to those considered strictly necessary by natural science knowledge if the normative quality of a risk is severe.

In the *Continued Suspension* case, the AB modified the criteria for determining the insufficiency of scientific evidence. It found that the appropriate

[21] A. Herwig, 'The Precautionary Principle in Support of Practical Reason: An Argument Against Formalistic Interpretations of the Precautionary Principle' in C. Joerges and E.-U. Petersmann (eds.), *Constitutionalism, Multilevel Trade Governance and Social Regulation*, (Oxford: Hart Publishing, 2006), 301–25.

level of protection (ALOP) against food-borne risk has some role to play in deciding on the sufficiency of scientific evidence.[22] According to the AB, the policy maker's ALOP can frame the risk assessment and influence the types of questions asked of experts, but the decision on whether or not the evidence is sufficient, ie, whether it has epistemological validity, belongs to the domain of the scientific experts.[23]

The SPS Agreement uses the term 'ALOP' to designate the level of risk tolerance/risk aversion of a WTO member.[24] The decision on the level of protection sought necessarily involves a normative weighing of costs and benefits in a broader factual context. Elements, such as how the risk is distributed across the population, how many people are likely to be affected, and the efficiency and cost of risk mitigation measures must be considered in order to establish legitimate regulatory priorities and goals (level of protection) where resources are finite. If resource constraints prohibit maximal protection against every risk possible, the setting of the ALOP becomes a question of a just distribution of a finite good (regulatory protection) for which a complete, reasoned analysis of the factual context of the risk is necessary. As a result, expert evidence only on the health hazards of a risk is insufficient for the legitimate determination of the ALOP; experts from other domains of science are also needed.

Note that the AB in *Continued Suspension* did not explicitly overrule its finding in *Japan–Apples* that scientific evidence is insufficient if the evidence does not allow a risk assessment as defined in the SPS Agreement. Assume that the AB had meant to overrule *Japan–Apples* implicitly. The result would be that the national policy maker could easily show that scientific evidence is insufficient in the sense of Article 5.7 because it does not include non-natural science expert evidence. However, once the non-natural science expert evidence is fully available and recourse to Article 5.7 is no longer needed, he or she could not set the ALOP at a higher level on the basis of this information than what the health experts' risk assessment considers necessary. This inability is explained by the interpretation of the obligation enshrined in Article 5.1, namely the requirement that an SPS measure be based on a risk assessment. According to the case law cited in note 5 above, a measure is based on risk assessment only if the assessment is specific

[22] AB Report, *US/Canada–Continued Suspension*, para. 534. [23] *Ibid.*
[24] SPS Agreement, Articles 5.4 and 5.5 and Annex A.5.

to the exposure targeted by the measure. Because food-borne risk assessment is understood as requiring natural science expert evidence, the non-natural science expert evidence is of no use to a WTO member in adopting the ALOP at a higher level. WTO members therefore are not better placed to use a plurality of experts in setting the ALOP for SPS measures under Article 5.1. Such an approach is not in accordance with the requirements set in the normative framework developed in this chapter. Assume now that the AB had not meant to overrule the decision in *Japan–Apples*. Following the *Continued Suspension* case, the national policy maker could request expert advice on the broader factual context from various scientific domains. However, the natural science experts employed to establish consistency with Article 5.1 for the framing of food-borne risk would have to assess whether any missing information from the non-natural sciences prevents a risk assessment of health effects. The only framing of risk assessment available to policy makers pursuant to this second interpretation of the *Continued Suspension* case would be to demonstrate the insufficiency of scientific evidence for a risk assessment by asking for a more detailed health risk assessment. Such a narrow framing fails to take account of the multidimensional nature of risk and is inconsistent with the normative framework because it prevents full consideration for all justice-related impacts of a health risk.

Nevertheless, the national policy maker could partially avoid the narrow framing of risk by asking strategic health-related questions of health experts he or she knows they cannot answer. For instance, he or she could ask experts to evaluate effects resulting from interaction with a host of other agents (whether plausible or not) that are very difficult for scientists to assess experimentally or for subgroups of the population, such as ethnic groups, children, the elderly, pregnant women, the poor, the rich and so on. It is likely that data on consumption patterns or health effects in some of these subgroups will not be available, so that no risk assessment can be performed. The problem with this approach would be that the national policy maker would have to disguise his or her non-health-based concerns in terms of health concerns and that he or she might engage in strategic questioning for illicit motives of self-interest or discrimination against foreign goods. The bottom line of my analysis is that the ruling in *Continued Suspension* does not cohere with the narrow framing of a risk assessment in the SPS Agreement. In other words, while this ruling suggests that risk can be framed more broadly, the definition of food-borne health risk in the SPS Agreement does not require broad expertise for the risk assessment.

10.3.1.4 Determination of the appropriate level of protection

Once the policy maker, in consultation with experts, has determined that an SPS health risk exists, he or she must decide what level of protection his or her policy shall achieve. The setting of the ALOP is often influenced by a variety of considerations besides health effects. I argue that the policy maker should involve experts for the factual assessment of all relevant aspects in order to set the ALOP legitimately

This sub-section analyses whether or not the provisions in the SPS Agreement allow the national policy maker to consider all the relevant dimensions of justice in setting the ALOP and which kinds of experts (if any) the policy maker must call on to justify its ALOP. Article 5.5 is the only mandatory provision explicitly governing the ALOP. It establishes a presumption that the regulatory policy of similar risks ought to exhibit a similar level of risk tolerance unless a difference in risk tolerance can be justified. If a difference in risk tolerance, i.e., the ALOP, cannot be justified, Article 5.5 examines whether the lack of justification for the regulatory policy under review results in discrimination against or disguised restriction on imports. Panels and the AB approach Article 5.5 by first examining whether or not there is a difference in ALOPs for comparable situations. The comparability criterion focuses on the same or similar end-point of risk (disease) or the same or similar agent of risk.[25] In addition, for animal diseases and pests, situations with the same biological and economic consequences are compared.[26] The first legal test is therefore formal and frames risk in terms typically used by natural scientists in accordance with the SPS Agreement's definition of a risk assessment.

The second step under Article 5.5 points to a substantive analysis, that is, the assessment of whether or not the difference in ALOPs is arbitrary or unjustifiable. Most SPS disputes concerning the arbitrarily and unjustifiably diverging ALOPs are decided on the basis of a comparison of the differences or similarities in the levels of risk associated with the substance subject to the SPS measure and with the comparator situation. Depending on how the parties present their arguments,[27] however, in some cases, policy-based considerations have been accepted as a

[25] AB Report, *EC–Hormones*, para. 235. Concretely, cancer risk from different forms of exposure to growth hormones were considered comparable, as were the health risks from hormonal growth promoters in cattle and anti-microbial growth promoters in pigs.

[26] AB Report, *Australia–Salmon*, paras. 146 and 147.

[27] AB Report, *EC–Hormones*, paras. 223–5; AB Report, *Australia–Salmon*, paras. 158, 219–26 and 234–6; Panel Report, *Australia–Salmon*, para. 8.141; Panel Report, *Australia–Salmon (21.5)*, paras. 7.100 and 7.101.

potential justification for a difference in ALOPs. In *EC–Hormones*, for example, the ALOP against the risks from growth hormones was higher than the ALOP against the risk from naturally occurring hormones and anti-microbial agents used in pig production. The AB found that there was a fundamental difference between hormones (and not the level of risk) that are naturally present and hormones that were added for growth-promotion purposes.[28] It accepted the differences in protection levels as justified based upon policy reasons.

The willingness of the panel and the AB to engage with the EC's policy arguments indicates that distinctions based on the qualitative evaluation of the risk are a possible justification for differences in ALOPs. This is confirmed, in principle, by the *US–Poultry* panel's analysis of the meaning of the terms 'arbitrary' and 'unjustifiable'. To interpret the term 'unjustifiable', the panel quoted the dictionary definition of the term 'justifiable' as 'capable of being legally or morally justified, or shown to be just, righteous, or innocent; defensible' and 'capable of being maintained, defended, or made good',[29] thereby clearly pointing to a normative standard of what justice requires. However, the *US–Poultry* panel then decided that only a difference in levels of risk between comparable situations justifies a difference in ALOP. The panel stated that 'in the context of Article 5.5 to show that the distinction in ALOPs is not arbitrary or unjustifiable, a Member *must* demonstrate that there are differing levels of risk between the comparable situations. We are of the view that such a demonstration requires scientific evidence'.[30] The panel thereby restricted the criteria for determining what is justifiable to those used by natural scientists in framing risk analysis. It also reduced the quintessential political cost–benefit evaluation of risk tolerance to one in which the policy maker is bound to follow the assessment of natural scientists, i.e., the possibility or probability of hazard. It is in effect these experts who determine the ALOP for all comparable risks. As a result, other justice-related aspects are excluded from decision making regarding ALOPs.

10.3.1.5 The role of experts in determining the sufficiency of evidence

This sub-section analyses the obligations applicable to the means used to control a previously established risk. Risk control measures, as part of the

[28] AB Report, *EC–Hormones*, para. 221.

[29] Panel Report, *United States–Certain Measures Affecting Imports of Poultry from China*, WT/DS392/R, adopted 25 October 2010, para. 7.259.

[30] Panel Report, *US–Poultry*, para. 7.263, emphasis added.

SPS measure under examination in a WTO dispute, must conform to the requirements of Articles 5.1 and 2.2 (unless Article 5.7 can be invoked successfully). Under Article 5.1, the risk control measure must be based on a risk assessment and, under Article 2.2, it must be maintained with sufficient scientific evidence. Article 5.6 also applies to risk control measures and requires that these be no more trade restrictive than *necessary* to achieve the WTO member's ALOP, taking into account technical and economic feasibility. It is logical and consistent with the normative framework that experts establish a credible factual basis for the policy maker's choice of a risk control measure. Establishing such a basis is important to help convince citizens that the measure is in the general interest and thus enhances output legitimacy.

Legally speaking, there are three ways to interpret the term 'necessity' in Article 5.6, namely as: (i) suitability; (ii) comparative effectiveness and trade restrictiveness; and (iii) proportionality *stricto sensu*. A suitability test focuses on whether the risk control measure makes a contribution to risk reduction – taking an aspirin to treat cancer is not a suitable measure. Comparative effectiveness considers which risk control measure works best while producing the slightest impact on trade. Proportionality *stricto sensu* is an assessment of the costs and benefits of the risk control measure. It considers whether the ALOP addresses issues which are serious enough to justify adverse impacts on trade and is always preceded by an analysis of suitability and comparative effectiveness.

In the development of the normative framework, I argued that legitimate risk policy making must consider all dimensions of risk relevant for justice and draw on a variety of experts to establish the broader factual context of risk. Proportionality *stricto sensu* acknowledges that the control of risk can produce justice-related impacts in other domains that are undesirable. Imagine that the most effective measure to reduce health risk from E. coli would be to prohibit trade from developing countries, resulting in an increase in poverty and a decrease in individual life prospects in these countries. On balance, one may think that these trade-related consequences are not justified by the anodyne nature of the risk. In short, proportionality *stricto sensu* requires the appraisal of the desired ALOP and the trade-related consequences of attaining it with risk control measures against the backdrop of what justice requires. This test comes close to deliberative processes of policy justification in which the impacts on everyone are considered and a justification is offered that everyone has reason to accept.

The question now arises whether the use of proportionality *stricto sensu* in SPS case law conforms with the normative framework and which role it assigns to experts. In *Japan–Apples* the panel and AB used each of the above-mentioned tests in their analysis of risk control measures under Article 2.2.[31] The case concerned two questions: first, whether or not fire-blight-infected apples that are immature or show symptoms of infection could introduce fire blight to Japan; and, second, whether or not mature, symptomless apples with surface fire-blight bacteria or a non-pathogenic infection could introduce fire blight to Japan. The experts acknowledged the existence of a negligible risk stemming from these potential exposures from different types of apples targeted by the eight Japanese risk control measures. They considered some of the measures to be too cautious and more trade restrictive than an available alternative, and others to be unsuitable.[32] In a decision that was upheld by the AB, the panel agreed with the experts and imposed the additional requirement that the protectiveness of the risk control measures must remain in proportion to the severity of the risk in order for the measure to be maintained with sufficient scientific evidence.[33]

The experts were of the opinion that there was no evidence that apples, whether diseased or not, could introduce fire blight into Japan, but did acknowledge that such a risk could not be totally excluded, characterizing it as remote, extremely low, negligible and close to zero, but not zero.[34] Therefore, they considered that phytosanitary controls on fire blight should not be totally abandoned, but that they should not be excessively costly or trade restrictive.[35] Even though the risk was negligible, the panel agreed with the experts that apples from severely blighted orchards should not be exported.[36] Implicitly, it seems, the panel and the experts considered that there was a proportional relationship between this risk control measure and the negligible nature of the risk. The experts acknowledged that the limits of science had been reached: the absence of evidence of risk does not equal the absence of risk because science cannot prove safety beyond doubt. This entails that

[31] Article 5.6 was also argued in *Japan–Apples*, but the panel exercised judicial economy on the Article 5.6 claim. Panel Report, *Japan–Apples*, para. 8.304.

[32] *Ibid.*, paras. 8.153 and 8.168.

[33] AB Report, *Japan–Apples*, paras. 162–3; Panel Report, *Japan–Apples*, paras. 8.101–8.103, 8.181 and 8.198.

[34] Panel Report, *Japan–Apples*, paras. 8.149, 329–30, 332, 372, 378, 383–6, 388, 393 and 395.

[35] Panel Report, *Japan–Apples*, paras. 419–23, 424, 8.388.

[36] *Ibid.*, para. 8.153.

the justification for limiting exports must come from a normative appraisal of the quality of the risk and the costs of the control measures (proportionality *stricto sensu*), which is the prerogative of the policy maker according to the normative framework.

Phytosanitary experts are experts on facts, not on theories of justice and are therefore the wrong people to assess SPS measures if the limits of science have been reached. What the panel and the AB should have done is to ask a broad range of experts from different scientific domains for a factual analysis of the phytosanitary and trade impacts of the risk control measure to ensure that the normative appraisal by the policy maker is likely to be factually correct and thus legitimate. It is not possible to judge the normative significance of a reduction in trade without looking at the broader factual context. A reduction in trade may not be relevant from the perspective of justice, even if it is high. It only becomes relevant because it affects important interests justice protects, such as poverty reduction or distributive equality. An analysis of the justice-related impacts of a reduction in trade therefore requires consulting experts on developmental economics. By asking only phytosanitary experts, the panel and AB failed to establish the complete factual record, which is needed to legitimize the choice for a certain risk control measure.

10.3.2 The Codex Alimentarius Commission

The SPS Agreement promotes the international harmonization of SPS standards. Where members follow international standards closely, they are deemed to take measures necessary for health protection and to comply with General Agreement on Tariffs and Trade (GATT) 1994.[37] Unless members can base their measures on risk assessment or avail themselves of Article 5.7, they have to base their measures on international standards.[38] In the area of food safety, the CAC is recognized as the relevant international standard-setter.[39] As a result, a discussion of the SPS Agreement would not be complete without considering the CAC. The CAC will be used as an example of international standardization through which expert knowledge is built into the political determination of risk acceptability and its appropriate mitigation. In other words, the CAC sets international ALOPs.

[37] SPS Agreement, Article 3.2. [38] *Ibid.*, Article 3.1. [39] *Ibid.*, Annex A3.

The CAC has a dual mandate: to protect the health of consumers and to ensure fair practices in food trade.[40] The framing of risk thus includes health risks and economic damage. Nevertheless, the Working Principles for Risk affirm that health protection should be the primary objective of CAC standards.[41] In the CAC, there is an institutionalized separation between risk assessment and risk management.[42] Risk assessment is performed by committees of experts, most of whom are located under the auspices of the Food and Agriculture Organization (FAO) and the World Health Organization (WHO), the two parent organizations of the CAC.[43] Risk management is carried out by specialized committees – composed of government specialists and industry and consumer organizations representatives – and the general CAC.[44] The members of the CAC are policy makers who are bound by the factual evaluation of the expert committees. The separation between risk assessment and management suggests a conception of risk regulation in which experts provide the factual basis for subsequent policy making. However, the institutional separation between risk assessment and management is not entirely rigid, since risk assessment policies are established by the specialized CAC committees and the general CAC in consultation with the FAO and WHO expert bodies.[45]

[40] Statutes of the Codex Alimentarius Commission in Codex Alimentarius Commission, 'Procedural Manual', twentieth edn, available at: www.codexalimentarius.org/procedures-strategies/procedural-manual/en, Article 1; General Principles of the Codex Alimentarius Commission, 'Procedural Manual', para. 1.

[41] Working Principles for Risk Analysis for Application in the Framework of the CAC, 'Procedural Manual', para. 27.

[42] *Ibid.*, para. 3.

[43] FAO and WHO, *Understanding the Codex Alimentarius Commission*, third edn, available at: www.codexalimentarius.org/about-codex/understanding-codex/en, at 22–4; Procedures for the Elaboration of the Codex Standards and Related Texts, 'Procedural Manual', Introduction and Part 3: 1.

[44] Working Principles for Risk Analysis for Application in the Framework of the CAC, 'Procedural Manual', para. 3.; A. Herwig, 'The Contribution of Global Administrative Law to the Legitimacy of the Codex Alimentarius Commission' in O. Dilling, M. Herberg and G. Winter, (eds.), *Transnational Administrative Rule-Making: Performance, Legal Effects and Legitimacy* (Oxford: Hart Publishing, 2011), 171–212; A. Herwig, 'Transnational Governance Regimes for Foods Derived from Bio-Technology and their Legitimacy' in C. Joerges, I. J. Sand and G. Teubner (eds.), *Transnational Governance and Constitutionalism* (Oxford: Hart Publishing, 2004), 199–221, at 199.

[45] Working Principles for Risk Analysis for Application in the Framework of the CAC, 'Procedural Manual', paras. 9, 13–16; Statements of Principle Relating to the Role of Food Safety Risk Assessment, 'Procedural Manual'.

A risk assessment policy can address most of the broader factual context of a risk by evaluating risk through various framings (e.g., of health risk, of distributive justice and of personal autonomy) and by informing the threshold of sufficient epistemological validity *for regulatory purposes* so that the threshold becomes sensitive to the normative context. For instance, if there is a lack of funding for particular types of research or the analytical methods for complex problems are imperfect, a legitimate policy should give weight to these types of deficiencies by introducing a more permissive standard of evidence for regulatory intervention.

The CAC prides itself in carrying out risk assessments that are based on sound science,[46] based on the functional separation between risk assessment and risk management. While risk management decisions can be based on legitimate factors other than human health protection and impacts on trade – so-called other legitimate factors (OLFs) – this must not affect the scientific basis of the risk assessment conducted by experts.[47] Note, however, that in the CAC context, there is no clear *a priori* restriction as to the issues on which a risk assessment may be sought. Its policies indicate that the health and safety aspects of CAC decisions and recommendations should be based on risk assessment as appropriate to the circumstances.[48] This provision establishes a floor, not a ceiling: at a minimum, the health and economic risks must be assessed by *some* experts, but this does not preclude seeking a risk assessment with a different framing of risk, which is to be welcomed in terms of the normative framework.

I see at least three main shortcomings in terms of the normative framework. First, in the CAC, the risk assessment policy must be framed in advance of the risk assessment.[49] Once the risk assessment policy has been framed, the standard of sufficiency for regulatory intervention

[46] Statements of Principle Relating to the Role of Food Safety Risk Assessment, 'Procedural Manual', note 49: 211, para. 2; Statements of Principle Concerning the Role of Science in the Codex Decision-Making Process and the Extent to which Other Factors are Taken into Account, 'Procedural Manual', 209, para. 1; Working Principles for Risk Analysis for Application in the Framework of the CAC, 'Procedural Manual', paras. 4 and 28.

[47] Statements of Principle Concerning the Role of Science in the Codex Decision-Making Process and the Extent to which Other Factors are Taken into Account, 'Procedural Manual', 209.

[48] Statements of Principle Relating to the Role of Food Safety Risk Assessment, 'Procedural Manual', 211, para. 1.

[49] Working Principles for Risk Analysis for Application in the Framework of the CAC, 'Procedural Manual', para. 14.

cannot be adjusted in light of further justice-related aspects from the broader factual context not considered in the risk assessment policy. Second, although the CAC in principle allows for engaging expertise beyond that provided by the natural sciences and allows risk managers to react to OLFs at the stage of risk management, the CAC Procedural Manual is conspicuously silent on several accounts. It does not consider how different forms of expertise are to be aggregated into one factual basis of scientific soundness, which factors other than health and fair practices in trade could be considered legitimate, and how they are to be weighed against each other. Third, while textually the framing of risk is not limited to health risks, and thus economic impacts and factors other than health and trade impacts can play a role as OLFs in risk management, the practice of the CAC has not yet evolved to taking on board experts from a much broader range of scientific domains.

10.4 Conclusion

On the basis of theories of deliberative democracy and equal respect for the moral autonomy of individuals, the normative framework provides systematic justification for two claims. First, normative justification by the policy maker is called for at each step in risk policy making. Even the step of evaluating whether or not there is a sufficient factual basis to regulate requires normative justification by policy makers and factual justification by experts. Normative justification is necessary because risk assessment provided by experts is not necessarily correct for each individual, given that experts employ models that simplify reality, employ a singular definition of risk and provide an assessment across a population. Furthermore, the amount of expert evidence is influenced by available funding and the ease with which a particular hazard can be researched. The resulting unequal distribution in levels of protection calls for normative justification. Normative justification for risk policy making must account for these justice-related impacts and requires consideration of the complete factual context of the regulatory problem. The second claim follows directly from the preceding claim. The issues of justice in addition to health impacts raise factual questions of their own that are in need of additional specific expert assessment because such assessment can show that normative propositions are truthful insofar as they are based on a factual assessment most likely to be correct.

Concerning the SPS Agreement, two main points need to be highlighted: first, food-borne risk is framed narrowly entailing the exclusion of other dimensions of justice and associated expertise from showing the insufficiency of evidence under Article 5.7; and, second, the differences in framing risk and the quantum of proof between food-borne risk on the one hand, and animal-borne, plant-borne and pest-borne risk on the other hand are arbitrary from the point of view of justice because the source of exposure is irrelevant.

Concerning the CAC, I suggested that the formulation of risk assessment policy potentially allows a broad array of normative justifications alongside factual elements to be taken into account, but that the actual practice of the CAC falls short of this ideal.

In conclusion, experts remain undervalued as policy legitimizers in the SPS Agreement and, to a lesser extent, also in the CAC, given the failure to involve a sufficiently broad range of experts who could address all justice-related aspects in risk policy making, for which the policy maker owes a deontological justification. Under the SPS Agreement, natural science experts on the risks framed by the Agreement are important. The Agreement delegates decision-making power on food safety risks to them because factual knowledge amounting to a risk assessment will preclude the policy maker from setting more conservative ALOPs in response to broader justice concerns as long as the risk assessment is not called into epistemological doubt from within its own discipline. More experts relevant to considerations of justice-related impacts from the broader factual context are essential for the risk assessment of animal-borne, plant-borne and pest-borne risks. *US–Poultry* gave experts decision-making power over the ALOP and *Japan–Apples* did likewise over the normative evaluation of different risk mitigation measures. The AB's decision in *Continued Suspension* seems to recognize that experts ought merely to be advisors. However, unless the framing of risk and the specificity requirement of risk assessment is adjusted, the revised role of experts remains partially an illusion.

11

The role of experts in environmental and health-related trade disputes in the WTO: deconstructing decision-making processes

LUKASZ GRUSZCZYNSKI

11.1 Introduction

Participation of scientific experts has become a characteristic feature of contemporary decision-making processes.[1] This widespread involvement of experts results not only from the increasing complexity of issues that need to be tackled, but can also be linked to the legitimizing role attributed to science, which is conventionally seen as a form of higher rationality. The presence of experts is particularly visible in the field of environmental and health protection, where they are expected to identify and characterize existing and emerging risks and validate the regulatory solutions chosen to control such risks.

The role played by experts is not limited to the national level; it is equally important at the international level. First, many contemporary health and environmental risks transgress national boundaries and can be effectively addressed and managed only through international cooperation. Second, the use of scientific experts can be regarded as a mechanism for improving the legitimacy of political and legal decisions taken by international institutions. Since they lack the democratic credentials that justify the exercise of power at the domestic level, international institutions need other compensatory mechanisms. Gráinne de Búrca has identified three broad groups of such mechanisms: (i) the quality of decision makers, i.e., expertise or special

This research was financed by the Foundation for Polish Science within its Housing Programme.

[1] The notion of decision making is understood here broadly and encompasses both adjudication and policy making. Although there are important differences between these two categories, the issues connected with experts' participation seem to be similar in both cases. Consequently, the term 'decision makers' in this chapter also encompasses adjudicators, unless stated otherwise.

qualifications possessed by the actors involved in the decision-making process and their independence from political influences;[2] (ii) the quality of decision-making processes, i.e., transparency, quality of deliberation and the inclusiveness of the processes; and (iii) the output of such processes, that is, the 'quality, efficiency or general acceptability of the norms that have been created'.[3] The first two mechanisms aim to improve input legitimacy (the process by which a decision is arrived at), while the third is used to test output legitimacy (i.e., substantive quality and acceptability of a final decision). There is a positive correlation between these two aspects of legitimacy since an outcome is always related to the underlying processes.

The legal system of the World Trade Organization (WTO) also mandates, either implicitly or explicitly, recourse to science to assess the legality of national measures that have an impact on international trade. The most elaborated framework is provided by the Agreement on the Application of Sanitary and Phytosanitary Measures (hereinafter 'the SPS Agreement'), which openly designates science as a criterion for distinguishing between permitted and prohibited sanitary and phytosanitary (SPS) measures.[4] This agreement also requires the involvement of scientific experts, who assist the WTO dispute settlement bodies in understanding the technical and scientific aspects of national measures.

This chapter analyses the organization of scientific experts' advice as well as the role of experts in the settlement of SPS-related trade disputes, linking these issues with the problem of input legitimacy. In particular, it argues that there are, as far as the participation of experts in the WTO proceedings is concerned, certain problematic aspects in the practice of dispute settlement bodies. The potential challenges relate to various issues, such as modes of consultation, guarantees for impartiality of experts or the communication process that takes place between panellist and scientist. The chapter submits that failures in those areas may compromise two compensatory mechanisms that are used to ensure input legitimacy and therefore affect the overall legitimacy of the rendered decisions. This area of research has received only limited attention in the literature, as most scholars have focused on the substantive rules (e.g., requirement of risk assessment). Although such an analysis is

[2] See also Klabbers, Chapter 5, this volume (discussing virtues as necessary element of expertise).

[3] G. de Búrca, 'Developing Democracy Beyond the State', *Columbia Journal of Transnational Law*, 46 (2007–8), 245–51.

[4] Articles 2.2 and 5.1 of the SPS Agreement.

essential, the *process* that leads to a final decision appears to be equally important, since the output of adjudication can only be as good as the underlying process.[5] The WTO Appellate Body (AB) also recognized the importance of processes when it observed that 'the manner in which [experts'] opinions are solicited and evaluated can have a significant bearing on a panel's consideration of the evidence and its review of a domestic measure, especially in cases ... involving highly complex scientific issues'.[6]

The chapter is organized as follows: it starts with a description of the scientific requirements of the SPS Agreement and procedural rules governing the participation of experts in SPS proceedings (sections 11.2 and 11.3). The next two sections (sections 11.4 and 11.5) identify various expert-related problems that have emerged in existing practice and inquire into the impact of the applicable standard of review on the role played by experts. The last section draws some overall conclusions on the relation between experts' participation and the legitimacy of decisions rendered by the WTO dispute settlement bodies.

Two preliminary issues deserve some explanation. First, while the discussion here is limited to experts' participation in the context of the SPS Agreement, the chapter recognizes that disputes that arise under other agreements, such as the Agreement on Technical Barriers to Trade, may also require recourse to specialists' knowledge. It is assumed that the potential problems are similar to those discussed here. Second, in the WTO context, experts play different roles and different types of expertise may be called upon. Panellists and AB members are themselves experts in trade issues. They may seek relevant information and technical advice on various issues. However, since in SPS practice the technical advice has been limited to natural science (e.g., biochemistry, epidemiology), this analysis is focused on this category of science.

11.2 Science and the SPS Agreement

Dispute settling within the WTO regime is assigned to the Dispute Settlement Body (DSB), where all WTO members are represented. In practice, disputes are decided by ad hoc panels and the standing AB, and

[5] See, e.g., C. Joerges and J. Neyer, 'Deliberative Supranationalism Revisited', EUI Working Paper Law No. 2006/20; Herwig, Chapter 10, this volume.

[6] Appellate Body Report, *United States–Continued Suspension of Obligations in the EC–Hormones Dispute*, WT/DS320/AB/R, adopted 14 November 2008, para. 436.

the role of the DSB is limited to formal approval of their decisions. Although both the panels and the AB are responsible for the administration of justice, their tasks are different. The panels are the sole fact-finders in dispute settlement proceedings (including the assessment of scientific evidence presented by the parties). A review of the AB is limited to issues of law covered in the panel report and legal interpretations developed by the panels.

The aim of the SPS Agreement is to limit the negative impact of national SPS regulations[7] on international trade, while providing WTO members with a wide margin of regulatory discretion. Consequently, although members are expected to observe certain requirements when introducing and maintaining SPS measures, they remain free to establish whatever level of protection they consider appropriate. The uniqueness of the SPS Agreement is its strong reliance on science and scientific expertise. Each SPS measure that does not conform to international standards has to be based on scientific principles and cannot be maintained without sufficient scientific evidence. This general obligation translates into the requirement to complete a scientific risk assessment to justify an SPS measure. The existence of risk may be expressed both in quantitative and qualitative terms. Quantitative measurement provides information on the statistical probability of the occurrence of adverse effects (e.g., 1:1,000); qualitative measurement concentrates on the possibility of the materialization of adverse effects (e.g., low, medium, high). The SPS case law has also recognized that risk assessment may be based on both mainstream science and on minority scientific opinions.[8] Moreover, if the scientific evidence is insufficient to perform an adequate risk assessment, a WTO member may adopt a provisional measure based on the available pertinent data.

Some argue that choosing science as a benchmark for deciding on the legality of national measures has important advantages.[9] Indeed, the use of science may be seen as a way of legitimizing decisions made by the panels through all three mechanisms identified by de Búrca. First,

[7] SPS measures are those measures that are directed against certain specific risks enumerated in the Agreement. This includes food safety, animal health and plant health risks (Annex A(1) of the SPS Agreement).

[8] Appellate Body Report, *EC–Measures Concerning Meat and Meat Products*, WT/DS26/AB/R, WT/DS48/AB/R, adopted 13 February 1998, para. 194.

[9] See generally G. Shaffer, 'Risk, Science and Law in the WTO: The Centrality of Institutional Choice (Proceedings of the 104th Annual Meeting of the American Society of International Law (2010)', Minnesota Legal Studies Research Paper No. 2010/20.

science can be regarded as a neutral criterion, thus providing a useful tool for assessing the competing claims made by the parties to a dispute. As noted by Haas, 'technical authority commanded by epistemic communities possesses some sort of neutrality/impartiality, which is attained through criteria for validating knowledge'.[10] This neutrality, by focusing on technical grounds, helps to depoliticize a dispute and ensures the quality of decision-making processes and decision makers (i.e., quality of deliberation and independence from political influences). This, in turn, improves input legitimacy. Second, science can give a panel's decision some additional persuasive force, emanating from the epistemic authority that is conventionally attached to science. An issue is decided in a specific way not because of any subjective preferences of a panel, but because science dictates the outcome (and as a consequence it improves the output of a decision-making process). Of course, the above understanding may be challenged on different grounds.[11] Without going into further details, as the subject would require a separate and extensive examination, it has to be recognized that science is not as neutral a criterion as one would expect. Scientific risk assessment is also infiltrated by non-scientific assumptions, policy considerations and value judgements.[12] Highly politicized disputes tend to remain politicized, irrespective of the criteria that one uses (scientific or non-scientific).

11.3 Law and practice of involving experts in SPS proceedings

WTO law explicitly acknowledges the possibility of engaging experts possessing specific technical and scientific knowledge in the dispute settlement process. The central provision in this context is Article 13 of the Understanding on Rules and Procedures Governing the Settlement of Disputes (DSU), which sets the limits for the investigative powers for WTO panels. As a general rule, a panel may seek information and technical advice from any individual or body that it deems appropriate (Article 13.1). In particular, it may request an advisory report from

[10] P. M. Haas, 'Epistemic Communities' in D. Bodansky, J. Brunnée and E. Hey (eds.), *The Oxford Handbook of International Environmental Law* (Oxford University Press, 2007), 791–806, at 802.

[11] See Werner, Chapter 3, this volume.

[12] See, e.g., D. Winickoff, S. Jasanoff, L. Busch, R. Grove-White and B. Wynne, 'Adjudicating the GM Food Wars: Science, Risk, and Democracy in World Trade Law', *Yale Journal of International Law*, 30 (2005), 81–123, at 95.

a special expert review group relating to any factual issue concerning a scientific or other technical matter raised by the parties to a dispute (Article 13.2). Appendix 4 of the DSU sets out special rules for the establishment of such a group and its procedures.

This general rule of the DSU is repeated in the SPS Agreement, which provides in its Article 11.2 that in disputes:

> involving scientific or technical issues, a panel should seek advice from experts chosen by the panel in consultation with the parties to the dispute. To this end, the panel may, when it deems it appropriate, establish an advisory technical experts group [another name for an expert review group], or consult the relevant international organizations, at the request of either party to the dispute or on its own initiative.

In practice, all SPS panels have decided to consult individual experts rather than to rely on expert review groups. However, since neither the DSU nor the SPS Agreement provides rules on consulting individual experts, the rules governing their input have been developed on an ad hoc basis. The early reports included very general guidelines, and the first elaborated guidance only appeared in 1998 in the *Japan–Agriculture Products* case.[13] In 2008, the panel in *US/Canada–Continued Suspension*[14] adopted a separate document that specifically addressed the provision of scientific and technical advice by individuals;[15] in *Australia–Apples* this aspect was governed by two documents that clarified further the applicable procedure.[16]

Based on the existing practice, the consultation process may be divided into four steps. It starts with the determination of the necessary fields of expertise and is followed by the identification of potential candidates. The panel normally decides on the areas of required expertise on the basis of the initial submissions by the parties. Panels tend to request specialized international bodies to indicate the persons who could serve as experts in a particular dispute (e.g., the Codex Alimentarius Commission (hereinafter

[13] Panel Report, *Japan–Measures Affecting Agricultural Products*, WT/DS76/R, adopted 19 March 1999.

[14] Panel Report, *United States–Continued Suspension of Obligations in the EC–Hormones Dispute*, WT/DS320/R, adopted 14 November 2008.

[15] The Working Procedures for Consultations with Scientific and/or Technical Experts (Annex A-5).

[16] Panel Report, *Australia–Measures Affecting the Importation of Apples from New Zealand*, WT/DS367/R, adopted 17 December 2010, Working Procedures for the Panel (Annex A-3) and Procedures for the Panel's Meeting with the Experts and Parties and the Panel's Second Substantive Meeting (Annex A-5).

'Codex') or the World Organization for Animal Health). Panels may also request (and have done so in practice) the parties to suggest potential candidates.[17]

During the second step, the panel will choose from a pool of available experts those to advise in a particular dispute. Except for the *EC–Hormones* case, where the parties were given the opportunity to nominate one expert each, experts are chosen by the panel in consultation with the parties.[18] While the opinions expressed by the parties are not binding, in practice, they are taken seriously and panels tend to avoid nominations that are opposed by one of the parties,[19] unless the objection is not sufficiently serious to undermine confidence in a particular expert.[20] As a standard practice, panels do not appoint experts who are nationals of any of the parties to the dispute unless the parties agree otherwise or the need for specialized expertise justifies it.[21] The selected experts must be independent and impartial, have no direct or indirect conflicts of interest, and respect the confidentiality of the proceedings.[22] To this end, experts are expected to sign special disclosure agreements.[23]

During the third step, the panel will draft questions relating to the specific scientific or technical aspects of a dispute. The parties are again consulted at this stage. Experts are expected to provide their answers in writing, but only to those questions that they feel competent to reply to. All experts are supplied, on a confidential basis, with the relevant parts of the parties' submissions. If it appears that some issues remain uncovered, a panel may prepare a supplemental list of experts, again based on prior consultation with the parties.[24] In practice, some questions are answered

[17] See, e.g., Panel Report, *Australia–Measures Affecting Importation of Salmon*, WT/DS18/R, adopted 6 November 1998, para. 6.2.

[18] To enable parties to have a meaningful participation in the appointment process, a panel normally solicits CVs from expert candidates and passes them on to the parties (e.g., Panel Report, *EC Measures Concerning Meat and Meat Products (Hormones)*, WT/DS26/R/USA, adopted 13 February 1998, para. VI.6).

[19] Panel Report, *Australia–Apples*, para. 1.26.

[20] Panel Report, *European Communities–Measures Affecting the Approval and Marketing of Biotech Products*, WT/DS291/R, WT/DS292/R and WT/DS293/R, adopted 21 November 2006, para. 7.21.

[21] Panel Report, *Japan–Agricultural Products*, para. 6.2.

[22] Rules of Conduct for the Understanding on Rules and Procedures Governing the Settlement of Disputes, WT/DSB/RC1, 11 December 1996.

[23] Self-Disclosure Requirements by Covered Persons Envisaged by the Rules of Conduct for the Understanding on Rules and Procedures Governing the Settlement of Disputes, 11 December 1996, WT/DSB/RC1.

[24] See, e.g., Panel Report, *EC–Biotech Products*, para. 7.27.

by all experts, while others only by some of them or even only by one. The answers are transferred to all parties and the other experts, who may comment on them. This procedure provides the experts with the opportunity to reconsider their replies and change their answers if they find this appropriate.

The final step is an oral hearing attended by the parties and experts. During this hearing, the panel asks questions aimed at clarifying those issues which remain unclear or contradictory. Parties can also cross-examine experts, but this process is mediated by the panel. If the panel is satisfied with the outcome, it may proceed to the next phase of the proceedings. If not, either an additional hearing or another round of written questions/answers might be arranged. Once the fact-finding process is closed, the panel will draft its report, the descriptive part of which will be sent out to the experts for final comments. The experts are expected to check whether their views have been properly reflected in the report. If not, the panel introduces the necessary changes. All the experts' answers to the panel's questions, as well as the transcripts from the oral hearings, are published alongside the panel's report.

11.4 Challenges to input legitimacy in the consultation process

The SPS case law demonstrates that specific aspects of the consultation process may be controversial. Potential problems include the way in which expert advice is sought (i.e., individual experts versus advisory expert groups (section 11.4.1)), guarantees of the quality and comprehensiveness of the scientific advice (i.e., the impartiality and objectivity of experts and their diversity (sections 11.4.2 and 11.4.3)) and the process of information exchange between experts and panels (section 11.4.4). These problems may undermine the legitimacy of the decisions rendered by WTO dispute settlement bodies by affecting the first two compensatory mechanisms discussed above.

11.4.1 Individual experts versus advisory expert groups

As mentioned above, a panel deciding an SPS dispute may either consult individual experts or establish an advisory expert group. In practice, all panels have preferred the first option. This approach can be justified on different grounds. First, the involvement of individual experts safeguards members' rights by allowing the panel to hear different scientific opinions (and each of them may in principle constitute a valid justification for a national SPS measure) as opposed to being confronted with a consensus text drafted by an expert review group. According to the *US–Continued Suspension* panel, 'an expert review group would only agree on a minimum common position, thus depriving the panel of a full picture of the problems'.[25] Second, the same panel held that the establishment of a review group would only make sense if its individual members had expertise in all or at least the majority of the required fields of competence. Since the extent of scientific advice sought in the *US–Continued Suspension* case was broad, it would have been difficult (if not impossible) to find a group of scientists with comprehensive knowledge of all the relevant subjects.[26] This difficulty reduces the value of an expert group, since in the end it will be individual members who will provide answers in any case. Third, the establishment of an expert group will most likely result in considerable delays in the settlement of disputes. The group would need to produce a separate report with the possibility for parties to comment on its first draft, and would be entitled to seek information from external sources.[27] As a consequence, panels may fail to meet the requirement of Article 3.3 of the DSU, that is, the prompt settlement of disputes.

The panels' preference for individual experts may also be motivated by more systemic reasons. As noted by Christoforou, such a choice indicates 'the way panels view the relationship of science and law [and] the role that panels should play in resolving scientific trade disputes'.[28] The appointment of individual experts allows a panel to control the overall dispute settlement process by weighing competing scientific views and choosing the one(s) that is (are) the most persuasive. The use of an expert group would considerably limit this discretion, as in most cases a panel would feel compelled to accept the report produced by such a group because of its superior epistemic value.[29]

While the use of an expert advisory group may be problematic, having the panel as the ultimate arbiter of competing scientific claims presented by individual experts seems to be even more challenging. WTO panels do not possess sufficient scientific literacy to decide which experts' views are

25 Panel Report, *US–Continued Suspension*, para. 7.71. 26 *Ibid.*

27 J. Pauwelyn, 'The Use of Experts in WTO Dispute Settlement', *International and Comparative Law Quarterly*, 51 (2002), 325–64, at 329.

28 T. Christoforou, 'Settlement of Science-Based Trade Disputes in the WTO: A Critical Review of the Developing Case Law in the Face of Scientific Uncertainty', *New York University Environmental Law Journal*, 8 (2000), 622–48, at 629.

29 Pauwelyn, 'The Use of Experts', at 328.

correct or scientifically more persuasive.[30] The SPS panels also seem to overestimate their skills in assessing the value of dissenting scientific opinions. Practice shows that the right of WTO members to base a measure on minority scientific views may remain theoretical, with panels tending, despite many statements to the contrary, to ascertain the 'best' or mainstream science.[31] Consequently, the potential for a mistaken finding resulting from misinterpretation or underestimation of certain facts or scientific claims is increased when consultations are based on the advice of individual experts.[32] This in turn may affect the quality of the decision-making process, which may undermine the legitimacy of the ultimate decisions. On the other hand, one could argue that the appointment of an expert advisory group would enhance the legitimacy of the decision-making process. Note that although individual experts are selected with the aim of covering relatively narrow fields of competence, in practice, they respond to questions which extend beyond their initially identified areas of expertise. One may therefore expect a meaningful dialogue between experts within an expert advisory group as well (since individual experts with narrowly identified expertise engage in discussion on other issues anyway). It also seems that some additional delay is a small sacrifice for a qualitative improvement of final judgements. It is after all preferable to have a sound rather than a quick verdict.

11.4.2 Criteria for guaranteeing the impartiality of experts

As noted above, the panels have introduced a number of criteria for ensuring the impartiality of experts. However, one issue has proven to be particularly problematic. The SPS Agreement requires scientific justification only for those measures that do not conform to international standards. This raises the question whether the scientists involved in the

30 See the discussion in section 4.4; and S. Jasanoff, *Science at the Bar: Law, Science and Technology in America* (Cambridge, MA: Harvard University Press, 1997), at 42–68.

31 See, e.g., Panel Report, *EC–Biotech Products*, para. 7.3300 (when examining the existence of insufficiency of scientific evidence for a safeguard measure adopted by France). In any case, a report of an expert group may equally include minority views, presenting them either as one of the available explanations or as dissenting opinions.

32 As noted by Christoforou, 'recourse to an expert review group is likely to provide an intellectually systematic, coherent, and non-polarizing approach to address and resolve scientific issues involved'. Christoforou, 'Settlement of Science-Based Trade Disputes in the WTO', at 640–1.

adoption of specific international standards should serve as experts in disputes over national measures diverging from these standards.

The early SPS case law did not consider this involvement a problem. Although the European Communities[33] argued in the *EC–Hormones* case that such experts should be excluded,[34] the panel appointed three experts who had close ties with the Codex and the Joint FAO/WHO Expert Committee on Food Additives (JECFA), the body that carries out risk assessment for international standards on several hormones. On appeal, the AB did not discuss the EC's argument and only stated that the rules pertaining to the selection of experts were agreed upon by the parties. The consent of the parties (to be bound by the relevant rules rather than to appoint specific experts), in the opinion of the AB, guaranteed the impartiality of the scientific advice.[35] A similar approach was taken in the *US–Continued Suspension* case when, after considering the concerns expressed by the EC, the panel refused to exclude experts solely on the basis of their ties with the JECFA. The panel justified its decision by the epistemic qualities of the individuals concerned, who were characterized as 'internationally recognized specialists'. This characterization immunized them from any prejudice. The panel also explained that the case required the involvement of specialists who understood the JECFA scientific framework.[36] It added, a bit naïvely, that:

> scientists would readily admit that science is constantly evolving and the fact that new studies are peer reviewed is evidence that assessing new ideas and findings is part of scientific work. Assuming that scientists may lack objectivity because they participated in the preparation and drafting of JECFA's risk assessments on the hormones at issue would call into question the whole principle of peer review.[37]

This time, the AB did not agree with the panel. It found that the experts' previous affiliation with the JECFA was an important factor to be taken into account when assessing their impartiality. It held that the qualifications and knowledge of the experts were not in themselves sufficient

[33] Until 30 November 2009, the European Union was officially known in the WTO as the European Communities (EC). This nomenclature changed with the introduction of the Treaty of Lisbon.

[34] Panel Report, *EC–Hormones*, para. VI.3.

[35] See also Christoforou, 'Settlement of Science-Based Trade Disputes in the WTO'.

[36] Panel Report, *US–Continued Suspension*, para. 7.85 (being a point of reference for many of the arguments made by the parties).

[37] *Ibid.*, para. 6.22.

guarantees.[38] It also noted that both of the experts challenged by the EC had close institutional connections with the JECFA[39] and used the JECFA's work as a benchmark against which the EC's risk assessment was probed and judged.[40] These elements gave rise to justifiable doubts as to the experts' independence or impartiality, and led the AB to conclude that the panel failed to guarantee the necessary due process rights to the EC.[41]

The approach proposed by the AB in the *US–Continued Suspension* case should be welcomed. It is clear that 'scientists coming from [specific] organizations may be unfairly biased in favor of maintaining their organization's standards and recommendations'.[42] Consequently, previous affiliation should be regarded as an important element when assessing the existence of potential conflicts of interest. Using experts who are potentially biased also negatively affects one of the compensatory mechanisms and reduces the legitimacy of the WTO dispute settlement system.

11.4.3 Ensuring expert diversity

A panel identifies the areas requiring expert advice at an early stage of the proceedings. The number of experts is determined in light of the issues on which advice is sought, as well as on the basis of the competences of the selected individuals. Unsurprisingly, both the nature of the expertise required and the number of experts to be involved may generate controversies between the parties. As noted by Timura, 'selection of one type of expert over another may favor a particular party's arguments',[43] because a specific scientific or technical problem may be looked at from different perspectives, all of which may be legitimate. In this context, Timura refers to the *Asbestos* case as an example, where the parties disagreed over the kind of expertise that was required. Canada, claiming that a French measure banning the marketing of asbestos

[38] Appellate Body Report, *US–Continued Suspension*, para. 459. [39] *Ibid.*, para. 460.

[40] *Ibid.*, para. 467. Dr Boisseau observed, for example, that: 'considering the conclusions of JECFA . . . it can be said that the scientific evidence relied upon in the SCVPH [Scientific Committee on Veterinary Measures relating to Public Health] Opinions does not support the conclusion that the carcinogenic effects of these five hormones are related to a mechanism other than hormonal activity'.

[41] *Ibid.*, para. 482.

[42] Christoforou, 'Settlement of Science-Based Trade Disputes in the WTO', at 630.

[43] C. Timura, 'Cross-examining Expertise in the WTO Dispute Settlement Process', *Michigan Journal of International Law*, 23 (2002), 709–32, at 720.

products was incompatible with WTO rules, favoured the appointment of experts specialized in the comparative toxicity of different types of asbestos fibres and substitute fibres, as well as in risk management of the controlled use of chrysotile asbestos.[44] The EC was in favour of the appointment of cancer epidemiologists, including specialists on asbestos-caused cancers.[45] Similarly, in the *US–Continued Suspension* case, the USA disagreed with the EC about the need to appoint an expert with experience in animal science, including good veterinary practices, pertaining to the administration of growth promotion hormones.[46] Thus, a preference for a specific type of expertise may reflect deliberate and strategic choices of the parties aimed at influencing the ultimate outcome of a dispute.

Procurement of the most complete coverage of different fields of expertise, to the extent practically possible, contributes to the quality of the decision-making process (and as a consequence to the overall legitimacy of a final decision). It also guarantees the inclusiveness of the process and helps to neutralize strategies by the parties aimed at influencing the outcome of a dispute by framing particular scientific problems from specific perspectives. At the same time, it must be admitted that including too many areas of expertise may be inadvisable as this can lead to a complete paralysis of the settlement process. An emblematic example is provided by the *Biotech* case, where the EC listed forty-four different fields of required expertise.[47] One solution would be to have experts only in those areas that are identified by the panel as the most crucial for the resolution of a dispute.

A related problem concerns the number of experts. Too many will slow down the resolution of a dispute and/or pose practical problems (e.g., finding the requisite number of experts) and too few will decrease the quality of the proceedings. A moderate approach would be to appoint at least two individuals each representing a specific field of expertise. This will allow a panel to draw a broader picture of the issues involved by the inclusion of, or at least by facilitating the inclusion of, different perspectives. Such an approach will also help to implement the standards envisaged in the SPS case law, i.e., the possibility of basing a measure on

[44] Panel Report, *European Communities–Measures Affecting Asbestos and Asbestos-Containing Products*, WT/DS135/R and Add. 1, adopted 5 April 2001, para. 5.2

[45] *Ibid.* [46] Panel Report, *US–Continued Suspension*, para. 7.91.

[47] Panel Report, *EC–Biotech Products*, para. 7.20 (to list just some of them: agrobiodiversity, DNA amplification, ecology, malherborology, phytopathology and soil sciences).

minority scientific views. In fact, there seems to be a tendency to involve larger numbers of experts. The *EC–Hormones* panel was advised by five individuals. This number dropped in subsequent disputes (e.g., *Australia–Salmon* and *Japan–Apples*), but later rose to six experts in *EC–Biotech Products* and *US/Canada–Continued Suspension* and seven in *Australia–Apples*. The last case is particularly interesting when one compares it with the *Japan–Apples* dispute. Although the scientific complexity involved in the cases was comparable, the panel almost doubled the number of experts. This may have been the result of the more sophisticated nature of the arguments put forward by the parties, but the need to cover all necessary fields of expertise, optimally with two experts on each issue, also seems important. Such an approach gives a panel the chance to obtain a fuller spectrum of available scientific views and improves the quality of the decision-making process by making it more inclusive.

11.4.4 Communicative process between panellists and experts

Expert participation in WTO dispute settlement proceedings also poses challenges to the communicative processes that take place between the panel and its experts. The basic premise underlying these challenges relates to the differences between legal and scientific language, and their supporting logics. Judicial decisions are expected to provide prompt and definitive answers to a legal controversy. This definitiveness is ensured by the mechanism known as the burden of persuasion. It is supposed to operate as a scale, i.e., the arguments of one of the parties must attain a certain weight over those of the other party in order for a particular claim to be established as true.[48] Moreover, in legal disputes, the facts have already occurred and the evidence may, in theory, be precisely weighed. In legal decisions involving scientific evidence, however, the evidence is never complete inasmuch as science may be seen as a process of falsification, where particular claims are constantly tested and valid only until they are refuted.[49] Thus, regulatory decisions that rely on scientific

48 D. Crawford-Brown, J. Pauwelyn and K. Smith, 'Environmental Risk, Precaution, and Scientific Rationality in the Context of WTO/NAFTA Trade Rules', *Risk Analysis*, 24 (2004), 461–9, at 462.

49 A. Eliason, 'Science versus Law in WTO Jurisprudence: The (Mis)Interpretation of the Scientific Process and the (In)Sufficiency of Scientific Evidence in *EC–Biotech*', *International Law and Politics*, 41 (2009), 341–406.

determinations may be seen as a snapshot of the scientific landscape at a particular moment in time. In the end, science, unlike law, does not provide definitive answers. This difference was captured by a US judge, who said that 'there are important differences between the quest for truth in the courtroom and the quest for truth in the laboratory. Scientific conclusions are subject to perpetual revisions. Law, on the other hand, must resolve disputes finally and quickly'.[50]

A practical consequence of these differences for WTO dispute settlement is that the answers of experts are frequently phrased in a tentative manner in order to reflect existing uncertainties. Consequently, a description of a particular risk may be phrased as follows:

> exposure to [X] carries with it a probability of adverse effect that varies from person to person, but is generally in the range of . . . one in a million to ten in a million; this range is subject to uncertainty and so the true range may be from one in a million to a hundred in a million, or may even be zero.[51]

This obviously makes the task of a panel difficult, because it must decide whether a particular SPS measure could be deemed necessary to mitigate a specific risk or whether there is any risk at all.

Even if there are no qualifications in experts' replies, they may be formulated in a manner that is not readily translatable into binary legal logic.[52] This difference in narrative creates a risk of misunderstanding by a panel. In particular, it may encourage a panel to simplify a specific problem or to choose an answer that appears to it to be the most direct and straightforward, thus corresponding more closely to legal logic.

The discussion on genotoxicity in *US/Canada–Continued Suspension* may serve as a good example. There was a fundamental disagreement between the parties as to whether there existed a safety threshold for oestradiol-17β. If there were no such threshold, as the EC argued, then no safe level for intakes from hormone residues could be established, and the fact that the doses used in the growth promotion process were low became irrelevant. Dr Boisseau was straightforward and held that the scientific evidence referred to by the EC did not demonstrate that there

50 *Daubert* v. *Merell Dow Pharms., Inc.*, 509 US 579, 596–7 (1993).

51 Crawford-Brown, Pauwelyn and Smith, 'Environmental Risk, Precaution, and Scientific Rationality', at 463.

52 See also M. Wagner, 'Law Talk v. Science Talk: The Languages of Law and Science in WTO Proceedings', *Fordham International Law Journal*, 35 (2011), 151–200.

was no threshold for oestradiol-17β.[53] Dr Cogliano was more ambiguous, noting that:

> the EC's statement that a threshold cannot be identified reflects their view of genotoxic mechanisms, just as the contrary statement that there is a threshold and that this threshold is above the levels found in meat residues reflects how Canada and the US view genotoxic mechanisms. Neither statement has been demonstrated by the scientific evidence, rather, they are different assumptions that each party uses in their interpretation of the available evidence.[54]

The panel agreed with Dr Boisseau's straightforward answer and found, without making any further inquiries, that there was no threshold for oestradiol-17β.

Another problem that may emerge in the communication process relates to the distinct methodologies employed by law and science. Law attaches great importance to the words used in a legal instrument under examination, i.e., a treaty. Different expressions are expected to have different meanings. For scientists, this may not be so obvious – they may not even realize that the specific wording in their answers could have far-reaching legal consequences. A discussion about 'possibility' in the context of risk assessment provides an example. As mentioned, the case law, based on the SPS treaty language, distinguishes between the assessment of possibility or potential (another name for possibility) for food-borne risks, and probability for quarantine risks. As explained by the AB in the *US–Continued Suspension* case, 'to examine the "potential" for adverse effects is to ask whether those adverse effects could ever occur'.[55] Probability, on the other hand, calls for an assessment of likelihood, which involves a higher threshold than possibility.[56] It is not certain whether this distinction was clear to the experts. One of them observed in the *Salmon* case that 'the requirement of a quarantine risk assessment is to evaluate the probability of risk ... [as] one can *always* construct a *possible* infection transmission scenario, however improbable and therefore demonstration of the possibility of successful transmission'.[57] If experts are so uncomfortable with the language of the SPS Agreement

[53] Panel Report, *US–Continued Suspension, Annex D, Replies of the Scientific Experts to Questions Posed by the Panel*, para. 182.

[54] *Ibid.*, para. 186. [55] Appellate Body Report, *US–Continued Suspension*, para. 572.

[56] See, e.g., Appellate Body Report, *Australia–Measures Affecting Importation of Salmon*, WT/DS18/AB/R, adopted 6 November 1998, para. 123.

[57] Panel Report, *Australia–Salmon*, para. 8.79, emphasis in original.

(e.g., 'almost anything is possible'), it is legitimate to ask whether their answers, when it comes to food-borne risks, really concern the specific threshold required in the Agreement.

Similarly, in some cases panellists tend to interpret non-scientific terms as objectively verifiable categories of a scientific nature. This is well illustrated by the analysis performed in the context of Article 5.7 of the SPS Agreement, i.e., whether the evidence is (in)sufficient to perform a risk assessment.[58] The *Biotech* panel rejected the idea that insufficiency, as a relativist concept, is determined not only by the quantity and quality of scientific evidence but also by other non-scientific considerations, such as the level of protection sought by the regulator. According to the *US–Continued Suspension* panel, the assessment of insufficiency is an objective determination that takes place in a purely scientific process isolated from non-scientific elements.[59] In a similar vein, the *Biotech* and *Suspension* panels saw only the temporal dimension of insufficiency, i.e., that insufficiency may re-emerge as a consequence of scientific developments that call into question previous evidence.[60] The spatial aspect, namely the possibility that insufficiency is recognized in some jurisdictions while not in others, was not recognized by either panel. However, as noted in the literature, 'there is no scientific definition of terms such as acceptable, reasonable and sufficient',[61] e.g., whether a given level of confidence is sufficient to establish a certain fact. These are normative terms whose appreciation depends on factors that are not reducible to scientific logic. The appreciations of these norms are instead subjective judgements of experts reflecting their attitudes towards particular risks, the values of particular communities in which the experts interact and the nature of the risk assessment. Consequently, 'evidence deemed reliable enough to generate a sufficient risk assessment in one regulatory context may fail in another context because of the different concerns, risk frames and particular circumstances'.[62]

This conceptual morass (i.e., considering non-scientific terms as objective categories of scientific nature) has had serious consequences

[58] For a more detailed discussion, see L. Gruszczynski, *Regulating Health and Environmental Risks under WTO Law: A Critical Analysis of the SPS Agreement* (Oxford University Press, 2010), 191–7.

[59] Panel Report, *US–Continued Suspension*, paras. 7.603–7.612.

[60] See, e.g., *ibid.*, para. 7.645.

[61] Crawford-Brown, Pauwelyn and Smith, 'Environmental Risk, Precaution, and Scientific Rationality', at 463.

[62] Winickoff et al., 'Adjudicating the GM Food Wars', at 114.

for the communication processes between the panels and their experts. For example, the *Biotech* panel, when examining the safeguard measures adopted by the EU Member States, simply concluded that since the EC Scientific Committee on Plants, a body responsible for risk assessment at the EC level, was able to perform risk assessment in reviewing the specific concerns raised by EU Member States, it was no longer possible for several EU countries to claim that there was an insufficient amount of scientific evidence.[63] Consequently, the panel failed to recognize the existence of the spatial aspect of insufficiency, namely that scientists from various jurisdictions can come to different conclusions on insufficiency. In this context, it is worth recalling the observation made by one of the *Biotech* experts, who explained that:

> when additional scientific knowledge is needed to evaluate new GM crops, each nation's regulators and scientific advisory committees are placed in the difficult position of choosing between expediency and greater certainty. It is not always clear where the distinction lies between what regulators 'need to know' vs. what is merely nice to know.[64]

It is difficult to propose any specific formal mechanisms that could address these concerns. As a starting point, panels need to acknowledge the existence of such challenges and recognize that they may seriously undermine the quality of both decision makers and decision-making processes (two crucial elements in construing the legitimacy of the whole system). Panels should also remain very careful and diligent when engaging in the communicative process with their experts. Conditional answers have to be deconstructed, while less direct responses need to be given proper appreciation. Panels should also ensure that legal and scientific categories are not confused, and that experts understand the meaning of the legal tests that are applied to national risk assessments in WTO proceedings.

11.5 Experts and the standard of review

One may also ask a more general question about the role that should be assigned to experts in the dispute settlement process. Should a panel request the experts to determine the current state of scientific knowledge with regard to a particular issue? Or should the experts' task be limited to

[63] See, e.g., Panel Report, *EC–Biotech Products*, para. 7.3300.

[64] Panel Report, *EC–Biotech Products, Annex H–Replies by the Scientific Experts Advising the Panel to Questions Posed by the Panel*, para. 14.

the assessment of the reasonableness of evidence put forward by the defendant?

The answer to these questions is contained in the concept of standard of review, which refers to the level of scrutiny applied by a panel to national scientific determinations. In theory, the applicable standard of review may vary from *de novo* review to full deference. Under the *de novo* review, a panel reviews all the determinations made by a national body and substitutes them with its own. A fully deferential standard would restrict the reviewing powers of the panel in assessing whether the prescribed procedures were followed and would prohibit any inquiry into the substance of the decision(s) taken. Between these two extremes are a number of intermediate standards of review. The standard of review employed by a panel obviously affects the role of experts. Some panels' questions and experts' answers may be permitted/legitimate under one type of review and prohibited/irrelevant under the other.

The SPS case law does not unequivocally determine the required level of scrutiny. The first case, the *EC–Hormones* case, employed a rather deferential approach, but subsequent decisions adopted increasingly intrusive assessments into the scientific back-up for national measures. The panels examined the persuasive force and quality of scientific findings made at the municipal level. The reports in *EC–Biotech Products* and *US/Canada–Continued Suspension* may be regarded as the culmination of that trend, with the panels engaging in an in-depth analysis of the scientific evidence and choosing between competing scientific views. The overall critical reaction of commentators to these developments was that panels lack the necessary competence to make complex factual findings involving scientific claims, even if they are assisted by experts. It was also argued that risk assessment depends on specific socio-cultural factors that remained unappreciated under the quasi-*de novo* review.[65]

In the *US/Canada–Continued Suspension* case, the AB moved back to a relatively deferential approach, recognizing the limited scientific competence of panels.[66] The panels were instructed not to decide whether municipal risk assessment was correct, but only whether it was based on coherent reasoning and respectable scientific evidence. This instruction was also relevant for the experts. According to the AB, a panel may seek

[65] See generally L. Gruszczynski, 'Standard of Review of Health and Environmental Regulation by WTO Panels' in G. Van Calster and D. Prévost (eds.), *Research Handbook on Environment, Health and the WTO* (Cheltenham: Edward Elgar, 2013).

[66] Appellate Body Report, *US–Continued Suspension*, para. 589.

their assistance in order to identify the scientific basis of an SPS measure, to determine whether such basis constitutes a defensible scientific claim and to review the quality of reasoning as to its objectivity and coherence. The AB warned that a panel should not attempt to test whether its experts would have undertaken the risk assessment in the same way as a particular WTO member. They are only expected to provide information whether a specific risk assessment is defensible in scientific terms.[67]

Regrettably, the case that followed, *Australia–Apples*, again obscured the whole picture. On the one hand, the AB explained that a panel is only expected to determine whether a specific claim can be regarded as 'legitimate' science, but on the other hand accepted a rather intrusive examination into the *reasoning* included in the risk assessment.[68] As a result, it is not enough for a panel to simply examine whether such reasoning falls within a range that could be considered legitimate by the scientific community.[69] Such reasoning is to be assessed against some benchmark of correctness. It is not clear why the AB decided to set two different thresholds: one for supporting evidence and one for reasoning. If the basis for the deferential approach with respect to scientific evidence was the limited epistemic competence of a panel in scientific matters, the same approach should be taken when analysing reasoning. A panel is in no way better equipped to decide on the correctness of the intermediate conclusions in a risk assessment or the expert judgements used to compensate for uncertainties. A more deferential standard that applies equally to both evidence and reasoning (in line with the *Suspension* case), from a legitimacy point of view, would be a preferable option.

11.6 Conclusions

The WTO dispute settlement system has developed mechanisms that strengthen input legitimacy. The whole process of consultation with experts is inclusive, as the parties are involved at every stage of the proceedings. The high quality of experts is ensured through the involvement of reputable international bodies specialized in a particular field of research and the standards set for experts. The publication of all experts'

67 *Ibid.*, para. 592.

68 Appellate Body Report, *Australia–Measures Affecting the Importation of Apples from New Zealand*, WT/DS367/AB/R, adopted 17 December 2010, para. 225.

69 *Ibid.*, para. 231.

answers in the final report provides, although *ex post facto*, additional external supervision by the relevant scientific community. The progressive formalization of the consultation process is also vital, as it increases the predictability and transparency of the proceedings.

At the same time, some flaws in the dispute settlement practice can compromise input legitimacy by affecting two compensatory mechanisms identified by de Búrca – the quality of the decision-making process and that of the decision maker. Procedural and communicative failures can also indirectly affect the outcome of the dispute settlement process (i.e., output legitimacy), as decisions taken in a deficient process are seldom of high quality or widely accepted by those concerned. Consequently, they may reduce the legitimizing character of science and scientific expertise.

Some problems identified above have been addressed in the SPS practice. The AB made clear that previous affiliation with one of the standard-setting bodies is relevant when assessing the impartiality and independence of experts. Panels have also made good progress as far as the diversity of experts is concerned, with the more recent disputes, e.g., *Australia–Apples*, reflecting a range of scientific advice. The practice of having at least two experts for every issue involved should be welcomed as well.

There are other issues that remain problematic. One of them is the continuing opposition of panels to the establishment of expert review groups. The reliance on individual experts, although not fatal to the operation of the WTO dispute settlement process, poses serious challenges for panellists. A report produced by an expert review group might help a panel to surmount some of the obstacles it encounters when weighing individual opinions. Another set of problems arises with the difference between scientific and legal logic, which may negatively affect the discursive process that takes place between panellists and experts. The qualified and indirect answers provided by experts, based on the existing scientific uncertainties and complexities involved, create the risk of being misunderstood and/or misinterpreted by a panel seeking to give them legal effect. Similarly, the conceptualization of certain categories as scientific when they are not may also lead to confusion. At the same time, experts may face difficulties in correctly appreciating the particular meanings attached to the specific legal terms or expressions. These problems are particularly troublesome because they are as yet unexplored in the literature and under-appreciated in WTO dispute settlement practice. Another point of concern relates to the standard of review used by SPS panels. The SPS case law seems to struggle in defining the appropriate level of scrutiny, with different panels applying standards that range from deferential to quasi-*de novo* review. The most recent reports offer some clarification, but also obscure certain issues (i.e., the standard to be applied to the reasoning in municipal risk assessments). This lack of clarity means that experts are assigned a somewhat ambiguous role, since it is not clear whether they should engage in testing the correctness or merely the reasonableness of national risk assessment.

PART IV

Experts in human rights-related decision-making processes

12

Human rights experts in the United Nations: a review of the role of United Nations Special Procedures

SURYA P. SUBEDI

12.1 Introduction: the significance of the United Nations Special Procedures for Human Rights

In the realm of human rights, the use of experts is widespread, especially within the United Nations (UN) system of human rights. This practice is probably due to what Christopher McCrudden has described as: 'The inevitably compromised, often ambiguous, usually open-ended nature of the legal texts advancing human rights [which] are the site of debates at the international, regional and national levels over their meaning and implications.'[1] His chapter on mainstreaming human rights was partly based on the concept of epistemic community, as defined and developed by Haas.[2] According to McCrudden:

> The debates about the extent to which human rights should play a central role in government decision-making can be seen to involve a clash of two different epistemic communities: one involving primarily professional administrators, and one involving those primarily with a human rights perspective. The latter often regard including the former in human rights interpretation as dangerous.[3]

These findings led McCrudden to point to the limits of mainstreaming human rights and to assert the need for involving human rights experts

The views expressed in this chapter are the personal views of the author and are not those of the United Nations Organization.

1 C. McCrudden, 'Mainstreaming Human Rights' in C. Harvey (ed.), *Human Rights in the Community: Rights as Agents for Change* (Oxford: Hart Publishing, 2005), 9–28, at 16.

2 Haas, Chapter 2, this volume.

3 McCrudden, 'Mainstreaming Human Rights'. In his chapter, McCrudden defined epistemic communities as 'a network of professionals with recognised expertise ... and an authoritative claim to knowledge ... who have a shared set of normative beliefs, shared causal beliefs, shared notions of validity, and a common policy enterprise'.

in the implementation of human rights, instead of leaving this to experts in other areas, such as trade law. By analogy, McCrudden's argument applies to the UN Special Procedures for Human Rights. The international human rights experts that operate within these Special Procedures interact with professional administrators or politicians, who are not necessarily human rights experts, in order to further the realization of human rights and thus operate within the tension signalled by McCrudden. Kofi Annan, the then Secretary-General of the UN, in a speech to the UN Human Rights Council in November 2006, also pointed to the tension between distinct epistemic communities in the context of the realization of the rule of law. While referring to the Special Procedures as the 'crown jewel' of the UN human rights procedures, Annan observed that: 'It has . . . been recognized in theory, and increasingly also in practice, that the rule of law cannot be left to the discretion of governments, no matter how democratically elected they may be.'[4]

Within the UN system, human rights experts work in various contexts, including as members of the human rights treaty bodies, as human rights professionals in the Office of the High Commissioner for Human Rights and as participants in the so-called 'Special Procedures' of the UN Human Rights Council.[5] The Council is the main political body responsible for promoting and protecting human rights within the organization, and the Special Procedures, including the Special Rapporteurs for Human Rights, or mandate-holders, operate under its auspices. It is these Special Procedures, and the Special Rapporteurs in particular, that are the focus of this chapter.

The Special Procedures are generally seen as highly relevant providers of important expert input into the work of the UN Human Rights Council. In addition, they may also report to or otherwise liaise with other UN bodies such as the General Assembly or the Security Council. As explained below, since the late 1960s, the UN Special Procedures for Human Rights have played an important role in promoting and protecting human rights in some of the most difficult

[4] See UN News Centre, 'Annan Calls on Human Rights Council to Strive for Unity, Avoid Familiar Fault Lines', 29 November 2006, www.un.org/apps/news/story.asp?NewsID=20770.

[5] Next to Special Rapporteurs, the Special Procedures also involve Independent Experts and Working Groups; see Office of the High Commissioner for Human Rights, 'Special Procedures of the Human Rights Council', www.ohchr.org/EN/HRBodies/SP/Pages/Introduction.aspx.

country situations (such as Myanmar or the occupied Palestinian territories) and on some of the most challenging issues (such as the situation of human rights defenders or the rights of indigenous peoples). According to Ted Piccone,[6] the UN Human Rights Council's Special Procedures 'bring truth to power in very important ways'.[7] Louise Arbour[8] and Navanethem Pillay,[9] respectively a past and the current UN High Commissioner for Human Rights, have also pointed to the importance of the Special Procedures in the efforts of the UN to protect human rights. Arbour also pointed to the characteristics that enable these experts to fulfil this role: their 'strength includes their independence, concerted focus on an issue or situation, ability to engage directly through country visits, on-going accessibility to victims and advocacy role in identifying implementation gaps'.[10] Independence, determination, focus, visibility and accessibility seem to be key to the influence of the human rights experts operating within the Special Procedures.

The influence of the human rights experts operating within the Special Procedures is also evidenced by the role that reports ensuing from these Procedures play in, for instance, the Universal Period Review (UPR) procedure. This procedure is the main and most visible human rights monitoring activity undertaken by the UN Human Rights Council. It entails a peer review of the human rights record of each UN Member State. Although there is no formal mechanism that involves the Special Procedures mandate-holders in the UPR process, the comments made by other states on the situation in the country under

6 T. Piccone, *Catalysts for Change: How the UN's Independent Experts Promote Human Rights* (Washington DC: Brookings Institution, 2012); and T. Piccone, *Catalysts for Rights: The Unique Contribution of the UN's Independent Experts on Human Rights* (Washington DC: Brookings Institution, 2010).

7 Transcribed from a video message by Piccone: www.brookings.edu/research/books/2012/catalystsforchange.

8 'Plan of Action Submitted by the United Nations High Commissioner for Human Rights', UN Doc. A/59/2005/Add.3, 26 May 2005, para. 101. According to Arbour, 'various rapporteurs, working groups and experts appointed by the Commission on Human Rights . . . an essential element of the efforts undertaken by the United Nations to protect human rights'.

9 Address by Ms Navanethem Pillay, 'UN High Commissioner for Human Rights – Introduction of the Annual Report', 4 March 2010, Geneva, on file with the author. According to Ms Pillay, the Special Procedures 'have continued to help the [Human Rights] Council, the General Assembly and other United Nations bodies and entities' in their endeavours to promote and protect human rights.

10 *Ibid.*

review are often informed by the reports and recommendations of the relevant Special Rapporteur(s).[11] Other indications of the significance of the Special Procedures exist in the realm of standard-setting or norm-creation. The knowledge of Special Rapporteurs, Independent Experts and Working Groups has been used for and has influenced the elaboration, interpretation and implementation of international human rights law in a number of areas. Two recent examples illustrate this point. First, there is the proposal for a possible draft convention on private military and security companies[12] by the Working Group on Mercenaries to the Human Rights Council. Second, the work of the then Independent Expert, Ms Catarina de Albuquerque, was instrumental in clarifying the legal content of the human rights obligations involved in access to safe drinking water and sanitation. Her work resulted in the recognition of these rights by the UN Human Rights Council and the General Assembly,[13] and at present Ms de Albuquerque is the first Special Rapporteur on the Human Rights to Safe Drinking Water and Sanitation.[14] Against this backdrop, the aim of this chapter is twofold. First, it examines the institution and practices of the Special Procedures for human rights in the UN, and more in particular the record of the expert human rights inputs into the UN system generated by these Special Procedures. Second, it explores the challenges embedded in these procedures in order to highlight some important features of human rights experts' involvement in international decision making.

After an introduction to the history, appointment and functions of Special Procedures mandate-holders, aspects of their legitimacy and accountability will be explored. Subsequently, three sets of major challenges to the work involved will be considered: the perceived focus of the work done by Special Procedures mandate-holders; their role in exposing shortcomings of governments and the tensions that may arise as a consequence thereof; and institutional issues. Finally,

[11] Where the text provides no specific references, the author drew on his personal experiences in the UN system.

[12] See, e.g., UN Doc. A/HRC/RES/15/25, 2 July 2010 and UN Doc. A/HRC/WG.10/CRP.1, 17 May 2011.

[13] See, respectively, for the Human Rights Council, UN Doc. A/HRC/RES/15/9, 6 October 2010, UN Doc. A/HRC/RES/16/2, 8 April 2011 and UN Doc. A/HRC/RES/18L.1, 23 September 2011, and for the General Assembly, UN Doc. A/RES/64/292, 3 August 2010.

[14] See Office of the High Commissioner for Human Rights, 'Overview of the Mandate', www.ohchr.org/EN/Issues/WaterAndSanitation/SRWater/Pages/Overview.aspx.

this chapter will draw conclusions that emerge from this example of expert inputs into international decision making on human rights matters.

12.2 The institution of Special Procedures mandate-holders: historical context, appointment and functions

The UN Special Procedures for Human Rights have been in existence in some form since the late 1960s. Over time, an increasing number of Special Rapporteurs, Independent Experts and Working Groups have been appointed on an ad hoc basis. Until 2006, these appointments were made by the Commission on Human Rights. Since then, its successor, the Human Rights Council, took over this role.[15] The Council was established in 2006 by the UN General Assembly as part of the ongoing general process of UN reform and, in particular, the reform of the UN human rights procedures.[16] After some discussion, the Special Procedures made the transition from the Commission to the Council and continued to exist in the new system.

[15] On Special Procedures generally, see S. P. Subedi, 'Protecting Human Rights through the Mechanism of UN Special Rapporteurs', *Human Rights Quarterly*, 33 (2011), 201–28; D. Weissbrodt, 'The Three "Theme" Special Rapporteurs of the UN Commission on Human Rights', *American Journal of International Law*, 80 (1986), 685–99; H. M. Cook, 'The Role of the Special Procedures in the Protection of Human Rights: The Way Forward after Vienna', *Review of the International Commission of Jurists*, 50 (1993), 31–55; M. J. Bossuyt, 'The Development of Special Procedures of the United Nations Commission on Human Rights', *Human Rights Law Journal*, 6 (1985), 179–210; L. S. Sunga, 'The Special Procedures of the UN Commission on Human Rights: Should They Be Scrapped?' in G. Alfredsson, J. Grimheden, B. G. Ramcharan and A. Zayas (eds.), *International Human Rights Monitoring Mechanisms: Essays in Honour of Jakob Th. Moller* (The Hague: Martinus Nijhoff Publishers, 2001), 233–77; P. S. Pinheiro, 'Musings of a UN Special Rapporteur on Human Rights', *Global Governance*, 9 (2003), 7–13; J. Gutter, 'Special Procedures and the Human Rights Council: Achievements and Challenges Ahead', *Human Rights Law Review*, 7 (2007), 93–107; I. Nifosi, *The UN Special Procedures in the Field of Human Rights* (Cambridge: Intersentia, 2005); M. T. Kamminga, 'The Thematic Procedures of the UN Commission on Human Rights', *Netherlands International Law Review*, 34 (1987), 299–323; B. Ramcharan, *The Protection Roles of UN Human Rights Special Procedures* (Leiden: Brill, 2009).

[16] The Human Rights Council was among others established as a result of the recommendations made by the UN Secretary-General High-Level Panel on Threats, Challenges and Change, *A More Secure World: Our Shared Responsibility*, UN Doc. A/59/565, 2 December 2004, especially Part XVIII. See also the report on UN reform by the then UN Secretary-General Kofi Annan, *In Larger Freedom: Towards Development, Security and Human Rights for All*, UN Doc. A/59/2005, 21 March 2005, paras. 181–3.

The UN human rights special mandate-holders are selected on the basis of criteria such as their expertise and experience in the area of the mandate, personal integrity, independence and impartiality and objectivity. The individuals who can be considered for appointment as Special Rapporteurs can be nominated by private individuals, civil society organizations or any other non-governmental or (inter) governmental institution, including UN agencies and governments. Until March 2011, there was no formal practice for selecting shortlisted candidates.[17] However, as part of the review of the Human Rights Council, in March 2011 the UN General Assembly determined that all shortlisted candidates for Special Procedures mandates would be interviewed.[18] The new system also allows individuals to nominate themselves by submitting an application for a specific mandate. These new procedures are likely to enhance the transparency of the appointment process for the experts involved and reaffirm the independent nature of the function of Special Procedures mandate-holder. These procedural arrangements might also help to expand the pool of potentially qualified and eligible candidates available for taking up these important positions.[19]

After appointment, the Special Rapporteurs exercise their powers and discharge their responsibilities under the Charter of the UN. Therefore, strictly speaking, they are not part of the Human Rights Council, an intergovernmental and political body. Accordingly, in principle, they can act independently and have the maximum freedom of action and flexibility. The special mandate-holders, however, are accountable to the Human Rights Council and the General Assembly of the UN to whom they present their annual reports. The UN High

[17] Informal, i.e., civil society organized public interviewing of candidates standing in elections for appointment on some of the UN human rights treaty bodies does exist, e.g., for the Committee on the Rights of the Child. See Child Rights Information Network, 'CRC Committee Elections 2012: Interviews with Candidates', www.crin.org/en/library/news-archive/crc-committee-elections-2012-interviews-candidates.

[18] UN Doc. A/HRC/16/L.39, 23 March 2011. See also www.ohchr.org/EN/HRBodies/SP/Pages/Nominations.aspx. The interviewing of shortlisted candidates is done by the Consultative Group of the UN Human Rights Council, which consists of five members representing the regional groups in the Council, i.e., respectively African, Asian, Eastern European, Latin American and Caribbean, and Western European and other states.

[19] See also T. Baldwin-Pask and P. Scanella, 'The Unfinished Business of a Special Procedures System' in M. C. Bassiouni and W. A. Schabas (eds.), *New Challenges for the UN Human Rights Machinery* (Cambridge: Intersentia, 2011), 419–78.

Commissioner for Human Rights is charged with providing logistical and technical support to the mandate-holders.

The appointment of Special Procedures mandate-holders has traditionally been seen as a response of the international community to situations of especially serious violations of human rights: either relating in general to violations of particular rights (thematic rapporteurs) or in a specific state or territory (country rapporteurs).

The total number of Special Rapporteurs has fluctuated throughout their existence. Towards the end of the 1990s, there were about twenty-six country mandates and twenty-seven thematic mandates. By April 2013, there were only thirteen country mandates left,[20] whereas the thematic mandates (which include Working Groups next to Special Rapporteurs) had grown to a total number of thirty-six.[21] Accordingly, in April 2013 there were forty-nine UN mandates altogether. The actual number of mandate-holders, including members of working groups, stood at seventy-two.

[20] They cover Myanmar (in operation since 1992), Cambodia (1993), the occupied Palestinian territories (1993), Somalia (1993), Haiti (1995), the Democratic People's Republic of Korea (2004), Sudan (2005), Iran (2011), Côte d'Ivoire (2011), Syria (2011, not yet operational – will start once the mandate of the Commission of Inquiry on Syria will have ended), Belarus and Eritrea. See www.ohchr.org/EN/HRBodies/SP/Pages/Countries.aspx.

[21] They include the following mandates: enforced or involuntary disappearances (established in 1980), extra-judicial, summary or arbitrary executions (1982), torture (1985), freedom of religion or belief (1986), sale of children, child prostitution and child pornography (1990), arbitrary detention (1991), freedom of opinion and expression (1993), racism and racial discrimination (1993), independence of judges and lawyers (1994), violence against women (1994), hazardous wastes (1995), right to education (1998), extreme poverty (1998), migrants (1999), right to food (2000), adequate housing (2000), human rights defenders (2000), foreign debt and related international financial obligations (2000), indigenous people (2001), people of African descent (2002), physical and mental health (2002), internally displaced persons (2004), trafficking in persons (2004), mercenaries (2005), minority issues (2005), international solidarity (2005), countering terrorism (2005), contemporary forms of slavery (2007), safe drinking water and sanitation (2008), cultural rights (2009), freedom of peaceful assembly and of association (2010), discrimination against women in law and in practice (2010), human rights and transnational corporations and other business enterprises (2011), democratic and equitable international order (2011), the promotion of truth, justice and, reparation and guarantees of non-recurrence (2011) and the enjoyment of a safe, clean, healthy and sustainable environment (2012). See www.ohchr.org/EN/HRBodies/SP/Pages/Themes.aspx.

While country rapporteurs are usually appointed for one year at a time,[22] their mandate being renewable up to a maximum of six years, the thematic mandate-holders are normally appointed for three years, which is usually renewable only once, resulting in a maximum of six years in office.

The primary tasks of UN Special Rapporteurs are fact-finding, reporting and advising on human rights in a specific country or on a particular human rights theme. In order to fulfil these tasks, they are vested with investigative, communicative and reporting powers, and within the UN system they are regarded as independent UN experts on mission. While working on their mandates, they thus enjoy functional diplomatic immunities in their capacity as Special Rapporteurs.[23] Their actual roles and functions vary according to the nature of their mandate and the situation or issue at stake. Generally speaking, the following six different principal functions feature in the package of functions of Special Procedures mandate-holders, including Special Rapporteurs:

(1) analysing the relevant thematic issue or country situation on behalf of the international community;
(2) advising on the measures to be taken by the government(s) concerned and other relevant actors;
(3) alerting UN organs and agencies and the international community in general of the need to address specific situations and issues (in this regard they have a role in providing 'early warning' and in encouraging preventive measures);
(4) advocating on behalf of the victims of violations, for example, through requesting 'urgent action' by relevant states and calling upon governments to respond to specific allegations of human rights violations and provide redress;

[22] In rare cases the mandate of country rapporteurs is renewed for more than one year at a time. The 2011 decision by the Human Rights Council to renew for two years the mandate of the UN Special Rapporteur for human rights in Cambodia is an example. See UN Doc. A/HRC/18/L.25, 26 September 2011.

[23] The status of 'expert performing missions for the United Nations' thus brings legal protection for the mandate-holders involved, e.g., in the form of privileges and immunities such as immunity from personal arrest or detention, from seizure of their personal baggage and from 'legal process of every kind' in relation to 'words spoken or written and acts done by them in the course of the performance of their mission', extended by Article 22 of the 1946 UN Convention on Privileges and Immunities.

(5) activating and mobilizing the international and national communities to address particular human rights issues and to encourage cooperation among governments, civil society and intergovernmental organizations; and
(6) devising follow-up to recommendations.[24]

Rather than taking decisions themselves, the special mandate-holders report and submit recommendations to the Human Rights Council, the General Assembly and occasionally to the Security Council, as well as to individual members of the United Nations. Usually, they convey their assessment of the situation concerning a country or a theme and recommend measures that in their view are necessary to improve the protection and promotion of the human rights covered by their mandates. The public advocacy role of the Special Procedures is especially important. While the human rights treaty bodies do not interact with the media much, Special Rapporteurs do and their work receives broad media attention, which serves as an additional source of pressure on the governments concerned. It is often said that the biggest sanction that international law has to offer against states that do not comply with it is public embarrassment or the 'mobilization of shame'. This assertion certainly applies to the work of the Special Procedures mandate-holders, who put the spotlight on the shortcomings of the governments concerned, but can only generate recommendations for promoting change.

Special Procedures mandate-holders have to find their way in a complex web of actors and activities involved in their tasks, both in the UN and in their activities in the field. In line with McCrudden's observations above, they have to navigate amidst the potential tensions that might arise between the different epistemic communities to which national administrators, state representatives on the Human Rights Council, human rights experts operating in various other UN bodies and Special Procedures mandate-holders possibly belong. This requires a great variety of different skills and talents, as in different contexts, at various moments or simultaneously, a Special Procedures mandate-holder will be more or less expected to be a human rights activist, a rallying point for human rights, an international diplomat, a human rights lawyer, a media specialist, a human rights academic and/or a government advisor.

[24] Manual of Operations of the Special Procedures of the Human Rights Council, Office of the UN High Commissioner of Human Rights, Geneva, August 2008, at 5.

12.3 Special Procedures mandate-holders as a community of experts: aspects of legitimacy and accountability

The generic name given to the Special Procedures mandate-holders within the UN human rights system is 'UN experts'. Several of the mandate-holders involved are explicitly appointed as 'Independent Experts'. All mandate-holders are expected to carry out their work independently, objectively and impartially. They act as experts in relation to the human rights situation in the country or concerning the particular theme assigned to them and may offer expert recommendations for addressing problems.

Since 1994, the Special Procedures mandate-holders meet once a year as an expert community to share experiences and to explore ways and means of making the special procedures more effective.[25] They elect a body known as the Coordination Committee to represent their collective views to other UN human rights mechanisms, including the UN High Commissioner for Human Rights and the UN Human Rights Council. Sometimes collective statements are issued on behalf of all Special Procedures mandate-holders. Recently, this has happened in relation to the human rights situation in Syria.[26] The Special Procedures mandate-holders also regularly interact with other human rights experts working within the UN system. For instance, during the above-mentioned annual meeting of the Coordination Committee, a special collective session was held with members of the UN treaty bodies to exchange views and information relating to the promotion and protection of human rights. Some treaty bodies have invited a country mandate-holder when they were considering the human rights report of a particular state. Thus, even in the absence of a formal mechanism to coordinate the activities of the Special Procedures mandate-holders with other UN human rights bodies, some coordination and sharing of information does take place. This kind of cooperation and interaction between the various human rights experts within the UN human rights system brings them together and, certainly

[25] See www.ohchr.org/EN/HRBodies/SP/AMeeting/Pages/AnnualMeeting.aspx.

[26] Statement delivered on behalf of all Special Procedures mandate-holders of the United Nations Human Rights Council at the nineteenth Special Session of the Human Rights Council on the situation of human rights in the Syrian Arab Republic, delivered on video by the Special Rapporteur on extra-judicial, summary or arbitrary executions, Mr Christof Heyns, Geneva, 1 June 2012, www.ohchr.org/EN/NewsEvents/Pages/DisplayNews.aspx?NewsID=12211&LangID=E.

from the perspective of the persons involved, including myself, gives the sense of belonging to an expert community.

The legitimacy of the appointment and the work of Special Procedures mandate-holders derives in part from the nature of their mandates, which are related to the obligations of UN members regarding human rights. First, all Member States of the United Nations have agreed to promote and protect human rights by joining the organization[27] and by ratifying different human rights treaties. The most specific body that the 193 UN Member States have created for the purpose of tackling human rights issues within the organization at present is the Human Rights Council. According to the General Assembly resolution that constituted the Council, its tasks are: to promote universal respect for the protection of all human rights; to 'address situations of violations of human rights, including gross and systematic violations, and [to] make recommendations thereon'; and to 'promote the effective coordination and the mainstreaming of human rights within the United Nations system'.[28] This mandate extends to the protection of human rights both globally and in individual countries. The Human Rights Council in turn charges Special Procedures mandate-holders with some of the activities that are required for the realization of the Council's tasks. Therefore, all members of the UN have agreed, either directly or indirectly, to the appointment of the Special Procedures mandate-holders. State consent thus provides the expert mandate-holders with input legitimacy in discharging their responsibilities and vests the Special Procedures system itself with a legitimate basis for making its contributions to the promotion and protection of human rights.

Another factor that contributes to the input legitimacy of the Special Procedures mandate-holders relates to the background and status of the specific persons involved. Since most of their work involves some legal element, and interpretations of legal texts referred to as 'open-ended' by McCrudden,[29] it is not surprising that most mandate-holders are either lawyers or have a legal background, and in most cases are from academia, the legal profession or the judiciary.[30] This legal

[27] See e.g., UN Charter, Articles 1(3), 55 and 56.

[28] UNGA Resolution 60/251, 3 April 2006, Doc. A/RES/60/251, 3 April 2006, paras. 2 and 3.

[29] McCrudden, 'Mainstreaming Human Rights', at 16.

[30] Where the text provides no specific references, the author drew on his personal experiences in the UN system.

background seems to have helped rather than hindered the work they carry out as human rights experts in the UN. Most likely, as implied above, the main reason for appointing persons with a legal background thus relates to the obvious legal dimensions to many human rights issues in terms of both the analysis of the issues involved and recommendations for improvement of the situation in a given country or countries, or on a particular theme. Until recently, the appointments have been quite homogeneous in other respects as well: a high number of individuals appointed as UN mandate-holders – especially for mandates dealing with civil and political rights – were male and originated from Western countries. But, gradually, the Human Rights Council seems to consider a larger variety of factors more explicitly in the appointment of mandate-holders, including gender, geographical origin, professional background and level of critical stance.[31] Consequently, nowadays the community of UN human rights experts is quite diverse, which serves to further strengthen their legitimacy as a group.

At first sight it may appear that the mandate-holders are not accountable to anyone since they are by definition 'independent', even from the Human Rights Council.[32] However, as mentioned above, they are clearly accountable to the Human Rights Council and/or the General Assembly, to which they report depending on the nature of the mandate. Furthermore, the Human Rights Council has the power to renew or not to renew the mandate, or to renew or not to renew the term of office of the particular mandate-holder. Beyond these formal procedures, UN Special Procedures mandate-holders, in practice, are accountable in a broader way and to a wider community of stakeholders. During, or in response to, the relevant public sessions of UN bodies or activities undertaken by Special Procedures mandate-holders outside such sessions, they can be challenged on their factual accuracy, the quality and content of their

[31] By 1 July 2012, all UN country rapporteurs were men and out of the nine operational mandates, two were taken up by rapporteurs from Western states (France and the USA). Among the almost sixty operational thematic mandates, the gender balance was almost equal and rapporteurs originating from Western states took charge of about one-quarter to at most one-third of the positions. See www.ohchr.org/EN/HRBodies/SP/Pages/Countries.aspx and www.ohchr.org/EN/HRBodies/SP/Pages/Themes.aspx.

[32] On the accountability of UN human rights experts, see P. Alston, 'Hobbling the Monitors: Should UN Human Rights Monitors Be Accountable?', *Harvard International Law Journal*, 52 (2011), 561–649.

findings, and recommendations not only by governments but also by non-governmental human rights organizations. As stated above, substantively the UN human rights experts in their work are to uphold the values enshrined in the Charter of the United Nations, the overall aims and objectives of the UN in general and the Human Rights Council in particular, and the UN human rights treaties. The work of the Human Rights Council, and therefore that of the Special Procedures, must furthermore be 'guided by the principles of universality, impartiality, objectivity and non-selectivity, constructive international dialogue and cooperation, with a view to enhancing the promotion and protection of all human rights'.[33]

Accountability aspects also come to the fore in the two major instruments that formally guide the UN Special Procedures for Human Rights. The first is the Code of Conduct adopted by the Human Rights Council in 2007 which presents 'the standards of ethical behaviour and professional conduct that special procedures mandate-holders of the Human Rights Council . . . shall observe whilst discharging their mandates'.[34] At present, there is an ongoing debate as to whether there should be a specific mechanism to entertain allegations of violations of this Code of Conduct. The special mandate-holders themselves largely oppose the creation of such a new mechanism and point to the already available procedures (e.g., in the form of the procedures for appointment, renewal of mandates or reporting referred to above). Many governments that are critical of the work and findings of some of the special mandate-holders have stated that they find the existing procedures for holding mandate-holders to account inadequate, and advocate the establishment of a new mechanism, such as a legal committee that could enforce the Code of Conduct through sanctions. Philip Alston, a long-serving former mandate-holder himself, proposed an alternative approach. He has advocated the establishment of a 'compliance body which would examine complaints by stakeholders in relation to the overall functioning of the Special Procedures system' so as to strengthen both

[33] UNGA Resolution 60/251, 3 April 2006, UN Doc. A/RES/60251, Preamble, para. 4.

[34] Human Rights Council, 'Code of Conduct for Special Procedures Mandate-Holders of the Human Rights Council', UN Doc. A/HRC/RES5/2, 18 June 2007, Article 2. For an analysis of the Code of Conduct, see M. Abraham, 'Building the New Human Rights Council: Outcome and Analysis of the Institution Building Year', *Occasional Papers No. 33*, Friedrich Ebert Stiftung, August 2007, 29–32.

the notions of independence and accountability, and 'to embrace the legitimacy of the system as a whole'.[35] The second major instrument formally guiding the Special Procedures is the Manual of Operations of the Special Procedures of the Human Rights Council, which was adopted by the meeting of Special Rapporteurs under the auspices of the Coordination Council of Special Procedures in June 2008. This document seeks to assist mandate-holders in their work and 'to facilitate a better understanding of their work by other stakeholders'[36] by providing basic factual and procedural information on the Special Procedures.

12.4 Challenges to expert input on human rights in the United Nations and attempts to reform

In practice, various challenges may complicate the functioning of the Special Procedures of the Human Rights Council and the expert input by the mandate-holders. As will be explained in this section, these challenges relate to the perceived focus of their work, their role in exposing the shortcomings of governments and institutional issues, and thus to output legitimacy.

In certain quarters there is a perception that the UN Special Procedures are designed to focus more on civil and political rights than on economic, social and cultural rights, and therefore to promote a 'Western' version of democracy or 'Western' political ideology. In these quarters the UN Special Procedures are seen as mainly focusing on developing countries, which is criticized as a bias. The reality is rather different. Individual mandate-holders have often spoken out against the failings of both developed and developing and both Western and non-Western countries. There are several examples of Special Rapporteurs who raised inadequacies of the Western powers in, for instance, the so-called War on Terror or in the treatment of migrants or minorities. For instance, Philip Alston, the then UN Special Rapporteur on extra-judicial, summary or arbitrary executions, criticized the US over drone killings in June 2010. He said that the use of targeted killings with weapons like drone aircrafts posed a growing challenge to the international rule of law: 'Intelligence agencies, which by

[35] Alston, 'Hobbling the Monitors', at 563.
[36] The Manual of Operations is available at: www.ohchr.org/EN/HRBodies/SP/AMeeting/Pages/AnnualMeeting.aspx, at 1.

definition are determined to remain unaccountable except to their own paymasters, have no place in running programmes that kill people in other countries.'[37] He went on to say that drone killings carry a significant risk of becoming war crimes because intelligence agencies 'do not generally operate within a framework which places appropriate emphasis upon ensuring compliance with international humanitarian law'.[38] Similarly, the UN Special Rapporteur on the human rights of migrants, Jorge Bustamante, and the Working Group on the Use of Mercenaries criticized the UK for its treatment of migrants in October 2010. Mr Bustamante stated that he was 'disturbed at seeing the manner in which migrants are being treated, with no dignity at all, due to the criminalisation of irregular migration'.[39] Other criticisms against the UK were voiced by the UN Special Rapporteur on housing and the UN Independent Expert on minority issues in relation to the attempted eviction by the Basildon Council in August 2011 of 400 travellers from Dale Farm in Essex.[40] Commenting on the killing of Osama bin Laden by US forces in Pakistan in May 2011, the newly appointed Special Rapporteur on extra-judicial, summary or arbitrary executions, Christof Heyns, and the then Special Rapporteur on the promotion and protection of human rights and fundamental freedoms while countering terrorism, Martin Scheinin, stated that the USA 'should disclose the supporting facts to allow an assessment in terms of international human rights law standards. For instance, it would be particularly important to know if the planning of the mission allowed an effort to capture Bin Laden'.[41] While the above illustrates that mandate-holders do criticize Western states when their human rights record so demands, the perception persists that the Special Procedures are over-focused on developing states. This situation is problematic because it to some extent delegitimizes the work of the mandate-holders, who can only rely on their independence, objectivity and impartiality to counter these arguments.

[37] 'UN Official Criticises US over Drone Attacks', 2 June 2010, http://news.bbc.co.uk/1/hi/world/us_and_canada/10219962.stm.

[38] *Ibid.*

[39] OHCHR, 'UN Experts Criticize Treatment of Migrants after Deportee Dies while in Custody of a UK Private Security Company', News Release, 21 October 2010.

[40] 'Eviction of 400 Travellers Defies Human Rights, Says UN Official', *Daily Telegraph*, 8 August 2011, at 11.

[41] OHCHR, 'Osama Bin Laden: Statement by the UN Special Rapporteurs on Summary Executions and on Human Rights and Counterterrorism', News Release, 6 May 2011.

Another challenge to the expert input delivered by Special Procedures mandate-holders arises in the realm of their role as 'bringing truth to power'.[42] This relates to the earlier raised potential differences that may arise – in terms of interests pursued and objectives set – between governments and Special Procedures mandate-holders. The introduction to this chapter portrayed these two sets of actors as possibly part of two different epistemic communities. In practice, the level of state cooperation with Special Procedures indeed leaves a lot to be desired. States regularly fail to accept requests to visit by mandate-holders or do not respond to the criticism of their human rights records. There is no mechanism to encourage, let alone force, states to cooperate. More broadly, states fail to make available adequate resources and, for instance, refrain from training local experts, both of which are needed to enhance the ability of special mandate-holders to work effectively. The level of state support for integrating the work done as part of the Special Procedures into the work of the Human Rights Council, including the UPR, can also be improved. It is no surprise that this applies especially to the work done by the country rapporteurs, which is likely to antagonize certain governments.

Concrete expressions of such differences in agendas and the tensions raised as a result are easily recognizable when mandate-holders criticize specific governments for their shortcomings. These mandate-holders often come under attack from governments arguing that the mandate-holders do not comply with the Code of Conduct or that they have exceeded their mandates. For instance, when the Special Rapporteur on torture, Manfred Nowak, in his final report to the Third Committee of the UN General Assembly in October 2010 criticized a number of governments for their failings in preventing torture and other cruel, inhuman or degrading treatment or punishment, some of these governments were vocal in their attacks on him.[43] The Special Rapporteur on the right to freedom of opinion and expression, Frank La Rue, encountered an equally critical, if less hostile, group of states in denial of their failings in upholding the right to freedom of opinion and expression when he presented his report to the Third Committee of

[42] Transcribed from video message by Piccone: www.brookings.edu/research/books/2012/catalystsforchange.

[43] International Service for Human Rights, 'Heated Exchange between States and Special Rapporteur on Torture Marks His Last Official Duty as UN', Geneva, 2 November 2010, www.ishr.ch/news/heated-exchange-between-states-and-special-rapporteur-torture-mars-his-last-official-duty-un.

the UN General Assembly in October 2010 and named twelve states having the highest rates of impunity for unresolved murders of journalists.[44] There is no mechanism yet to protect Special Procedure mandate-holders against these kinds of attacks by states. As mentioned above, independence, objectivity and impartiality is all the mandate-holders can rely on to counter such attacks.

An institutional challenge to the work of Special Procedures mandate-holders lies in the fact that these Procedures were created in an ad hoc manner and with varying mandates, entailing that the system is not maximally cohesive. As a result, all mandate-holders face institutional constraints when fulfilling their tasks. The absence of a follow-up mechanism to the recommendations resulting from the Special Procedures is a key illustration of the fact that the Special Procedures were not set up in a systematic and comprehensive manner. Indeed, one of the major differences between the Special Procedures and the UN treaty bodies is that the Special Procedures cannot benefit from a formal follow-up mechanism similar to those available to the treaty bodies. The absence of such a mechanism makes monitoring and ensuring the follow-up of the mandate-holders' recommendations an even bigger challenge than is the case for treaty body recommendations.

On the basis of the experiences of its first five years of activities, the Human Rights Council reviewed the Special Procedures as part of its 2011 general review.[45] However, the review has not generated much that can help to tackle the above-mentioned challenges.[46] For instance, the Council failed to adopt means to enhance the cooperation of states and, more broadly, their engagement with Special Procedures; it did not introduce concrete ways to follow up on the recommendations generated by the Special Procedures; and no measures were taken to enhance the visibility of the work of the special mandate-holders in the UPR, for example, through making it possible for mandate-holders who have visited states under review to be invited to participate in the UPR review session. The outcome document only

44 International Service for Human Rights, 'SR on Freedom of Expression Calls on 12 States to End Impunity of Journalists' Killings', Geneva, 10 November 2010.

45 This was provided for by the UN General Assembly Resolution that created the Council back in 2006; see UNGA Resolution 60/251, 15 March 2006.

46 See Human Rights Council, 'Outcome of the Review of the Work and Functioning of the United National Human Rights Council', UN Doc. A/HRC/16/L.39, 23 March 2011.

underlined that 'States should cooperate with and assist special procedures in the performance of their tasks'.[47] It also urged states 'to cooperate with and assist special procedures by responding in a timely manner to requests for information and visits, and to study carefully the conclusions and recommendations addressed to them by the special procedures'.[48]

Although the Human Rights Council did not go far enough in including provisions designed to address some of the serious challenges faced by the Special Procedures, some satisfaction was expressed that it did not decide to increase the level of supervision of the Special Procedures. Certain groupings of states that seek to undermine the role of the Special Procedures submitted proposals directed at overseeing the way in which mandate-holders determine their priorities and activities, which would have curtailed their independence. Both the proposal to establish a legal committee to monitor the implementation of the Code of Conduct by Special Procedures mandate-holders and a related proposal to establish a roster of lawyers to advise the President of the Human Rights Council on the implementation of the Code of Conduct were ultimately not included in the outcome document. The proposal to restart the review and seek further rationalization and improvement of mandates – which was designed to reduce the number of mandates, to merge them or to convert certain Special Rapporteurs into working groups – was also not adopted. As stated by a seasoned diplomat from a Scandinavian country, the overall end result for the Special Procedures could have been much worse!

However, the USA was dissatisfied with the outcome and disassociated itself from the resolution. A coalition of civil society human rights organizations, including Amnesty International and Human Rights Watch, also criticized the outcome of the review, qualifying it as disappointing in relation to state obligations. This latter group called upon the UN General Assembly to endorse an annual 'cooperation audit' whereby the General Assembly reviews and assesses the state of cooperation with the Human Rights Council and the Special Procedures by UN Member States who would be candidates for election to the Council.[49] The civil society organizations went on to state that, in

[47] *Ibid.*, para. 23. [48] *Ibid.*, para. 26.

[49] Letter from Civil Society Organisations to Representatives of Member States of the United Nations General Assembly, 31 March 2011, on file with the author.

order to help evaluate the records of UN Member States who sit or aspire to have a seat on the Council, a public up-to-date record of such cooperation should be kept. They added that the Council should define and elaborate the meaning of cooperation between states and Special Procedures, and should set guidelines on how to measure whether states are abiding by their commitments. In their view, the minimum benchmark for state cooperation with the Special Procedures should include issuing standing invitations, responding within a specific timeframe to requests for visits, accepting the standard terms of reference for such visits and responding to all communications in a timely and substantive manner.[50]

The General Assembly followed the proposals contained in the review document of the Human Rights Council, even if in its resolution it elaborated on the procedure for the appointment of Special Rapporteurs. In addition to the existing entities that are eligible to nominate candidates as Special Procedures mandate-holders, the Assembly made it possible for national human rights institutions that comply with the Paris Principles[51] (concerning their independence) to nominate potential candidates as well. The resolution also required nominated candidates to submit a short motivation letter in support of their nomination. Furthermore, as referred to above, for the first time, provision was made for the shortlisted candidates to be interviewed. The General Assembly also stuck with the Human Rights Council decision not to establish the proposed legal committee to hold the Special Procedures mandate-holders to account or to entertain allegations of breaches of the Code of Conduct.

The final outcome of the Human Rights Council review process is definitely not as encouraging as many would have liked to see, and UN members have missed opportunities to further enhance the scope and quality of expert human rights input into the organization through the Special Procedures. However, it can also be argued that, on the whole, it is positive that the Special Procedures were not significantly weakened by this exercise either. In addition, as indicated above, the General Assembly even decided on a few minor procedural improvements concerning the nomination and appointment of mandate-holders.

[50] *Ibid.*

[51] 'Principles Relating to the Status of National Institutions', Annex to UNGA Res. 48/134, 4 March 1994, UN Doc. A/RES/48/134, at 4–7.

12.5 Concluding observations

By analogy to McCrudden's findings on mainstreaming human rights, it is now asked whether ultimately UN Special Procedures mandate-holders can be seen as 'ensuring that a wider epistemic community is formed that is favourable to human rights thinking, one that avoids handing over human rights interpretation to ill equipped or hostile public servants?'.[52] The conditions for and the practice of UN Special Procedures outlined in this chapter suggest that this is only partly the case. For example, continuous tensions occur between the by-and-large human rights-oriented special mandate-holders and the often more narrowly state interest-oriented members of the Human Rights Council.

Despite all the challenges and constraints inherent in the UN system and human rights law at large, the special mandate-holders have built a record of positive contributions to important human rights causes. After conducting a study of UN Special Procedures, they were referred to as 'one of the most effective tools of the international human rights system' in the 2010 Report of the Brookings Institute.[53] The Report concluded that:

> The UN's independent experts on human rights are *catalysts for rights*, helping to convert abstract principles into meaningful change. Thanks to their status as *independent* experts mandated by the United Nations, most Special Procedures have played, and continue to play, a critical role in shaping the content of international human rights norms, shedding light on how states comply with such norms, and influencing how governments behave, to the benefit of millions of people.[54]

Nevertheless, the Report also stated that: 'Written communications from Special Procedures . . . to governments have some limited impact on influencing state behaviour but in general are ineffective.'[55] After analysing nearly 9,000 communications sent over a five-year period by seventeen mandate-holders to 174 states, the report concluded that 58 per cent received no or only immaterial responses by governments: 'In 18 per cent of responses, governments took steps to address the underlying allegation in some way, while 21 per cent showed rejection

[52] McCrudden, 'Mainstreaming Human Rights', at 24.
[53] Piccone, *Catalysts for Rights*, at ix. [54] *Ibid.*, at viii–ix, emphasis in original.
[55] *Ibid.*, at ix.

of the allegation with no evidence of an investigation of the underlying claim.'[56] However, the fact that states do not respond formally to the communications by Special Procedures mandate-holders does not necessarily mean that the communications have no impact. In some cases, the very fact that the matter under consideration has been brought to international attention can deter governments and galvanize them into action. Furthermore, the effectiveness of the work of the Special Procedures cannot be measured by the rate of response alone. It is the quality of the response that matters. A state may respond, but the response may be no more than a formality. The effectiveness of the Special Procedures should thus be measured against the overall impact of their work on the government, on the victims of human rights violations, the position taken by local human rights organizations and so on.

Spreading human rights values and protecting the defenders of human rights has become more challenging today than ever. While the mechanism of Special Procedures was seriously challenged and suffered some setbacks during the journey from the Human Rights Commission to the Human Rights Council, including attempts to abolish the country mandates altogether, a reasonable new balance seems to have been reached by the outcome of the 2011 Human Rights Council review. Recent decisions of the Human Rights Council to establish new mandates for Special Rapporteurs on human rights in Iran, Côte d'Ivoire and Syria, and for an Independent Expert on cultural rights are examples of positive developments. Likewise, the unprecedented renewal of the country mandate for Cambodia held by the present author for two years instead of the usual single year,[57] coming so soon after the completion of the review of the work and functioning of the Human Rights Council, is certainly another good omen for the institution of Special Procedures. The *Cambodia Daily*, an independent and critical newspaper, published the following comments on this decision of the Human Rights Council:

> The extension came only two days after the envoy, Surya Subedi, delivered a strongly worded report on the shortcomings of the National Assembly and urged the government not to pass a controversial law on NGOs ... Deviating from the usual one-year renewal, though, the

[56] *Ibid.*, at x.

[57] Human Rights Council, 'Advisory Services and Technical Assistance for Cambodia', Res. 18/25, 30 September 2011, UN Doc. A/HRC/RES/18/25, 17 October 2011, para. 9.

> Council agreed to extend Mr Subedi's term to allow the envoy to better plan his future moves and save itself the trouble of revisiting the issue a year from now.[58]

Despite these positive developments, much can and should be improved in relation to the Special Procedures, and the procedures for mandate-holders in particular, as suggested in this chapter.[59] Moreover, new challenges have presented themselves, in particular regarding anti-terrorist measures adopted by the UN Security Council and by individual states.[60] UN human rights experts, including the special mandate-holders, in advocating these improvements and addressing these challenges, as an epistemic community of human rights experts, will have to continue to engage with 'the other' epistemic community of professional administrators, within states and in international bodies, such as the Human Rights Council. As this chapter and McCrudden's work illustrate, characterizing these distinct communities as epistemic has proven to be analytically useful because it enables us to distinguish the role of human rights experts, even if doing so might offend the analytical rigour that Haas brings to the concept. Might human rights experts also be characterized as norm entrepreneurs, as Haas suggests?[61] Indeed, this characterization may be correct, given that it is precisely norms, that is, human right norms, that are the core of the authoritative claim to knowledge, the shared normative beliefs, causal beliefs and notions of validity, and the common policy enterprise that human rights experts share.

[58] 'UN Envoy Gets New Two-Year Term Extension', *Cambodia Daily*, 3 October 2011.

[59] Letter from Civil Society Organisations to Representatives of Member States of the United Nations General Assembly, 31 March 2011, on file with the author.

[60] On UN Security Council anti-terrorist measures and human rights, see United Nations, Press Conference by Special Rapporteur Martin Scheinin on protecting human rights while countering terrorism, New York, 26 October 2010, www.ohchr.org/Documents/Issues/Terrorism/statement_GA26.10.10.pdf. Scheinin's full report is available in UN Doc. A/65/258, 6 August 2010. On national measures to counter terrorism and human rights, see e.g., Philippe Sands, *Lawless World: America and the Making and Breaking of Global Rules* (London: Allen Lane, 2005); European Center for Constitutional and Human Rights, 'CIA Extraordinary Rendition Flights, Torture and Accountability – A European Approach', 2nd edn (Berlin, 2009); International Commission of Jurists, 'E-Bulletin on Counter-Terrorism and Human Rights', www.icj.org/default.asp?nodeID=401&langage=1&sessID=.

[61] Haas, Chapter 2, this volume.

13

'Experts': the mantra of irregular migration and the reproduction of hierarchies

JEFF HANDMAKER AND CLAUDIA MORA

13.1 Introduction

The movement of people around the globe is connected to a larger set of economic, transnational and geopolitical trends. Migrant flows are part of the global exchange of people, capital, goods and intangibles.[1] Inequalities among different global regions are among the factors that have fostered the displacement of large numbers of people. Hence, the direction and characteristics of some migration flows suggest the workings of overlapping patterns of stratification and inequality.[2] These are reinforced by legal distinctions between those subject to special protection (such as refugees) and other migrants, who have limited or no access to state social welfare and economic systems. The latter category is in fact the majority of migrants in the world. This has led to a structural dependence by wealthier, migrant-receiving countries on (im)migrant labour.[3] In this broad context, migration experts have emerged.

Migration experts from non-governmental organizations (NGOs), research institutes, corporations and international organizations have long been involved in the formulation and implementation of migration policies. International organizations, platforms and networks involved in developing migration policy, including the UNHCR, the Hague Process on the Future of Asylum and Migration, and most especially the IOM, the main international organization devoted to migrant issues,

Handmaker was a participatory observer in the migration policy discussions, which were organized by the International Organization for Migration (IOM)/ United Nations High Commissioner for Refugees (UNHCR) and the Hague Process.

[1] S. Sassen, *Globalization and its Discontents: Essays on the New Mobility of People and Money* (New York: New Press, 1999).

[2] Migration flows are comprehensively documented by organizations such as the Migration Policy Institute in Washington DC. See www.migrationinformation.org.

[3] S. Castles, 'Why Migration Policies Fail', *Ethnic and Racial Studies*, 27 (2004), 205–27, at 210.

have highlighted the importance of expertise from non-state actors. The IOM in particular has emphasized that these partnerships help it to provide 'substantive, expert and organizational assistance to governments and other institutions'.[4] According to the IOM, partnerships with NGOs, research institutes, corporations and international organizations 'provide an important platform for advancing cooperation on migration'.[5] IOM spokesperson Irena Vojackova-Sollorano has highlighted the importance of expertise from different sources and has stressed the need for the following: 'Cooperative approaches that bring together governments, the shipping industry, NGOs and international organizations are therefore urgently needed if we are to ensure the safety and protection of all people rescued at sea.'[6] In practice, as this chapter will reveal, migration experts have not only been involved in framing the content of policy discussions, but also in assisting states in the implementation of migration policies. However, the close, albeit always secondary involvement of experts in state-led policy discussions and implementation programmes cannot be said to be free of challenges.

The content and practical implementation of migration policies is oriented around 'irregular migration', a very problematic concept. Uncritical use of this concept results in the reproduction of what we will argue is a false dichotomy between regular and irregular migrants. In this chapter, we will first explain how the concept of irregular migration has become a policy mantra, rooted in notions of state security and reinforced by the use of strict enforcement measures to stem the flow of migrants, and why this is problematic.[7] We will substantiate this by explaining that the enforcement of border controls, which often involves a number of migration experts, is an extension of a state-centred, extraterritorial and often privatized interdiction and/or deterrent measures, including detention and carrier sanctions. Alternatively, a migrant-centred perspective reveals both the social exclusion and the liminal

[4] See www.iom.int/jahia/Jahia/partnerships/ngos/lang/en.

[5] The IOM's cooperation with NGOs and research institutes is very close, occurs 'in various contexts and reflects the diverse relationships between the two actors. . . . IOM and NGOs may act as equal partners, or complement each other's activities'. See IOM, 'Civil Society and NGOs', www.iom.int/cms/en/sites/iom/home/about-iom-1/members-and-observers/civil-society–ngos.html.

[6] IOM, 'Expert Meeting on Refugees and Asylum Seekers in Distress at Sea Opens in Djibouti', www.iom.int/cms/en/sites/iom/home/news-and-views/press-briefing-notes/pbn-2011/pbn-listing/expert-meeting-on-refugees-and-asylum-se.html.

[7] B. Ghosh, *Huddled Masses and Uncertain Shores: Insights into Irregular Migration* (The Hague: Kluwer Law International, 1998).

legality[8] to which all migrants are relegated as a result of measures aimed at 'combating' irregular migration.

Second, this chapter will substantiate that, with some exceptions, migration experts have become involved in reproducing binary explanations of contemporary migration by using the regular versus irregular distinction in relation to transnational migrants.[9] We will provide one example where experts from NGOs challenged the concept of irregular migration, and another example where experts from NGOs and corporate backgrounds who advise states and international organizations reproduced the irregular migration mantra rather than critically engaging with the concept. This binary notion of transnational migration reinforces patterns of social exclusion, based on the possession of social, economic and human capital (knowledge migrants and refugees), and deepens the marginalization of those lacking this capital (most other migrants). In other words, by emphasizing a distinction between certain privileged categories of migrants and others, experts reproduce state-created hierarchies or categories of 'worthiness' within the discourse on migration. This distinction may add to existing public and political pressures to take an uncompromising stance on undocumented migrants that has a significant external impact on migration policy discourses, and reinforces the normative vulnerability of the vast majority of migrants.

The reality of contemporary migration and border control enforcement measures has overwhelmingly been focused on what Helton has referred to as containment measures designed to combat irregular migration.[10] Consequently, as we will substantiate later in this chapter, migration experts have become a core component in giving legitimacy to the enforcement of migration policies and border controls, as a direct extension of state-centred efforts to contain and control migrants. We will also show that migration experts from NGOs, academia and elsewhere engaged in migration policy discussions and enforcement measures are fulfilling central roles as policy advisors and even implementers,

[8] Liminal legality refers to a form of 'in-between' legal status which falls short of the legal status held by others and fails to allow migrants to protect their rights. The concept has been developed and applied by various authors, notably C. Menjivar, 'Liminal Legality: Salvadoran and Guatemalan Immigrants' Lives in the United States', *American Journal of Sociology*, 111 (2006), 999–1037; and E. Glenn, 'Constructing Citizenship: Exclusion, Subordination and Resistance', *American Sociological Review*, 76 (2011), 1–24.

[9] The term 'transnational migrants' refers to migrants who travel between different nation-states.

[10] A. Helton, *The Price of Indifference: Refugees and Humanitarian Action in the New Century* (Oxford University Press, 2001).

and that their unquestioning acceptance of the concept of irregular migration is problematic. We conclude that the consequences of this are not only worrying from a human rights perspective, but that containment measures by states to address migration flows will continue to fail so long as policy makers continue to focus on a state-centred approach and lack a deeper and more contextualized understanding of both the dynamics of migration and the relationship between private/civic actors and the government.

13.2 Contextualizing the role of experts: the mantra of irregular migration

The context in which migration experts have contributed to migration policy discussions and measures for the implementation of these policies has overwhelmingly been framed by the notion of irregular migration. It is not clear when the term 'irregular migration' first came into use, although the IOM provided the following definition at a workshop in its World Migration Report of 2008, referring in particular to states' practices:

> The term 'irregular' may refer variously to conditions of entry, stay and employment, including possession of appropriate documentation. Most commonly, irregularity is determined by reference to the norms of the country of destination or transit, although recent research has shown that irregularity is a multifaceted concept that is often not reflected in policy responses.[11]

Despite this lack of clarity, the term has been propagated extensively by both states and the IOM, and has been perceived as a desirable alternative to other terms that were either less clear (e.g., undocumented migrants) or denigratory (e.g., illegal migrants). Elspeth Guild has noted that irregular migration 'occupies a central place on the European Union's area of freedom security and justice'.[12] Guild acknowledged the ambiguity of IOM and states' definitions, arguing that irregular essentially means 'illegal' and that states are notoriously reluctant to define what it means exactly to be either irregular or illegal.

So, what do other experts understand to be irregular migration? Bimal Ghosh, a long-time advisor to the IOM, argued in 1998 that 'there is still no

[11] IOM, *World Migration Report 2008* (IOM, 2008).

[12] E. Guild, 'Who is an Irregular Migrant?' in B. Bogusz, R. Cholewinski, A. Cygan and E. Szyszczak (eds.), *Irregular Migration and Human Rights: Theoretical, European and International Perspectives* (Leiden: Martinus Nijhoff, 2004), 3–28, at 3.

clear or universally accepted definition of irregular migration'.[13] According to Ghosh's broad formulation, irregular migration is 'any inter-country movement that takes place outside the regulatory framework of the sending country, or the receiving country, or both'.[14] Referring to an expert round-table in Lisbon in 2002, Koser argued that the term 'irregular migration' should relate exclusively to the 'secondary movement' of asylum seekers and refugees that decide to travel onwards to a country other than the one in which they originally applied for, or had been granted refugee status.[15] Similar to Guild, Koser explained that there is a lack of conceptual clarity in the use of the term. Like many other migration experts, Koser is exclusively focused on a particular category of irregular migrants (asylum seekers and refugees) whose legal status is explicitly protected in international law. This exclusive focus has had a (perhaps unintended) consequence. As we will discuss later on in this chapter, states have directed their efforts at combating irregular migration through introducing ever-stringent restrictions on applying for refugee status, making it increasingly difficult for irregular migrants to obtain this status.

Pécoud and Guchteneire, for their part, argue that irregular migration is a central feature of migration policy that suggests that borders are porous and thus need greater surveillance.[16] However, the authors condemned the impact that restrictive policies, aimed generally at irregular migrants, have had on both asylum seekers and economic migrants:

> The measures meant to stop irregular migration have direct consequences on the asylum principle, according to which all human beings are entitled to seek protection from persecution. The lack of legal migration channels incites some economic migrants to present themselves as asylum-seekers, which, in a self-nurturing process, then casts doubts on all refugees and leads to even more restrictive measures.[17]

The use of the term 'irregular migration' has been reflected in three particular, state-led trends in which migration experts have fulfilled an important, albeit secondary role. First, conceptually, the term has been

[13] Ghosh, *Huddled Masses*, at 1. [14] *Ibid.*, at 34.

[15] Koser went on to explain that there are multiple reasons for secondary movement, including a 'lack of access to legal migration opportunities'. K. Koser, 'Irregular Migration, State Security and Human Security: A Paper Prepared for the Policy Analysis and Research Programme', (Geneva: Global Commission on International Migration, 2005), at 5–7.

[16] A. Pécoud and P. Guchteneire, 'International Migration, Border Controls and Human Rights: Assessing the Relevance of a Right to Mobility', *Journal of Borderlands Studies*, 21 (2006), 69–86, at 70.

[17] *Ibid.*, at 73.

invoked in unilateral and collective state efforts to combat irregular migration. The mantra of irregular migration has underpinned the efforts of states to interdict migrants, both in-country (through strict border controls)[18] and extra-territorially (for example, interdictions at sea).[19] Second, governments have invoked the term in their efforts to prioritize knowledge migrants, recognize refugees and exclude all other categories of migrants. Third, the mantra has been invoked to justify the detention of migrants as well as to justify sanctions against private carriers,[20] both in an effort to contain irregular migration.[21] We will discuss each of these trends in turn.

13.2.1 Combating irregular migration and the transnationalization of border controls

Efforts to combat irregular migration have taken similar forms in jurisdictions around the world and have also taken on a transnational dimension. In Europe, the principal institution established to interdict migrants and enforce border control at a collective level is the European Agency for the Management of Operational Cooperation at the External Borders of the Member States of the European Union (Frontex). A significant feature of Frontex is the Rapid Border Intervention Teams or 'Rabit'.[22] The Regulation setting up the Rabit system in 2007 aimed at:

> Effective management of the external borders through checks and surveillance . . . to combat illegal immigration and trafficking in human beings and to prevent any threat to the internal security, public policy, public health and international relations of the Member States.[23]

18 *Ibid.*; Ghosh, *Huddled Masses.*

19 A. Fischer-Lescano, T. Löhr and T. Tohidipur, 'Border Controls at Sea: Requirements under International Human Rights and Refugee Law', *International Journal of Refugee Law*, 21 (2009), 256–96.

20 The latter is explained in depth by Scholten and Terlouw, Chapter 14, this volume.

21 A fourth and relatively more recent trend in the development of the irregular migration mantra is the containment of migrants through social and economic measures, designed to compel irregular migrants who have failed to obtain – or lost – their legal residential status to return home.

22 EU, 'Regulation (EC) No. 863/2007 of the European Parliament and of the Council establishing a mechanism for the creation of Rapid Border Intervention Teams and amending Council Regulation (EC) No. 2007/2004 as regards that mechanism and regulating the tasks and powers of guest officers', Official Journal L 199 (2007), 31 July 2007, 30–9.

23 *Ibid.*, at 30.

After vaguely asserting that the Regulation respects 'fundamental rights', the Rabit Regulation refers explicitly to the rights of 'refugees and persons requesting international protection, in particular as regards non-refoulement'.[24] Such an exclusive focus on refugees, we argue, is problematic as it disregards the vast majority of migrants.

Frontex is not the only agency coordinating border enforcement. As Saskia Sassen has noted, there has been a proliferation of transnational regimes aimed at regulating temporary labour migration, much of which has been privatized. This proliferation of these transnational regimes, she argued, has seriously undermined state sovereignty. She described this phenomenon as:

> part of the larger institutional reshuffling of some of the components of sovereign power over entry and can be seen as an extension of the general set of processes whereby state sovereignty is partly being decentred onto other non- or quasi-governmental entities for the governance of the global economy.[25]

The privatization of border control has been especially problematic.[26] Interdictions of irregular migrants, especially outside a state's physical borders, have fuelled an economically significant and technology-driven industry. Insurance companies sell 'risk management' policies to companies with expertise in interdicting, detaining and deporting irregular migrants. Denmark, Israel, South Africa, the UK, the USA and other countries with large security industries offer a range of products and advisory services to countries interested in strengthening their physical borders against irregular migrants.[27] The euphemistically named 'immigration liaison officers' (ILOs) are hired by states as security experts with very little (if any) knowledge or training in the field of migrant protection or human rights. ILOs appear in airports around the world, screening passengers from the manifest list, to the final point of physical embarkation of the aircraft.[28] They have

[24] *Ibid.*, at 31–2.

[25] S. Sassen, 'Regulating Immigration in a Global Age: A New Policy Landscape', *The Annals of the American Academy of Political and Social Science*, 570 (2000), 65–77, at 71.

[26] See also Scholten and Terlouw, Chapter 14, this volume.

[27] Elbit systems, an Israeli company, provides various surveillance, detection and other equipment to manage border control, including at the US/Mexico border – see www.elbitsystems.com. P&I (Personal and Indemnity) Associates is an Australian/South African company that specializes in migrant deportations – see www.pandi.co.za. G4S is a UK/Danish company involved in various forms of migrant interdiction and detention. In 2002 it bought the US firm Wackenhut, which had long been involved in migrant detention – see www.g4s.com.

[28] Interview on 9 March 2011 by Handmaker with an official (details on record) of the IOM who was responsible for liaising with ILOs.

been contracted by the governments of European countries, the USA, Australia and others in an effort to interdict irregular migrants before they physically travel to these countries. With a drop in the cost of air travel, these countries have become a popular destination for largely middle-class, irregular migrants seeking to better their economic situation or protection from persecution.[29]

Interdiction at land and sea borders targets the remaining 'irregular' migrants. States have constructed formidable physical barriers to keep them out. Some of the most notorious have been technology-enhanced barriers erected by the USA along its border with Mexico, with substantial assistance from private corporations and advisors.[30] The significant increase in US border controls has led to a substantial increase in migrant deaths.[31] In Europe, Frontex coordinates the interception of irregular migrants on land, particularly in Eastern European countries, and also at sea, in cooperation with European Union (EU) Member States. Fischer-Lescano and colleagues explored the extent to which countries in the EU claimed jurisdiction not only in their own territory, but also extra-territorially, both on the high seas and in the territorial waters of third countries. Their principal concern was whether states' obligations to refugees extended to these extra-territorial interdictions, and they concluded that this was the case.[32] It was, however, notable that the authors did not express a view as to the (il)legality of extra-territorial interdictions regarding irregular migrants more generally. Their focus was on refugees, the implication being that their status as (potential) refugees invoked these protective obligations.

13.2.2 Prioritizing knowledge migrants, recognizing refugees and condemning others

In individual states, such as the Netherlands, the irregular migration mantra has led to a highly confusing situation. Dutch immigration policy is, officially, based on the protection of human rights, while simultaneously it is intolerant towards immigrants. Between October 2010 and the end of April 2012, the then government of the Netherlands ('Rutte 1')

[29] *Ibid.*

[30] A. Aradas, 'US–Mexico Border: Efforts to Build a Virtual Wall', *BBC Mundo*, 29 August 2012, www.bbc.co.uk/news/technology-19409682.

[31] W. A. Cornelius, 'Death at the Border: Efficacy and Unintended Consequences of US Immigration Control Policy', *Population and Development Review*, 27 (2001), 661–85.

[32] Fischer-Lescano, Löhr and Tohidipur, 'Border Controls at Sea'.

had the basis for its migration policies enshrined in a so-called *gedoog-akkoord* ('Tolerance Agreement'),[33] which stated that:

> Asylum and migration policy is strict but fair ... The Netherlands will continue to protect and absorb refugees in terms of the Refugee Convention ... This cannot apply to asylum seekers who appear to be economic migrants. Therefore, it will be determined as soon as possible in which category the applicant belongs and whether they can stay here or must leave the Netherlands.[34]

Accordingly, the then Dutch Minister for Immigration, Gerd Leers, enforced this policy with little exception, including in the well-publicized case of an 18-year-old Angolan simply known as 'Mauro'.[35] While Mauro originally arrived as an under-aged asylum seeker, by reaching the age of majority, with little prospects to continue his education (which would have placed him in the desirable category of 'knowledge migrant'), he was subsequently regarded as an economic migrant (a migrant in search of labour or a labour migrant) and should, according to Minister Leers' interpretation of the government's 'Tolerance Agreement', be removed 'as quickly as possible'.[36]

Furthermore, the Dutch government's favouring of 'knowledge migrants'[37] who migrate in an orderly manner has been accompanied by

[33] This agreement was the outcome of government coalition negotiations between the anti-immigration Freedom Party (PVV), the socially conservative Christian Democrats (CDA) and the liberal VVD Party.

[34] Tolerance Agreement, *Gedoogakkoord VVD-PVV-CDA*, signed on 30 July 2010, www.kabinetsformatie2010.nl, at 4.

[35] See e.g., www.rtl.nl/components/actueel/editienl/nieuws/2011/w43/Mauro-moest-al-eerder-het-land-uit.xml; http://nos.nl/op3/artikel/307808-stemming-mauro-na-cdacongres-online-acties-voor-de-angolees.html.

[36] On 30 March 2013, it was reported that Mauro received a permanent residence permit for the Netherlands as part of the 'children's pardon' applied by the Dutch government. See Defence for Children International, 'Finally Certainty for Mauro' (translation), www.defenceforchildren.nl/p/21/2675/mo89-mc21.

[37] According to the Dutch government, a knowledge migrant is one who has graduated with a Master's degree or PhD from a university ranked in one of the recognized World University Rankings, who obtained this higher degree not more than three years ago (or graduated from a Dutch university). Additionally, the knowledge migrant should earn at least €51,239 (or €37,575 if younger than 30 years). This income criterion does not apply to a person who is admitted for doctoral studies at a Dutch university or if the person is fulfilling a medical residency as a specialist. This information is difficult to find and changes frequently. The above-mentioned criteria were obtained from the Dutch government's website (www.rijksoverheid.nl/onderwerpen/buitenlandse-werknemers) and in a document (in English) provided to prospective knowledge migrants: Immigration and Naturalisation Service, *A Highly Educated Migrant Seeking Employment*, Ministry of the Interior and Kingdom Relations, 30 August 2012, www.ind.nl/en/Customer-Information/Documents/1211.pdf.

a shift away from labour migrants. The promotion of knowledge migrants has become a cornerstone of European governments' migration policies. Faist put it as follows:

> In immigration countries, notions of economic globalisation have led to an increased effort by companies and states to attract post-secondary international students and future scientists. OECD countries have thus changed their legislation, moving from a 'red card' to a 'red carpet' strategy. The hunt for knowledge workers is nonetheless reminiscent of 'body shopping' and the poaching of workers ... The difference is, however, that nowadays it is not the countries catching up that engage in poaching, but those who are furthest ahead.[38]

According to this 'red carpet' treatment, Leers also made it clear that the government ought to be able to 'choose' who arrives and works in the Netherlands. The criteria for choosing are tied to the paternalistic assumption that it is only those with a real chance of success that ought to be formally admitted to the Netherlands.[39]

13.2.3 Detention and carrier sanctions

The rapid growth in the border control industry, fuelled by global efforts to combat irregular migration, has included detention facilities, both within a state's territorial boundaries and abroad. For example, Morocco has hosted Spanish-run detention centres in Ceuta and Melilla in an attempt to interdict and deter would-be migrants.[40] This has been further reinforced by a Spanish-funded 'early warning radar system' to control Spanish maritime borders.[41]

At home, states have spent relatively large portions of their budget on the detention of irregular migrants. The Dutch government spends well over €250 million per year on the detention of migrants and asylum seekers.[42] Recorded as overseas development assistance, this amount

[38] T. Faist, 'Migrants as Transnational Development Agents: An Inquiry into the Newest Round of the Migration–Development Nexus', *Population, Space and Place*, 14 (2008), 21–42, at 33.

[39] A. Smit, 'De kansrijke migrant bestaat niet', *De Volkskrant*, 25 October 2011; M. E. van Bochove, K. M. Rusinovic and G. B. M. Engbersen, 'Over de rode loper: Kennismigranten in Rotterdam en Den Haag', Research Report, Faculty of Social Sciences, Erasmus University Rotterdam (2010).

[40] M. Carr, 'Policing the Frontier: Ceuta and Melilla', *Race and Class*, 39 (1997), 61–6.

[41] H. de Haas, 'The Myth of Invasion: The Inconvenient Realities of African Migration to Europe', *Third World Quarterly*, 29 (2008), 1305–22, at 1309.

[42] Netherlands Parliament, *HGIS-Jaarverslag 2010, Homogene Groep Internationale Samenwerking*, presented to Parliament on 18 May 2011, at 19.

substantially exceeds the Dutch government's annual non-earmarked contribution of €2.9 million to the budget of UNHCR.[43]

Following general global trends of detaining irregular migrants, an increasing number of migrant detention facilities have been privatized. Describing the treatment of irregular migrants in secure detention in the USA, which are often run by large corporations, Dow described the well-documented 'beat and greet reception' by correctional officers there, which has included:

> kicking, punching, and . . . plucking detainees' body hairs with pliers, forcing detainees to place their heads in toilet bowls, encouraging and ordering detainees to perform sexual acts upon one another, forcing detainees to assume unusual and degrading positions while naked and cursing at and verbally insulting the detainees.[44]

In South Africa, the 'inadmissibility facility' at Johannesburg Airport and 'Lindela Accommodation Centre', both run by private corporations, are responsible for the detention of irregular migrants. Lindela[45] is run by Bosasa and is located in a former mine outside Johannesburg. The Lindela facility's management persistently distinguishes itself from its contractor, the South African Department of Home Affairs, making clear that the management 'has no authority over the apprehension, detention or release of any person at Lindela'. And yet, it offers services in: 'Capturing of finger prints, induction programme to inform detainees of their legal rights [and] visiting procedures.'[46] The South African Human Rights Commission has issued at least two reports describing the deplorable conditions in the facility[47] and lawyers acting on behalf of detainees have taken legal action against the facility, albeit mainly in relation to the detention of asylum seekers and refugees.[48]

Finally, emphasizing states' transnational approach to combating irregular migration, in addition to internal controls, extra-territorial

43 *Ibid.*, at 34.

44 M. Dow, *American Gulag: Inside US Immigration Prisons* (Berkeley: University of California Press, 2008), at 143–4.

45 'Lindela' means 'wait here' in several South African indigenous languages.

46 PMG, 'Bosasa briefing to the Parliamentary Committee on Home Affairs on 11 August 2005' (Cape Town: Parliamentary Monitoring Group, 2005).

47 SAHRC, *Lindela at the Crossroads for Detention and Repatriation: An Assessment of the Conditions of Detention* (Johannesburg: South African Human Rights Commission, 2000), www.queensu.ca/samp/migrationresources/xenophobia/reports/sahrc1.pdf.

48 Human Rights Watch, *Living on the Margins: Inadequate Protection for Refugees and Asylum Seekers in Johannesburg* (New York: Human Rights Watch, 2005), www.hrw.org/reports/2005/11/16/living-margins, at 48.

interdictions and detention, states have introduced carrier sanctions. The idea is to push responsibility for border control away from states and towards private actors. For example, airlines that transport migrants lacking legal travel documentation are fined large sums of money per migrant.[49]

13.3 Migration experts and their reproduction of the term 'irregular migration'

As mentioned above, the movement of people around the globe is connected to a larger set of economic, transnational and geopolitical trends. The realities of migration are in tension with the containment-oriented migration policies that states use in their efforts to combat irregular migration.

This section will show that the realities of migration have not been a central feature of most migration policy debates involving the contributions of migration experts. In particular, the sparse efforts of migration experts to seriously critique the concept of irregular migration has led to a reproduction and normalization of the concept. The importance of examining migration from a migrant-oriented rather than a state-oriented perspective has not been a mainstream view.[50] In this section, the involvement of migration experts in reproducing the irregular migration mantra is analysed in three forms, namely: through promoting the link between asylum and (orderly) migration; through giving a 'human face' to state-led efforts to interdict migrants; and, more broadly, through failing to speak out and address the efforts of governments to 'combat' irregular migration.

13.3.1 Migration experts and the asylum–migration nexus

In the context of refugee and asylum, experts have responded to IOM-led and UNHCR-supported initiatives to promote a nexus between the provision of asylum for political refugees and the promotion of orderly migration more generally.

Correspondingly, the casual use of the term 'irregular migration' by many migration experts has reinforced states' efforts to combat irregular migration in a similar way to how states combat crime. In his 1998 book,

[49] See Scholten and Terlouw, Chapter 14, this volume.

[50] See T.-D. Truong, D. Gasper, J. Handmaker and S. I. Bergh (eds.), *Migration, Gender and Social Justice: Perspectives on Human Security* (Frankfurt: Springer, 2014). Available at: www.iss.nl/IRDC.

Ghosh already forewarned policy makers of the potential dangers involved in what others (including Helton) later referred to as containment measures.[51] He argued there was a 'real danger' on the part of states' policy makers that:

> in their anxiety to curb irregular migration as quickly as possible, the receiving industrial countries might attach a disproportionate importance to a set of narrow and ad hoc measures, focusing on short-term cures through border control and punitive action.[52]

The concept of irregular migration and the resulting policies of containment long pre-date the rigorous, state-centred responses to the events of 11 September 2001. Immigration control was, in fact, already a big issue since the 1980s.[53] The so-called War on Terror brought with it additional pressures to protect industrialized states from terrorist attacks in future through further curtailing the already-restricted possibilities for migration. In short, the War on Terror has justified new and ever-more draconian measures against migrants, including the use of biometrics.[54]

As confirmed by Koser and others, a trend in the use of the term 'irregular migration' has been to deliberately link it to the need for legal protection and institutional arrangements for asylum seekers and refugees. This was, in fact, the central topic of policy discussions in 2001, when the IOM sponsored an initiative designed to address the so-called asylum–migration nexus as part of the UNHCR's 2001 Global Consultations on International Refugee Protection.[55]

A document was produced by IOM and was formally, albeit reluctantly, endorsed by the UNHCR,[56] clearly implying that asylum reception systems were to be the primary target of states' individual and collective

[51] Helton, *The Price of Indifference*. [52] Ghosh, *Huddled Masses*, at 46–7.

[53] B. Chiswick, 'Illegal Immigration and Immigration Control', *Journal of Economic Perspectives*, 2 (1988), 101–15, at 101.

[54] L. Amoore, 'Biometric Borders: Governing Mobilities in the War on Terror', *Political Geography*, 25 (2006), 336–51.

[55] Leading up to the fiftieth anniversary and second meeting of states party to the 1951 United Nations Convention Relating to the Status of Refugees, the UNHCR held a series of meetings as part of the 'Global Consultations on International Protection'. For more information, see www.unhcr.org/pages/4a16b14b6.html.

[56] United Nations, 'Refugee Protection and Migration Control: Perspectives from UNHCR and IOM', *Refugee Survey Quarterly*, 22 (2003), 111–25. At a June 2001 meeting to discuss this document (attended by Handmaker), the then Director of International Protection, Erika Feller, made clear that she was not in favour of the UNHCR's endorsement of the IOM document, but that it had been made clear to her that the UNHCR had 'no choice' but to be involved.

efforts to deal with irregular migrants. The document placed substantial attention on state security and control. It furthermore confused notions of who should qualify as an irregular migrant by conflating irregular migrants with the even more vague characterization of a 'broader mixed flow' of migrants:

> Refugees are not migrants in the lay sense of the word. They move through compulsion, not on the basis of meaningful choice, and their immediate objective is to seek protection, not a migration outcome. This being said, refugees may also move – in fact increasingly do so – within a broader mixed flow which includes both forced and voluntary movements. They may even resort to migrant smugglers as one way to leave their country. At the same time, in the absence of viable, legal migration options to pursue, persons who are not refugees are nevertheless seeking to enter countries of their choice through the asylum channel, it being often the only entrance possibility effectively open to them. So the line between migrant and asylum-seeker progressively blurs in the public mind, just as does the distinction between migration control and refugee protection in the policies of some States.[57]

The document further stressed elaborate interdiction or 'interception' measures as 'one of the most effective measures to enforce their domestic migration laws and policies'.[58] By contrast, the document dedicated only minimal attention to migrant or refugee protection by way of a variety of unelaborated 'safeguards'.[59] Although the document acknowledged the complex realities of migration, it still focused on measures to discourage 'root causes' of migration in order to 'maintain the integrity of the institution of asylum'.[60]

Migration experts responded to the document in a variety of ways.[61] First, the document's cursory treatment of the root causes of movement was criticized, based on the argument that more complex reasons as to why people were moving were being avoided. As an alternative to the restrictive line proposed by the IOM–UNHCR document, NGO experts, led primarily by Human Rights Watch, collectively promoted a rights-based normative discourse, emphasizing that 'all human beings have inalienable rights', but that refugees have 'additional rights'.[62] Some

[57] *Ibid.*, at 1. [58] *Ibid.*, at 5. [59] *Ibid.*, at 8–9. [60] *Ibid.*, at 10.

[61] Human Rights Watch et al., 'NGO Background Paper on the Refugee and Migration Interface (28–29 June 2001)', *Refugee Survey Quarterly*, 22 (2003), 373–89. The original version of this NGO paper, which lists the full set of organizations that contributed, is available on the website of Human Rights Watch, www.hrw.org/en/node/77559.

[62] *Ibid.*, at 375.

critique of the concept of irregular migration noted that there were 'grey areas' involved in avoiding the 'orderly' migration channels. For example, they argued that some irregular or undocumented migrants may have a valid asylum claim and very good reasons for not presenting themselves to the authorities.[63] The experts further critiqued the perception by IOM that migrants were merely abusing the system, which tended to ignore the very stringent measures involved in migrating in an 'orderly' manner.[64] Finally, the experts criticized the interception of irregular migrants as a key policy strategy, which often took place in unmonitored zones.[65]

In other words, NGO-affiliated migration experts in this policy discussion critiqued the enforcement of border controls, as well as certain questionable assumptions underpinning the concept of irregular migration. While asylum seekers and refugees were noted as particularly vulnerable in these circumstances, the NGO-affiliated migration experts on this occasion did not reinforce the hierarchical division between 'orderly' and other migrants. By contrast, as will be explained in the next section, a rather different approach was taken where migration experts strove to present a 'positive' face to orderly migration.

13.3.2 Giving migration a 'positive' face?

Another example of the involvement of migration experts in global migration policy processes is one in which the concept of irregular migration was uncritically reproduced and hierarchies of migrants were reinforced, despite the emphasis placed by these experts on giving migration a 'positive' face. In 2000, under the auspices of the Netherlands Society for International Development, an initiative was launched that eventually became known as 'The Hague Process', supported by a panel of experts known as the 'Club of The Hague'.[66] A series of meetings was held that led to a Declaration of The Hague, eventually adopted by the UN General Assembly on 23 December 2002.[67] Arguing

[63] *Ibid.*, at 376–7. [64] *Ibid.*, at 378. [65] *Ibid.*, at 380–1.

[66] This initiative involved a network of hundreds of representatives from NGOs, policy institutes, governments and international organizations in the 'Club of The Hague'. Participating organizations included the European Council on Refugees and Exiles, the Brookings Institute, the Danish Institute for Human Rights and many others. More information about the history of the process leading up to the document and follow-up can be found at www.thehagueprocess.org.

[67] United Nations, *Declaration of The Hague on the Future of Refugee and Migration Policy*, United Nations General Assembly, A/57/693 (2002), http://thehagueprocess.org/wordpress/wp-content/uploads/2012/12/Declaration-English.pdf. Although technically this

that migration should be viewed as 'a normal phenomenon which can contribute positively to economic and social development, cultural richness and diversity', the preamble to the Declaration further argued that 'no state can any longer act alone', effectively shifting the responsibility for migration policies towards collective efforts. The preamble further stated that 'refugees and migrants matter enormously to the international community' and that it was 'time for a major change of focus'.[68]

The migration experts involved in drafting the Declaration of The Hague adopted a rights-based approach, insisting that 'powerful instruments of human rights, international humanitarian law and refugee law already exist to protect refugees, and to a lesser extent migrants'.[69] The Declaration reflected a similar bias as the IOM–UNHCR document towards refugees and the promotion of 'orderly' migration.[70]

By promoting 'orderly legal migration' and discouraging 'disorderly migration', the migration experts who drafted the document explicitly endorsed the efforts of states and international organizations to combat irregular migration. Neither in the document nor during the processes leading up to the drafting of the document was the concept of irregular migration questioned.[71] Accordingly, by adopting a consensual, non-confrontational approach, and notwithstanding the 'positive' and rights-based approach adopted by the experts, specific problems relating to migration enforcement were left unaddressed.

13.3.3 Mixed efforts to address the problems of migration enforcement

A third example of the role of migration experts in the development of migration policy is their failure to critique a range of problems in states' and private companies' efforts at border control. An example of this was revealed in South Africa, where Dutch and South African experts, associated with NGOs, paralegal advice offices and church groups, became engaged in a well-intentioned but highly problematic project to assist the South African government in the return or regularization of several

document was the outcome of a state process, in fact the Declaration was adopted with little to no debate by the General Assembly.

[68] *Ibid.*, Preamble. [69] *Ibid.*, Principle 12. [70] *Ibid.*, Commentary, point 7.

[71] Handmaker attended nearly all meetings of the Hague Process from 2000 to 2002, as well as meetings of the strategy and drafting group that produced the Declaration.

hundred thousand former Mozambican refugees residing in South Africa without residence papers.[72]

By failing to confront the government with their primary responsibilities to administer these programmes and to a large extent taking on the responsibilities themselves, a chaotic situation emerged. The roles of the government and the mainly South African NGOs assisting the government became blurred. This situation was further complicated by a non-transparent political lobby by a Dutch NGO that was driven more by the demands of financial donors than by sound management, let alone the protection concerns of the migrants themselves.[73] With unclear responsibilities, the former Mozambican refugees became squeezed in the middle, with several thousand being denied any form of residential status and only very limited possibilities for legal appeal.[74]

The failure of NGO migration experts to adequately address the problems of migration policy enforcement does have some notable exceptions. For example, Menjivar has gone to exceptional lengths to challenge arguably the most insidious form of migrant interdiction and control, that is, the social control of migrants, by denying them access to basic services such as healthcare or labour rights.[75] Migrants' liminal status is furthermore well understood by two migration experts and lawyers, Pim Fischer and Jelle Klaas, who have been litigating against the Dutch government's policies aimed at the containment of migrants by way of targeted, restrictive social policies. They have challenged the exclusion of their clients as a result of what they refer to as the 'breakdown of the welfare state'.[76] They base their arguments on Dutch legal and constitutional obligations and international human rights instruments. These Dutch lawyers challenge what they see as 'degradation'. As quoted by Westerin and De Waard:

> an ideology has advanced according to which you have to be able to take care of yourself and it is your own fault if you live in poverty. Migrants and refugees without papers and without a right to facilities are being told: you have made the choice to come here, and now that your application for a residence title failed, you must also sort things out yourself.[77]

[72] J. Handmaker, *Advocating for Accountability: Civic–State Interactions to Protect Refugees in South Africa* (Cambridge: Intersentia, 2009), at 123–52.

[73] *Ibid.*, at 145–6. [74] *Ibid.* [75] Menjivar, 'Liminal Legality'.

[76] H. Westerink and E. de Waard, 'Leftist Lawyers in Action against Exclusion' (translation), *De Fabel van de Illegaal*, 89/90 (2008), www.doorbraak.eu/gebladerte/11375f89.htm.

[77] *Ibid.*

Fischer and Klaas have broken with the mainstream and conservative tradition of legal practice in the Netherlands by persistently litigating their cases, which few practising lawyers, including those with expertise in migration matters, have tended to emulate. Oomen has observed that Fischer and Klaas' break with tradition also extends to their extensive use of international law in cases that are brought before the Dutch court, which few Dutch lawyers do.[78]

Apart from their unconventional legal practice, Fischer and Klaas are unique in other ways as well. As experts in what can be broadly termed migration law,[79] they depart from most other migration experts. They do not focus their attention on 'orderly migrants' and asylum seekers, but on the largely forgotten category of irregular migrants who have lost, or never had in the first place, their legal residential status in the Netherlands and who face often profound social exclusion. As exceptions to the general rule that migration experts tend to privilege refugees and knowledge migrants, Fischer and Klaas, as well as Menjivar,[80] highlight a number of issues and concerns faced by the majority of so-called irregular migrants that most migration experts overlook.

13.3.4 Issues and concerns overlooked by most migration experts

In each of the aforementioned examples of policy formulation or (privatized) implementation measures aimed at combating irregular migration, particular issues and concerns arise that tend to be overlooked by migration experts. First, migration experts have tended to focus their attention on state responsibility, overlooking the increasingly private and for-profit nature of migration policy enforcement. State-defined security needs have increasingly shifted to companies, who deploy their state-given mandate with patently economic goals. This has a potentially perverse effect on the implementation of containment policies, for example, where restricting food rations offered to detained migrants in privately run detention facilities results in a raise for prison employees and the escape of a detainee harms the stock price of the private detention facility.[81]

[78] B. Oomen, 'Small Places: The Homecoming of Human Rights in the Netherlands', inaugural lecture, Utrecht University, delivered in Middelburg, 2 December 2011, at 38. Oomen went on to explain that this attitude reflects the 'primacy of parliament in political and legal decision-making'.

[79] P. Boeles and M. den Heijer, *European Migration Law* (Antwerp: Intersentia, 2009).

[80] Menjivar, 'Liminal Legality'. [81] Dow, *American Gulag*, at 97.

Second, if one regards – as we do – the proliferation of privatized enforcement measures as an inevitable harshening of the measures of containment, then migration experts would also be expected to question, equally harshly, the broader effects of for-profit containment of labour migrants in the labour market more generally. It has been discussed how the lack of attention to an already vulnerable labour force furthers their exploitation in labour markets profiting from migrants' inability to claim rights, but further attention could be paid to the structural dimensions of this issue.[82]

Third, and perhaps more importantly, migration experts often fail to appreciate how these developments reveal the normative persistence of the notion of the Westphalian state, which is being simultaneously challenged by the extension, velocity and depth of the movements of people, capital and intangibles. For example, contemporary patterns of migration challenge traditional notions of citizenship, understood as the bond between individuals, their rights and responsibilities, and a nation-state. In a highly mobile world, immigrants do not always become, or want to become, national citizens, or even to become visible. Hence, states are unable to deny these rights to non-citizens.[83] Rights claimed by immigrants could be derived from the legal status accorded them by a nation-state or by supranational norms entitling individuals to new avenues of citizenship participation, from accessing basic services such as health and education to labour protection. In other words, nationality (and citizenship) is no longer the only possible link to a political community, which an influential community of experts and policies seem to ignore in their reification of a self-contained nation-state.

As highlighted above, the reproduction by migration experts of the migration–asylum nexus, coupled with their failure to give migration a positive face, while simultaneously failing to address the problems of migration regulation and enforcement thereof, leads to a situation where migration experts overlook a range of highly relevant issues and concerns. Accordingly, larger questions can be asked, including about the social legitimacy that these experts have to participate in migration policy discussions, to assist in the implementation of migration policies or to consider alternative approaches for evaluating the scope and dynamics of migration.

82 C. Cranford, 'Networks of Exploitation: Immigrant Labor and the Restructuring of the Los Angeles Janitorial Industry', *Social Problems*, 52 (2005), 379–97.

83 I. Bloemraad, *Becoming a Citizen: Incorporating Immigrants and Refugees in the United States and Canada* (Berkeley: University of California Press, 2006).

13.4 Experts and output legitimacy

As discussed in the previous sections, the involvement of migration experts has the potential to reproduce bland policy mantras and to promote – intentionally or not – hierarchical categories of migrants. In this section we evaluate the roles that these experts have, either in formulating policy or assisting states with the implementation of that policy according to Abels' notion of input and output legitimacy.

According to Abels:

> Input legitimacy pertains to participation, i.e. the social dimension insofar as it considers who actually has access to the policy process and who can influence policy-making ... Output legitimacy, in contrast, builds on a concept of policy-making as problem-solving in the interest of the general public. The criterion here is functional, i.e. utilitarian effectiveness ... Input and output legitimacy are not disconnected, but closely interlinked. Output legitimacy actually builds on some form of political inclusion and representation, whereas input models argue that inclusion allows achieving a better quality of the output such as enhanced acceptance and compliance.[84]

By preoccupying themselves with refugees and migrants' knowledge and skill contributions, and by neglecting the pernicious nature of migration policies and enforcement measures, many migration experts involved in the migration and asylum debate neglect the vast majority of migrants.

Some migration experts, including Menjivar, take a more nuanced approach. Referring to the circumstances of labour migrants and their social exclusion in Canada, Menjivar explained that the 'in between' or liminal legal status 'shapes who [migrants] are, how they relate to others, their participation in local communities, and their continued relationship with [their countries of origin]'.[85] Although the uncertain legal status they possess can be 'long-term',[86] the 'grey areas' of possessing a liminal status have not been widely explored,[87] let alone incorporated into migration policies.

Similarly, Glenn explained that the notion of a liminal legal status transcends fixed categories of legal and illegal.[88] She referred to the

[84] G. Abels, 'Citizen Involvement in Public Policy-Making: Does it Improve Democratic Legitimacy and Accountability? The Case of PTA', *Interdisciplinary Information Sciences*, 13 (2007), 103–16, at 106–7.

[85] Menjivar, 'Liminal Legality', at 1000. [86] *Ibid.*, at 1001. [87] *Ibid.*, at 1004.

[88] Glenn, 'Constructing Citizenship', at 3. See also C. Mora and E. A. Undurraga, 'Racialisation of Immigrants at Work: Labour Mobility and Segmentation of Peruvian Migrants in Chile', *Bulletin of Latin American Research*, 3 (2013), 1–17.

hidden nature of segregation, both legal and social,[89] which was further manifested in the existence of internal organizations and activities 'allowing for emancipation' and 'external institutions of the political order, where non-whites were disenfranchised'.[90] The in-between status that irregular migrants claim, she argued, 'disturbs the coherence of the legal-illegal dichotomy'.[91]

Similar to Menjivar, Glenn's explanation represents a departure from the conventional binary understandings of migrants. By avoiding a characterization of migrants as being either 'orderly' (i.e., documented) or in search of protection in terms of international and national refugee and humanitarian laws or, on the other hand, irregular and falling outside either of these two categories, Glenn and Menjivar contributed to the output legitimacy of migration experts by resisting a binary categorization of migrants.

Experts engaged in migration policy discussions and even in the course of enforcement – also a component of the policy-making process – are clearly involved in what Abels referred to as a form of 'problem-solving in the interest of the general public'.[92] There are three categories that form a useful basis for testing the output legitimacy of these experts, namely whether the roles of migration experts: (1) are irrelevant; (2) position them as policy advisors; and/or (3) render them (administrative) decision makers. In each of these categories, the public role of the state as policy maker and implementer will have been brought into question.

Whether based at NGOs, research institutions or in corporations, the relevance of these experts' roles in policy making seems clear at first glance, although it may be overstated by themselves. However, influencing policy makers will be of little to no effect if experts fail to appreciate that certain structural boundaries exist in the relationship between civic actors and states. For example, it is primarily the role of governments to develop migration policies. In order to be of influence, NGOs could be recognized for their expertise and as 'concerned stakeholders', while by no means regarding themselves as irrelevant or replacing the role of government.[93] Furthermore, experts concerned with refugee protection could enhance the relevance of their role by not only taking heed of migrants more generally, but also of states' interests and global trends,

[89] Glenn, 'Constructing Citizenship', at 4–7. [90] *Ibid.*, at 8. [91] *Ibid.*, at 16.
[92] Abels, 'Citizen Involvement', at 105.
[93] Handmaker, *Advocating for Accountability*, at 202–3.

and by illustrating the direction that refugee policy could take by way of 'scenario analysis'. Explaining this approach, Helton wrote:

> The future of refugee policy is contingent upon a myriad of decisions within and outside of officialdom. Circumstances in the real world will impose constraints and create opportunities for policy development . . . leaders and thinkers must attempt to see forward: to expect the unexpected.[94]

That migration experts qualify as policy advisors also seems clear, although the (democratic) legitimacy of this role may be questioned. Experts often do fulfil the role of policy advisors, either as invited participants to a policy process[95] or as policy advocates or practising lawyers campaigning for a particular position.[96] NGO experts in particular are increasingly expected by their donors to support government through providing advice rather than resorting to confrontation. At the same time, the constituencies that NGOs often claim to represent expect experts to distance themselves from the governments they criticize, or at least not appear to be too influenced by the government. As explored elsewhere, the dual-roles fulfilled by NGO experts in particular involve an inevitable tension between engaging constructively in a government-led policy process and maintaining their critical independence.[97]

Nevertheless, identifying migration experts as administrative decision makers is increasingly a reality. As sub-contracted immigration liaison officers, deportation escorts and other private-run interdiction and risk-management operations or even as NGOs assisting government in the implementation of a migrant return programme,[98] migration experts fulfil a growing number of roles traditionally performed by politicians and bureaucrats administering the state. Furthermore, corporate migration experts are also carrying out central roles traditionally fulfilled by states.

However, a key point to note in all these cases is that in the diverse roles that they fulfil, as both advisors and implementers, experts are – perhaps inadvertently – privileging certain groups of migrants over others, and namely refugees and victims of humanitarian emergencies, as well as knowledge migrants who enter through orderly or regular channels.

[94] Helton, *The Price of Indifference*, at 257.

[95] Handmaker, *Advocating for Accountability*, at 91–122.

[96] J. Handmaker, J. Klaaren and J. Dugard (eds.), *South African Journal on Human Rights: Special Issue on Public Interest Litigation*, 27 (2011).

[97] Handmaker, *Advocating for Accountability*, at 5–8. [98] *Ibid.*, at 123–54.

13.5 Conclusions

This chapter has argued that based on a state-centred approach, the reproduction by some migration experts of the term 'irregular migration' has reinforced a false distinction between regular and irregular migrants. Other migration experts who take a more grounded and nuanced approach have avoided this problem. The former categorization has become increasingly problematic in a globalized and conflict-ridden world, where the movement of people is becoming the norm. A further classification reproduced by migration experts has emerged within the concept of 'irregulars': that of refugees and knowledge migrants, on the one hand, and labour migrants, on the other. This appears to be based on an assumption that the forces propelling migration and the human capital of knowledge migrants constitute different subjects, with different rights attached. The efforts of experts are then directed to the protection of refugees, while the economic system serves to 'protect' highly qualified knowledge migrants. Irregular migrants are hence seen as a problem to be solved.

This idea of regarding irregular migrants as a problem was confirmed by sociologist Saskia Sassen, who has argued that we are witnessing the emergence of two different circuits of migration – skilled migration and claims for refugee protection – that leave social stratification unchallenged.[99] There has been greater mobility of highly skilled professionals on the one hand, which more closely resembles the relatively free movement of capital. On the other hand, the vast majority of informal migrants are, by comparison, largely ignored. Concerning the latter category, a further distinction is made between labour workers and refugees. Labour workers are subject to increasing constraints of movement. This leads to flows 'outside the regulatory framework' of the sending and/or receiving country.[100] In short, the motivations for movement by refugees are valued by migration experts and policy makers as more worthy of protection than the economic deprivation of migrant labourers.

Experts engaged in migration policy discussions and enforcement measures fulfil central roles as policy advisors and even implementers. This is potentially problematic, not only because many of these experts do not address the negative effects of combating irregular migration but

[99] Sassen, 'Regulating Immigration'.

[100] S. Sassen, 'Informalization in Advanced Market Economies', *Issues in Development Discussion Paper*, 20 (Geneva: ILO, 1990), at 2.

also because they reinforce the protection of certain, privileged categories of migrants – namely refugees and knowledge migrants – to the detriment of the vast majority of migrants. Accordingly, migration experts without a more nuanced appreciation of migration miss an important opportunity to address the core issue at stake, that is, the inherent contradiction between the nature of migration and the reductionism of the irregular migration concept.

Consequently, many if not most migration experts have failed to address the complicated liminal legal and social status or associated marginalization that awaits migrants in their country of destination. A more grounded position is that the interests and concerns of refugees and other legal categories of migrants should be seen as fundamentally intertwined in terms of their legal and social exclusion.

The consequences of experts' involvement in migration policy discussions and enforcement measures are not only worrying from a human rights and social justice perspective. A closer look at the consequences of migration policies and the roles of experts in the construction of these policies aimed primarily at combating irregular migration reveals the failure of containment measures to address migration flows. As Stephen Castles has maintained:

> Policies that claim to exclude undocumented workers may often really be about allowing them in through side doors and back doors, so that they can be more readily exploited. This, in turn, could be seen as an attempt to create a transnational working class, stratified not only by skill and ethnicity, but also by legal status. The vast disparities of wealth and power in the emerging global order mean that not all citizens are equal and that some passports are better than others. Such hierarchies may be the basis of a new system of global economic stratification, in which migration – in all its guises – is a key element. In this context, migration control is really about regulating North-South relationships and maintaining inequality.[101]

We pose that this will continue to be the case so long as states, and the experts that advise and assist them, lack a deeper and more contextualized understanding of the dynamics of migration and the tense relationship between private actors and the government.

The implications of this are that experts engaged in migration policy discussions and implementation programmes would be regarded as more relevant and legitimate if they were more conscious in: (1) recognizing the primary responsibility of government, as well as the narrow but

[101] Castles, 'Why Migration Policies Fail', at 210.

significant possibilities to influence the direction of policy in state-led processes; (2) openly challenging one of the primary concepts underpinning state-centred international migration policies and implementation programmes, namely the concept of irregular migration; and (3) developing a more grounded and migrant-centred understanding of the realities of migration, and in particular the social stratification and liminal legality that many migrants face.

14

Private carriers as experts in immigration control

SOPHIE SCHOLTEN AND ASHLEY TERLOUW

14.1 Introduction

Since the 1980s, carriers have been increasingly involved in immigration control through the so-called carrier sanctions policies. Carrier sanctions policies generally impose financial sanctions on carriers that transport passengers who do not possess the required travel documents. They are further obliged to return the refused passenger(s) and can be held liable for any costs connected with the return and/or stay of the migrant(s). Private actors thus have become key players in a process that used to be subject to state control exclusively: immigration control.

In this chapter we consider how this involvement of carriers might be understood. Carriers can be seen as operating in a number of semi-autonomous social fields.[1] They are autonomous in making their own norms about transport conditions and their business, but semi-autonomous when they implement government rules about immigration control. In this latter role carriers may to some extent be regarded as part of an epistemic community, as defined by Haas:[2] their involvement in immigration control entails that carriers can be regarded as belonging to the community of experts in travel documents, identity papers and entry requirements. Although carriers might feel co-responsible for exercising this government task, they can – in our view – never really become an epistemic community because their first interest will always be commercial. Nevertheless, we will investigate whether carriers are moving in the direction of becoming an epistemic community or are forced to behave as an epistemic community. We do this by posing two sets of questions. First, what are the interests of the private carriers and governments

[1] S. F. Moore, 'The Semi-autonomous Social Field as an Appropriate Subject of Study', *Law and Society Review*, 7 (1973), 719–46.

[2] P. M. Haas, 'Introduction: Epistemic Communities and International Policy Coordination', *International Organization*, 46 (1992), 1–35.

involved; where do these interests collide and where do they meet? And to what extent are carriers willing partners in this process of border control? This leads to the second set of questions: what is the position of carriers in immigration control? What are their tasks, what expertise do they need to fulfil these tasks and which norms do they have to observe in relation to these tasks? With regard to these questions, the content and nature of carrier sanctions policies in the Netherlands and the UK are investigated, focusing on the airline industry. Finally, this chapter will critically assess the effects of allocating responsibilities for immigration control to private carriers. In particular, it will examine whether the involvement of carriers enhances output legitimacy. The core of the research presented in this chapter is based on interviews with representatives of airlines and various government officials that were conducted by one of the authors, Sophie Scholten.[3]

14.2 The rationale of involving carriers in immigration control

The involvement of private carriers is a response by governments to the difficulties that they encounter in controlling the entry of undocumented passengers and 'unwanted' immigrants. The importance of immigration control as a political issue grew in the 1980s when the number of immigrants and asylum seekers travelling to Western Europe increased rapidly, while a growing number of them did not possess the necessary travel documents. In response, governments introduced tougher immigration control mechanisms designed to check the flow of immigrants, especially asylum seekers.[4] Carrier sanctions were one of the measures introduced.

The question whether states have lost control over immigration has been the subject of debate. Some scholars argue that states hardly ever succeeded in managing migration.[5] Others argue that states have lost

[3] Semi-structured interviews were conducted during the period 2007–09 with representatives of the Dutch and British government and immigration authorities, private transport companies (KLM, Transavia, British Airways, British Midlands and EasyJet) and trade associations, both at the top (management) and the work-floor level.

[4] E. Feller, 'Carrier Sanctions and International Law', *International Journal of Refugee Law*, 1 (1989), 48–66.

[5] H. van Amersfoort, 'Migration: The Limits of Governmental Control', *New Community*, 22, (1996), 243–57; W.A. Cornelius, P.L. Martin and J.F. Hollifield, *Controlling Immigration: A Global Perspective* (Stanford University Press, 2004); W. A. Cornelius, 'Controlling Unwanted Immigration: Lessons from the United States', *Journal of Ethnic*

control over immigration – due to, for example, globalization.[6] Yet others suggest that Europeanization may offer states a possibility to regain control over migration.[7]

The inclusion of carriers in immigration control constitutes an attempt to control unwanted immigration. Lahav argues that 'shifting' competences and responsibility, and involving other actors such as carriers, has been the strategy of governments to 'extend their realm of action and overcome certain constraints'.[8] By changing the gatekeepers to include private, local and international or supranational agents, governments have enlarged the 'migration playing field' and so have been able to 'solve the control dilemma in ways that can at once appease public anxiety over migration and security, short-circuit judicial and normative constraints (by involving actors that are not bound by the international rules concerning human rights protection) and still promote trade and tourist flows'.[9] By 'privatizing' immigration control and handing it over to a carrier who operates before the physical border, governments avoid having to employ and train staff to execute control functions abroad and circumvent sovereignty issues. They also reduce the costs of accommodation, the assessment of asylum claims and expulsions. By using a private carrier to perform part of the control tasks, governments have circumvented practical and possible legal problems, and have 'externalized' part of the costs associated with migration control to private actors.[10] Carriers thus have become an essential part of state border control mechanisms.

The carrier sanctions legislation can be understood as a system of third-party liability[11] or as third-party policing.[12] As is characteristic for

and Migration Studies, 31 (2005), 775–94; W. A. Cornelius and I. Salehyan, 'Does Border Enforcement Deter Unauthorised Immigration?', *Regulation and Governance*, 1 (2007), 139–53; T. de Lange, *Staat, Markt en Migrant. De regulering van arbeidsmigratie naar Nederland 1945–2006* (The Hague: Boom Juridische Uitgevers, 2007).

[6] S. Sassen, *Losing Control? Sovereignty in an Age of Globalisation* (New York: Columbia University Press, 1996).

[7] A. Geddes, 'International Migration and State Sovereignty in an Integrating Europe', *International Migration*, 39 (2001), 21–42; V. Guiraudon and G. Lahav, 'A Reappraisal of the State Sovereignty Debate: The Case of Migration Control', *Comparative Political Studies*, 33 (2000), 163–95.

[8] G. Lahav, 'Migration and Security: The Role of Non-state Actors and Civil Liberties in Liberal Democracies', www.un.org/esa/population/meetings/secoord2003/ITT_COOR2_CH16_Lahav.pdf.

[9] *Ibid.*, at 89. [10] Guiraudon and Lahav, 'A Reappraisal of the State'.

[11] J. A. Gilboy, 'Compelled Third-Party Participation in the Regulatory Process: Legal Duties, Culture, and Noncompliance', *Law and Policy*, 20 (1998), 135–55.

[12] L. Mazerolle and J. Ransley, *Third Party Policing* (Cambridge University Press, 2006).

this kind of a third-party liability system,[13] the private carrier whose help is enlisted by government is neither the primary author nor the (direct) beneficiary of the misconduct it polices. This arrangement therefore differs from forms of third-party involvement in which the third parties stand to benefit from their cooperation with government.[14] In third-party liability systems, third parties are made responsible for the performance of tasks, while control remains with the state. They are used as 'sheriffs' deputies'[15] or as 'cops on the beat'.[16] In immigration control, 'misconduct' is interpreted as travelling undocumented or inadequately documented – trying to access a state's territory without possessing a (valid) passport or visa.

In the case of carriers' sanctions, opposing interests between carriers and governments are at play, which make it difficult for the state to assume that a carrier will willingly fulfil its duties. The commercial objective – and internal norm – of carriers is to transport as many passengers as possible in the most cost-efficient manner. Transferring responsibilities regarding the checking of documents will cost carriers time and money, mainly for hiring and training extra staff. Through the carriers' liability regime, de facto the passenger is transformed into a potential economic threat to the carrier, since the carrier might be fined for bringing an undocumented passenger into a country. Carriers have repeatedly stated they are unwilling to take on the role of immigration officers. Mazerolle and Ransley note that the use of a range of civil, criminal and regulatory rules and laws to encourage (or force) third parties into taking some crime control responsibility is central to third-party policing.[17] With the carriers' liability regime, states have introduced legislation which goes against the pre-existing internal norms of the carriers and thereby forced carriers to cooperate in complex immigration processes.

14.3 Private carriers as an epistemic community?

How might the involvement of carriers in immigration control be conceptualized? Haas developed a framework for comprehending the

[13] Gilboy, 'Compelled Third-Party Participation'.
[14] *Ibid.*; see also R. Kraakman, 'Gatekeepers: The Anatomy of a Third-Party Enforcement Strategy', *Journal of Law, Economics and Organisation*, 2 (1986), 53–104.
[15] J. Torpey, *The Invention of the Passport: Surveillance, Citizenship and the State* (Cambridge University Press, 2000), at 9.
[16] Kraakman, 'Gatekeepers', at 53. [17] Mazerolle and Ransley, *Third Party Policing*.

involvement of non-governmental communities in governance.[18] He uses the term 'epistemic communities' for a 'network of professionals with recognized expertise and competence in a particular domain and an authoritative claim to policy relevant knowledge within that domain or issue-area'.[19] Epistemic communities further share a set of normative, principled and causal beliefs as well as notions of validity, and a common policy enterprise.[20]

The natural task of carriers is to transport people and/or goods from one place to another. In exercising this commercial task, carriers mainly deal with private law and customary law norms. They are experts in transporting, in selling seats and in offering a good balance between service, speed and security, taking into account the applicable norms. This is the nucleus of their expertise. What states are most interested in is the access that carriers have to persons before they travel. This access is exactly what governments lack. Carrier sanctions involve a legal task and force carriers to become experts in immigration regulations, identity documents, passports, visa falsifications and so on. This expertise does not belong to the natural habitus of the carrier and is far removed from the natural nucleus of carrier expertise. Finally, in order not to risk *refoulement*, the carrier should develop some level of expertise in asylum law. This task, however, is a moral one, since the legal responsibility for *non-refoulement*[21] at all times rests with the state.

The broadening of tasks and the necessary expertise to fulfil these tasks thus expands the range of norms that a carrier needs to comply with and forces carriers to be experts in fields other than the core of their expertise. Figure 14.1 below depicts how carriers are forced to expand their expertise beyond their nucleus task – that of transporting people and goods.

Carriers cannot be said to hold a common set of principles and causal beliefs – an important element of Haas' definition of epistemic communities. However, they can be seen as a 'network of professionals with recognized expertise and competence in a particular domain and an authoritative claim to policy relevant knowledge within that domain or issue-area'.[22] Accordingly, carriers can be understood as an expert

[18] Haas, 'Introduction: Epistemic Communities'. [19] *Ibid.*, at 3. [20] *Ibid.*

[21] The principle of non-refoulement is, among others, laid down in Article 33 of the 1951 Refugee Convention. It prohibits the expulsion or return by a state of a refugee, in any manner whatsoever, to a country where his or her life or freedom will be threatened.

[22] Haas, 'Introduction: Epistemic Communities', at 3.

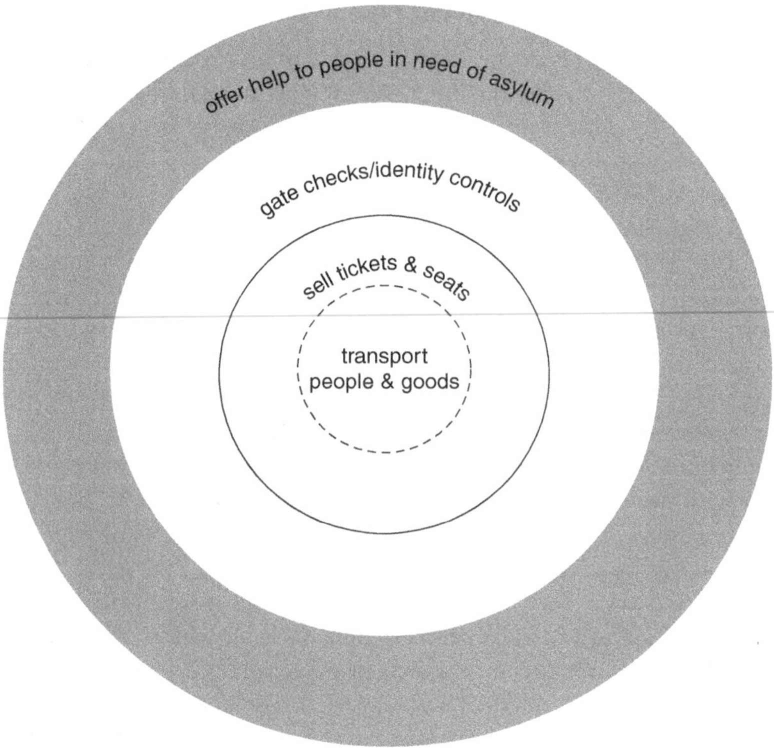

Figure 14.1 Carriers as experts

group, mainly because they have access to groups of people which a government cannot reach but whose behaviour it nonetheless desires to control. The fact that governments now also require carriers – in the fight against terrorism – to forward passenger data prior to departure corresponds with Haas' finding that decision makers turn to epistemic communities when they experience uncertainty about an issue area.[23] Carrier involvement in migration control might thus be regarded as the top-down enforced establishment of an expert group rather than of an epistemic community. Furthermore, unlike epistemic communities, carriers have a commercial interest, which makes their involvement not value-free. The latter aspect in particular prevents carriers from ever becoming an epistemic community.

[23] *Ibid.*, at 29.

14.4 Carriers as actors in semi-autonomous social fields

Carriers are thus forced to become experts in an area that is outside the scope of their day-to-day business. But why would a carrier agree to this expert role? To better understand the behaviour of the community of carriers, we draw on the work of Sally Falk Moore on semi-autonomous social fields (SASFs).[24] Moore suggests that it is useful to study a social field in terms of its semi-autonomy, that is, 'the fact that it can generate rules and customs and symbols internally, but that it is also vulnerable to rules and decisions and other forces emanating from the larger world by which it is surrounded'.[25] A social field, moreover, develops its own customs and rules, and the means of coercing or inducing compliance.[26]

Carriers can be regarded as a semi-autonomous social group on at least two levels. First, a private carrier on its own can be viewed as a semi-autonomous social field, where employees are subject to internal norms and regulations which can be enforced by management but where simultaneously the company must comply with government legislation. Second, many carriers are members of national and international trade associations such as the International Air Transport Association (IATA) and the Association of European Airlines (AEA), which maintain their own norms and interests and which interact with various governments on behalf of their members. These associations then can also be viewed as SASFs. In addition, we need to remember that many other relations also come with the carrier sanctions. Relevant relationships include at least the seven relations listed here and illustrated in Figure 14.2 below:

(1) between the carrier and the individual traveller (asylum seeker or other migrant);
(2) between the carrier and the country of reception (which can fine the carrier);
(3) between the carrier and the country of origin or transit country (which can prevent the individual from leaving or push or otherwise force the person to leave);
(4) between the carrier and the European Union (EU);
(5) between the carrier and other carriers;
(6) between the carrier and international trade associations;
(7) between the carrier and its employees and shareholders.

[24] Moore, 'The Semi-autonomous Social Field'. [25] *Ibid.*, at 720. [26] *Ibid.*, at 721.

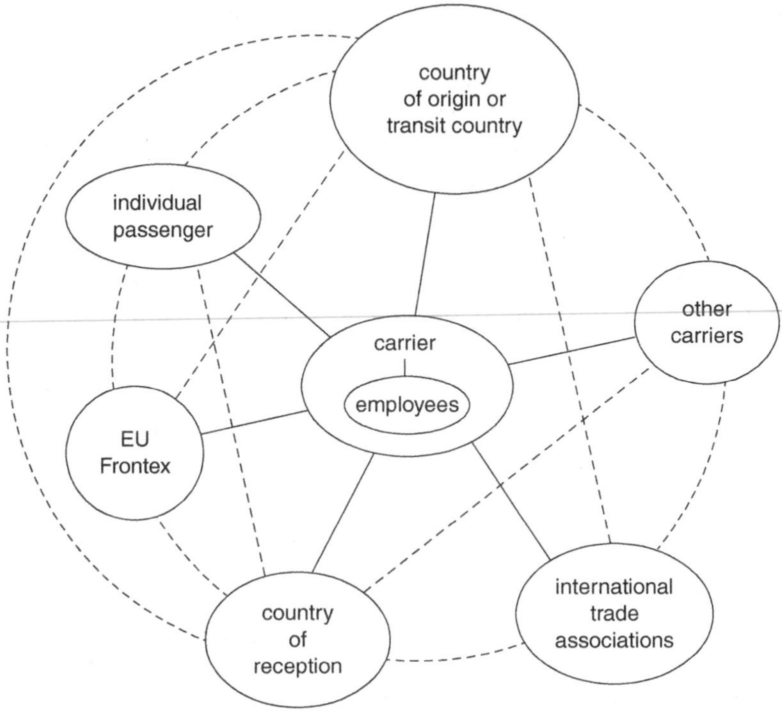

Figure 14.2 Carriers as actors in semi-autonomous social fields

This chapter focuses primarily on the relationship between the carrier and the country of reception, because it is this country that requires the carrier to become an expert in immigration control. This role of the carrier in turn directly affects the relationships between the individual and the carrier and between the country of reception and the individual. These last two relationships will thus also be referred to in this chapter.

Moore's idea about SASFs concerns conflicting and overlapping norm systems within different social fields. This is relevant for our subject, as carriers are burdened with three systems of – not necessarily legal – norms, assignments or interests, which might be in conflict: customers' interests, shareholders' interests and the interests of the various states they interact with. Does this lead to a purely economic balancing of conflicting requirements and cost–benefit thinking, in which the price of the fine and the risk to get one are weighed against the opportunity to sell a ticket? Or do moral ideas and norms also play a role? For instance, how is the risk of leaving behind a person in danger assessed?

The carrier has to deal with various and often contradictory (legal) norms, depending on its location and flag of registration. Moore's concept of SASFs is therefore useful, as it accommodates legal pluralism and norm pluralism. Does that make the carrier free to pick and choose the most convenient norms or is the carrier not autonomous or even semi-autonomous anymore? We assume that in the case of carrier sanctions, the freedom of carriers is curtailed. They are treated as experts of travel and identity documents and entry requirements, and as agents of immigration control. Consequently, state norms will have a great impact on their decisions concerning the transport of undocumented passengers.

14.5 Specific case examples: carrier involvement in the Netherlands and the UK

The circumstances sketched above raise questions about the nature of the relationship between commercial carriers and the state. We have seen the rationale behind involving private transporters in immigration control and suspect that carriers do not view this development positively. We question whether sanctions are the most effective way to make carriers exercise these tasks. Instead, agreements and partnerships might lead to better results. According to authors such as Tyler and Kagan, people obey the law if they believe it is legitimate, useful or to their benefit, not because they fear punishment.[27] Law makers and law enforcers thus would do much better by developing legal systems worthy of respect than to try to instil fear of punishment. Tyler has also found that people obey law primarily if two prerequisites are met: first, if the people concerned find the authority to be legitimate and worthy of respect; and, second, if the norms at stake conform with their own value system and norms. Under these circumstances, there is no need to force compliance; people – and in our case carriers – will feel involved or even co-responsible for enforcement.

To explore how governments have succeeded in involving carriers as expert communities, we will now turn to the implementation of the

[27] T.R. Tyler, *Why People Obey the Law* (Princeton University Press, 2006); R.A. Kagan, *Regulatory Justice: Implementing a Wage-Price Freeze* (New York: Russell Sage Foundation, 1980).

policy involved in two EU Member States: the Netherlands and the UK. In both countries private carriers are involved in immigration control processes. Although legislation in the Netherlands and the UK differs somewhat, the basic provisions are similar. The measures were introduced in the UK in the late 1980s and in the Netherlands in the early 1990s.[28]

In the Netherlands the duty for carriers to check passenger documents was introduced in 1994. The Dutch government, however, did not hold private transporters to these obligations by imposing sanctions immediately, but considered fines to be an ultimate remedy.[29] As a result of growing numbers of undocumented arrivals, this lenient style of enforcement was abandoned in the second half of the 1990s and was replaced by a harsher approach towards carriers, with fines used as a deterrent. The first official reports of breaches of the carrier sanctions legislation in the Netherlands were forwarded to the public prosecutor's office in early 1998. KLM, the largest airline flying to and from Schiphol Airport then and now, received the major part of the fines. In May 1998 the public prosecutor served KLM with 277 summons[30] and in the four and a half months between 1 December 1997 and 12 April 1998, more than 4,000 reports were filed against KLM for transporting undocumented passengers.[31]

In the UK the imposition of fines started roughly half a decade earlier with the Implementation of the Immigration (Carriers' Liability) Act (ICLA) in March 1987. The British government strictly implemented its carriers' liability policy and in the first nineteen months 8,502 notices of liability were issued to carriers, totalling more than £6 million in fines.[32] This rose to 14,295 cases after three years, giving rise to charges equalling over £14 million, with no less than 242 different air and sea carriers who were issued with a fine.[33] These numbers show that the impact of the

[28] Information in this section has been supplemented by data from interviews; see above, note 3.

[29] Annex to Kamerstukken II 1995/6, no. 914, at 1857.

[30] Kamerstukken II 1999/20000, 19637, no. 502. In the Netherlands fines imposed under the carrier sanctions legislation are penal sanctions; hence, a criminal procedure is followed.

[31] Annex to Kamerstukken II 1997/8, no. 1208, at 2471.

[32] Hansard HC Deb. (1988) 139 col. 647W.

[33] Hansard HC Deb. (1990) 173 col. 5–8W; see also A. Cruz, *Shifting Responsibility: Carriers' Liability in the Member States of the European Union and North America* (Oakhill: Trentham Books, 1995).

policy in the UK was considerable. More than other transport businesses, airlines had to deal with negative publicity, especially because some of them had organized their own procedures to prevent the arrival of undocumented passengers and in other instances had attempted to avoid liability under the carriers' liability legislation. Studies reported that some passengers were not allowed to leave the plane because of the fear among airlines of being fined and charged for the costs of detention and re-transportation.[34] From the carriers' perspective, they were punished by the state for being callous, through sanctions, and they were punished by the media for being overzealous, through negative publicity. This enticed a trade association chief executive to state that airlines are 'the evil villain. Damned if we do, damned if we don't'.[35]

Moore notes a tendency in SASFs to 'fight any encroachment on autonomy previously enjoyed'.[36] Considering the fact that obligations under the carrier sanctions policy can negatively impact the commercial interests of carriers, it shall come as no surprise that, both in the Netherlands and in UK, carriers were up in arms against the legislation that introduced financial sanctions for carrying undocumented passengers.

Both states installed a combination of sanctioning and monitoring measures to stimulate carriers to exercise their task with diligence.[37] With the imposition of fines, both the Dutch and the British governments clearly counted on the cost–benefit rhetoric of commercial airlines to take measures to avoid the costs of fines. In 2001 a Dutch government representative noted that 'the results of the fines are

[34] Hansard HC Deb. (1991) 531, col. 454W; Cruz, *Shifting Responsibility*, at 3; J. Forster 'Sanctions Imposed on Carriers: Impact on Migration Flows and Asylum Requests' in C. Faria (ed.), *Managing Migration Flows and Preventing Illegal Immigration* (Maastricht: EIPA, 2002), 25–8, at 27; J. Morrison, *The Cost of Survival* (London: British Refugee Council, 1998); J. Morrison and B. Crosland, 'The Trafficking and Smuggling of Refugees: The End Game in European Asylum Policy?', UNHCR Working Paper No. 39 (2001); House of Commons Home Affairs Committee Immigration Control Fifth Report of Session 2005–06, Volume I Report, together with formal minutes HC 775-I, at 52–3.

[35] *The Independent*, 10 July 1991, cited in F. Nicholson, 'Implementation of the Immigration (Carriers' Liability) Act 1987: Privatising Immigration Functions at the Expense of International Obligations', *International and Comparative Law Quarterly*, 46 (1997), 586–634, at 591.

[36] Moore, 'The Semi-autonomous Social Field', at 744.

[37] S. Scholten and P. Minderhoud, 'Regulating Immigration Control: Carrier Sanctions in the Netherlands', *European Journal of Migration and Law*, 10 (2008), 123–47.

encouraging' and the effect of the fines was that 'the carriers take document checks far more seriously'.[38]

The above shows that the Dutch and British governments used economic coercion to incorporate carriers in the immigration process and make them use their expertise, knowledge and access to would-be immigrants. Carriers, however, remained reluctant and resisted either by not paying the fines or by disputing liability in court. This resistance has made both governments and carriers in the UK and the Netherlands realize that an alternative solution should be sought so as to better attune their various interests.

14.5.1 Alternative solutions in the Netherlands

In the Netherlands, KLM found the imposition of financial sanctions problematic, while the Dutch government found their enforcement problematic. A case in which KLM was sentenced to pay a fine of about €4.5 million triggered the start of negotiations with the aim of developing an alternative solution for dealing with undocumented arrivals. Representatives of the Dutch government and KLM reached agreement on a joint effort.[39] They negotiated a Memorandum of Understanding (MoU), specifying KLM's obligations and stipulating various working arrangements between government agencies and KLM.[40]

The MoU was signed on 24 January 2000 and came into force on 1 April 2000. The intention was to achieve the goals of the carrier legislation without imposing fines on the carrier.[41] The MoU provided that KLM would be considered to be in compliance with the legislation if before every flight it would check whether passengers were in possession of the correct travel documents. Furthermore, KLM was made responsible for ensuring that its employees had sufficient expertise and knowledge to perform their tasks. KLM was also to ensure the availability of technical appliances for checking the relevant documents. The Dutch government agreed to provide training and expertise for KLM employees concerning the recognition of false or falsified documents. The MoU also

[38] IRU (International Road Transport Union), 'Minutes of the Meeting: Round Table on Carriers: Liability Related to Illegal Immigration' (30 November 2001), at 38.

[39] Interview with a former KLM senior vice-president security services, Schiphol Airport, 6 November 2008.

[40] Kamerstukken II 1999/00, 19 637, annex to no. 502 (Memorandum of Understanding).

[41] *Ibid.*

set targets, including quotas for the numbers of undocumented or inadequately documented passengers that KLM could carry without being criminally prosecuted. The quotas were to be reduced gradually, with the number of 'inadmissible' passengers transported by KLM being reduced to 215 in 2003.

The objective of the agreement was to regulate compliance through the MoU and avoid criminal prosecution. The negotiation of the MoU illustrates the existence of heightened levels of trust between the actors involved. It also indicated that the government regarded KLM as an actor which could be entrusted with expert tasks, without the direct threat of sanctions. As a result, KLM, involuntarily, started to behave as if it belonged to an epistemic community of experts in migration matters. The MoU's most important result is the creation of an extensive consultative structure between KLM and various government agencies, which facilitated the development of relations based on mutual trust. According to several respondents, the willingness to cooperate at the highest management levels was essential in the negotiation of the MoU. One KLM respondent remarked:

> In this domain it goes a lot like 'who knows who' ... if you have a commitment at the top then we can align our organisations [by instructing employees to] cooperate and try to share as much data as possible between ourselves.[42]

These remarks support Moore's assertion that laws are often made operative when within a social field individuals are in a position to threaten or press for enforcement.[43] They are even more effective if they are in accordance with the norms of the norm addressees. So, in the event of carrier sanctions, it is of utmost importance that the norms are shared by the carriers as they have considerable power to resist them.

Several interviewees indicated that the relationship between KLM and the various government agencies involved developed and improved over the years.[44] Regular formal and informal contacts exist between the

42 Interview with a former KLM senior vice-president security services, Schiphol Airport, 5 November 2008. See also interview with a former KLM senior vice-president security services, Schiphol Airport, 6 November 2008.

43 Moore, 'The Semi-autonomous Social Field'.

44 Interviews with a KLM senior vice-president security services, Schiphol Airport, 5 November 2008; a KLM security manager, Schiphol Airport, 1 November 2007; a former KLM senior vice-president security services, Schiphol Airport, 6 November

parties. The carrier sanctions policy thus seems to have developed from fining KLM, via fighting over fines in court, to negotiating the MoU, into developing structured cooperation and a climate suitable for consultation. What started out as a one-way-street for developing the carrier sanctions policy and the imposition of sanctions by the government has developed into a structural and collaborative working relationship that is embedded in various layers of both the government and KLM. KLM is clearly perceived as an expert in the field and the MoU working arrangements have stimulated cooperation between the airline and the government. On a more fundamental point, cooperation between KLM and the Dutch government has also slowly changed KLM's approach to its responsibilities. Where KLM's feeling of responsibility concerning the transport of undocumented passengers used to be weaker,[45] the MoU created a common goal. Despite the fact that the actors involved have their own interests, the common interest became the transportation of as few inadmissible passengers as possible. Through the MoU, rules that were prescribed by the government were gradually embraced by KLM and enforced in the organization. This attunes with Moore's finding on how an SASF can make law its custom.[46] Interestingly, we have the impression that this development has made KLM move from acting as an expert in the direction of acting as belonging to an epistemic community of experts on travel and identity documents and entry requirements. When government attention focused less on the enforcement of norms and more on collaboration with the carriers, the latter began to internalize the norms and to use their expertise in immigration control of their own accord. They began to feel co-responsible for exercising this task.[47]

2008; a KMar staff member, The Hague, 7 November 2008; KMar employees of the border control division at Schiphol Airport, Schiphol Airport, 20 November 2008. KMar, the Dutch Royal Marechaussee, is responsible for entry controls at all border crossing points in the Netherlands for laying claims with airlines for re-transportation and imposing fines on carriers. The IND (the Immigration and Naturalisation Service) is part of the Ministry of the Interior and Kingdom Relations and is responsible for carrying out immigration regulations and policy and deciding on admissibility to the Netherlands and on residence permit requests.

45 Interview with a KLM security manager, Schiphol Airport, 1 November 2007.

46 Moore, 'The Semi-autonomous Social Field', at 744.

47 Interviews with a KLM security manager, Schiphol Airport, 1 November 2007 and with a former KLM senior vice-president Security Services, Schiphol Airport, 6 November 2008.

14.5.2 *Alternative solutions in the UK*

The UK government also experienced problems in convincing carriers to assume liability for transporting undocumented passengers. British Airways was the biggest airline at the time and clearly expressed its concerns about the carriers' liability regime. At a time when British Airways was 'absolutely hammered' by fines, the UK government, in collaboration with British Airways, developed a scheme to exempt from liability carriers who made an effort to prevent the transport of undocumented passengers.[48] This was the Approved Gate Check (AGC) scheme. Carriers are given a special status at airports of departure, based on an 'audited high standard of document checking and security procedures at the port of embarkation, a good level of co-operation from the carrier, and a satisfactory record in respect of its responsibilities under the [carriers' liability policy]'.[49] The Border Agency normally waives fines relating to undocumented passengers (or passengers with damaged documents) arriving from ports where a carrier has obtained an AGC status.[50] However, carriers may still be fined when, for example, passengers arrive with forged passports of which the falsity is reasonably apparent, or for inadequately documented passengers, such as when passengers fail to present the required visa.[51] The AGC system is thus deployed as an incentive for carriers to put in place an effective system for checking documents. Carriers can apply for an AGC status per departure airport. The Dutch carrier Transavia, for example, has an approved gate check status at Rotterdam Airport.[52] The AGC scheme was introduced in October 1992 and is available to all air carriers.

The UK Home Office reported that the AGC scheme has been an 'extremely effective tool' in encouraging carriers to ensure that passengers travelling to the UK are correctly documented. In 2010 the UK Border Agency revealed that the numbers of inadequately documented arrivals on Egypt Air dropped by 66 per cent following security improvements required by the AGC scheme.[53]

48 Interview with a British Airways representative, Heathrow, 25 November 2008.
49 UK Border Agency, 'Charging Procedures: A Guide for Carriers', www.gov.uk/government/collections/check-passenger-documents.
50 If, for example, a carrier has AGC status at Schiphol Airport, all flights from that carrier to any airport in the UK are covered by the AGC.
51 Home Office Consultation, 'Copying Passenger Documentation: A Voluntary System for Carriers', January 2005.
52 Interview with a Transavia representative, Schiphol Airport, 27 November 2009.
53 UK Border Agency, 'UK Border Agency News', Issue 4, November 2010.

The AGC scheme has also been important in developing the relationship between carriers and the government. Comparable to the Dutch MoU, the AGC scheme is a way of stimulating cooperation with carriers in immigration control. Instead of punishing carriers for non-compliance, the AGC scheme rewards carriers for improving compliance. A British Airways representative emphasized that being awarded AGC status is a 'big prize'.[54] The representative is not alone in this perception as airlines often proudly announce the fact that they have been awarded AGC status at an airport. Commercial companies also use the AGC status as a way to advertise their expertise and reliability as an airline. A government inspector emphasized that the AGC scheme can also contribute towards defining shared goals between the government and the carriers:

> What we would like is for the airlines to understand why they are doing these document checks, gate checks, border checks ... rather than they just say: 'it's not my job it's Immigration's'.[55]

This respondent thus highlights the importance of carriers understanding the reasons for their new responsibilities. The AGC scheme clearly constitutes an attempt by the UK government to influence the attitude of actors in the social field vis-à-vis the carriers' liability policy. Again, this confirms the ideas of Moore, Kagan and Tyler discussed above about norm compliance. When the UK government opted for a cooperation model, let go of its previous top-down enforced policy and treated carriers as belonging to an epistemic community of experts on travel and identity documents and entry requirements, carriers themselves started to behave as members of an epistemic community and began to feel co-responsible for immigration control.

Like the Dutch MoU, the British AGC introduced an alternative to a command-and-control style of enforcement. The development of the AGC status moved the regulation and enforcement from a one-sided, top-down enforcement style by the immigration authorities towards cooperation between carriers and the government. Through the AGC inspections and the annual AGC reviews, regular contacts exist between the carrier liability department and carriers that have AGC status.

[54] Interview with a British Airways representative, Heathrow, 25 November 2008.

[55] Interview with employees of the Carriers' Liability Unit of the UK Border Agency, Heathrow, 8 April 2009. CLU is the Carriers' Liability Unit of the UK Border Agency and is responsible for the enforcement of the UK's carrier sanctions policy.

Both carriers and government officials in the UK consider their cooperation a partnership which has grown and developed over the years, with the government defining carriers as 'key partners'. Comparable to the Dutch MoU, changes in the interaction between the actors involved seem to indicate a shift whereby the penalty aspect of the policy has diminished and cooperation with carriers has become more important. In both countries the imposition of fines led to protests from carriers, which in turn led the actors involved to search for new ways of cooperation. This shift in regulatory style with the aim of getting the social field to comply with state regulations can be discerned both in the Netherlands and the UK. In short, we see a development, where the carrier was first involved as a forced expert to where the carrier is becoming an epistemic actor, being co-responsible for immigration controls and accepting this responsibility.

14.6 Enhancing output legitimacy?

Haas assumes that the involvement of epistemic communities in decision making can enhance output legitimacy.[56] Considering the involvement of carriers in migration control, we conclude that they do not qualify as epistemic communities, but rather as expert communities or groups. The question remains whether the involvement of private carriers in immigration control enhances output legitimacy. When exploring output legitimacy, it is useful to look at the effects and the question of effectiveness. We distinguish three ways of looking at the effectiveness of carrier sanctions. First, there is a narrow approach: does the carrier comply with the law? As we already analysed, sanctions and a top-down approach might not be the best way to achieve compliance with the law. Second, there is a broader way of conceiving the topic: is the aim of the law attained, i.e., are undocumented travellers refused entry? Third, and even broader, are there no unwanted side-effects, such as refusing asylum seekers and preventing asylum seekers from lodging claims?

We question whether the carriers involved are impartial and neutral, and also suggest that they will try to prioritize their own interests of not being fined and selling as many seats as possible. Related to this is the question of what the effects are of involving carriers in immigration control for the position of (would-be) asylum seekers and the protection of human rights.

[56] Haas, 'Introduction: Epistemic Communities'.

Privatization of migration control makes employees of private companies responsible for checking passports and visas. Carriers thereby serve as 'refugee screening agencies' and are forced to make decisions about whether asylum seekers are allowed to travel or not.[57] However, privatization of migration control makes employees of private companies only partly responsible for checking passports and visas; states ultimately remain fully responsible. As Den Heijer has argued: 'When European states endeavour to control the movement of asylum-seekers outside their territories, they remain responsible under international law for possible wrongdoings ensuing from their sphere of activity.'[58]

Nevertheless, carriers also have a responsibility of their own. Faced with a would-be asylum seeker with inadequate documentation who claims to be in need of protection, the question is whether a private carrier is able to judge an asylum seeker's account. And, moreover, the question is whether a commercial organization will risk the costs of re-transportation, the costs of accommodation for the alien and possibly a fine, or whether it will choose the safe side and refuse the passenger, and so avoid liability. Non-governmental organizations (NGOs) argued in 2005 that:

> corporate interests, including the overriding interest carriers have in maximising their profits, result in companies striving to avoid fines by refusing to let passengers board unless they are convinced that their documentation is valid. In doing so, private companies, which are not themselves bound by the 1951 Convention, may be undermining the fundamental right to asylum and forcing refugees to remain in countries where their lives are at risk.[59]

The carrier is punished for allowing a person with irregular status access to the territory, but is not punished for refusing to take on board a refugee in breach of international law. Worries about the protection of asylum seekers have been voiced since the introduction of carrier sanctions. These critical views concentrated on the difficulties that asylum seekers may face in trying to reach safe countries where they can lodge an asylum claim. Various authors submit that these difficulties that arise as a result of the use of carrier sanctions may amount to a violation of a

57 Meijers Committee (Standing Committee of experts in international immigration, refugee and criminal law), 'Schengen and Carrier Sanctions: International Law Objections', *Nieuwsbrief Asiel en Vluchtelingenrecht*, 4 (1992), 320 and supplement at 339.

58 M. den Heijer, *Europe and Extraterritorial Asylum* (Oxford: Hart Publishing, 2012), at 1.

59 Oxfam/Refugee Council, 'Joint Refugee Council and Oxfam GB Response to the Home Affairs Committee Inquiry into Immigration Control', December 2005, at 6.

state's obligations under international law.[60] Refugees often do not have the time or means to acquire full travel documentation and those fleeing persecution may be refused passports and/or exit visas. Indeed, it may be too dangerous for them to approach the authorities. This makes them especially vulnerable to the detrimental effect of the provisions on carrier sanctions which, according to Feller, 'undermine . . . basic provisions of refugee protection' and are 'fundamentally flawed'.[61] The 1951 Refugee Convention contains explicit provisions for this type of scenario. These provisions oblige the state to take into account its obligations of non-refoulement under international law, also in situations where carrier sanctions apply.

Besides refusing to transport passengers, carriers may also show other risk-avoiding behaviour. Gilboy notes that third parties may find it advantageous to extract themselves from the circumstances giving rise to their third-party duties. In the event that they find their duties too costly to perform, they may avoid burdensome or risky situations altogether.[62] Cruz found that in some cases:

> airlines have been refusing to allow asylum seekers to board flights, flagrantly discriminating against non-European passengers, and even going so far as to kidnap passengers to prevent them from presenting themselves to airport immigration authorities. Of course this is done to avoid having to pay fines, clearly putting individual rights below economical ones.[63]

Similarly, a 1999 report of the Parliamentary Assembly of the Council of Europe stated that the application of carrier sanctions has provoked airline companies to take certain 'preventive' measures. They described the example of the Czech national airlines that marked with a G – for 'Gypsy' – the passengers with Roma names or who looked like Roma,

[60] A. Cruz, 'Carrier Sanctions in Four European Community States: Incompatibilities between International Civil Aviation and Human Rights Obligations', *Journal of Refugee Studies*, 4 (1991), 63–81; Cruz, *Shifting Responsibility*; Feller, 'Carrier Sanctions and International Law'; Meijers Committee, 'Schengen and Carrier Sanctions'; M. Kjærum (ed.), *The Role of Airline Companies in the Asylum Procedure: Group of Experts under the Auspices of the European Consultation on Refugees and Exiles (ECRE)* (Copenhagen: Danish Refugee Council, 1988); M. Kjærum (ed.), *The Effects of Carriers Sanctions on the Asylum System* (Copenhagen: Danish Refugee Council/Danish Centre of Human Rights, 1991); J. C. Hathaway, 'Harmonizing for Whom: The Devaluation of Refugee Protection in the Era of European Economic Integration', *Cornell International Law Journal*, 26 (1993), 719–36.

[61] Feller, 'Carrier Sanctions and International Law', at 64.

[62] Gilboy, 'Compelled Third-Party Participation', at 144.

[63] Cruz, *Shifting Responsibility*, at 3.

with the intent of alerting the British authorities about potential Roma asylum seekers.[64] Another example of carrier practices was provided by a British Airways official who claimed that one carrier on arrival checked passenger documents prior to immigration control. Those passengers who were found to lack proper documentation were 'forcibly put back on the aircraft, to be flown against their will to where they had come from'.[65]

The criticism of carrier sanctions was mainly voiced shortly after they were introduced in the 1980s and 1990s. Nowadays, criticism has reduced considerably, especially criticism by NGOs. This might imply that the possible negative effects of carrier obligations for asylum seekers are nowadays less controversial than they were in the beginning, although the measures have not become less strict and fines are generally higher now than they were in the 1990s.

With the 'externalization' and 'de-territorialization' of immigration control, governments have in fact distanced themselves – legally and geographically – from immigration control. Control is no longer conducted in the country itself, but at a distance – in the country of origin or transit. Guiraudon and Lahav argue that the involvement of private carriers is a response to constraints that migration control policy faces in a national setting.[66] Immigration control through 'remote control' is being used to 'circumvent legal constraints absent in the early twentieth century'.[67] By preventing migration at source and making sure that would-be asylum seekers do not reach the territory of receiving countries, governments no longer have to refuse possible asylum seekers and other migrants at the border. They no longer need to expel failed asylum claimants – with the risk of violating the prohibition of refoulement – they simply make sure that asylum seekers cannot reach the border, let alone enter their territory.

Beyond carrier sanctions, criticism also extends to the broader trend of 'exporting' the borders, whereby states – according to Gibney, driven by an 'insatiable appetite for control'[68] – use non-arrival measures such

[64] Council of Europe, Parliamentary Assembly, 'Restrictions on Asylum in the Member States of the Council of Europe and the European Union', Doc. 8598 (1999).

[65] Forster, 'Sanctions Imposed on Carriers', at 27.

[66] V. Guiraudon, 'Before the EU Border: Remote Control of the "Huddled Masses"' in C. A. Groenendijk, E. Guild and P. Minderhoud (eds.), *In Search of Europe's Borders* (The Hague: Kluwer Law International, 2003), 191–214; Lahav, 'Migration and Security'.

[67] Guiraudon, 'Before the EU Border', at 195.

[68] M. J. Gibney, 'Beyond the Bounds of Responsibility: Western States and Measures to Prevent the Arrival of Refugees', *Global Migration Perspectives*, 22 (2005), 1–24, at 9.

as carrier sanctions, interception practices and visa regimes. With these practices, states move the border outside their geographical territory and 'export' their immigration control mechanisms abroad. These practices can have appalling implications for the institution of asylum.[69] The fact that non-arrival measures are indiscriminate – that is, they make no distinction between genuine refugees and other potentially irregularly arriving immigrants – means that they will be as effective in keeping genuine refugees out as they are at preventing illegal immigration. According to Hathaway, carrier sanctions policies are a 'crude instrument' since they do not discriminate between asylum seekers and ordinary passengers.[70] This means that both real and bogus asylum seekers may be forced to use illegal means, such as human smugglers, to reach the territory of Western states. In effect, this means, as argued by Gammeltoft-Hansen, that 'placing obligations upon private actors such as carriers . . . not only shifts responsibility for migration control but in effect equally the responsibility for asylum seekers and refugees'.[71]

A consequence of moving border control away from the state is that controls and the way in which they are executed are no longer subject to democratic control mechanisms. For example, it is not clear how many passengers are being refused by airlines. Various authors have raised questions concerning the lack of judicial remedies, democratic control and accountability.[72] Salter even claims that the lack of judicial remedies – which are available in a face-to-face asylum claim – is an expression of Foucault's statement that 'tactics [are used] rather than laws, and even . . . laws themselves [are used] as tactics'.[73] In immigration control, but possibly also in other situations in which experts are involved in rule making and implementation, the expert will not be bound by international rules. Expert involvement then might not only be triggered by a desire to better the policy, but can also be an attempt by government to avoid existing constraints.

[69] *Ibid.*, at 11. [70] Hathaway, 'Harmonizing for Whom', at 724.

[71] T. Gammeltoft-Hansen, *Access to Asylum: International Refugee Law and the Globalisation of Migration Control* (Cambridge University Press, 2011), at 188.

[72] See e.g., M. B. Salter, 'Governmentalities of an Airport: Heterotopia and Confession', *International Political Sociology*, 1 (2007), 49–66; M. den Boer, 'Out of the Blue: Policy Perspectives on Europe, Governance and Accountability', inaugural lecture, Free University Amsterdam, 2004.

[73] Salter, 'Governmentalities of an Airport', at 57, referring to M. Foucault, *The Foucault Effect: Studies in Governmentality*, G. Burchell, C. Gordon and P. Miller (eds.) (Boston: Harvester Wheatsheaf, 1991), at 95.

Criticism by academics and NGOs was voiced mainly in the period when carriers' liability policies were introduced. Critical views on the compatibility of carrier sanctions policies and refugee protection are still occasionally expressed, but in general the measures now seem to be largely accepted as part and parcel of existing immigration policies.

States are responsible for the legitimacy of the output of their policies. They have to guarantee non-refoulement, but also access to a procedure in conformity with the requirements of EU regulations. However, according to the arrangements described above, states involve carriers in the performance of immigration control and the latter have their own norms, tasks, fields and relations to consider. These carriers then become 'agents' of the state, which might enhance the output legitimacy of carrier sanctions because the trust-based ways of regulation facilitate cooperation and have proven to be effective, in the sense that they enhance compliance and seem to prevent the entry of bogus asylum seekers. However, due to conflicting norms and responsibilities, carrier involvement may also reduce output legitimacy by way of the negative side-effects that might also emerge. While states remain responsible if asylum seekers are refused by a carrier trying to avoid a fine, the system does not ensure that asylum seekers have access to procedures that enable them to submit an application for asylum. This negative side-effect is inherent in the situation where carriers are forced to act as if they belong to an epistemic community of experts, since: (a) their principal interest is a commercial one; (b) they do not have an intrinsic interest in immigration control; and (c) acting as experts on travel and identity documents and entry requirements in the context of immigration is not value-free, since many contradicting interests play a role.

A carrier has primary tasks as depicted in the inner circle of Figure 14.3, must have expertise to fulfil these tasks and there are norms to comply with when exercising these tasks. As stated above, transporting people and selling tickets are at the nucleus of this task. To do this, a carrier must be an expert in the means of transport involved (e.g., the plane, vessel or vehicle), in the outside conditions (such as wind, air pressure or roads) and in the legal and commercial norms of the contract with the passenger (e.g., regarding safety, service and speed).

The middle circle concerns tasks that force the carrier to gain expertise in fields outside its natural scope and to comply with legal and moral norms which do not form part of the original commercial contract. If the scope of tasks is widened, so is the scope of the necessary expertise and applicable norms.

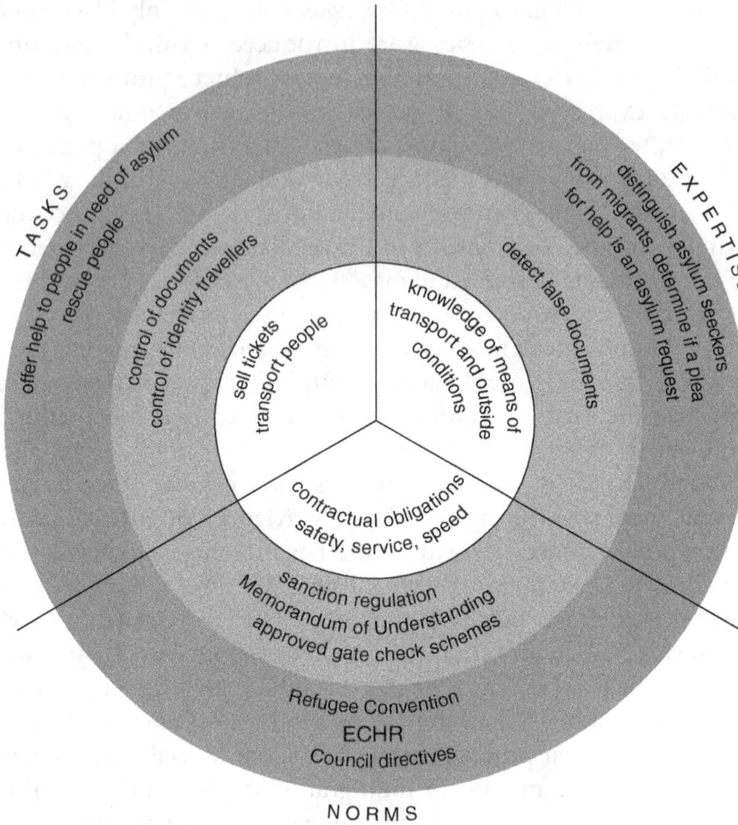

Figure 14.3 Carriers' tasks, expertise and norms

However, with the tasks in the middle circle comes an additional task: responsibility for asylum seekers. It is this task that harbours the danger of resulting in negative side-effects in the sense that legitimate asylum seekers might not be able to access procedures for submitting an asylum application and thus remain unprotected. Do carriers have the duty to protect asylum seekers and, if so, would this task fit their norms? While carriers clearly do not have a legal duty to protect asylum seekers, it might be argued that this task fits their norms in the sense that rescuing people in danger also belongs to the nucleus tasks of carriers.[74]

[74] International Convention for the Safety of Life at Sea (SOLAS), 1 November 1994, V/31, V/32 and V/33, and the International Convention on Maritime Search and Rescue

14.7 Conclusion

We discussed the involvement of private carriers in immigration control by addressing three topics: the position of carriers in immigration control; the nature of the relationship between carriers and governments; and whether the involvement of private carriers contributes towards the enhancement of output legitimacy in the area of immigration control.

Although carriers do not meet Haas' definition of an epistemic community, they have been forced to act as experts in the field of immigration control.[75] Due to the threat of sanctions when transporting undocumented migrants, carriers have been forced to expand their expertise and were confronted with other norm systems. Their involvement in immigration control is considered indispensable by states and leads to high-impact decisions. Private carriers, however, have not always been willing partners in this process. To understand the relationship between carriers and governments, we turned to Moore's notion of the SASF. This helped to illustrate that carriers' liability policies went against the pre-existing organizational beliefs and objectives.[76] The top-down approach initially deployed both by the Netherlands and the UK led to considerable protests from private carriers whose commercial interests and objectives are far removed from those of the state. Through alternative arrangements, the Dutch and British governments were able to connect to norms already held by the carriers, making the legislation more effective. As a result, carriers voluntarily started to act more like epistemic communities, who in (semi-)free cooperation with governments carry out expert tasks, which governments alone cannot provide as effectively as the carriers can. However, carriers can never become an epistemic community, as the nucleus of their task and interest is commercial: transporting goods and people on a commercial basis.

The measures analysed in this chapter in practice amount to non-arrival measures that enhance the capacity of the state to control its borders and to circumvent legal constraints. They may be characterized as enhancing efficiency and thus contribute to output legitimacy, in this

(SAR), 27 April 1979. In addition, for example, Article 255 of the Dutch Penal Code prohibits bringing or leaving someone in a situation of helplessness, while Article 450 prohibits refusing help to persons whose life is in danger. See also den Heijer, *Europe and Extraterritorial Asylum*, at 242 ff.

75 Haas, 'Introduction: Epistemic Communities'.

76 Moore, 'The Semi-autonomous Social Field'.

sense. However, complications also arise concerning output legitimacy. These complications concern the fact that the control measures are performed extra-territorially and by private carriers that are not bound by refugee law or international human rights obligations, placing those individuals seeking asylum in a very precarious situation.

PART V

Experts in decision-making processes of the European Union

15

The European system of financial supervision: a technology of expertise

MICHELLE EVERSON

15.1 Technocracy in crisis

Financial and sovereign debt crises have ushered in an unprecedented era of technocracy within the European Union (EU), with, for example, establishment of technocratic and semi-technocratic regimes in Italy and Greece. Vitally, however, a European trend away from democratic governmental structures is not merely a crisis-driven phenomenon. Instead, it is a far deeper historical progression, which has given rise to fundamental questions about the governing relationships within Europe between legitimate democratic process, the effective exercise of political and administrative power, the deployment of technical expertise and the (autonomous) operation of market forces.[1] Against this backdrop, the establishment in late 2010 of a European System of Financial Supervision (ESFS) might be understood as an immediate EU response to financial meltdown. Yet, the creation of the ESFS, comprising three European Supervisory Authorities for financial services (ESAsfs), the European Systemic Risk Board (ESRB) and national regulators, is also one further chapter in the ongoing efforts to balance functional demands for effective supervision of intricate European integration processes (output legitimation) against the democratic imperatives of the EU (input legitimation).

The need to balance output against input legitimation is not peculiar to the EU, nor is it new within the general constitution of government. The term 'government' simultaneously captures the Enlightenment concept of popular sovereignty and entails the

[1] Debates positing a 'technocratic' character for European integration versus the political union of Europe are as old as the European Economic Communities. See C. Joerges, 'What is Left of the European Economic Constitution?', EUI Working Paper, 2004, No. 2004/13.

establishment of the democratic process, which ensures that government *for* the people is also government *by* the people. But good governing also requires that government is functionally effective and can ensure that the people's will *is* done through the executive imposition of democratic mandates on a social environment beyond political discourse. The subsequent spectre, however, is the usurping administration; an unchecked executive which, if given too great a margin of discretion, might wield power to the detriment of the people. By the same token, the conventional response to this danger – or 'transmission-belt model' of administration – is by now so well entrenched within modern states as to be a constitutional truism: the strict hierarchy of legislative and administrative norms must be complemented by a ban on the delegation of discretionary powers to the executive.[2]

The Lisbon Treaty reproduces this truism within primary European law. Article 290 of the Treaty on the Functioning of the European Union (TFEU) establishes a hierarchical distinction between legislative and non-legislative acts, introduces a strict ban on the delegation of 'essential' legislative matters to the expanding administrative arm of the European Commission, and subjects all delegations of powers to it to ongoing 'democratic' supervision by the European Council and the European Parliament by means of a primary legal norm of recall of powers. Yet, the belated appearance of the transmission-belt concept within the TFEU cannot disguise the obvious fact that tensions between input and output legitimacy in the EU are necessarily amplified by the remarkable degree of reliance that Europe has placed on technocratic structures in the three decades since commencement of the Single Market Programme.

The roots and consequences of this technocratic reliance are twofold. First, the establishment of myriad ad hoc expert institutions – committees (comitology) and semi-autonomous 'agencies' (as well as the European Central Bank (ECB)) – outside the institutional structures of the EU treaties has met the supranational demand for increased administrative capacity to oversee the integration of national markets. But it has also given rise to increased concerns about the dangers of executive alienation of democratic competence,

[2] R. Stewart, 'The Reformation of American Administrative Law', *Harvard Law Review*, 88 (1975), 1667–813.

especially on the part of the European Parliament.[3] The vast number of technocratic bodies now operating at EU level[4] has led to a re-characterization of the EU as a 'regulatory state',[5] which both rebuffs parliamentary doubters and legitimates technocratic supranational oversight within a justificatory narrative of 'governance' as distinct from 'government' – a discourse which privileges mechanisms of expertise, transparency and deliberation above traditional democratic instruments of representative accountability.[6]

Second, the turn to European technocratic governance has also been encouraged by national movements and, above all, by the 'permissive consensus', which has, since the early 1980s, seen the governments of EU Member States lose confidence in the steering capacities of the welfare state and place their faith in the wealth-creating powers of the market.[7] Designed by the French socialist Jacques Delors, the Single Market Programme was not a neoliberal design, but was instead conceived as one further step in the federalization of Europe. Nonetheless, in a context of permissive consensus at the national level, 'economic rationality' subsequently became the dominant theme to the tune of which all European policy was forced to dance.[8] This led to a liberalization agenda, which had fundamental consequences for the constitution of relations between politics and the market.

Traditional government in Europe is now in retreat, not simply because constructs of democratic process underlying notions of 'good' governing are themselves mutating as governments, challenged by globalization processes, seek to reinforce their limited functional capacities within supranational governance institutions. Instead, liberalizing market integration, as well as increased EU reliance upon technocratic expertise, are facilitated as the commanding constitutional relationship between the polity and the market is altered. The 'legally

[3] K. Bradley St Claire, 'The European Parliament and Comitology: On the Road to Nowhere?', *European Law Journal*, 3 (1997), 230–54.

[4] Committee activity is striking: 270 committees delivered 2,185 opinions in 2008. See http://ec.europa.eu/transparency/regcomitology/docs/com-2009-0335_en.pdf.

[5] G. Majone, *Regulating Europe* (London: Routledge, 1996).

[6] See European Commission, 'White Paper on Governance', COM(2001) 428 final.

[7] C. Crouch, *The Strange Non-Death of Neo-Liberalism* (London: Polity Press, 2011).

[8] M. Everson and C. Joerges, 'Reconfiguring the Politics–Law Relationship in the Integration Project through Conflict-Law Constitutionalism', *European Law Journal*, 18 (2012), 644–66.

secured' private sphere of market operation, once characterized only by the safeguarding of individual (contractual) rights, has now been radically expanded in order to create a realm in which the 'rationalities'[9] of market operation are shielded from majoritarian political influence. Technocratization – or 'scientification' – entails the wholesale transfer of political steering capacities to rationalities that evolve within the market, as well as a commitment to protect the autonomous market sphere within which such rationalities unfold free from political interference.

At a time of a sovereign debt crisis in the eurozone, one paradox of this technocratization has become impossible to ignore. The striking point is not simply that European politics has been unable to assert itself against the institutionalized monetarist rationality of the Maastricht Treaty, but, rather, a more complex one – that parallel to political inaction, the ECB has found itself locked into the pursuit of price stability, perhaps even to the catastrophic point of systemic collapse.[10] Given this contemporary example of technocratic crisis, the following analysis revisits tensions between input and output legitimacy in the light of the radical (constitutional) re-alignment of relationships maintained between the democratic polity, the functional administration and the market. Reviewing the ever-present 'executive spectre' with reference to the EU response to the financial crisis, it asks a question mostly overlooked within the traditional EU governance debate: to what degree has the trend towards expert governance augmented a general crisis of political capacity in Europe? Has it nurtured a dominantly unavoidable rationality or, in theories borrowed from Michel Foucault,[11] a technology of expertise that usurps democratic process and sovereign will? Moving on, first, to assess technocratic structures of EU financial regulation and, second, to examine the capture of EU regulation by a rationality of risk, this analysis concludes that expert governance has played its part in denuding political capacity within Europe; however, vitally, not because

[9] The term is taken from Michel Foucault, from his assertion that the evolution of 'savoir-faire', or technical knowledge, has fundamentally altered modes of human governing – see M. Foucault, *Birth of Biopolitics: Lectures at the College de France, 1978–79* (Basingstoke: Palgrave Macmillan, 2008), at 291–313.

[10] Everson and Joerges, 'Reconfiguring the Politics–Law Relationship'; G. Majone, *The EU in Comparative Context: Regional Integration and Political Transaction Costs* (Cambridge University Press, forthcoming).

[11] Foucault, *Birth of Biopolitics*, at 216–313.

the executive itself seeks dominance, but because a no longer sovereign polity has abdicated all socio-political responsibility for the exercise of executive power.

15.2 Governance versus expert government of financial markets[12]

The ESFS was established by a series of EU regulations in 2010.[13] It comprises:

(1) The ESRB, chaired by the President of the ECB and including governors of national central banks (NCBs), a Commission representative and the chairs of the three ESAsfs. The role of the ESRB is to provide 'macro-prudential' supervision, combating 'systemic risks' or hazardous financial activities, which threaten the functioning of the ESFS.
(2) Three ESAsfs that administer a complex series of common financial regulations for banks, insurers and financial markets by means of the establishment of the Binding Technical Standards (BTS) and jointly established practices which inform micro-prudential supervision of financial institutions at the national level. ESAsfs are also charged with the identification of systemic risks.
(3) National Supervisory Authorities (NSAs), formally responsible for micro-prudential supervision at the Member State level.

The ESFS is not the first endeavour to coordinate financial supervision at the supranational level. It builds upon the national regulatory networks and European standard-setting committees for the financial services, established following the report of the Lamfalussy Committee on the

[12] Please note that, at the time of writing, it is envisaged that the regime for the supervision of financial markets within the eurozone will be significantly enhanced by establishment of a Banking Union, including enhanced ECB supervision of national banks and direct ECB control of national banks (Proposal for a Council Regulation conferring specific tasks on the European central Bank concerning policies relating to the prudential supervision of credit institutions, COM(2012) 511 final).

[13] Regulation (EU) No. 1092/2010 (ESRB Regulation); Regulation No. 1096/2010 (ECB Regulation); Regulation (EU) No. 1095/2010 (European Securities and Markets Authority); Regulation (EU) No. 1093/2010 (European Banking Authority); Regulation (EU) No. 1094/2010 (European Insurance and Occupational Pensions Authority) ('EIOPA Regulation').

Regulation of European Securities Markets in early 2001.[14] However, lying between the Commission's establishment of its own comitology system and a far broader EU commitment to the ESFS, we find the collapse of Lehman Brothers in late 2008, a significant change in the rhetorical justification for institutional reform at the EU level, a host of new financial regulations and a significant widening of supranational regulatory structures founded in independent expertise.

The Lamfalussy Committee was primarily concerned with the establishment of a globally competitive European market for financial services. Unwieldy EU regulation and discrepancies in terms of national implementation were seen as regulatory failings because they led to the differential treatment of financial instruments, both 'violating the pre-requisite of the neutrality of financial supervision' in the EU market and delaying the adaption of European financial services 'to the pace of global financial market change'.[15] By rhetorical contrast, the 'high-level' de Larosière group on EU financial supervision convened in response to the financial meltdown appeared to have returned to a more traditional concept of market failure, concluding that the system of European financial regulation must be strengthened: first, to improve an 'inadequate mix' of regulatory and supervisory skills, which had seen too little information gathered and shared 'on the global magnitude of global leveraging', and had exhibited a catastrophic failure to 'fully understand or evaluate the size of the risks'; and, second, to create a coordinated early warning system 'to identify macro-systemic risks of a contagion of correlated horizontal shocks'.[16]

In addition to the imposition of straitened capital requirements on financial institutions, the regulatory and supervisory structure was significantly enhanced with the creation of new, semi-autonomous authorities – or EU agencies – for the regulation and supervision of securities, banking and insurance. This final development is particularly significant. Facing crisis, the European Parliament 'enthusiastically'

[14] Known as the European Financial Services Action Plan and comprising, in particular, Commission Decisions, 2001/527/EC and 2001/528/EC (EU Securities Committee and Committee of European Securities Regulators); Commission Decision 2004/10/EC (Committee of European Banking Supervisors); Commission Decision 2004/9/EC (Committee of European Insurance and Occupational Pensions Supervisors). See also Knio, Chapter 16, this volume.

[15] See http://ec.europa.eu/internal_market/securities/docs/lamfalussy/wisemen/final-report-wise-men_en.pdf.

[16] See http://ec.europa.eu/internal_market/finances/docs/de_larosiere_report_en.pdf.

welcomed the ESFS, discarding its long-standing opposition to further consolidation of EU technocratic governance,[17] in particular by means of supranational 'agencification'.[18]

15.2.1 Autonomy and accountability in EU financial governance

The current Commission preference for European governance by means of agencies, or semi-autonomous expert bodies, may be traced back to the failings in comitology structures exposed by the bovine spongiform encephalopathy (BSE) or 'mad cow disease' crisis. BSE still functions as a potent warning to proponents of technocratic governance, especially with regard to the problem of what to do when technical expertise can no longer provide answers, or of how to respond when diffuse hazards cannot be concretized as risk 'because the science has run out'.[19] In the 1990s, however, the failure of scientific expertise was primarily viewed within an institutional paradigm stressing the need to act to improve its quality and delivery. A lack of transparency within ad hoc scientific committees established by the Commission to ensure food security had exacerbated a lack of scientific expertise at the EU level and foreclosed the potential for epistemic scientific review. Highlighting the 'obscurantism' of the comitology model,[20] the BSE saga also revealed a need for permanently funded EU expertise in order to facilitate long-term research into the basis on which hazards could be transformed into manageable risks, as well as a demand for permanent oversight of the implementation of EU standards at the Member State level.[21]

[17] The Parliament had rejected a proposed Institutional Agreement on a common operating framework for EU agencies (COM(2005) 59 final) creating a factual moratorium on their establishment by demanding that the Commission undertake further review of the operations of such bodies already operating at the EU level; see 'European Agencies – The Way Forward', COM(2008) 159 final.

[18] N. Moloney, 'The European Securities and Markets Authority and Institutional Design for the EU Financial Market – A Tale of Two Competences: Part 1: Rule-Making', *European Business Organization Law Review*, 12 (2011), 41–86, at 42.

[19] M. van Asselt and E. Vos, 'Science, Knowledge and Uncertainty in EU Risk Regulation' in M. Everson and E. Vos (eds.), *Uncertain Risks Regulated* (London: Routledge), 359–88, at 359.

[20] R. Dehousse, 'Comitology: Who Watches the Watchmen?', *Journal of European Public Policy*, 10 (2003), 798–813, at 798.

[21] E. Vos, 'EU Food Safety Regulation in the Aftermath of the BSE Crisis', *Journal of Consumer Policy*, 23 (2000), 227–55.

Since transparency and permanence are the hallmarks of the operation of expertise within regulatory agencies,[22] a radical expansion in their use followed in the wake of the BSE crisis. Article 290 TFEU's restriction of delegated powers stands as testament to continuing parliamentary reservations about the European executive spectre. Nonetheless, governance continues to compensate for the lacking EU government and, in the case of the European agency model, forcefully to assert its own pragmatic-normative claim to legitimacy. The existence of autonomous regulatory agencies operating at arm's length from government has long been justified by the argument that areas requiring complex technical oversight are best governed by 'experts'.[23] However, 'autonomous market governance' is now further justified by alterations in the manner in which the relationship between the exercise of political power and economic operation is viewed. The argument traditionally used to justify independent central banks – the prevention of governmental manipulation of exchange rates for short-term political gain[24] – finds far more general application within the permissive consensus that market operation should take place within its own autonomous sphere. 'Efficiency' is the leading criterion within a modern regulatory paradigm that seeks to refashion regulation in order to separate out the pursuit of general redistributive goals from sectoral regulatory aims. Assuming a higher normative commitment to autonomous market operation, efficiency-based regulatory models argue that the distorting statist tendency to conflate micro-economic market regulation with redistributive macroeconomic policies can be combated by establishing independent regulatory expertise.

Autonomous regulatory models also gain in normative legitimacy as the postulation of a concept of Pareto efficiency itself mediates against concerns that executive power should never be endowed with too broad a mandate. Discretionary powers may be delegated to independent agencies where they have no redistributive consequences – which will always require majoritarian political oversight – or the

[22] D. Demortain, *Scientists and the Regulation of Risk: Standardising Control* (Cheltenham: Edward Elgar, 2010).

[23] F. Vibert, 'Better Regulation and the Role of EU Agencies' in S. Weatherhill (ed.), *Better Regulation* (Oxford: Hart Publishing, 2007), 387–404.

[24] Majone, *Regulating Europe*.

subject matter of regulation is value-neutral in terms of general welfare losses.[25] Accordingly, and to the degree that the pursuit of economic efficiency has become a self-limiting principle within the polity, the independence of regulatory agencies is transformed from a constitutional spectre to a positive constitutional good that must be protected from potential political perversion. In this analysis, an 'independent fourth branch of government' is no stranger to the transmission-belt model of administration, but is instead its modern manifestation securing the long-term will of the polity for efficient regulation by shielding regulatory expertise from political contingency.

At the same time, the modernized transmission-belt construct demands that an independent administration of expertise must be subject to control in order to ensure that it is capable of fulfilling its regulatory functions and performs them well. A 'transparent' agency must consequently be made accountable to traditional constitutional institutions (government, legislature and courts) and to the general public in a manner that does not endanger its own autonomy. This is generally achieved by applying a plural scheme of multiple institution oversight – drawn from US experience – which determines that 'no-one controls the agency, yet the agency is under control'.[26]

European modes of ensuring the independence and accountability of operation of EU agencies are due primarily to the continuing impact of the '*Meroni* doctrine' – a ban on the delegation of powers to ad hoc institutions not named within the EU treaties established by the Court of Justice of the European Union (CJEU).[27] Despite the fact that the fait accompli of the European agency has belatedly been recognized within the Lisbon Treaty,[28] the doctrine continues to preclude the full independence of agencies at the EU level. Accordingly, EU agencies are only ever 'semi-autonomous', independent in fact rather than law and operating under the umbrella of the European Commission, which retains final decision-making power. The Commission's relations with its own agencies are consequently

[25] G. Majone, 'Independence v. Accountability: European Non-majoritarian Institutions and Democratic Government in Europe', EUI Working Papers (SPS), 1994, No. 1993/09.

[26] See T. M. Moe, 'Political Institutions: The Neglected Side of the Story', *Journal of Law, Economics and Organization*, 6 (1990), 213–53; See also M. Everson, 'Independent Agencies: Hierarchy Beaters?', *European Law Journal*, 1 (1995), 180–205.

[27] Case 9/56 *Meroni* v. *High Authority* [1957–8] ECR 133.

[28] But only to the degree that Article 263 TFEU expressly establishes a right of review of the CJEU over the acts of agencies.

often strained; after all, semi-autonomous agency operation threatens to alienate the competences of a Commission, which will be held accountable for the impacts of agency decisions.[29] Nevertheless, the agency vehicle provides the Commission with a vital increase in its functional capacities, making it an institutionally powerful if reluctant proponent of autonomous European market governance.

15.2.2 *A legitimately effective response to the crisis?*

Historically, the supranational regulatory interest in financial services sought only to create a 'level competitive playing field' between EU and US regulatory structures.[30] Once it had established the credit-worthiness of individual financial institutions to allow for the creation of 'one-seat authorizations' for Europe-wide market actors, the system restricted itself to cooperative standard-setting. The implementation of EU prudential legislation and the material supervision of financial products was a matter for the national authorities alone. Since the financial crisis, however, EU financial services regulation has burgeoned.[31] Major initiatives have focused on the implementation of the Basel III international regulatory framework for banks; in particular, the strengthening of each of its three pillars encompassing quantitative requirements (regulatory and economic solvency), qualitative requirements (risk management and supervisory oversight, including 'stress tests'), as well as market discipline (disclosure and transparency). The regulatory initiatives have demanded a significant strengthening of EU legislation (the Capital Requirement and Solvency Directives)[32] and of supranational standard-setting and supervisory oversight.[33]

[29] Everson and Vos (eds.), *Uncertain Risks Regulated.*

[30] P. O. Mülbert and A. Wilhelm, 'Reforms of EU Banking and Securities Regulation after the Financial Crisis', *Banking & Finance Law Review*, 26 (2011), 187–232.

[31] See, for details as of late 2011, Mülbert and Wilhelm, 'Reforms of EU Banking and Securities Regulation'.

[32] The Capital Requirements Directive (CRD III), 2010/76/EU (OJ L329/3 of 12 October 2010) for banks and the Solvency Directive (Solvency II), 2009/138/EC (OJ L335/1 of 17 Deember 2009) for insurers.

[33] In addition, the EU has introduced important measures in securities markets. See the Securities Regulation on Credit Rating Agencies (Regulation (EC) No. 1060/2009), the Directive on Alternative Investment Funds (Directive 2011/61/EU, OJ L174/1 of 1 July 2011), as well as proposed regulation on over-the-counter derivatives and short-selling: COM(2010) 484/5 and COM(2011) 482.

Charged with overseeing this enhanced regulatory framework are the ESAsfs, which are amongst the most powerful autonomous institutions ever established at the EU level by virtue of their dual character as rule-making and supervisory authorities. Broadly similar to one another, the agencies are mandated with 'improving the functioning of the internal market', 'ensuring the integrity, efficiency and orderly functioning' of markets, combating 'regulatory arbitrage', 'consumer protection' and strengthening the 'international supervisory co-ordination' (Article 1 Founding Regulations).[34] They are also afforded one major domain of rule-making powers:[35] the power to make BTS. These standards comprise Technical Regulatory Standards for the harmonization of the provisions of EU regulation and Implementing Technical Standards to be applied at the national level. Formally exercised by the Commission under competences delegated to the Commission by the Parliament and the Council under Articles 290 and 291 TFEU, BTS are nonetheless subject to a 'regulatory with scrutiny procedure',[36] which determines that, if opposed to the BTS proposed by an ESAsfs, the Commission has the power only to delay its full adoption as a regulation or decision, subject to the scrutiny of the Parliament and the Council.[37]

The supervisory functions of the agencies are wide-ranging, relating primarily to the cooperative establishment of joint (risk-based) methodologies for national supervisory authorities through peer review and the issuing of recommendations and guidelines (Article 16 Founding Regulations). However, 'soft' supervision hardens in important situations, when the relevant agency makes recommendations to national supervisors and private actors, and pursues (Commission) enforcement proceedings: first, in 'emergency' cases of threats to systemic coherence where the relevant agency acts under the guidance of the ECB, addressing decisions to national authorities and, where necessary, financial institutions; and, second, with regard to threats

[34] The term 'Founding Regulations' refers to the three regulations that established the ESAsfs. See the last three regulations referred to in note 13.

[35] Founding Regulations, Articles 10 and 15. Similarly, the ESAs may contribute to the making of rules within the relevant 'College of Supervisors' – see Moloney, 'The European Securities and Markets Authority: Part 1'.

[36] Reproducing the traditional procedures of the Comitology Decision (1999/468/EC), which provides the procedures for decision making within comitology.

[37] As a result, ESAs may be argued to exercise a 'hard power', backed by law rather than a 'soft power', which is dependent upon their abilities to influence the Commission.

posed to the consumer by financial innovation, where the relevant agency may temporarily prohibit detrimental activities or products (Articles 17, 18 and 19 Founding Regulations).

15.2.2.1 Autonomy and efficiency

With regard to the question of whether the ESFS is both a legitimate and effective response to the crisis, primary doubts arise by virtue of the potential for inefficiency and political interference within the ESAsfs. If the purpose of the ESFS is to promote a permissive consensus underlying expert-led market regulation, the partially autonomous status of the ESAsfs could prove to be the worst of all possible worlds.[38] The *Meroni* doctrine applies, determining that agency chairs – enjoined 'neither [to] seek or [to] take instruction from the Union institutions' (Article 49 Founding Regulations) – may find themselves in disruptive conflict with the Commission, which is held accountable for the operations of ESAsfs. Certainly, Commission–agency conflict is not new and has largely been negotiated without fundamental upheaval.[39] Nonetheless, additional strain arises as the sphere of delegated powers is also subject to Article 290 TFEU transmission strictures, encompassing a permanent threat of recall of powers by the Parliament and the Council, and a 'sunset clause', in any case limiting delegation of the competence (exercised by ESAsfs) to the Commission to issue BTS for a period of four years (Article 11 Founding Regulations). Although sunset clauses have proved to be a powerful tool within the USA, ensuring that independent agencies are narrowly focused upon their mandates, their impact may prove to be counter-productive within this unusual constellation, whereby semi-autonomous institutions exercise the mandated competences of a Commission, thus made vulnerable to censure by the Council or the Parliament. Further, where BTS are issued by agencies under the 'regulatory with scrutiny procedure', potential for inter-institutional conflict heightens, both placing regulatory efficiency in doubt as renewed political influence may give rise to interventionism and casting the Commission as a perpetually rancorous loser in an institutional game of competence accrual.

[38] Moloney, 'The European Securities and Markets Authority: Part 1'.
[39] Everson and Vos (eds.), *Uncertain Risks Regulated.*

Efficiency concerns have also been raised about the expansion of the oversight of the ESAsfs at the national level. In part, these concerns echo objections to the general widening in the supranational regulatory competence, which, it is argued, has seen 'stealthy' neo-functionalist efforts to effect political integration by means of intensified EU market regulation and frustrate efficiency-oriented regulatory programmes at all levels.[40] Nevertheless, the prevalence of regulatory arbitrage and contagion within the less intrusive Lamfalussy system[41] weighed in favour of a hardening of the supranational supervisory competence and now gives rise to worries about potential for NSA–ESAsfs conflict within hierarchical EU financial supervision.[42] Possible discord arises by virtue of the fact that regulatory standard-setting cannot easily be divorced from supervisory implementation. Instead, the relationship between standards and their ongoing application is necessarily complex, not simply because understandings about regulatory aims may differ at each supervisory level, but rather because their successful achievement is necessarily context-dependent.[43] Several factors militate in favour of local flexibility in the implementation of BTS. First, ESAsfs are relatively inexperienced and are currently understaffed. Second, regulatory goals will also necessarily require adaptation in view of the varied national institutional supervisory structures. Above all, complex Basel III regulatory methodologies not only require an intense degree of local knowledge in order to overcome informational asymmetries, but also demand regulatory implementing flexibility to allow for experimentation with regard to rapid financial innovation, as well as for an immediate response to systemic shock. Equally, experimentalist localism may act as a 'safety valve' within the system, easing the potential for contagion through a supervisory plurality that guards against the danger that undue centralization will itself facilitate systemic shock.[44]

[40] G. Majone, *Dilemmas of European Integration: The Ambiguities and Pitfalls of Integration by Stealth* (Oxford University Press, 2005).

[41] P. Snowden and S. Lovegrove, 'The New European Supervisory Structure', *Compliance Officer Bulletin*, 83 (2011), 1–31.

[42] J. Black, 'Restructuring Global and EU Financial Regulation: Capacities, Coordination and Learning', LSE Law, Society and Economy Working Papers, 2010, No. 18/2010.

[43] N. Moloney, 'The European Securities and Markets Authority and Institutional Design for the EU Financial Market – A Tale of Two Competences: Part 2: Rules in Action', *European Business Organization Law Review*, 12 (2011), 177–225.

[44] Black, 'Restructuring Global and EU Financial Regulation'; Moloney, 'The European Securities and Markets Authority: Part 2'.

15.2.2.2 Accountability and transparency

An interesting peculiarity of the structure of the ESAsfs, which may mediate inefficiency effects, is the self-contained nature of expertise assembled within the authorities. Possibly as a consequence of the heightened influence afforded to the Parliament and the Council, the desire for political presence at the agency level is dampened: ESAsfs have not experienced the unseemly scramble for parliamentary representation *within* the agency more generally witnessed within the EU.[45] Instead, expertise headlines the agency in the character of the Board of Supervisors, which is made up of the heads of each NSA, as well as non-voting representatives from the Commission and the ESRB (Article 40 Founding Regulations), and is subject to a concept of 'technocratic excellence'. The chairperson of the insurance ESAsfs, for example, is to be appointed 'on the basis of merit, skills, knowledge of financial institutions and markets and of experience relevant to financial supervision and regulation' (Article 48(2) EIOPA Regulation). National interest is also purged with regard to the duties of independence of ESAsfs (Article 42 Founding Regulations). Political arbitrage is combated by simple majority voting in both the Supervisory and Management Boards: the sole decisional criteria are technocratic in nature, shorn of political interest and thus – under theories of expert deliberation[46] – facilitative of the objectivity and epistemic cooperation that might ensure ESFS efficiency.

Given the technocratic coherence of the ESAsfs, the primary legitimating mechanism for their operation is the establishment of an effective scheme of plural accountability, which ensures that each agency is both competent and acts within its technical mandate. In this case, all common control mechanisms apply: the *ex ante* control of multi-annual work programmes and budgets by multiple EU institutions, including the Court of Auditors (Article 62 Founding Regulations); the ongoing control of agency activities by means of parliamentary committee hearings; and the *ex post* multi-institutional control both of budgets and annual reports. In addition, agency decisions addressed to individual actors may be reviewed by an independent Board of Appeal and by the CJEU (Article 61 Founding

[45] M. Everson, 'Good Governance and European Agencies: The balance' in D. Geradin (ed.), *Which Regulatory Authorities in the EU?* (Cheltenham: Edward Elgar, 2005), 141–63.

[46] Majone, *Regulating Europe*.

Regulations). Despite doubts about the budgetary adequacy of the agencies,[47] it appears fair to state that, in structure at least, 'no-one controls the ESAsfs, yet the ESAsfs are under control'.

Concerns about the accountability of agencies nonetheless remain, particularly with regard to their transparency and public responsiveness. These worries have accompanied the operation of agencies from the outset.[48] However, the concern that EU agencies are unable to generate their own public communities of review is heightened in the case of ESAsfs. In contrast to the USA,[49] EU institutional literature is strangely devoid of the theme of agency capture.[50] Instead – in line with the efficiency-based consensus – industry actors are regarded as 'stakeholders' within the regulatory process, representatives of autonomous market process whose views must be taken seriously in the establishment of sensitive oversight schemes.[51] The same philosophy has been applied to ESAsfs that are mandated to establish 'stakeholder' groups (Article 37 Founding Regulations) – comprising market actors as well as consumers and academics – and to consult them prior to issuing BTS. However, within the financial services sector, it was precisely this close relationship that facilitated the financial collapse.[52] The joint application of risk-based models of economic solvency fostered particularly intense relations between the regulators and the regulated within which the fatal complacency arose that tolerated and even welcomed unsustainable business models as wealth-creating vehicles of innovation, which were also of benefit to (disadvantaged) consumers. Agency capture potential was instead replaced with the far more subtle, but no less catastrophic danger posed by the creation of a dominant 'rationality', a shared mode of thinking – or cognitive failure[53] – which could not recognize, let alone tolerate, dissent. Accordingly, in establishing its own epistemic community of review, the ESFS as a whole is surely charged with identifying voices not of partnership, but of maverick methodological dissent. In this regard, a vital question remains: where might these malcontents come from?

47 Moloney, 'The European Securities and Markets Authority: Part 2'.

48 Everson, 'Good Governance and European Agencies'.

49 M. Shapiro, *Who Guards the Guardians? Judicial Control of Administration* (Athens, GA: University of Georgia Press, 1988).

50 J. E. Stiglitz, *The Economic Role of the State* (Oxford: Basil Blackwell, 1989); Shapiro, *Who Guards the Guardians?*

51 Vos, 'EU Food Safety Regulation'.

52 Black, 'Restructuring Global and EU Financial Regulation'.

53 *Ibid.*

Within the USA, a vital element of legitimate agency operation is the identification of the broader public with the institution's work, such as is the case with the Environmental Protection Agency. In its three decades of operation, and despite the use of modern transparency methods (websites), no such public agency has arisen within the EU. In part, the problem is one of a lack of a European press – the absence of a European public sphere of communication and a tendency to renationalize European decision making within a fragmented media. The problem is also institutional: no *general* public right to challenge the actions of European agencies has been established. Even if the reformulated Article 263 TFEU widens the scope of the parties who might request the review of the ESA implementing acts conducted by the CJEU, a European Procedures Act has yet to be established. The publicity and post-legislative control generated by class action claims is still absent from the EU system.[54] The problem, however, is also specific to financial services. Confidentiality matters: in the case of emergency action to combat systemic risk, there are powerful reasons that weigh against the large-scale provision of public information.

15.3 A rationality of risk

15.3.1 'Government in miniature' and reinstated political steering capacity?

To the degree that models of agency governance are founded in the postulate that Pareto-efficient regulation is best conducted behind a firewall guarding against political contingency, the primary concerns in terms of legitimating institutional design must be those of the establishment of the independence and accountability of a shielded core of expertise. Nevertheless, such starting assumptions and institutional conclusions may be doubted. Influential and sophisticated sections within (national) regulatory debate maintain a far more optimistic view of the continuing vitality of political steering mechanisms within the market. In this view, the trend to an autonomous market is wholly overstated. Although the grand ideological battle between command interventionism and market autonomy has been lost, seemingly slight typological distinctions within 'autonomous'

[54] See, for the publicity generated by the US Administrative Procedures Act, Stewart, 'The Reformation of American Administrative Law'.

regulatory models do matter to the extent that they reflect our reality of how steering capacities within the modern economy are exercised and to what end.[55] Autonomous regulation is not an act of deregulation or a mandated imposition of Pareto efficiency, but merely the establishment of a 'regulatory enterprise',[56] within which the sharp divides made between public and private spheres, between efficiency-led regulation and the continuing pursuit of social goals necessarily dissolve within a conventional praxis of discretionary supervision; a melange of radicalized delegation in which all competing regulatory rationales of efficiency and consumer choice, the pursuit of legal rights, social solidarity and consumer protection are fought out.[57]

Typological regulatory distinctions are argued to represent different models and rhetorical strategies detailing exactly how social and institutional resources might be utilized, regulatory actors might be incentivized and macroeconomic goals might be assured.[58] Depending on the regulatory variant chosen, emphasis is laid upon learning within a networked regulatory environment, wherein the cognitive capacities of the regulator and the regulated are expanded and enhanced within a sliding enforcement scale, ranging from common suasion to rare sanctioning,[59] or, upon the perceptions of private actors, whereby command is replaced with incentive and sanctioning with the steering-capacity of 'nudge', or the cognitive re-alignment of private to public interest.[60] In response to the financial crisis and the rapid spread of systemic risk, these functional efforts to improve the effectiveness and sensitivity of regulation have similarly been augmented by a 'performance-based element' within regulation,[61] which seeks to re-establish the missing-link or component of macroeconomic control not through defunct commands, but through better enunciation and coordination of micro- and macroeconomic goals.[62]

[55] F. Vibert, 'Regulation in an Age of Austerity: Reframing International Regulatory Policies', LSE Working Paper, 2011, No. WP 03/2011.

[56] T. Prosser, *The Regulatory Enterprise: Government Regulation and Legitimacy* (Oxford University Press, 2011).

[57] *Ibid.* [58] Vibert, 'Regulation in an Age of Austerity'.

[59] R. Baldwin and J. Black, 'Really Responsive Risk-Based Regulation', *Law and Policy*, 32 (2010), 181–213.

[60] R. Thaler and C. Sunstein, *Improving Decisions about Health, Wealth, and Happiness* (Yale University Press, 2008).

[61] J. Black, 'Tensions in the Regulatory State', *Public Law*, (2007), 58–73; Baldwin and Black, 'Really Responsive Risk-Based Regulation'.

[62] Vibert, 'Regulation in an Age of Austerity'.

In this view, the creation of the ESFS is not a particular problem of delegation of oversight capacities, but rather a long-overdue recognition that political steering capacities over financial markets can now only be effectively exercised within autonomous regulatory structures that are sensitive to learning, incentives and public–private coordination. The clear political elaboration of a series of regulatory goals that emphasize the macroeconomic goal of 'financial stability'[63] overcomes the existing state of nature within the European financial markets. Meanwhile, close coordination between micro- and macroeconomic supervision is assured by institutional obligations placed upon ESAsfs to alert the ESRB of operational malfunctions that might endanger the 'orderly functioning' of financial markets. The potential problems posed by ESAsfs operations may – in this view – be re-characterized as habitual characteristics of the regulatory space; commonly manifested features to be managed rather than viewed with suspicion. Above all, sunset and revocation clauses are a simple, if messy, manifestation of the ongoing political steering capacity; a means to adjust ongoing market operation to regulatory-political goals. Equally, the apparent tension within the agencies between their market innovation functions – clearly enunciated within the preambles of founding regulations – and their precautionary role with regard to product regulation suggest a lack of clarity within the regulatory mandate afforded to agencies.[64] However, this is also a simple reflection of the necessary tensions that arise in any regulatory enterprise between notions of consumer choice, consumer protection and macro-steering: is the regulator a representative of consumer interests that defy commodification, a vital coordinator between micro- and macroeconomic policy or a facilitator for 'marketized' consumer opportunity – a choice that is to be made in the instantiated light of expert-regulatory deliberation?

All is well in the world of European financial services regulation. Or is it? On a brief reading, sophisticated regulatory debate also presents a curious mix of blind optimism and equally unsighted rationalism, at least with regard to steering that might accomplish (social) macroeconomic goals. Diffuse, rights-based feelings of social solidarity within 'government in miniature' are to be welcomed, but are surely

[63] Article 2 of Regulation (EU) No. 1092/2010 of the European Council and Parliament on macro-financial oversight of the system and establishing a European Systemic Risk Board.

[64] Moloney, 'The European Securities and Markets Authority: Part 1'.

no substitute for the majoritarian self-dedication to comprehensive social redistribution, being necessarily piecemeal and subject to potentially distorting acts of juridical application. Likewise, 'nudge' is itself inexorably founded within the market-leaning rationalities of behavioural economics and would seem singularly ill-designed to implement a wholesale challenge to the rationalities in which it is rooted. This final point is vital: optimistic regulatory debate itself identifies a conceptual problem of 'cognition failure' to which 'risk-based regulation' is particularly prone.[65] Although underestimated within that debate itself, the problem of cognition failure, as will be demonstrated below, highlights a potential for rationality capture within modern regulation, which is facilitative of the socio-political abdication of responsibility for the exercise of executive power.

15.3.2 Radical rationality capture

The underlying regulatory scheme established by the ESFS implements the Basel III Accords of the Basel Group of International Banking Supervisors that sought to overcome the deficiencies of the risk-based regulatory scheme introduced by Basel II – a scheme which inexorably contributed to the financial meltdown.[66] Accordingly, it is founded on a process of: (1) debt de-leveraging through enhanced regulatory solvency; (2) the discouragement of systemically inappropriate debt resecuritization by means of better coordinated oversight of the economic solvency and risk management processes of individual financial institutions; and (3) the imposition of stringent market discipline and transparency to discourage further stealthy resecuritization. Reform entails better oversight of the Value at Risk (VaR) methodology of prudential financial supervision[67] introduced by Basel II: first, in order to minimize its internal 'pro-cyclical' impacts, whereby strong markets encourage hazardous debt resecuritization; and, second,

[65] Black, 'Restructuring Global and EU Financial Regulation'.

[66] The accords were ratified by the G20 in November 2010. See, for the crisis inducing pro-cyclical bias of Basel II, *ibid.*; and Snowden and Lovegrove, 'The New European Supervisory Structure'.

[67] Requiring financial institutions to assess their own liabilities with regard to calculations offsetting debt risks against credit potential within wider financial markets.

to improve external supervision with regard to VaR's methodological application and potential for the transmission of systemic shock.[68]

Vitally, and beyond increased regulatory capital requirements, Basel III and the ESFS do not represent a radical re-evaluation of the founding risk-based regulatory philosophy of Basel II. Instead, they may be characterized as making corrective modifications to the existing scheme of supervision and, in the case of the insurance sector, as a dangerous radical extension of it.[69] The continuing dominance of the rationality of risk-based regulation – or, more cogently, the failure to engage in explicit questioning of it – is nonetheless highly incongruous, given the central role that it played in the financial meltdown. A risk-based approach to regulation radically increases the risk of cognition failure – particularly with regard to a fragmented and decentralized regime of control – where supervisory or self-regulatory failure to identify and to communicate risks can and did cause systemic shocks of epic proportions.[70] More significantly, risk-based models of regulation may also create a lack of political accountability on the part of regulators: 'Framing regulatory problems as risks allows regulators to argue that certain regulatory failures are not regulatory failures at all, but normal events, which are to be expected, and for which they are not to blame.'[71]

To radicalize this statement with regard to a European regulatory space, the following can be stated. Where permissive consensus at the national level has played its own role in the evolution of a European technocracy, a 'normalization of inevitability' translates into regularized denial of political accountability. Here it may be argued that an ideological battle has been replaced not by a new political reality, but by a seductive formula of political abdication. The process

[68] With a focus on the insurance industry, see I. Holzmüller, 'The United States RBC Standards, Solvency II and the Swiss Solvency Test: A Comparative Assessment', *Geneva Papers on Risk and Insurance*, 34 (2009), 56–77.

[69] To the degree that regulatory convergence in the financial services industry would seem to find its limits in its lack of recognition that the insurance *product* is 'different' – not a means of speculative financial securitization, but rather a product, which is bought to offset concrete contingencies – see A. Beltratti and G. Corvino, 'Why are Insurance Companies Different? The Limits of Convergence among Financial Institutions', *Geneva Papers on Risk and Insurance*, 33 (2008), 363–88.

[70] Recognized as a major cause of financial collapse, 'The whole is only as strong as its weakest link'; see IMF, 'The Fund's Mandate – An Overview' (January 2010), www.imf.org/external/np/pp/eng/2010/012210a.pdf, at 12.

[71] Black, 'Tensions in the Regulatory State', at 58.

of wealth-maximization is a universal good – or normality – to which all conflicting political positions might commit without fear of blame for its collapse. Equally, the need for the *ex ante* political identification of what constitutes market failure is obviated. No break on autonomous market operation need ever be applied and political responsibility for the lost benefits of potential market innovation need never be assumed. Instead, the potential for the collapse of wealth-maximizing markets becomes the norm as it is re-characterized as a 'risk' that might be quantified and assessed within expert-led processes of evidence-gathering, to then be managed within a neutered 'political' process that also lends itself to the expert techniques of cost–benefit analysis. The contrasting regulatory goals of consumer choice, consumer protection and macro-steering do not represent opposing political aims, but are, instead, neutral regulatory goods, the quantitative benefits of which might be objectively balanced against one another.

In this far more critical light, the problem is not that regulators might deny blame for market failure, but that the concept of market failure has itself been expunged and that the distinction between uncertainty and risk made by Frank Knight has been collapsed, such that the question of political accountability for financial collapse need never arise.[72] Rather than being founded upon a differentiation between risk and 'uncertainty' – or a situation of immutable hazard (social externalities) to which politics once responded by limiting the sphere of free operation of the market – modern economic policy is based upon the distinction between risk and a 'normality' of market collapse, to which politics need not respond.

In this setting, the specific constellation of expert oversight within a European regulatory enterprise matters and gives rise to disturbing conclusions. First, at a pragmatic level, the EU has not only experienced 'normal collapse' within its risk-based schemes of governance; instead, its precautionary response has also proved inadequate with regard to the re-entry of social concerns within EU policy.[73] The BSE crisis, in particular, still teaches us that evidence-based models of risk regulation can never furnish universally objective truths. Scientific method is only scientific method. Risk can only be modelled where evidence has been garnered demonstrating its existence. Permissively translated into regulatory models of wealth-maximization, the notion

[72] F. Knight, *Risk, Uncertainty and Profit* (Boston: Houghton & Mifflin, 1921).
[73] Van Asselt and Vos, 'Science, Knowledge and Uncertainty'.

of 'quantifiable risk' becomes the spectre that promises to deceive; a social construction that disguises the reality of uncertainty, for which no one holds themselves accountable. Similarly, the ideologically neutered response to scientific uncertainty – or principle of 'precaution', secured at the EU treaty level (Article 191 TFEU) – has confounded all mechanisms of judicial control. In a world dominated by the rationality of innovation and wealth-maximization, courts will not reinstate political process, overturn expertise with reference to social or ethical concerns, or substitute their will for that of political process. Instead, courts still demand – in defiance of all logic – an (impossible) evidentiary base for the existence of a 'risk' that cannot be quantified, with the consequence that harm potential remains unchecked.[74]

Second, where a rationality of risk has established itself at the core of the regulatory regime, it can only ever be challenged where political channels of influence are particularly strong. Nonetheless – as ECB actions during the sovereign debt crisis teach us – the autonomous institutions of European governance, discursively legitimated *only* by their autonomous expertise, are inevitably resistant to all contingent political influences that contradict their mandated regulatory objectives, and are so even to the point of systemic collapse. The strength of parliamentary oversight over ESAsfs might thus be particularly doubted, especially where it urges precautionary approaches to financial innovation. For a telling example, all parliamentary efforts to enjoin the pursuit of broader economic policy upon the ECB have been rebuffed within a cognition dissonance of epic proportions.[75] Where the justificatory discourse of independent European governance has hardened into law, the ESAsfs may, as a simple result of their own self-justificatory legitimacy, find it hard to accept interference with their evidence-based mandates.

The cognition gap identified as a major cause of the financial collapse is radical in its extent and is only accentuated by efforts to correct financial dysfunction within regimes of regulatory response that disguise

[74] Ethical and social concerns about the impacts of GMOs have found it particularly difficult to assert themselves against the 'governing rationality' of the EU Commission and the refusal of the CJEU to afford a legal value to hazard – see Van Asselt and Vos, 'Science, Knowledge and Uncertainty'.

[75] F. Amtenbrink and K. van Duin, 'The European Central Bank before the European Parliament: Theory and Practice after Ten Years of Monetary Dialogue', *European Law Review*, 4 (2009), 561–83.

the ideological abdication of political responsibility for the construction of market failure and instead create an appearance of objective truth and evidence-based 'certainty' where none may exist. To this extent, the problems of agency capture by economic interests are surely dwarfed by the *self-capture* of the system by a governing rationality of risk – a methodology of regulation that owes its existence not to sovereign intent, but to sovereign abdication. The hope that cognitive failure, even in relation to initially quite limited instances of financial innovation, can be overcome by malcontents who question both the economic 'science' of VaR as well as the construction of a normality of market collapse is a faint one.

15.4 The technology of EU expertise

The problems of control of exercise of expert-based executive power are greatly magnified at the EU level where the traditional democratic process is in any case weak. They are further radicalized where permissive consensus and dominantly unavoidable risk rationality substitute for democratic will formation. The core issue, however, is not one of a lack of justification or an absence of attempts to legitimize the sphere of governance beyond traditional government. The governance enterprise is replete with justificatory discourse, of debate about a sphere of technocratic and market autonomy within which constitutional tradition (transmission) reacts against and is interwoven with expert-led and evidence-based regulatory strategies; a realm of radicalized delegation where social and ethical concerns seek re-entry within the technical regulatory process.

To contemporary regulatory debate, competing justificatory discourses and the contradictions inherent to the endeavour to establish an autonomous sphere of regulation within which continued engineering is the norm do not recall historical spectres of the usurping administration. Instead, the blurring of the public and the private and the flattening of distinctions between the governors and the governed are no more than an overdue pragmatic recognition that steering capacities cannot be assured through political fiat. Steering is possible only where political capacity acts radically *within* a network of public–private relations. Pareto-efficient regulation is revealed as the purely theoretical construct even its supporters concede it to be[76] – a

[76] Majone, *The EU in Comparative Context*.

putative limitation of the regulatory sphere which has no concrete meaning. Meanwhile, even Michel Foucault's famous formulation of 'governmentality' – the spread of a power of rationality across the web of human relations – finds its curious place within sections of contemporary regulatory theory not simply as a characterizing tool, which might be used to describe the modern operations of steering capacity within autonomous market operation, but also as a regulatory tool in its own right.[77]

The regulatory deployment of the work of Foucault is illuminating to this analysis. Certainly, (slightly) more conventional analyses of modern power relations, which continue to posit the existence of sovereign will, might provide regulatory debate with useful techniques to enforce steering capacity within autonomous market logics; that is, a means of establishing an 'unobservable' power that impacts upon the minds of its subjects by usurping the environment of debate 'such that the subject cannot recognise that other opportunities for action exist'.[78] However, the 'power' of governmentality and 'political technology' is a very different creature indeed, attaching to rationalities, or savoir faire, that are authored by and within human affairs, but of which man is no longer the subject but the object instead.[79] The scientification of the social is radical in its extent and entails a negation not of political steering capacity, but of political subjectivity itself. Rationalities are authored, but the political subject stands in a necessarily 'agonistic' relationship with them. Simultaneously, their 'scientific object', or a politically denuded entity, permanently struggles with negating technology.[80] Foucault is not a thinker who might aid in overcoming the perennial danger of usurped executive power; instead, he is the thinker who demonstrates just how dark this spectre is.[81]

Seen in this light, the construction or 'fiction' of Pareto efficiency and the modern transmission-belt model of administration take on a far more significant constitutional meaning. The core message that regulatory agencies, as a fourth branch of government, should only be

[77] C. Scott, 'Regulation in the Age of Governance: The Rise of the Post-regulatory State' in J. Jordana and D. Levi-Faur (eds.), *The Politics of Regulation: Institutions and Regulatory Reforms for the Age of Governance* (Cheltenham: Edward Elgar, 2004), 145–74.

[78] S. Lukes, *Power: A Radical View* (2nd edn, Basingtoke: Palgrave Macmillan, 2005), at 14–29.

[79] M. Foucault, *Power: Essential Works of Foucault, 1954–1984 (Volume 3, Power)*, J. D. Fabian (ed.) (London: Penguin, 1994), at 416.

[80] *Ibid.*, at 343. [81] M. Foucault, *Birth of Biopolitics*.

established where regulation has no redistributive consequences may entail a radical extension of the self-limiting of the polity witnessed in the eighteenth-century creation of constitutionalized property rights. Nonetheless, the sphere of market rationality is itself subject to limits. Finance or monetary policy with all of its redistributive consequences can never be viewed as a suitable object for supervision.[82] Certainly, independent central banks might still be established, but their creation must be understood as political projects with political consequences, for which political accountability must be assumed.[83] To this degree, the modern transmission-belt model reveals itself as the other side of the coin of renewed post-war or Hayekian commitments to the constitutionally secured sphere of private autonomy. Where Hayek emphasizes the importance of establishment of spheres of autonomy *outside* of the technology of the state and in defence against it, the modern transmission-belt model raises a normative expectation that technology will also be overcome *within* the state; markets may be made 'free', but, by the same token, political accountability must be explicitly assumed for political projects.

The emergence of permissive compromise and a rationality of risk within the EU – and, more particularly, their impacts within the ESFS – might accordingly be characterized not as a radical extension of the traditional constitutionally secured sphere of (market) autonomy, but rather as a final perversion of it. Following the abdication of political accountability, the market becomes subject to the technology of expertise. Where permanent innovation within financial services markets – or the substitution of ever more refined debt financing mechanisms for the (politically) defined, though admittedly lacklustre, *product* of traditional markets – forms a part of the permissive consensus, which has also seen (Keynsian) debt privatized in ever more refined, but ever more illusionary, debt securitization mechanisms,[84] we are all complicit with a rationality that entails the abdication of political accountability for public welfare. Where a rationality of risk normalizes the permanent potential for the failure of financial markets, Foucault's final and unexpected observations on the slow passage from Hayek's self-limiting philosophies to the

[82] Majone, *Regulating Europe*.

[83] Majone, *Dilemmas of European Integration*; Majone, *The EU in Comparative Context*.

[84] Crouch, *The Strange Non-Death of Neo-Liberalism*, especially Chapter 1.

expansive rationalities of neoliberalism or anarcho-liberalism prove topical and highly uncomfortable. The rationality of wealth-maximization, married with the behavioural sciences (economics), heightens permanent agonism between the political subject and rationality, and does so to the point of systemic collapse. Where expressions of political subjectivity or attempts to influence autonomous expertise on the part of the Parliament, the Council or the public are dismissed within the science or rationality of regulation as instances of 'risk aversion' within 'economic objects', political capacity and democratic will have been wholly usurped.

16

The role of experts and financial supervision in the European Union: the de Larosière Commission

KARIM KNIO

16.1 Introduction

The process of European integration can be regarded as always having been fuelled by the notion of 'crises'. The process itself emerged as a response to various political, social and economic governance problems facing many European states towards the end of the Second World War. After the formation of the European Coal and Steel Community, the European Economic Community and the European Atomic Energy Community in the 1950s, European integration has swung pendulum-like from the heights of strong, rapid and intense regional integration mechanisms in the 1960s to the lows of 'multiple sclerosis' and the 'doldrums years'[1] of the 1970s and early 1980s when national economic protectionism resurfaced. Even after the establishment of the single market and the launch of the euro, the process of European integration has continued to exhibit the same alternating movements. In addition, problems accruing from an enlarged European Union (EU), for example, relating to the liberalization of services or to Common Agricultural Policy reforms following the 2004 enlargement round, questioned the EU's capability to withstand new external threats while simultaneously deepening its own institutional architecture after the coming into force of the Lisbon Treaty. Despite the EU's remarkable resilience in the face of different crises, it cannot be denied that it is currently facing its biggest and deepest crisis ever. The sovereign debt problem that swamped the Irish, Portuguese, Greek and Spanish economies now threatens Italy.

[1] J. Caporaso and J. T. S. Keeler, 'The European Union and Regional Integration Theory' in C. Rhodes and S. Mazey (eds.), *The State of The European Union, vol. iii, Building a European Polity?* (Boulder, CO: Lynne Reinner and Longman, 1995), 29–62, at 37.

These developments have, among other things, posed serious concerns over whether the euro, once the symbol of a high level of economic integration, is sustainable or whether certain Member States need to abandon the eurozone.[2]

Due to the ongoing nature of the current crisis, the lack of an immediate, detailed and comprehensive reform strategy on the part of the EU is hardly surprising. As the German Chancellor Angela Merkel recently reminded the Bundestag: 'There are no quick and easy answers. Resolving the sovereign debt crisis is a process and this process will take years. We have started a new phase in European integration.'[3] Yet, a broad tripartite strategy seems to be emerging within the EU. It is aimed at tackling three specific inter-related objectives: the reinforcement of economic governance with close EU supranational supervision, the stabilization of the eurozone's public finances and the repair of the financial system.[4]

This chapter focuses on the role of a particular set of experts in driving the reforms currently being undertaken in the field of financial supervision, which falls under one of the EU strategy objectives, namely the repairing of the financial system mentioned above. In particular, it will shed light on the role of the High-Level Group on Financial Supervision in the EU, also known as the de Larosière Commission, which brought together financial experts and policy makers. It was established by the European Commission in 2009.[5] The experts involved were invited to write a scientific report on the manner in which the EU could supervise and coordinate its financial reforms during and in the aftermath of the ongoing crisis.

The de Larosière Commission significantly influenced the design of the new European System of Financial Supervision (ESFS). This chapter corroborates the view of many institutional constructivist scholars[6] who, contrary to many structuralist and functionalist views, have prioritized

[2] F. Serricchio, M. Tsakatika and L. Quaglia, 'Euroscepticism and the Global Financial Crisis', *Journal of Common Market Studies*, 51 (2013), 51–64.

[3] K. Chibber, 'What is Germany's Vision for Europe?', 8 December 2011, www.bbc.co.uk/news/business-16030374.

[4] European Commission, 'Europe 2020: Priorities and Economic Governance', http://ec.europa.eu/europe2020/priorities/economic-governance/index_en.htm.

[5] L. Seabrooke and E. Tsingou, 'Responding to the Global Credit Crisis: The Politics of Financial Reform', *British Journal of Politics and International Relations*, 12 (2010), 313–23.

[6] M. Blyth, 'Structures Do Not Come with an Instruction Sheet: Interests, Ideas and Progress in Political Science', *Perspectives on Politics*, 1 (2003), 695–703; R. Abdelal, M. Blyth and C. Parsons, *Constructing the International Economy* (Ithaca, NY: Cornell University Press, 2010).

the importance of ideas held by experts and their pivotal importance during crises. Despite the many strengths of this constructivist analysis, I argue that these ideas need to be situated within the material socio-economic milieu from which they emanate. Drawing on a French *Régulation* analysis of capitalist restructuring processes during crises,[7] I will show how experts' ideas tend to reform and normalize existing practices instead of providing novel solutions to problems. The implications of such an argument invite us to rethink the relationship between experts, ideas and policy making in the context of the EU where legitimacy is constantly derived from the technical expertise of unelected officials.

To clarify these points further, I will first present the major analytical framework of this chapter, which centres around the complex interplay between experts' ideas and interests and their potential effects on policy making. Then, the two theoretical lenses (constructivist institutionalism and French *Régulation*) that are used to examine this nexus will be presented. This will be followed by a brief overview of the EU tripartite strategy of reform and an analysis of the composition of the de Larosière Commission and its appointment process. The chapter concludes by linking these two theories to the case study and discussing the implications of these theoretical insights in relation to the de Larosière Commission.

16.2 Experts' ideas and interests: a complex analytical framework

The role of ideas in political analysis and social science research is currently gaining significant weight, as exemplified by the rising number of scholarly publications dealing with this subject matter.[8] This 'ideational turn' can largely be interpreted as a post-positivist epistemological reaction against the shortcomings of multiple rationalist/utility maximization and structuralist agendas of research that are still dominant in various academic and policy-making circles. Consequently, if we

[7] R. Boyer and Y. Saillard, 'A Summary of *Régulation* Theory' in R. Boyer and Y. Saillard (eds.), *Régulation Theory: The State of The Art* (London: Routledge, 2002), 36–44.

[8] A. Gofas and C. Hay (eds.), *The Role of Ideas in Political Analysis* (New York: Routledge, 2010); D. Béland and R. H. Cox (eds.), *Ideas and Politics in Social Science Research* (Oxford University Press, 2011).

take the inseparability thesis[9] of subjects and objects in social sciences seriously, the role of subjective interpretation and the privileging of meaning in our everyday lives become paramount. This means that concepts such as experts' interests do not refer to anything real in or by themselves and do not come with 'instruction sheets', as Mark Blyth has humorously noted.[10] The implication of this ideational analysis is that actors' interests are not real *per se*, but their perception of them is. In other words, the social construction of interests means that ideas create interests and not the other way round.

This 'ideational turn' stands in opposition to positivist analyses, usually articulated by rationalist, structuralist and Marxist theories, which treat interests as a material given. From these perspectives, despite the variety of forms they can occupy in the policy process, ideas are nothing more than instrumental auxiliary variables in the overall analysis. For instance, whether ideas were analysed as 'road maps' and/or 'focal points',[11] as 'false consciousness' or as justifications for interests,[12] the common thread among all of these propositions was that ideas are residual variables always related to a given, defined and fixed notion of interests. In this vein, interests create ideas.

Clearly, the advent of this 'ideational turn' has advanced our understanding of this complex ideas–interests nexus. Simply put, interests cannot be axiomatically defined and should not be assumed to exist independently of our minds. However, in recent years, this turn has propelled a resurgence of critical realist arguments warning us about its idiographic excesses and the absence of a material dimension of analysis necessary for any thorough explanation of social reality.[13] Therefore, the social construction of interests thesis does not necessarily mean that only perceptions of interests exist. Instead, critical realists argue that interests possess intrinsic qualities and capabilities (causal powers) in their own right and are independent of our minds. However, these capabilities are

9 This thesis refers to the position that subjects and objects are intertwined simultaneously. A meaningful social science analysis cannot study one without the other. See M. S. Archer, *Realist Social Theory: The Morphogenetic Approach* (Cambridge University Press, 1995).

10 Blyth, 'Structures Do Not Come with an Instruction Sheet'.

11 J. Goldstein and R. O. Keohane, 'Ideas and Foreign Policy: An Analytical Framework' in J. Goldstein and R. O. Keohane (eds.), *Ideas and Foreign Policy: Beliefs, Institutions and Political Change* (Ithaca, NY: Cornell University Press, 1993), 3–30.

12 J. L. Hochschild, 'How Ideas Affect Actions' in R. E. Goodin and C. Tilly (eds.), *The Oxford Handbook of Contextual Political Analysis* (Oxford University Press, 2006), 284–96.

13 A. Sayer, *Realism and Social Science* (London: Sage, 2000).

only activated via the perceptions that actors have of them and their subsequent interaction with other interests, ideas and events. In so doing, critical realism shows us how interests are both independent of and dependent on our minds. In other words, interests nurture ideas, but do not determine them.[14]

In sum, the analytical relationship between ideas and interests is inconclusive. It rests largely on the theoretical lenses one deploys to study the subject matter in question. This is precisely why in the next section I introduce the two theoretical tools used in this chapter to explain the role of experts in the field of financial supervision. The theory of constructivist institutionalism fits within the 'ideational turn' discussed above where interests are constructed by ideas, while the French *Régulation* approach corresponds to a critical realist mode of investigation where interests exist independent of our perception of them, but are necessarily nurtured by ideas.

16.3 Situating theory within the analytical framework: constructivist institutionalism and the French *Régulation* school

16.3.1 Constructivist institutionalism and the role of ideas in crises

Constructivism as an intellectual movement and theoretical approach started to gain prominence in social sciences, and more specifically in international relations, by the early 1990s. Its ascendency was primarily due to the unexpected fall of the Soviet Union and the inability of various structuralist, functionalist or rationalist theories to anticipate this change, despite the empirical and analytical rigorousness of their concepts and methods. By focusing ontologically on the mutual constitutiveness of structure and agency, constructivists highlighted the intersubjective nature of social reality.[15] Hence, social reality does not have an *a priori* meaning in and of itself. It is only through discursive interactions concretized via various processes of shared meanings between actors that particular realities exist. Consequently, the continuous construction and deconstruction of these realities on the one hand problematizes the essentialization of identities and meanings. On the other hand, these processes of construction or deconstruction imply an analytical tendency geared towards revealing the

[14] *Ibid.*; Archer, *Realist Social Theory*.

[15] A. Wendt, 'Anarchy is What States Make of it: The Social Construction of Power Politics', *International Organization*, 46 (1992), 391–425.

historically contingent nature of such meanings. Focusing on the role of perception, interpretation and social learning performed by reflexive social agents, constructivism highlights the importance of the role of ideas in explaining political, economic and social change.[16]

Nonetheless, constructivism cannot be seen as only a critique of structuralism, functionalism and/or rationalism; it also poses a serious challenge to post-structuralism. Although both constructivism and post-structuralism epistemologically emphasize relativism and the situated nature of our knowledge of the world, given the concomitant interaction between subjects and objects, constructivism differs ontologically from post-structuralism in according equal weight to objects in its overall analysis. From this perspective, objects not only acquire their meaning from discursive interactions but also influence the way in which we construct such a discourse. In other words, constructivism widens the manner in which discourses influence practice by incorporating the opposite movement, namely how practices influence discourses.[17] In so doing, it focuses on the content and nature of ideas and simultaneously questions when these ideas have been vocalized, how, by whom, to whom, and how they objectivize, restrict and constrain reality. These two analytical movements shift the focus of post-structuralism on meaning towards meaning-making since haphazard, subjective yet dominant epistemes are not only imposed on actors, but are also crafted, negotiated, deliberated and persuaded. This is why Schmidt referred to constructivism as an approach exhibiting 'logic of communication'.[18]

Constructivist or discursive institutionalism (CI/DI, hereinafter 'CI') carries these ideas and applies them through a sociological interpretation of institutions.[19] It emphasizes the endogenous nature and social construction

[16] T. Risse-Kappen, 'Ideas Do Not Float Freely: Transnational Coalitions, Domestic Structures, and the End of the Cold War', *International Organization*, 48 (1994), 185–214; E. Adler, 'Seizing the Middle Ground: Constructivism in World Politics', *European Journal of International Relations*, 3 (1997), 319–63.

[17] T. Diez, 'Speaking Europe: The Politics of Integration Discourse', *Journal of European Public Policy*, 6 (1999), 598–613; T. Risse, 'Social Constructivism and European Integration' in A. Wiener and T. Diez (eds.), *European Integration Theory* (Oxford University Press, 2001), 159–76.

[18] V. Schmidt, 'Discursive Institutionalism: The Explanatory Power of Ideas and Discourse', *Annual Review of Political Science*, 11 (2008), 303–26.

[19] Blyth, 'Structures Do Not Come with an Instruction Sheet'; C. Hay, 'Constructivist Institutionalism' in R. A. W. Rhodes, S. A. Binder and B. A. Rockman (eds.), *The Oxford Handbook of Political Institutions* (Oxford University Press, 2006), 56–74; Schmidt, 'Discursive Institutionalism'.

of political institutions, in particular, the relationship between institutional characteristics, political agency, performance and change. Thus, expert discourses have become the units of analysis, especially in relation to the formation of preferences. These units of analysis further comprise norms, narratives, discourses and frames of reference that serve to (re)construct actors' understandings of interests, hence redirecting their actions within institutions.

Seeking to grapple with complex questions of (post-)formative institutional change, CI focuses on the independent causal role of the ideational and the discursive in its analysis. Institutions therefore exist permanently in a state of disequilibrium due to the constant construction/deconstruction of ideas and their appropriation by human agency. To capture the ideational/discursive links analytically between formative and post-formative institutional junctures, CI deploys 'path shaping' or 'ideational path dependency', a concept coined to mark its distinctiveness from the more deterministic and structural legacy of path dependency-led types of arguments. As Hay put it: 'It is not just institutions, but the very ideas on which they are predicated and which inform their design and development, that exert constraints on political autonomy. Institutions are built on ideational foundations which exert an independent path dependent effect on their subsequent development.' Consequently, institutional change 'is best understood in terms of the interaction between strategic conduct, the strategic context within which it is conceived, and the unfolding of its consequences, both intended and unintended'.[20]

Given this paramount relevance of ideas in explaining change and institutional outcomes, ideational change invariably precedes institutional change in constructivist institutionalism. The causal and independent role of ideas in this perspective matters more in periods of crises, exhibiting more radical uncertainty or what Blyth calls 'Knightian moments' than in 'normal' relatively stable time junctures. Crises entail fluid times characterized by fluxes of uncertainty where the core and basis of the perception of experts of their interests, goals, techniques and objectives are seriously shaken. Different ideas about how to solve emerging problems, the ideational contestation between the holders of these ideas (experts) and the subsequent power struggles it generates, and the extent to which these ideas resonate with other important players (logic of communication)

[20] Hay, 'Constructivist Institutionalism', at 64.

explain to a large extent why institutions in crises from this perspective favour a particular course of action over the other.[21]

16.3.2 French Régulation[22] *and capitalism*

The French *Régulation* body of analysis (hereinafter 'FR') provides a relevant and unique understanding of contemporary capitalism(s). It delves further into the deeper processes and inner social forces that essentially shape and support institutional variations of various regimes of accumulation. Drawing on the techniques of the French *Annales* School in studying history,[23] the FR approach highlights how different social groups continuously produce and reproduce the values, norms, rules and ideas of their ever-changing, material, socio-economic living conditions through historically contingent institutional compromises and political pacts. In so doing, it addresses, for instance, the centrality of the 'political' and the 'cultural' in our understanding of 'economic' institutions, and offers a dynamic analysis of social relationships of production and their evolution over time.[24]

From this perspective, the subjectivity of experts' ideas in policy making cannot be divorced from the material practice and vested interests among which they are nurtured and conditioned. Compared to CI, the social construction of interests within an FR framework does not necessarily overlook the fact that interests are objectively defined prior to our perception of them. Interests are considered both real and constructed, and independent of and dependent on our minds.

Although the FR lexicon is vast and encyclopaedic in its own right, three important concepts lie at the heart of its analysis: Regimes of

[21] M. Blyth, *The Great Transformations* (Cambridge University Press, 2002); Blyth, 'Structures Do Not Come with an Instruction Sheet'.

[22] The proponents of this school of thought remind us that the French language distinguishes between *régulation* and *réglementation*. The former deals with the notion of transformation, while the latter is synonymous with the meaning of 'regulation' in the English language. The research focus of this school of thought is on *régulation* and not *réglementation* or regulation. See R. Boyer, 'The Origins of Régulation Theory' in R. Boyer and Y. Saillard (eds.), *Régulation Theory: The State of The Art* (London: Routledge, 2002), 13–20.

[23] F. Braudel, *La Méditerranée et le monde méditerranéen à l'époque de Philippe II*, 2 vols. (Paris: Armand Colin, 1947); J. Clio, 'Régulation et histoire: je t'aime, moi non plus' in R. Boyer and Y. Saillard (eds.), *Théorie de la Regulation: L'état des savoirs* (Paris: La Découverte, 1998), 49–57; P. Verley, 'Histoire économique et théorie économique' in R. Boyer and Y. Saillard (eds.), *Théorie de la regulation: L'état des savoirs* (Paris: La Découverte, 1995), 521–29.

[24] Boyer, 'The Origins of Régulation Theory'.

Accumulation (RoA), Modes of Regulation (MoR) and crises. RoA represent an abstraction used to describe how repeated social and economic patterns facilitate the creation of particular types of growth trajectories between two structural crises in the long term. In Boyer's words, they are 'the set of regularities that ensure the general and relatively coherent progress of capital accumulation, that is, which allow for the resolution or postponement of the distortions and disequilibria to which the process continuously gives rise'.[25]

MoR are an abstraction that primarily refers to the way in which socio-economic, legal and political adjustment processes ease ever-present tensions within RoA. According to Boyer and Saillard: 'A mode of *régulation* establishes a set of procedures and individual and collective behaviour patterns which must simultaneously reproduce social relations through the conjunction of institutional forms which are historically determined and supported by the current accumulation regime. Furthermore, a mode of *régulation* ensures the compatibility of a set of decentralised decisions, without requiring agents to internalise the principles governing the overall dynamics of the system.'[26]

As the definition implies, MoR are codified within five institutional forms, encompassing monetary constraints, the wage–labour nexus, competition, incorporation of the state into the international economy and form of state. It is noteworthy that MoR are not a mirror reflection of RoA, since the former steer and regulate the institutional forms that are eventually supported by the latter. The 'codification' of MoR or the manner in which they intervene within the institutional forms is mediated through: (i) formal rules and laws; (ii) social pacts and deals generated by institutionalized compromises; and (iii) the body of ideas, norms and routines that define the overall system. From this perspective, the FR's central argument rests on the dialectic interaction between RoA and MoR as manifested through the five institutional forms.[27]

Crises occupy an important space in the FR framework given the literature's meticulous distinction between five types of crises categorized by their increasing severity: exogenous crises, endogenous or internal crises, crises of MoR, crises of RoA and crises of the mode of production.[28]

[25] R. Boyer, *The Regulation School: A Critical Introduction* (New York: Columbia University Press, 1990), at 35–6.
[26] Boyer and Saillard, 'A Summary of *Régulation* Theory', at 41.
[27] Boyer and Saillard, 'A Summary of *Régulation* Theory'.
[28] Boyer, *The Regulation School*, at 35–6.

Exogenously triggered crises, or crises of external disturbances, occur when the economic reproduction of a country is interrupted due to natural disasters or war.[29] Endogenous or cyclical crises 'correspond to the phase in which tensions and disequilibria accumulated during periods of expansion are wiped out. They take place within the existing economic mechanisms and social patterns, and thus within the prevailed mode of *régulation* in a given country and era'.[30] Both exogenous and endogenous crises are considered minor since they do not affect MoR, RoA or the interaction between the two. The other three variations of crises are called structural or organic crises, since their implications force profound changes on the whole system of production and exchange. Consequently, crises of MoR occur when the modes are 'incapable of overcoming unfavourable short term tendencies, even though the regime of accumulation was at least initially viable'.[31] A good example of this could be the wave of institutional reforms that swamped the finance industry after the collapse of Lehman Brothers (2008–present). On the other hand, crises in RoA reflect a disruption to the growth regime and seriously alter the productive infrastructure of the ailing economy.[32] A good example of this is the shift from Taylorist to Fordist techniques of production in the USA after the Great Depression in the 1930s. A mode of production crisis refers to the collapse of the specific set of social relationships and institutional compromises that define the genesis of the whole system.[33] This happens when institutional forms reach their limits and new RoA do not seem to emerge. The crisis of the feudalist mode of production in fourteenth-century Europe is an example.

In a nutshell, all organic or structural crises configure a disjoint between RoA and MoR. The degree of severity depends on whether the exhaustion of the institutional apparatus can be overcome (crises in MoR), or whether new socio-economic practices and technological innovations are needed to surpass the crisis in question (crises in RoA), or whether the overall system of production, appropriation, distribution and exchange is simply no longer viable (crises of the mode of production).

16.3.3 Constructivist institutionalism and French Régulation

Compared to CI, the FR framework presents a different explanatory pathway in relation to the nature of experts' knowledge and the typology

[29] *Ibid.*, at 49. [30] *Ibid.*, at 50. [31] *Ibid.*, at 52. [32] *Ibid.*, at 56. [33] *Ibid.*, at 58.

of crises. Unlike under CI, experts' knowledge in FR is not only subjectively constructed but is also conditioned by concrete social milieu characterized by their own everyday material routines and biases. In other words, experts' ideas are necessarily shaped by the material environment in which they exist (situated in MoR but conditioned by RoA).

Crises in FR, on the other hand, are not monolithic and do not necessarily exhibit change. The nuanced typology of crises in FR reveals to us how experts' ideas, for example, can: (i) contribute towards the stability of the system (exogenous or endogenous crises); (ii) reform the system (crises in MoR); (iii) revolutionize the system (crises in RoA); or (iv) simply not matter at all (crises of the mode of production). After this I will continue with the discussion on the de Larosière Commission, which serves here as a case study, and I will explain how these two theoretical perspectives relate to the subject matter.

16.4 Case study: EU reforms and the de Larosière Commission

The de Larosière Commission was a body of experts invited by the European Commission to provide advice on how to reshape the field of financial supervision in light of the current financial crisis. Since financial supervision cannot be seen in isolation from the other reforms stipulated by the EU's broad tripartite strategy[34] mentioned earlier in the chapter, this section will first provide some background information about the other two areas of reform (i.e., the reinforcement of economic governance and the stabilization of the eurozone's public finances) before delving into the de Larosière Commission.

Committed to Europe 2020 targets,[35] the first area of reform (economic governance) focuses on the complementarities between the Euro

[34] European Commission, 'Europe 2020'.

[35] The EU targets for 2020 centre around employment, innovation, energy/climate, education and poverty. Under employment, the EU aims to have 75 per cent of the population aged between twenty-four and sixty employed. In parallel, 3 per cent of GDP is to be invested in Research and Development (R&D) schemes to enhance innovation. With respect to energy, the EU's tripartite strategy aims to reduce greenhouse gas emissions by 20 per cent, improve the share of renewable energy by 20 per cent and increase energy efficiency by 20 per cent. For education, the target is to limit the share of early school dropouts to 10 per cent. Also, 40 per cent of the younger generation should have a degree or diploma. Finally, the targets seek to lift 20 million people out of poverty. For more detailed information, see European Commission, 'Europe 2020: Reaching the Goals', http://ec.europa.eu/europe2020/europe-2020-in-a-nutshell/targets/index_en.htm.

Plus and the renewed Growth and Stability Pacts. The Euro Plus Pact refers to a series of reforms agreed upon by the eurozone members plus six additional Member States (Bulgaria, Denmark, Latvia, Lithuania, Poland and Romania). It revolves around the sustainability of public finances, the reinforcement of financial stability and the strengthening of employment and competitiveness levels across the Euro Plus area.[36] The 'new' Growth and Stability Pact aims to strengthen and monitor the compliance of member countries with the strict budgetary and public debt rules enshrined in the Maastricht criteria.[37] Unlike the previous Growth and Stability Pact, the new one will include preventive and corrective elements. In the realm of prevention, the European Commission will have the power to offer recommendations to countries at risk of non-compliance with the Maastricht criteria.[38] It can also alert the Council of Ministers about possible cases of excessive budget deficit. For correction purposes, the Excessive Deficit Procedure (EDP) can be used, whereby the Commission not only issues recommendations about how to address the problem(s) at hand but can also impose a range of penalties. These new economic governance measures envisage greater surveillance by the Commission in relation to macroeconomic

[36] The sustainability of public finances will be enhanced by monitoring national fiscal rules across pensions, healthcare and social benefits schemes. Financial stability will be reinforced through national legislation for banking resolution and regular bank stress tests. Similarly, fostering competitiveness will require the monitoring of wages and productivity trends, as well as the introduction of measures to increase productivity. Finally, fostering employment will be undertaken via labour market reforms, lifelong learning and tax reform to raise labour participation. European Council, 'Conclusions', (24/25 March 2011) EUCO 10/1/11 REV 1; European Commission, 'Background on the Euro Plus Pact: Information Prepared for the European Council' (9 December 2011), http://ec.europa.eu/europe2020/pdf/euro_plus_pact_background_december_2011_en.pdf; European Commission, 'Taking Stock of the Euro Plus Pact', presentation of J. M. Barroso, President of the European Commission, to the European Council (9 December 2011), http://ec.europa.eu/europe2020/pdf/euro_plus_pact_presentation_december_2011_en.pdf.

[37] K. McNamara, 'Economic and Monetary Union' in H. Wallace, W. Wallace and M. A. Pollack (eds.), *Policy-Making in the European Union* (5th edn, Oxford University Press, 2005), 141–60.

[38] The Maastricht criteria comprise five elements: (i) the budget deficit may not be more than 3 per cent of GDP; (ii) the public debt may not amount to more than 60 per cent of GDP; (iii) the level of inflation may not be higher than 1.5 percentage points above the average level achieved by the three states with the lowest levels of inflation; (iv) interest rates may not be higher than 2 percentage points above the average level achieved by the three states with the lowest levels of interest rates; and (v) the normal fluctuation margins of the Exchange Rate Mechanism (ERM) have to be on record for two years.

imbalances such as property bubbles, growing current account deficits and faltering competitiveness rates.[39]

The second area of reform (stabilization of the eurozone's public finances) deals with crisis management. To respond to the diverse and immediate problems created by the sovereign debt crisis, the EU introduced a special purpose vehicle known as the European Financial Stability Facility (EFSF) in May 2010. Based in Luxembourg and owned by the eurozone Member States, the EFSF's mandate includes: safeguarding financial stability in the eurozone by providing loans to affected countries, intervention in primary and secondary debt markets, and the recapitalization of financial institutions via loans dedicated to governments. The EFSF undertakes these activities by issuing bonds or other debt instruments in capital markets. It is backed by guarantee commitments from its Member States for a total of €780 billion and possesses a lending capacity of €440 billion. The EFSF is rated 'AAA' by Standard & Poor's and Fitch ratings, and 'Aaa' by Moody's.[40] In parallel, an emergency funding mechanism, the European Financial Stabilisation Mechanism (EFSM), was created to provide financial stability and assistance to all EU Member States, including those that are not part of the eurozone. The EFSM is backed by all the Member States within the EU and has a capacity to raise up to €60 billion. Both the EFSF and the EFSM were superseded by the more permanent European Stability Mechanism (ESM) in 2013.[41]

16.4.1 Financial supervision and the de Larosière Commission

Prior to the financial crisis, the European system of financial supervision operated along the Lamfalussy institutional model that sought to provide an evolutionary and gradual road map to converge with the supervisory practices of Member States and procedures towards an EU-wide system of financial integration.[42] Accordingly, the Lamfalussy institutional model consisted of four sequential levels of action that required the following steps:

[39] European Commission, 'Reinforcing Economic Policy Coordination', COM(2010) 250 final; European Commission, 'Enhancing Economic Policy Coordination for Stability, Growth and Jobs-Tools for Stronger EU Economic Governance', COM(2010) 367 final; European Commission, 'Europe 2020'.

[40] European Commission, 'Europe 2020'.

[41] See http://ec.europa.eu/economy_finance/economic_governance/sgp/index_en.htm.

[42] Lamfalussy Committee Report, 'The Final Report of the Committee of Wise Men on the Regulation of European Securities Markets' (15 February 2001).

(1) Initiation of legislative proposals agreed upon through an EU co-decision process.
(2) Agreement among EU finance ministers to implement measures for Member States based on these proposals.
(3) Liaison and coordination between Member State regulators and EU finance on implementation procedures.
(4) National compliance and legal enforcement.[43]

By following this logic, the implementation of the Lamfalussy model in the third step given above has indirectly allowed existing regulatory and supervisory committees[44] to have some influence over Member States' supervisory mechanisms. In response to a greater cross-border financial integration in the EU and the more recent financial crisis, the European Commission appointed a high-level expert group on financial supervision in the EU, chaired by Jacques de Larosière. The de Larosière Commission was requested to provide recommendations on strengthening and transforming a nationally fragmented, partially converged EU financial supervision system into a more efficient, integrated and sustainable one, thus addressing the third step in the logic set out above.[45]

In addition to de Larosière, the Commission included seven members: Leszek Balcerowics, Otmar Issing, Rainer Masera, Callum McCarthy, Lars Nyberg, José Pérez and Onno Ruding.[46] These experts hail from various European countries and are well-known figures in the banking and financial industry. De Larosière was the Managing Director of the International Monetary Fund (IMF) in the 1980s and became the Governor of the Bank of France nearly a decade later. He then served as the head of the European Bank of Reconstruction and Development (EBRD) until 1998. Currently, he is an advisor to Michel Pébereau, the Chairman of BNP Paribas. Balcerowics is a former chairman of the National Bank of Poland and the architect of Poland's shock therapy macroeconomic structural reforms of the early 1990s. Issing's career shifted between the German Bundesbank and the European Central

[43] *Ibid.*

[44] The Committee of European Banking Supervisors (CEBS), the Committee of European Securities Regulators (CESR) and the Committee of European Insurance and Operational Pensions Supervisors (CEIOPS).

[45] Report of the High-Level Group on Financial Supervision in the EU, chaired by Jacques de Larosière, (25 February 2009), http://ec.europa.eu/internal_market/finances/docs/de_larosiere_report_en.pdf.

[46] *Ibid.*

Bank (ECB), where he was known for developing the 'two pillar' approach of monetary policy. He also advises Goldman Sachs.

Masera was head of the Lehman Brothers' branch in Italy and served for a long time as a member of the board of the European Investment Bank (EIB). McCarthy is a former chairman of the Financial Services Authority in the UK and has held senior positions in Barclays Bank and the UK Department for Trade and Industry. Nyberg worked for twenty years in the private financial sector before being appointed the Deputy Governor of Sweden's central bank in 1999. Pérez worked for a long time in the Spanish central bank before acting as the Managing Director of a private-sector bank, Banco Bilbao Vizcaya Argentaria (BBVA). Ruding worked for the IMF and the Dutch bank ABN AMRO before assuming the role of Minister of Finance in the Netherlands between 1982 and 1989. In 1992, he became the Vice Chairman of Citibank and acted as a lobbyist for Dutch and European employer associations. Although he retired in 2003, he is still part of Citigroup's international advisory committee and is a board member of the Brussels-based Centre for European Policy Studies (CEPS).

The European Commission set a tripartite mandate of investigation for the de Larosière Commission of experts which revolved around: (i) how to best organize the supervision of European financial institutions and markets to ensure the prudential soundness of institutions, the orderly functioning of markets and thereby the protection of depositors, policy holders and investors; (ii) how to strengthen European cooperation on financial stability oversight, early warning mechanisms and crisis management, including the management of cross-border and cross-sectoral risks; and (iii) how to structure cooperation between the supervisors in competent EU authorities and other major jurisdictions to help safeguard financial stability globally.[47] In order to address these issues, the de Larosière Commission conducted hearings and organized consultations with various personalities,[48] representatives of European financial services associations and international institutions.[49]

[47] *Ibid.*, at 69.

[48] An overview of the personalities involved in these hearings is provided in the de Larosière report at p. 70. The chairs of the Lamfalussy level-three committees (the CEBS, the CESR and the CEIOPS), the President of the ECB at the time Mr Jean Claude Trichet, the Governor of the Bank of Italy and current ECB President Mr Mario Draghi, Baron Alexander Lamfalussy, and European Commissioners Charlie McCreevy and Joaquin Almunia were among the interviewees in these meetings.

[49] Report of the High-Level Group on Financial Supervision in the EU, at 70.

The de Larosière report argued that despite the initial success of the third level of the institutional model of Lamfalussy, it was no longer capable of dealing with the demands of a new regulatory and supervisory era. The report noted that there were many inconsistencies between macroeconomic and regulatory policy in the EU, and that more attention needed to be paid to the link between macroprudential oversight and microprudential supervision and regulation. Drawing on thirty-one recommendations, the report called for the creation of the ESFS and a college of supervisors consisting of two bodies: the European Systemic Risk Board (ESRB) and the European Supervisory Authorities (ESAs).[50] The ESRB's mandate would deal with macroprudential oversight and surveillance of systemic risk in EU and global financial markets. It would also have the power to issue legally non-binding recommendations and warnings to Member States. The ESAs' mandate would focus on microprudential supervision and resolving potential disputes between Member States and supervisory authorities over the implementation and interpretation of EU legislation.[51]

After a round of consultation, the European Commission largely accepted the de Larosière report and issued four regulations respectively calling for the establishment of the ESRB, the EBA, the EIOPA and the ESMA.[52] The regulations were accepted by the European Parliament in September 2010 and by the ECOFIN Council (the economic ministers' meeting under the umbrella of the Council of Ministers) in November 2010. The ESRB and the three ESAs came into force in January 2011.[53]

[50] The ESAs listed in the report should replace the previous supervisory committees. They would consist of three authorities: (i) the European Banking Authority (EBA) based in London; (ii) the European Insurance and Occupational Pensions Authority (EIOPA) based in Frankfurt; and (iii) the European Securities and Markets Authority (ESMA) based in Paris. See Report of the High-Level Group on Financial Supervision in the EU.

[51] *Ibid.*; K. Alexander, 'Reforming the European Financial Supervision: Adapting EU Institutions to Market Structures', *ERA Forum*, 12 (2011), 229–52.

[52] European Commission, 'Proposal for a Regulation on Community Macro Prudential Oversight of the Financial System and Establishing a European Systemic Risk Board', COM(2009) 499; European Commission, 'Proposal for a Regulation Establishing a European Banking Authority', COM(2009) 501; European Commission, 'Proposal for a Regulation Establishing a European Insurance and Occupational Pensions Authority', COM(2009) 502; European Commission, 'Proposal for a Regulation Establishing a European Securities and Markets Authority', COM(2009) 503.

[53] European Commission, 'Financial Supervision' (2012), http://ec.europa.eu/internal_market/finances/committees/index_en.htm.

16.5 Linking the theoretical perspectives to the case study: the role of experts

CI has improved our understanding of the role of experts in policy making in a variety of ways. It allows us to see how the production of knowledge structures are primarily intersubjective before they become locked in particular frameworks or policies. Consequently, experts' knowledge is not necessarily 'neutral' or 'impartial', but situated within humanly devised constructed contexts. In addition, CI pertinently shows us how ideas held by experts play an important role in setting up policies, especially during crises.

This CI problem setting speaks to a large extent to the 'politics' and 'sociology' of the de Larosière Commission. Confronted by one of the most existentialist crises in its history, the European Commission invited eight fully respected experts to generate ideas for outlining a road map for the EU to pursue in the field of financial supervision. Clearly, the knowledge base generated by these experts is not technically neutral, despite their undisputed professional qualifications, since their expertise does not and cannot exhaust all pertaining views on regulatory supervision within the financial industry. Nonetheless, both the 'intersubjectivity' and 'intrasubjectivity' of the ideas held by these experts (or the subjective non-neutral expertise of these experts who work in the same field) were locked into a structure (the de Larosière Commission) that exerted a major influence on financial supervision reforms in its own right by virtue of its resonance with the European Commission first and then with the rest of the EU's institutions (when it was translated into the new ESFS). This finding corroborates the CI view on the role of ideas and experts, and resonates with Haas'[54] argument about the role of epistemic communities in policy making.

Drawing on an FR line of analysis, I argue that constructivist institutionalism does not address two specific lacunae. First, it remains silent about the origins of ideas and how they are nurtured and inscribed within particular contexts. Thereby, it denies the objective[55] existence of interests and ignores that these can be both independent of and dependent on our mind and understanding of the world. Second, CI's

[54] See Haas, Chapter 2, this volume; and P. M. Haas, 'Introduction: Epistemic Communities and International Policy Coordination', *International Organization*, 46 (1992), 1–35.

[55] The word 'objective' is used here within a critical realist lexicon. It does not mean 'value-neutral' or 'true', but refers to the nature of social/physical objects, regardless of what we think of them. See Sayer, *Realism and Social Science*, at 58.

interpretation of how ideas held by experts and elites can influence policy making during crises does not take into consideration how ideas can also be used as tools to normalize and regularize existing power configurations. Rather than only being constitutive and causal, ideas can also be constraining and reformist. It follows that ideas need to be analysed through the social and material environments within which they are located and not as independent variables in their own right.

The detailed FR analysis of capitalism(s) shows how ideas, norms and values that regulate and steer the economy (located in MoR and codified through the five institutional forms) dynamically correspond to how different social groups relate to the formation, circulation and distribution of capital in a particular space and time (RoA). Hence, the production and reproduction of ideas through law, social pacts and institutional compromises speaks to the dispositions articulated by various social groups, given their praxis-led objective existence within specific socio-economic fields. From this perspective, the explicit critical realist theme evident in the FR analysis problematizes material and ideational reductionism, and portrays a sociological concept of interest that can be both materially situated and socially constructed.

Accordingly, the commonalities that cut across all intersubjectivities are lost from the CI analysis on experts' knowledge. This is important because one should not underestimate the fact that all of the personalities in the de Larosière Commission worked in the same industry (the financial sector) and that all the public hearings undertaken by this Commission were with personalities also located within the same industry.[56] Therefore, all the personalities involved shared particular ways of thinking in relation to certain common themes, issues, problems and solutions, given their everyday life practices that conditioned the contours of the possible solutions for them. Consequently, their intersubjective expertise cannot be detached from their vested interests that nurture their knowledge and positions about contemporary developments in financial supervision in the EU. Clearly, the fact that these personalities have vested interests does not imply that they all interpret their interests in a similar vein. Nonetheless, this also does not mean that interests are simply ideational constructions as CI maintains; interests are real and have real consequences.

In parallel, the role of experts' ideas in setting policy during crises is equally one-sided. If we locate ideas again within their respective social

[56] Report of the High-Level Group on Financial Supervision in the EU, at 70.

and economic environments, it follows that ideas perform a variety of roles defined by the situational positions in which they are embedded. Drawing on the FR analysis of crises, one can distinguish between different roles of ideas depending on the type of crises. As was explained earlier, crises in MoR refer to situations where the institutional linchpins of the system are exhausted. Ideas here play an important role in normalizing and legitimizing new reforms that do not necessarily seek to shake the system, but opt to refine it. Crises in RoA, on the contrary, witness the unsustainability of the growth regime where ideas play a crucial role in identifying new potential RoA that can viably supersede the previous one.

Apart from the fact that the CI argument does not incorporate the multiplicity of ideational routes in policy settings, it is important to stress that the current financial crisis is one of MoR and not RoA. Obviously, this crisis could progress and it could transform in various ways. But whether this will happen or not is an empirical question which needs to be seen over time. At the moment, however, this is a crisis where the current institutional forms cannot be sustained, inviting a revision of the system's ideational and institutional requirements.

The content of the de Larosière report epitomized this mode of analysis. In fact, all the thirty-one recommendations made in this report sit very congruently with the Europe 2020 strategy where financial markets should play an important role in maintaining a high level of competitiveness, job creation, employment and social cohesion. The report was more critical about the current institutional set-up in the EU that permitted a structural rupture between macroeconomic policy and regulatory frameworks. From this perspective, the report suggested further institutional engineering to ensure better coordination between macroprudential and microprudential supervision. Hence, the ideas expressed in this report are *reformist par excellence* and do not entail a path-shaping mechanism as the CI analysis implies. This should hardly come as a surprise given that the personalities within the de Larosière Commission had no vested interests in shaking a system of their own design. From this perspective, reformism can be the only expected outcome of such a commission.

In conclusion, the role of experts and the ideas they hold in policy making is very important. However, if we do not place these ideas within their socio-economic terrains, we risk not seeing how those who supposedly influence policies (experts) are themselves also influenced by material, ideational and institutional considerations. Such a scenario further obfuscates our understanding of power relations, legitimacy considerations and governance regimes, in particular geographically situated institutional settings. This theoretical elaboration is very relevant to the current EU financial supervision set-up for, if the vested interests of a committee (de Larosière) are validated by another body that is similarly appointed (the European Commission), then the risk of a more socially detached technocratic mode of governance (promoted through the involvement of experts) becomes increasingly more evident, thereby also risking the further widening of the democratic deficit in the EU.

17

Expertise at the crossroads of national and international policy making: a public management perspective

ADRIAAN SCHOUT AND JAAP SLEIFER

17.1 Introduction

Over the past few years, the work of civil servants in many European Union (EU) countries has changed to ensure a better – more structured and more transparent – handling of expertise. The work of EU and national civil servants has become a more formalized balancing act between political assessments, fact-finding and analysis.[1] In a sense, civil servants have had to develop expertise and expert-like work processes of their own. New requirements have been imposed on them in terms of their own expertise and how they respond to new and integrated political preferences, using a multitude of insights from experts in and around government. The expertise that the civil servants need to be able to work with covers a variety of areas (e.g., environment, spatial planning, finance and social security), political insights (e.g., for ensuring political and societal support), legal expertise and relevant management information (related to the choice of instruments, implementation aspects and the assessment of effectiveness). As a result, civil servants are forced to move outside the confinements of working with specific epistemic communities and are required to think in integrated, or 'joined-up', ways, and to include a variety of objectives and information sources in their decision-making processes.[2] This variety of input is seldom available in a ready-made way and needs to be compiled, filtered, interpreted and weighed in terms of competing objectives and sources of information, and then communicated. Accordingly, expert communities

[1] J. B. Wiener, 'Better Regulation in Europe', *Current Legal Problems*, 59 (2006), 447–518.
[2] A. Schout and A. Jordan, 'The European Union's Governance Ambitions and its Administrative Capacities', *Journal of European Public Policy*, 15 (2008), 957–74.

and expertise are not only affecting external dimensions of administrations but are also transforming the work of civil servants in profound ways from the inside.[3]

A public management perspective helps to shed light on the changing roles and sources of expertise in policy processes and to broaden the discussion beyond the relevance of epistemic communities. The organization of the policy process determines the scale, scope, timing and sources (such as impact assessments, hearings and input from experts) of the expertise used in that policy process, and thereby impacts the quality of the policy-making process.[4] The way in which the variety of inputs from experts is organized also influences the transparency of and the extent to which politicians can exercise control over the policy-making processes.

The advancements in the use of expertise and the related administrative innovations in the policy processes in EU Member States have occurred under the heading of 'better regulation' (BR) initiatives. Radaelli defines BR as a type of meta-regulation which steers the processing of external and internal expertise during rule formulation, adoption, enforcement and evaluation.[5] BR agendas focus on increasing the legitimacy of governance by ensuring that appropriate and reliable information is gathered and analysed, and by offering means for public and political control of sources and the use of information. In the context of this chapter, legitimacy is understood as grounded in the trust that people, industry and other relevant actors have in the rules and actions of government. The public has to trust the policies produced by the systems that governments have in place for taking informed decisions. Scharpf's distinction between input and output legitimacy is closely related to the different steps involved in directing and processing expertise through institutional arrangements and the setting of objectives. He states that 'legitimacy has come to rest almost exclusively on *trust in institutional arrangements* that are thought to ensure that governing processes are generally responsive to the manifest preferences of the governed (*input legitimacy*...) and/or that the policies adopted will generally represent

[3] A. Schout, 'Organizational Learning in the EU's Multi-level Governance System', *Journal of European Public Policy*, 16 (2009), 1124–44.

[4] J. P. Olsen, 'Maybe it is Time to Rediscover Bureaucracy', Arena Working Paper, No. 10 (March 2005), Centre for European Studies, University of Oslo.

[5] C. Radaelli, 'Whither Better Regulation for the Lisbon Agenda?', *Journal of Public Policy*, 14 (2007), 190–207.

effective solutions to common problems of the governed (*output legitimacy*...)'.[6]

Input legitimacy relates to the arrangements that govern and control the ways in which expertise is used in day-to-day decision making. It concerns what we might regard as the 'micro-level' of decision making and the political supervision of the policy processes. Therefore, input legitimacy relates to work planning (the setting of the policy agendas), including the planning of the required expert input in the form of obligatory hearings and impact assessments, regular evaluations of policies, tenders for reports, careful assessment of the instruments chosen, and rules to regulate expert consultations and transparency.[7] These administrative guarantees direct when, where and how expertise is to be used, and how decisions are to be made. They also facilitate the hierarchical control of these otherwise technocratic processes and offer the public access to policy making. Output legitimacy includes the setting of targets by the political level and entrusting independent expert bodies with the monitoring of these targets. It prevents having to impose detailed (micro-)instructions on what expertise to use at what stage in the policy process and how it is gathered and processed. Setting outcome indicators offers leeway to civil servants and other actors in the policy process to solve problems and leaves the control of outputs to expert bodies with independent supervisory authorities, which are better equipped to monitor specific trends than before. An example of an output legitimacy process is the objective to reduce administrative costs in the Netherlands by 25 per cent, leaving the ministries more or less free to implement this target under the watchful eye of a ministerial regulatory reform group and an independent authority ('Actal').

With the BR agendas, EU Member States have attempted, in different ways, to improve the use and control of expertise through input and output mechanisms.[8] In addition to the legal and political perspectives on the role of expertise and experts addressed in other chapters of this

[6] F. Scharpf, 'Problem-Solving Effectiveness and Democratic Accountability in the EU', MPIfG Working Paper 03/1 (February 2003), Max Planck Institute for the Study of Societies, emphasis in original.

[7] A. Schout, 'Framework for Assessing the Added Value of an EU Agency', *Journal of Public Policy*, 31 (2011), 363–84.

[8] European Commission, *Reducing the Administrative Burdens in the European Union* (Brussels: European Commission, 2009); A. Jordan and A. Schout, *The Coordination of European Governance: Exploring the Capacities for Networked Governance* (Oxford University Press, 2008); O. Treib, H. Bähr and G. Falkner, 'Modes of Governance: Towards a Conceptual Clarification', *Journal of European Public Policy*, 14 (2007), 1–20.

book, this contribution considers the involvement of various different forms of expertise in the decision-making process as a public management challenge. Importantly, the fact that the EU is a multilevel governance system complicates the efforts towards the better use of expertise in the European policy processes.[9] The success of the Commission's BR agenda is in many ways related to BR innovations in national administrations. For example, the Commission is dependent on expertise available at the national level. In other words, the quality of expertise at the EU level is related to the gathering and processing of information at the national level.

Despite massive investments, evaluations of BR have been lukewarm. Many changes have been introduced under the heading of BR, but there is little evidence that EU policies have actually improved as a result.[10] One explanation might be that there are concerns about 'de-politicized decision making' through independent authorities.[11] Another explanation might be that the multilevel challenges of managing expertise have been ignored. While EU governance literature increasingly considers the developments of better regulation policies at both the national and European levels,[12] the interdependence between BR systems has hardly been explored.[13]

This chapter examines how the EU and Dutch better regulation agendas treat expertise, and whether these agendas are developing towards similar and interconnected systems. The Dutch example provides a critical case as the Netherlands has been one of the frontrunners in better regulation, together with the UK, Germany and Denmark. If we find diverging patterns in better regulation policies, we may speculate what our findings from the Dutch case might imply for the treatment of expertise in the EU more generally.

To examine the match between the EU and national BR initiatives, the next section discusses the interdependence in the use of expertise at the EU and national levels of government. Limiting the research period to between 2000 and 2010, section 17.3 analyses the EU's BR agenda and

9 Schout, 'Organizational Learning'.

10 European Court of Auditors, *Impact Assessments in the EU Institutions: Do They Support Decision-Making?* (Luxembourg: COA, 2010).

11 G. Majone, *Regulating Europe* (London: Routledge, 1996); Everson, Chapter 15, this volume. For a critique, see S. Kettell, 'Does Depoliticisation Work?', *British Journal of Politics and International Relations*, 10 (2008), 630–48.

12 L. Allio, 'The Emergence of Better Regulation in the European Union', unpublished PhD thesis, Exeter University (2008).

13 Schout, 'Organizational Learning'.

shows that it has been focusing on 'input' legitimacy (and especially on procedures to guide micro-policy processes), but has gradually started to also emphasize 'output' legitimacy (in the form of top-down imposed targets to regulate policies in specific sectors). Section 17.4 illustrates that the Netherlands seems to have moved the other way round: from an initial focus on output legitimacy now complemented with input legitimacy. Innovations in tools of government should be considered in the context of actual concerns and perceived weaknesses in administrative systems.[14] Hence, discussions on the reforms in the Netherlands and the Commission start with short descriptions of the specific backgrounds of the BR agendas. Section 17.5 subsequently presents the major developments in BR and ends with a short discussion on the achievements. Finally, the concluding section will discuss whether the two systems converge in their handling of information and whether they are becoming interconnected instead of remaining separate BR policies.

17.2 Better regulation as a multilevel challenge

At the end of the 1990s, governments, particularly in the EU, started to explore new ways of managing policy making, which became known as the 'governance turn' in European public policy.[15] The debate on EU governance, defined here as value setting, contributed to systematic attention for a wide range of quality standards, including the choice of instruments, integration of horizontal objectives, transparency and use of expertise in decision making.[16] At first, these specific foci of attention multiplied into a host of unrelated BR approaches geared towards improving policies in specific areas such as environmental policy.[17] Later on, they were mainstreamed in general approaches to improving policies and policy making.[18]

This search for better governance is closely linked to the role of expertise in the policy process. Expertise should become deeper as well as broader. Officials have been advised to 'think outside their box'[19] and to become less

[14] H. Kassim and P. Legales, Exploring Governance in a Multi-level Polity: A Policy Instruments Approach, *West European Politics*, 33 (2010), 1–21.

[15] Treib, Bähr and Falkner, 'Modes of Governance'.

[16] European Commission, *Reducing the Administrative Burdens.*

[17] Schout and Jordan, 'The European Union's Governance Ambitions'.

[18] A. Jordan and and A. Lenschow (eds.), *Environmental Policy Integration: Defining and Developing the State of the Art* (Cheltenham: Edward Elgar, 2010).

[19] European Commission, *Reducing the Administrative Burdens*, at 10.

dependent on sectoral interests (which are often related to more narrow epistemic communities and representatives from the private sector). Integrating horizontal objectives – such as integration of environmental objectives, subsidiarity and deregulation – into decision making and policy making has meant that civil servants have had to incorporate vast amounts of information from adjacent fields in decision making and better assess costs of policies in relation to their expected benefits. Similarly, the increased attention for the selection of instruments has shifted the preference from regulation to softer tools and implies that EU civil servants are expected to be able to manage the expertise need for deciding which instruments are most suitable and cost-efficient in specific contexts. This implies that civil servants have to combine different ways to gather and process expertise through studies, social hearings – to get soft information and to use exchange of expertise as a tool for finding social consensus[20] – and consultancy reports. New transparency requirements have, furthermore, opened up the available expertise and its use to the scrutiny of the world outside the policy circles involved.

These innovations in instrumentation, broadening of policy objectives, transparency and public consultations have been condensed to more concrete better regulation agendas of the European Commission and national governments.[21] At the core of the BR agenda is the Commission's impact assessment (IA) system in which attention for these innovations has been formalized – and which, as will be discussed below, has influenced the Member States significantly. The EU's BR agenda now comprises a range of objectives including subsidiarity, proportionality, providing empirical proof for policies, sustainability, reducing administrative burdens by 25 per cent or using the least disruptive instruments. It applies to all phases of EU policy making, including the planning of comitology[22] decisions and other (legal) policy instruments. BR principles and the use of expertise they impose are now well founded in the Commission's IA system and are supported by the European Parliament and the Council.[23]

[20] M. Jachtenfuchs, 'Theoretical Perspectives on European Governance', *European Law Journal*, 1 (2009), 115–33.

[21] Radaelli, 'Whither Better Regulation'; A. Alemanno, F. den Butter, A. Nijsen and J. Torriti, *Better Business Regulation in a Risk Society* (New York: Springer, 2013).

[22] Comitology is a system of committees comprised of Member State representatives controlling the Commission's implementing powers. See Everson, Chapter 15 and Busuioc, Chapter 18, both this volume.

[23] Council of the European Union, *Better Regulation – Handling of Impact Assessments*, COMPET DS 150/06, (Brussels, 1 March 2006).

The fact that the EU is a multilevel governance system complicates this drive towards BR because it requires combining expertise that is scattered throughout the EU.[24] Communication between the levels of government becomes difficult if one level, e.g., the European Commission, is more advanced in the use of expertise while another level, e.g., the Member States, lag behind in their better regulation efforts. To succeed in working with more and better information, the Commission needs facts and figures from the Member States to be able to argue that the subsidiarity or proportionality principles are complied with.[25] Moreover, if national officials want to influence Commission initiatives, they need to follow the ways in which expertise is defined and used by the Commission. For example, the previous Dutch government, supported by Geert Wilder's Freedom Party, tried to find support for a stricter EU asylum policy by producing a short political paper outlining Dutch ambitions in controlling migration.[26] Commission officials responded by asking what the problems were, which alternatives were available and how the results would compare to doing nothing. The Dutch agenda was predominantly political and clashed with the more fact-based procedures used by the Commission when formulating policies.[27] As a result, the Dutch proposals hardly influenced the Commission's asylum-related policies, such as the EU's family reunification policy.[28]

Working with compatible BR principles is also relevant from the point of view of ensuring continuity between the various stages of the EU decision-making process.[29] For example, it makes little sense if the Commission, based on expert impact assessments, prepares proposals

[24] Schout, 'Organizational Learning'; S. Piattoni, 'Multi-level Governance in the EU. Does it Work?', Globalization and Politics: A Conference in Honor of Suzanne Berger (MIT, 8–9 May 2009)

[25] Schout, 'Organizational Learning'. Determining whether a measure is proportionate or if the subsidiarity principle applies (i.e., whether regulation at the EU level is appropriate) can require a considerable amount of information on objectives and actual effects, including insights into the administrative and enforcement costs: European Commission, *Reducing the Administrative Burdens.*

[26] C. Groenendijk, 'Asylum and Migration' in A. Schout and J. Rood (eds.), *The Netherlands as an EU Member State: A Normal Partner at Last?* (Portland: Eleven International Publishing, 2013).

[27] A. Schout, 'Expert: Asielplan Leers ergert EU', *NRC Handelsblad*, 21 April 2011.

[28] EC2011, 'Green Paper on the Right to Family Reunification of Third-Country Nationals Living in the European Union', COM(2011) 735 final; E. Akse, *Influencing the Preparation of EU Legislation. A Practical Guide to Working with Impact Assessments* (London: John Harper Publishing, 2013).

[29] Schout, 'Organizational Learning'.

for discussion in the European Parliament and the Council (Member States), and these latter two bodies continue with 'politics as usual', paying little or no attention to the expertise-based evidence submitted. Hence, at different levels in the EU's multilevel administrative system, both between the EU institutions and between the EU and the Member State authorities, BR initiatives need to follow parallel trajectories to allow for a useful exchange of expertise and effective fact-based communication between policy makers.

Although different in background and form, national and European public authorities have opted for 'fewer and better' policies[30] and have imposed requirements to incorporate expertise in the policy processes on deregulation, weighing costs and benefits, and in the choice of instruments. However, there have been marked differences between BR agendas in the EU and in the Member States. In relation to the EU's agenda, better regulation has concentrated on tools to improve the preparation of new regulations (input legitimacy) in a similar manner to the now popular better regulation vocabulary, such as evidence-based law making and *ex ante* and *ex post* evaluations.[31] In addition to improving the micro-level, better regulation also encompasses macro-policy objectives by setting specific targets and formulating horizontal objectives. Together, the input (micro) and the output (macro) tools help to implement BR objectives. The balance between the micro- and macro-approaches, however, has differed between levels of government, complicating the communication between expertise at the EU and the national levels.

17.3 Better regulation at the EU level: from micro to macro

The European Commission's BR policy has to be seen in relation to its own growing pains. One of the weaknesses in EU policy making was that originally expertise did not play a prominent role in decision making – political considerations dominated the scene. Up until approximately 2000, expertise was largely provided through expert committees advising the Commission.[32] What the Commission did with the information remained unclear because it operated primarily as a political organization.[33] Also, the negotiations on the basis of the Commission proposals

30 R. Baldwin, 'Is Better Regulation Smarter Regulation?', *Public Law* (2005), 485–511.
31 Schout, 'Organizational Learning'.
32 R. Pedler and G. Schaefer, *Shaping European Law and Policy: The Role of Committees and Comitology in the Political Process* (Maastricht: EIPA, 1996).
33 Majone, *Regulating Europe*.

between the European Parliament and the Council were driven by politics. The link between expert input and policy output was weak. As a result, EU policy witnessed a legitimacy crisis at the end of the 1990s following major upheavals over food safety. There were also numerous complaints over inconsistent policies with too many and too detailed obligations. Scandals such as the bovine spongiform encephalopathy (BSE) crisis had proven that expert input from comitology committees was neither transparent nor reliable. The BSE investigation concluded that it was unclear who had provided what information and how that information was used in decision making.[34] This crisis and other similar ones highlighted that EU policy making suffered from a credibility crisis that in part resulted from an unreliable and opaque handling of information.[35]

A second weakness in EU policies originated from the internal fragmentation of the Commission.[36] Internal coordination was compounded by political appointments, Directorates-General (DGs) working independently, and a lack of agreement on policy priorities among DGs.[37] Policy processes were hardly formalized and officials were working in relative isolation from other Commission units. As a result, it was difficult for officials to combine the relevant expertise from policy areas outside their own DG.

Furthermore, a sectoral instead of an integrated policy approach clashed with the increased number of horizontal objectives (e.g., ensuring sustainable development attention for regional consequences and subsidiarity). As a result, the Commission was forced to integrate expertise from different areas to ensure that policies reflect different horizontal objectives and to ensure transparency. Scharpf has pointed out that the Commission was initially behind in terms of working with reliable and interconnected expertise when compared with the Member States.[38]

Yet, the systematic use of expertise that BR agenda imposed has helped to develop the EU administration from a backward policy system towards a better planned policy system in which expertise is better

[34] Medina Report, *European Parliament Final BSE Inquiry Report*, A4-0020/97/A (Brussels: European Parliament, 1997).

[35] M. Everson, G. Majone, L. Metcalfe and A. Schout, *The Role of Specialised Agencies in Decentralising EU Governance* (Brussels: European Commission, 1999).

[36] Mandelkern Group, *Mandelkern Group on Better Regulation*, Final Report (13 November 2001), at 64.

[37] Schout and Jordan, 'The European Union's Governance Ambitions'.

[38] Scharpf, 'Problem-Solving Effectiveness'.

managed.[39] As is to be expected in a deeply fragmented organization, earlier attempts failed to get IAs accepted since these emerged from the sectoral DGs,[40] with each DG expecting its IAs to be applied by other DGs. However, the BR agenda also gathered momentum because it was supported by the Commission Presidents Romano Prodi and José Manuel Barroso, and by the modernization led by Commissioner Neil Kinnock. The latter resulted in a system of activity-based management backed up by the strategic planning and programming (SPP) cycle to focus the Commission's activities, resources and processes for gathering information.[41] This planning cycle now starts every year around February with rough ideas about the policy initiatives that the DGs plan to develop and an indication of the expertise that is required to develop them. The planning cycle ends with a reduced realistic legislative programme that is presented to the Council and the Parliament at the end of the year.

IAs are an obligatory part of this planning system. A legislative proposal can only be included in the work programme if it is complemented by an initial IA ('road map'). The content of the assessments is formalized[42] in accordance with the IA guidelines which direct the gathering and processing of expertise and include questions about risk assessments, baseline scenarios, choice of instruments, etc. IAs are explicitly eclectic (or 'integrated'), covering a range of horizontal objectives, including environmental, regional and social consequences as well as concern for gender equality, proportionality and subsidiarity. According to the IA guidelines, an IA should be presented in a condensed form of about thirty pages reflecting the expertise originating from hearings and studies, and an assessment of the internal quality control board (the Impact Assessment Board (IAB) – see below).

The modernization of the work planning has necessitated new organizational roles and rules and therefore has contributed to the much-needed bureaucratization of the Commission and to the streamlining of the role and use of expertise in the policy processes. The Secretariat-General (SG) of the Commission was never as powerful as the nationally appointed Commissioners who have exercised strong control over 'their'

[39] M. Bauer, 'Introduction: Organizational Change, Management Reform and EU Policy-Making', *Journal of European Public Policy*, 15 (2008), 627–47.

[40] Schout and Jordan, 'The European Union's Governance Ambitions'. [41] *Ibid.*

[42] European Commission, *Impact Assessment Guidelines*, SEC(2009)92 (Brussels: European Commission, 2009).

DGs and could easily overrule the SG (as well as the President of the Commission). Barroso has reinforced the role of the SG to strengthen his grip on the management of the Commission, also with a view to strengthening the SG's influence vis-à-vis the President of the European Council, the European Parliament and European Central Bank. Barroso's more 'presidential' approach to the management of the Commission has upgraded the SG's horizontal authority in work planning and IAs. The DGs take the lead for developing new proposals and hold the first responsibility for writing the IAs and for setting up a steering group with other DGs involved in a particular IA.[43] The SG monitors the writing of IAs and participates in this steering group. In 2006 the Commission also established the IAB. The IAB is a high-level team which cements the horizontal coordination and supervision of the quality of IAs. It monitors the development of the IAs and checks the assessments when proposals are sent to the College of Commissioners. The IAB's comments are available to all on the Commission's website. This shows a remarkably high level of transparency, opening up the Commission's internal deliberations to public scrutiny. The College of Commissioners by a simple majority decides whether the proposal moves forward, based on the proposal, the accompanying IA and the comments of the IAB.

The BR agenda has changed the work practices of officials significantly. Its operating style has moved from being hierarchical and focused on political decision making towards planned policy making with careful attention for content, expert input and transparency. The effects of these reforms are still under discussion. One remaining point of concern is that it is difficult to tell what the impact of IAs is on actual policy decisions.[44] In 2010 the Court of Auditors pointed out that the main results of the IAs are not always easy to gather and that the used expertise is often qualitative rather than quantitative due to, among other things, the difficulties and costs involved in collecting expertise from the different Member States. Similarly, specifying alternative policy options and instruments in IAs seems to be difficult due to the amount of expertise required. Moreover, even when a new proposal is assessed, it often remains unclear on what grounds policies are selected and why some

[43] Schout and Jordan, 'The European Union's Governance Ambitions'.

[44] The Evaluation Partnership, *Evaluation of the Commission's Impact Assessment System* (Brussels: European Commission, 2010); European Court of Auditors, *Impact Assessments in the EU Institutions*.

alternatives have been ignored.[45] Even though the EU's BR agenda is the shared agenda of the Council, the Commission and the Parliament, and should therefore speak to the concerns of inter-institutional decision making, in practice the BR agenda is mainly the responsibility of the Commission. The Council and the Parliament have been much less involved due to their strong political (i.e., less expert) concerns and their internal fragmentation resulting from differences between political parties in the Parliament and from negotiations in the sectoral Councils.[46]

It still seems to be the case that DGs use the IAs to justify a particular piece of legislation rather than use the gathered expertise to explore the value of alternatives.[47] In addition, the quality of the assessments leaves room for improvement.[48] The Commission also needs to improve communication to enterprises and the public on how it has used the feedback it has received during the consultation phases. However, being aware of the learning process it is in, the Commission regularly evaluates its system for processing expertise.[49]

One result of the IA system is that it has contributed to the external and internal transparency of decision making. Hiding plans and information from colleagues in other DGs has become difficult because steps in the decision-making process and the results from hearings, studies and IAs are publicly available.[50] Hence, although actual differences in policies or quality are difficult to prove, gains have been achieved in terms of internal coordination, transparency and communication.

The persistent fears that IAs would remain 'box-ticking' exercises highlight the dilemma of creating ownership for the IAs and for the range of horizontal objectives. DGs have budgets for making IAs, involving experts, using consultants and setting up industry-based focus groups. However, ownership of horizontal objectives related to concerns of other DGs remains difficult because officials find it hard to be closely

[45] European Commission, *Impact Assessment Board Report for 2010* (Brussels: European Commission, 2010).

[46] Scharpf, 'Problem-Solving Effectiveness'; A. Schout and A. Mijs, *Administratieve Lastenverlichting voor Burgers. Een uitdaging op verschillende bestuurlijke niveaus* (The Hague: Netherlands Institute of International Relations, 2010).

[47] The Evaluation Partnership, *Evaluation of the Commission's Impact Assessment*; European Court of Auditors, *Impact Assessments in the EU Institutions.*

[48] European Commission, *Impact Assessment Board Report for 2010.*

[49] See the annual IAB reports on the Commission's website: http://ec.europa.eu/smart-regulation/impact/iab/iab_en.htm.

[50] Schout and Jordan, 'The European Union's Governance Ambitions'.

involved and engage their networks in IAs that fall primarily under the responsibility of other DGs.

In 2007, an external advisory body, the High-Level Group of Independent Stakeholders (also known as the 'Stoiber Group') was created to mobilize external political pressure behind BR and to help focus expertise on cost reduction. This group of experts from business, environmental and social organizations scrutinizes EU policies from an output perspective to assess how the *acquis*, the entire body of EU law, affects the EU's integrated objectives. The focus of this Group at first was on a reduction of administrative costs. Since August 2010, the mandate of the Group also encompasses the assessment of best practices in Member States for the implementation of EU policies.[51]

17.4 From input legitimacy to output legitimacy

Priorities and terminology have changed over the past decade. For example, Barroso rephrased better regulation into 'smart regulation', but the Commission still uses the BR terminology in practice.[52] However, the work of the Stoiber Group shows that the Commission has started to experiment with an output-oriented approach. In fact, the 'input'-oriented approach of IAs was never meant to stand on its own. The Lisbon agenda was already largely output-oriented with its ambition to make the EU the most dynamic knowledge-based economy in the world. Similarly, the Commission report on simplifying and improving the regulatory environment[53] outlined the twin approaches of combining the systematic use of integrated IAs when preparing new policies (to improve input legitimacy) and programmes to simplify and update the existing body of European law in order to improve output legitimacy. The famous Kok Report,[54] which assessed the failures of the Lisbon process, also highlighted the importance of output targets, placing the reduction of administrative burdens on the EU agenda and stressing the

51 EC2010, Commission Decision amending Decision 2007/623/EC, 2010/C 223/03 (Brussels: European Commission, 2010).

52 For example, European Commission, 'Smart Regulation in the European Union', COM (2010) 0543 final.

53 European Commission, 'Simplifying and Improving the Regulatory Environment', COM(2012) 0278 final.

54 The High-Level Group, *Facing the Challenge. The Lisbon Strategy for Growth and Employment. Report from the High-Level Group Chaired by Wim Kok* (Luxembourg: Commission of the European Communities, 2004).

importance of deregulation, an output objective, to make it easier to start an enterprise. Similarly, ambitious reduction targets have also been used in the field of environment. However, partly due to the multilevel complexity of the EU's administrative system, these targets have never really materialized.

The development of output objectives has marked a next step in directing and supervising the use of expertise in the policy process. Imposing and monitoring macro-objectives – particularly the quantitative reduction of regulation – has become an additional way to create ownership of the process of incorporating expertise about deregulation and cost reduction. Quantitative reduction of the administrative burdens originating from EU policies has become a major objective in the EU's BR agenda over the past few years, as have other objectives such as quantitative emission reductions, 3 per cent research and development spending, the use of renewable energy targets and the 75 per cent employment target.[55]

Limiting the discussion to burden reduction, the existing stock of European regulation is addressed through the Action Programme for Reducing Administrative Burdens in the European Union.[56] It has set the objective of a 25 per cent reduction target of administrative costs. Thirteen priority areas have been selected for cost reduction: agriculture and agricultural subsidies, annual accounts/company law, cohesion policy, the environment, financial services, fisheries, food safety, pharmaceutical legislation, public procurement, statistics, tax law, transport, and working environment and employment relations. The burden reduction priorities force officials to develop or assemble the expertise in order to assess the impact of objectives, implementation systems, information and administration burdens on industry, and how these costs are influenced by different instruments. DG Enterprise has carried out a large-scale baseline measurement to quantify objectives in these areas and to specify the final achievements. The baseline scenario assessed the administrative costs incurred by businesses on their legal obligations to provide information to public authorities or third parties (such as costs related to reporting, inspection and statistics) and concluded that €38 billion could be saved out of a total amount of €124 billion of administrative costs.[57]

[55] European Commission, 'Europe 2020: A Strategy for Smart, Sustainable and Inclusive Growth', COM(2010) 2020 final.

[56] European Commission, *Reducing the Administrative Burdens.*

[57] European Commission, 'Smart Regulation in the European Union'.

However, the 25 per cent target is not a 'net' target so that the costs of introducing a new policy do not have to be reduced elsewhere. As a result, the suggested opportunities are discussed within the isolated perspective of the relevant policy area, and not in the light of overall cost reduction or broader economic reform agendas (e.g., the EU's 2020 agenda). Moreover, one of the main difficulties with the EU's output approach is that many of the costs incurred by industry result from the national implementation of EU legislation. It is therefore quite difficult to impose a 25 per cent reduction target at the EU level. Hence, the Commission has emphasized the need for national and EU administrations to work together on implementing the 25 per cent target. Despite these difficulties, the baseline scenario and the quantitative objectives have helped to put pressure on the Commission, DGs and Member States to place more emphasis on the expertise needed to make the internal market more competitive and to ensure that the least burdensome measures for industry are adopted.[58]

The BR agenda first focused on broadening and integrating expertise at the micro-level. To reinforce the ownership of the incorporation and elaboration of expertise guided by the IA system, the Commission subsequently imposed macro-objectives (overall cost reduction) to direct policy processes and the use of expertise towards the reduction of regulatory burdens. This combination of micro- and macro-approaches offers additional incentives to guide and solidify the incorporation of expertise in the EU's policy processes, and to monitor changes in policies.

17.5 Better regulation in the Netherlands: from macro to micro; from narrow to broad

The Netherlands introduced macro-objectives by prioritizing cost reduction. Subsequently, it broadened its BR objectives by creating an integrated IA system for day-to-day policy processes. The Netherlands was originally a tightly regulated market economy in which the public sector played an important role.[59] From the early 1980s onwards, administrative reform processes have concentrated on quantity (reducing the size of government) and on market liberalization. The first Cabinet of Wim Kok formulated the ambition of 10 per cent cost reduction in 1994. This was raised to 25 per cent in 1998 and the cost reduction agenda was continued by the various Cabinets that were in place from 2002 onwards.

[58] *Ibid.* [59] P. O. de Jong and M. Herweijer, *Alle regels tellen* (The Hague: WODC, 2004).

With already considerable progress achieved in terms of cost reduction, the Rutte-Verhagen Cabinet agreed in 2010 to a cost reduction of a further 10 per cent by 2012. This was followed by a further 5 per cent reduction target for the following years.

These targets have resulted in a stream of cost reduction activities that have helped to focus the use of expertise in the Dutch policy processes. It is important to realize that these objectives are net targets so that administrative costs arising from new regulations have to be compensated by reducing administrative costs elsewhere. In addition to reducing costs for industry, burden reduction for citizens was also added to the agenda in 2005.

The Dutch administration was originally based on the assumption that ministries make their policies independently, implying rather narrow foci on the primary objectives of the responsible ministry, as well as when it comes to the use of expertise. As a result, policy makers have had close ties with the traditional epistemic communities in their specific policy fields. Furthermore, policy making has not been a very transparent process, making the incorporation of horizontal objectives or objectives from other ministries difficult.[60] Since output-oriented net targets for administrative burden reduction require less horizontal coordination, hierarchically imposed targets have been a way to avoid the coordination of expertise in day-to-day policies. Ministries 'own' objectives and compensate for any administrative burden resulting from new policies due to the hierarchically imposed net target, which is rooted in Cabinet decisions.[61] To operate effectively, the Slechte Commission (1999) recommended extending the Dutch burden reduction agenda and keeping to this narrow scope instead of opting for a broader impact assessment system.[62] A broader scope would introduce the risk of increasing internal opposition and complicating management of the objectives. Hence, at the start of the 2000s, the emphasis in the Netherlands was on targets (i.e., improving output legitimacy) and specifically on cost reduction.

[60] P. Popelier, R. van Gestel, K. van Aeken, V. Verlinden and P. van Humbeek, *Consulteren over ontwerp-regelgeving: alibi voor vrijblijvendheid of prikkel tot actie? Een inventarisatie van de Nederlandse consultatiepraktijk* (The Hague: WODC, 2007).

[61] R. Linschoten, J. Nijland and J. Sleifer, 'Institutions for Better Regulation: The Example of the Netherlands' in A. Nijsen, J. Hudson, K. van Paridon, C. Müller and R. Thurik (eds.), *Business Regulation and Public Policy: The Costs and Benefits of Compliance* (New York: Springer, 2009), pp. 217–28.

[62] Commissie Slechte (Commissie Administratieve Lasten), *Regels zonder overlast* (The Hague: Dutch Ministry of Foreign Affairs, 1999).

The hierarchically imposed output objective, and the related quality control, had a narrow focus – even though it has been successfully implemented. According to the World Bank, the Dutch government has become a 'world leader' in cost reduction due to its clear and simple structure, a strong coordinating minister of finance and the support of an independent advisory and monitoring body (Actal).[63] Actal monitors the cost reduction programme and scrutinizes assessments *ex ante* to ensure that ownership of the targets is indeed reflected in the actions of the individual ministries. In addition, the Netherlands has developed two baseline measurements to track the actual reductions. The first (base year 2002) focused on the costs of information that industry has to provide to public authorities and third parties (other businesses or citizens). The second baseline (base year 2007) concerned information obligations to public authorities only. In spite of narrowing the baseline, the BR agenda was actually broadened because compliance costs were included (i.e., information costs plus costs related to investments need to comply with the rules). As is typical for the loosely coupled – rather fragmented – Dutch administration, the first baseline scenario was primarily done by the individual ministries. The second baseline scenario was more of a collective exercise led by the coordinating ministries (economic affairs, finance and home affairs).

Despite discussions on whether the business sector has actually noticed any reductions and on the dangers of ignoring the benefits of regulation, the assessments of actual cost reductions indicate substantial results on meeting the 25 per cent reduction targets.[64] Moreover, the BR policy has contributed to a culture that is more conscious of the costs that policies impose on business.[65] Van Bockel and Sleifer concluded that a structure with an independent agency (such as Actal) scrutinizing the administrative costs assessments and monitoring progress in reaching the reduction targets was one of the success factors.[66] Hence, the output focus, supported by an independent monitoring mechanism, has helped

63 World Bank, *Review of the Dutch Administrative Burden Reduction Programme* (Washington DC: World Bank, 2007); P. O. de Jong and S. E. Zijlstra, *Wikken, wegen en (toch) wetgeven. Een onderzoek naar de hiërarchie en omvang van wetgeving in vijf Europese landen* (The Hague: Boom, 2009).

64 Schout, 'Organizational Learning'.

65 Linschoten, Nijland and Sleifer, 'Institutions for Better Regulation'.

66 J. van Bockel and J. Sleifer, 'Internal Pressures – External Safeguards' in A. Alemanno, F. den Butter, A. Nijsen and J. Torriti (eds.), *Better Business Regulation in a Risk Society* (New York: Springer, 2012), pp. 147–56.

to establish ownership and to steer the policy processes and the required expertise towards cost reduction.

The progress achieved in the cost reduction programmes meant that reform debates could, from the 2000s onwards, broaden towards additional objectives so that different areas of expertise could be incorporated. This refocusing of the required expertise was supported by reviews of the Dutch output-oriented programme among others by the Organisation for Economic Co-operation and Development (OECD) and the World Bank.[67]

The emphasis on output targets related to administrative costs does not mean that the Netherlands lacked IAs and tests related to expertise concerning wider objectives. In fact, it has had many types of IAs, but these were largely unknown to policy makers, not integrated in decision making, not publicly available and, consequently, rather ineffective. An estimation of the Ministry of Justice in 2007 uncovered 110 tests and criteria that steered the use of expertise in the preparation of new policies.[68] These included assessments of environmental effects, tests related to establishing the effects of proposed measures on small and medium-sized enterprises, and different kinds of social, regional and economic effects. Yet, most of these impacts were neither examined systematically nor properly documented. Moreover, these assessments suffered from shortcomings in data and were mostly qualitative.[69]

The final scrutiny of a new policy takes place in the Council of State, which assesses the overall quality of a proposal, including the justifications put forward for adopting it and evidence in support of those justifications, before it goes to the Cabinet and the Parliament for final approval. It is only when the proposal is sent to the Parliament that the various assessments, the work of the independent advisory board on the administrative burden (Actal) and the views of the Council of State become publicly available. In fact, this means that the public cannot follow the steps leading to the adoption of a policy. Furthermore, not all background studies, including the expertise that has been used in

[67] Organisation for Economic Co-operation and Development, *Cutting Red Tape: Administrative Simplification in the Netherlands* (Paris: OECD, 2007); World Bank, *Review of the Dutch Administrative Burden Reduction Programme* (Washington DC: World Bank, 2007).

[68] Schout, 'Framework for Assessing the Added Value of an EU Agency'.

[69] Instituut Onderzoek Overheidsuitgaven (Institute for the Investigation of Government Expenses), *Praktijkonderzoek Regeldruk Toetsen* (Zoetermeer, the Netherlands: Instituut Onderzoek Overheidsuitgaven, 2008).

preparing them, are made available, nor can arguments for not adopting a policy be traced. Clearly, the Dutch system is less transparent compared to the Commission's BR procedures.

As the exploration of horizontal tests in 2007 has highlighted, the Dutch government has started to move away from the burden reduction programme towards a web-based system of impact assessments.[70] This has complemented the output-oriented approach based on targets with a BR approach focusing on the input side (policy procedures). The different tests or assessments have been reduced to eighteen new IA systems. The effectiveness of the new policy procedures remains to be seen as they are currently under construction. For a while, supervision of the IA systems was carried out by a commission (*Commissie Effect Toetsing* (CET)). This consisted of civil servants and was chaired by a (senior) civil servant of the Ministry of Economics, Innovation and Agriculture. Actal will execute an annual audit on the quality of the assessments as well as on the IA systems as a whole. It remains to be seen whether the shortcomings in the available expertise can be identified since the methods for calculating the (unintended) effects of policies in areas other than administrative costs are probably much less developed.

17.6 Conclusions: towards converging and interconnected expertise agendas?

Responding to weaknesses in policy making, governments in the EU have been searching for new ways to improve fact-based policies at all stages of the process. Better regulation agendas have steered and formalized the use of expertise and have improved the transparency and control of the expertise on which decisions are based. As discussed, it is important that BR systems allow effective communication between the administrative systems in the EU's multilevel governance system.

The EU and Dutch BR approaches have been converging in many ways over the past decade. The Commission agenda was primarily concerned with input legitimacy through modernizing its work planning. Consequently, it now includes an integrated IA system. The recently improved procedures for formulating new policies implied a move towards output-oriented programmes in the Commission by including targets for reducing administrative costs. The Dutch

[70] Tweede Kamer der Staten-Generaal (Dutch Second Chamber), *Kamerstuk 29515 nr. 330*, 14 April 2011.

developments started from a focus on output (through cost reduction) and are now in the process of being broadened towards a (more or less) integrated agenda related to policy processes (to improve input legitimacy). Although coming from different starting points, both systems are now experimenting with complementary mechanisms to increase the amount and control of expertise.

To manage these input- and output-oriented programmes, both levels of government have invested in setting up new planning and monitoring institutions, both within the administrations (the IAB and the CET) as well as outside them (the Stoiber Group and Actal). Nevertheless, both levels of governance also suffer from difficulties in assessing and quantifying the different kinds of costs and benefits associated with the streamlining of expert involvement in decision making.

It is not by accident that the systems for structuring expertise are converging. The Netherlands has been lobbying together with other leading EU Member States in BR for simplification and cost reduction at the European level of decision making. In parallel, governments have been lobbying for coordinated agendas concerning environmental impacts and regional consequences.[71] Additional reports and position papers that have been produced to influence the EU's agenda include the 2010 'Smart Regulation' Report and the 2009 position paper 'Achieving a Sustainable Reduction of Administrative Burdens in the European Union'.[72]

Governments have met in formal and informal working groups to discuss better regulation activities at the national and EU levels. The Commission has kept close contact with better regulation developments in the Member States and the so-called Single Point of Contact[73] was set up in 2009 in the Member States to facilitate the emerging convergence of the national and EU BR agendas.

There are also differences. First, the Commission has invested heavily in the transparency of policy processes. Work plans, road maps, background studies, input from governments and from the private sector in hearings and online consultations, IAs and the (sometimes critical) reports from the IAB display all the expert input and deliberations

[71] C. Radaelli and F. DeFrancesco, *Regulatory Quality in Europe* (Manchester University Press, 2008).

[72] Produced by Actal (the Netherlands), Nationaler Normen kontrollrat (Germany), Regelrådet (Sweden) and the Regulatory Policy Committee (UK) in 2009.

[73] See www.epractice.eu/en/library/292999.

during the writing of new policy initiatives, and the input involved can be found on the Commission's website. The transparency of assessments and expertise used in the Netherlands has been less advanced. Eventually, all background documents are attached to the proposal that goes to the Dutch Parliament. However, these documents only become accessible at the end of the process and only if the policy is adopted. Second, whereas the Commission's assessment system aims at integrated expertise, the Dutch system consists of (fragmented) parallel assessments of policy proposals. In addition, there are concerns about the ownership of the BR programmes at both levels of governance. In the Commission, oversight is organized through the IAB operating under the Commission President in the SG and through the external Stoiber Group. External control in the Netherlands has focused on administrative costs through an independent monitoring body (Actal), but is now being broadened into an integrated assessment system that is somewhat comparable to the EU's IA system.

One problem remains: the programmes have converged but have not become mutually interconnected. The EU BR developments have largely concerned the formulation of policies at both levels of government, but have not produced a wealth of actual interactions in the day-to-day policy processes. A study found that EU coordination in the Netherlands focuses on EU policies at the Council phase. Hence, the Dutch involvement in the development of the EU's impact assessments has remained modest.[74] In fact, reflecting the Dutch reactive approach to EU policy making,[75] Dutch EU policy coordination starts in the inter-ministerial committee assessing new Commission proposals when a Commission proposal is ready to be sent to the European Parliament and national parliaments. But even at this stage, little attention is paid to the expertise embodied in the IAs of the Commission because the ministries doubt whether the European assessments are sufficiently relevant to the specific Dutch situation. Hence, the Commission assessments are often not included in the Dutch assessments of new Commission proposals.[76]

Similarly, although the Commission has various different ways of finding information, interviews in the SG show that 'there is a hunger

[74] KPMG, *Onderzoek nieuwe Europese regelgeving: 'Impact Assessed'* (The Hague: KPMG, 2010).
[75] H. Ten Broeke and G. Schouw, *Bovenop Europa* (The Hague: Tweede Kamer, 2011).
[76] KPMG, *Onderzoek nieuwe Europese regelgeving.*

for information' on how policies affect the twenty-eight Member States. There are only a few examples of efforts by which the Dutch government has actually tried to influence EU decision making early on in the process by providing relevant information on, for example, the expected effectiveness and implementation costs of a certain policy measure.[77] As also indicated by interviews that were conducted in the Commission, managing the interdependence between the national and the EU BR agendas remains critical for the success of both.[78] Given the great differences among the twenty-eight Member States in terms of population density, climate, soil conditions and so on, the Commission can often produce accurate assessments only when the Member States provide it with relevant and timely information. Moreover, the administrative demands of a multilevel IA system require that the Member States incorporate the IA logic in the Council at the negotiation stage, otherwise the Commission will feel few incentives from the Council to perform assessments or to identify and act upon the variety of objectives requiring (occasionally painful) coordination among DGs.

Therefore, more attention is needed to further coordinate the systems for gathering and processing expertise between the Commission and the Member States. If in the case of the Netherlands (a leader in terms of BR) there is a need for deepening the links between the national systems and those of the EU, then the situation is probably not much better with regard to other EU Member States. This situation shows that while national and EU officials have been heavily involved in defining BR policies, attention for managing the actual implications on the ground of a multilevel administrative system has been lacking.

A lot of work still needs to be done to strengthen the use of expertise in the EU's multilevel governance system.[79] Moreover, in setting up parallel IA systems, officials should be more aware of the interdependence between European and national administrative expertise-related innovations. There is a lot of 'sending' when it comes to lobbying for effective European BR programmes, but there does not appear to be enough attention for 'receiving' – i.e., for what the efforts to build EU systems might imply in terms of adapting national programmes to ensure that systems of expertise communicate effectively.

[77] Schout and Mijs, *Administratieve Lastenverlichting voor Burgers.*
[78] Schout, 'Organizational Learning'; KPMG, *Onderzoek nieuwe Europese regelgeving.*
[79] European Commission, 'Smart Regulation in the European Union'.

18

Blurred areas of responsibility: European agencies' scientific 'opinions' under scrutiny

E. MADALINA BUSUIOC

18.1 Introduction: peering into blurred areas of responsibility

The process of agencification at the European Union (EU) level started in 1975, when the first two European agencies were created, and has intensified in recent years. There are currently over thirty European agencies, exercising a variety of powers at the EU level, ranging from informational and management tasks to quasi-rule-making and decision-making powers. These agencies operate in, and often regulate, a multitude of policy fields such as food safety, pharmaceuticals, law enforcement, air safety, border control, telecommunications, financial supervision, etc., and have come to be regarded as a pervasive feature of the European executive order.[1]

One of the main reasons for the adoption of the agency model at the EU level has been the technical expertise that they would inject into the EU regulatory processes. Their 'neutral' expert advice or input, removed from direct political control, was to improve the quality of the EU's regulatory output.[2] Technical and/or scientific considerations rather than political concerns would form the basis of EU regulatory measures, even more so at a time when the European Commission, in the aftermath of multiple food crises[3] (e.g., bovine spongiform encephalopathy (BSE), dioxin contamination), was increasingly losing face as a credible regulator.

[1] M. Busuioc, M. Groenleer and J. Trondal, *The Agency Phenomenon in the European Union: Emergence, Institutionalisation and Everyday Decision-Making* (Manchester University Press, 2011). On the European executive more generally, see D. Curtin, *Executive Power of the European Union: Law, Practices, and the Living Constitution* (Oxford University Press, 2009).

[2] Schout and Sleifer, Chapter 17, this volume.

[3] Everson, Chapter 15 and Schout and Sleifer, Chapter 17, both in this volume.

As the EU agencification process gained a foothold and momentum, the rise of agencies has become controversial,[4] precisely because of their non-majoritarian character and operation at arm's length from direct political control. As agencies have grown not only in numbers but also in terms of their powers, most visibly exemplified by specific agencies' mandates to adopt binding decisions vis-à-vis third parties, the extent to which their powers have been matched by countervailing checks has increasingly been signalled as a matter of concern and has formed the subject of academic scrutiny.[5]

Furthermore, beyond their formal decision-making powers, equally significant are the powers that agencies can exercise in a less obvious fashion. These are the powers they exercise informally, under the guise of expert opinions. Specific European agencies are endowed with the power to adopt scientific opinions (e.g., on the safety of food, pharmaceuticals, chemicals, etc.), which are formally endorsed into binding decisions by the European Commission. To be able to deal with such complex technical and scientific issues, agencies rely on the input of their expert committees, with distinct scientific competence and composed of experts appointed on the basis of their specialized knowledge and expertise. Given this high level of agency expertise and ensuing informational asymmetries running in agencies' favour, their opinions are in practice often simply 'rubber-stamped',[6] as we will see below, into binding decisions by the European Commission, the formal decision maker.

[4] M. Busuioc and M. Groenleer, 'The Theory and Practice of EU Agency Autonomy and Accountability: Early Day Expectations, Today's Realities and Future Perspectives' in M. Everson, C. Monda and E. Vos (eds.), *European Agencies in between Institutions and Member States* (Alphen aan den Rijn: Kluwer Law International, 2014), 175–200.

[5] See, among others, M. Everson, 'Independent Agencies: Hierarchy Beaters?', *European Law Journal*, 1 (1995), 180–204; M. Shapiro, 'The Problems of Independent Agencies in the United States and Europe', *Journal of European Public Policy*, 4 (1997), 276–91; E. Vos, 'Reforming the European Commission: What Role to Play for EU Agencies?', *Common Market Law Review*, 37 (2000), 1113–34; D. M. Curtin, 'Delegation to EU Non-majoritarian Agencies and Emerging Practices of Public Accountability' in D. Geradin and N. Petit, *Regulation through Agencies in the EU: A New Paradigm of European Governance?* (London: Routledge, 2005), 88–119; D.M. Curtin, 'Holding (Quasi-) Autonomous Administrative Actors to Public Account', *European Law Journal*, (2007), 523–41; M. Busuioc, 'Accountability, Control and Independence: The Case of European Agencies', *European Law Journal*, 15 (2009), 599–615; E. M. Busuioc, *European Agencies: Law and Practices of Accountability* (Oxford University Press, 2013).

[6] T. Gehring and S. Krapohl, 'Supranational Regulatory Agencies between Independence and Control: The EMEA and the Authorization of Pharmaceuticals in the European Single Market', *Journal of European Public Policy*, 14 (2007), 208–26; R. Dehousse,

The decision of the Commission is a formal binding legal act and is subject to review by the Court of Justice of the European Union (CJEU) under Article 263 of the Treaty on the Functioning of the European Union (TFEU). The question arises, however, whether these agency expert opinions can also be subject to judicial checks and, if so, on what aspects. Whereas the notion of judicial reviewability of non-binding acts seems counter-intuitive and perhaps even somewhat provocative, some form of judicial review in such cases is not only desirable but is in fact necessary, as in its absence the agency involvement in decision making runs the risk of becoming a source of unchecked power. After all, as observed by Craig, 'if judicial review is to be effective it must be capable of being applied to the institution that made the operative decision ... If review is to be effective it is necessary for the ... Community courts to be able to go behind the Commission decision and consider the agency reasoning'.[7] The absence of possibilities for review of the agency opinion informing the Commission decision would amount to a shortcoming in judicial protection shading the de facto decision maker from responsibility, scrutiny and accountability.

Against this backdrop, this chapter aims to explore one of the most blurred areas of agency responsibility – agency scientific opinions – and investigate to what extent judicial scrutiny of such opinions is possible. Is the CJEU able to peer into these muddy waters and shed light on this hidden (exercise of) power? How has responsibility been disentangled, hashed out and assigned by the Court?

The present chapter investigates issues concerning judicial review of the use of agency powers by analysing the relevant case law of the CJEU[8] on this matter. With this aim in mind, in section 18.2 below, the stage is set for the ensuing discussion by examining more generally the topic of judicial review in the context of European agencies. It will also analyse how judicial review has evolved in recent years, on a par with the growth in agency power. Section 18.3 brings the reader to the crux of the matter: the de facto decision-making powers of agencies and the risks inherent in the exercise of such powers. On this basis, section 18.4 investigates possibilities for judicial review of the exercise of such powers before the CJEU and the role that the Court has played in addressing the concerns surrounding

'Delegation of Powers in the European Union: The Need for a Multi-principals Model', *West European Politics*, 31 (2008), 789–99.

[7] P. Craig, *EU Administrative Law* (Oxford University Press, 2006), at 167.

[8] Comprising of the Court of Justice (CJ) and the General Court (GC) (pre-Treaty of Lisbon, the Court of First Instance (CFI)).

this judicial review process. The conclusion (section 18.5) contains a reflection on the current system of expert decision making and its impact, and on the adequacy of existing (judicial and political) checks in scrutinizing this underlying source of power.

18.2 Judicial review of agencies' binding acts: an evolving process

A limited number of European agencies have been granted final decision-making powers, i.e., the power to adopt decisions that are binding upon third parties. It should be stressed, though, that these legally binding decisions are restricted to the application of general rules to specific cases. In other words, the powers at stake are individual decision-making powers as opposed to rule-making powers. Examples of agencies that have been granted such powers are the Office for Harmonization in the Internal Market (OHIM), the European Aviation Safety Agency (EASA), the European Chemicals Agency (ECHA), the Agency for the Cooperation of Energy Regulators (ACER) or the three European financial supervisory authorities. In line with their (decision-making) powers, the basic regulations of these agencies also contained from their very set-up a layered system of (judicial) review. A two-tier appeal structure was provided for, with a first internal appeal before the agency's Boards of Appeal followed by an appeal before the CJEU.

In the case of agencies whose basic regulation did not explicitly provide for decision-making powers but only provided for executive or advisory functions (i.e., the great majority of European agencies), judicial review was not provided for in their constituent acts. It remained debatable and open to speculation for a long time, in the absence of explicit provisions in this direction in either the Treaty or secondary legislation, whether binding measures of such agencies – on organizational/management matters (i.e., tendering or recruitment) or at the administrative phase of an application procedure – could nevertheless be reviewable by the Court. Commentators generally believed this to be the case and expected that, should a related complaint arise, the Court would use a similar line of reasoning as in *Les Verts*[9] to justify an expansion of its scope of review to

[9] *Parti Ecologiste 'Les Verts'* v. *European Parliament* [1986] ECR 1339. In the case, the Court extended the scope of reviewable acts to those of the European Parliament, which were not included in the scope of the Court's purview at the time (ex-Article 173 EC).

agencies.[10] The Court of First Instance (CFI) confirmed this expectation at the end of 2008 in the *Sogelma Srl* v. *European Agency for Reconstruction (EAR)* case.[11]

In the latter case, the applicant brought an action for annulment of administrative decisions of the EAR concerning the cancellation of a tender procedure and the organization of a new one. The case was directed against the EAR under Article 230 EC (currently Article 263 TFEU), the annulment provision provided in the Treaty, even though this Article did not list acts of European agencies as reviewable by the Court. Furthermore, the EAR basic regulation (like most agencies' regulations) did not contain any provisions granting jurisdiction for the Court to review such decisions, i.e., the jurisdiction of the Court was restricted to contractual and non-contractual liability cases and EAR decisions relating to access to documents, which was explicitly provided for in its constituent act.

The Court nevertheless claimed jurisdiction over the case and accepted the action against the EAR decisions. In the words of the Court:

> the general principle to be elicited from that judgment [i.e., *Les Verts*] is that any act of a Community body intended to produce legal effects vis-à-vis third parties must be open to judicial review. It is true that *Les Verts*, paragraph 24, refers only to Community institutions and the EAR is not one of the institutions listed in Article 7 EC. Nonetheless, the situation of Community bodies endowed with the power to take measures intended to produce legal effects vis-à-vis third parties is identical to the situation which led to the *Les Verts* judgment: it cannot be acceptable, in a community based on the rule of law, that such acts escape judicial review.[12]

The CFI's stance was foretelling of the changes that were to be ushered in by the Treaty of Lisbon. By virtue of the Treaty of Lisbon, the Court was explicitly granted jurisdiction over agencies' binding acts. Article 263 TFEU now explicitly provides for judicial review of agencies' binding acts on a par with those of the European Parliament, the Council, the Commission, the European Council and the European Central Bank. This amounts to the culminating act of an evolving process, in which the system of judicial review in respect of agencies has been progressively improved and expanded through the activist role of the Court. The

[10] See, for instance, Craig, *EU Administrative Law*; E. Chiti, 'An Important Part of the EU's Institutional Machinery: Features, Problems and Perspectives of European Agencies', *Common Market Law Review*, 46 (2009), 1395–1442.

[11] Case T-411/06, *Sogelma* v. *EAR* [2008] ECR II-2771.

[12] *Ibid.*, para. 37.

Lisbon Treaty 'codified' this system, remedying what had been described as 'a significant and salient treaty lacuna'.[13]

18.3 Agencies as informal decision makers

As mentioned above, most of the EU agencies do not have the capacity to adopt binding acts. Certain agencies are endowed with only advisory or so-called 'instrumental' powers.[14] They provide scientific advice, in the form of opinions, to the Commission in the context of market authorization procedures, but the latter retains the final and binding decision-making powers. Notable examples of agencies possessing such 'instrumental' powers are the European Food Safety Authority (EFSA), the European Medicines Agency (EMA/EMEA)[15] and partly the powers held by the ECHA.[16]

18.3.1 An attempt at demarcating science and politics

The rationale for the division of labour between science and politics goes back to the aftermath of the highly politicized food crises of the 1990s and the ensuing policy of the Commission for a clear institutional separation between risk assessment and risk management, i.e., between science and politics. The former was to be the domain of 'independent' agencies, insulated from politics. The latter, involving the balancing of public interests, was to be carried out by the European Commission. Following this premise, agencies such as the EFSA and the EMA have a mandate in risk assessment (and risk communication), advising the Commission, while the Commission is responsible for the risk management, weighing the various factors and adopting the final formal decision.

This set-up is also to no small extent the result of the institutional and political constraints represented by the *Meroni* case,[17] which acted as a

[13] Curtin, *Executive Power*, at 162. [14] Chiti, 'An Important Part', at 1403–7.

[15] The name of the agency was changed from the European Medicines Evaluation Agency (EMEA) to the European Medicines Agency (EMA). 'EMEA' is referred to in this chapter when directly quoting cases or literature from before the date that the name change took place.

[16] The ECHA also has decision-making powers. However, part of its responsibilities, particularly in the authorization and restriction stages of REACH (see note 39 below), is to issue opinions on measures to be adopted by the European Commission. See further M. Bronckers and Y. van Gerven, 'Legal Remedies under the EC's New Chemicals Legislation REACH: Testing a New Model of European Governance', *Common Market Law Review*, 46 (2009), 1823–71.

[17] Case 9/56, *Meroni & Co, Industrie Metallurgiche SpA* v. *High Authority* [1958] ECR 133.

break on the delegation of further reaching powers to agencies. The case has been used by the Commission to justify its preference for non-delegation. Thus, as observed by Dehousse with respect to the EMA:

> a system in which the [EMA] would have been granted the power to adopt marketing authorizations would have been perfectly in line with the *Meroni* doctrine, provided that the Commission retained the power to disallow the decisions. In other words, even accepting that the *Meroni* precedent was relevant for the new agencies . . . other control devices that are more respectful of agency autonomy might have met the demands of the Court of Justice. Another option was chosen nonetheless. This clearly suggests that, in addition to legal concerns, considerations of political opportunity obviously played a role in the definition of agencies' power.[18]

Regardless of whether the reasons behind this set-up were functional, institutional and/or political, this original demarcation between the official decision maker and the opinion provider is not tenable in practice. As will be explained below, there has been a blurring in practice between the scientific opinion and the final decision, with advisory agencies often in the seat of the decision maker.

18.3.2 The sources of the de facto impact of agency opinions

The substantial de facto 'weight' that agency opinions can carry is due to a variety of reasons: (1) the lack of expertise of the European Commission to second-guess expert agency opinions; (2) the need to safeguard the independence of the agency; and (3) procedural safeguards in the set-up of the system as such, which make it very cumbersome for the Commission to disregard the agency's opinion.[19] With regard to the first reason, one of the central motivations for the creation of European agencies was the need for scientific expertise of a highly technical nature, which was not readily available within the Commission. In parallel, this has also allowed for a reduction in the workload of the Commission, which could delegate part of its technical tasks and focus on its 'core tasks'. The result is that whereas agencies have built up expertise, the Commission has seen a reduction of in-house technical expertise on issues that fall within agencies' mandates. This state of affairs makes it difficult for the Commission to have the

[18] R. Dehousse, '*Misfits:* EU Law and the Transformation of European Governance', Jean Monnet Working Paper 2/02 (2002), at 14.

[19] S. Krapohl, 'Credible Commitment in Non-independent Regulatory Agencies: A Comparative Analysis of the European Agencies for Pharmaceuticals and Foodstuffs', *European Law Journal*, 10 (2004), 518–38.

expert capacity to second-guess agency opinions. The Commission simply lacks a comparable scientific apparatus for examining each authorization opinion, leading to significant informational asymmetries in the favour of agencies. Thus, in the case of EMA, for instance, it has been observed that this general policy of endorsement of scientific opinions by the Commission is an indication of 'the strength of science (and/or the Commission's lack of capacity to validate it)'.[20]

Second, if the Commission would recurrently refuse to endorse agency expert opinions, this could easily delegitimize the agency, call into question the quality of its science and thus deal a serious blow to the credibility of its expertise and to its authority as an independent regulator. The legitimacy of an agency, as is the case for most public organizations, is highly dependent on the political support it receives.[21] An important indicator of political support in the case of European agencies is whether the Commission (but more generally also other EU institutions and the Member States) follow agency opinions, decisions and recommendations.[22] In other words, as observed in relation to the EFSA, for instance, its 'credibility will depend on the Commission's willingness to act on its advice'.[23] These credibility considerations alone can act as incentives to follow agency advice unless there are strong reasons against it.

The third inter-related rationale concerns the general set-up of the system, which contains a set of institutional incentives towards endorsing agencies' opinions in order to protect the aforementioned independence of their science. Thus, in the context of pre-market authorization procedures for foodstuffs (i.e., food additives, food enzymes and food flavourings, and genetically modified food and feed), if the decision drafted by the Commission diverges from the EFSA opinion, the Commission 'shall provide an explanation for the differences'.[24] Therefore, the Commission is under a clear obligation to justify any deviation. Moreover, it has to find

[20] G. Permanand and E. Vos, 'Between Health and the Market: The Roles of the European Medicines Agency and European Food Safety Authority', Maastricht Faculty of Law Working Paper 2008/4 (2008), at 22.

[21] For an in-depth discussion of the topic, see M. Groenleer, *The Autonomy of European Union Agencies: A Comparative Study of Institutional Development* (Delft: Eburon, 2009), at 52–6.

[22] *Ibid.*, at 77–8.

[23] House of Lords Select Committee on European Union, Seventh Report, 'A European Food Authority', 16 May 2000, available at: www.publications.parliament.uk/pa/ld199900/ldselect/ldeucom/66/6605.htm, para. 61.

[24] See Articles 7(1) and 19(1) of Regulation (EC) No. 1829/2003 of the European Parliament and of the Council of 22 September 2003 on genetically modified food and

equivalent scientific evidence to that of EFSA and give reasons justifying its reliance thereon.[25] Similarly, in the case of the EMA, if the decision of the Commission diverged from that of the agency, the Commission would have to justify this deviation by providing 'a detailed explanation for the reasons for the differences'.[26] Furthermore, additional institutional features and procedural rules strengthen the role of the EMA and its expert committees, and entice the Commission to follow the EMA's opinions.[27] For instance, the EMA committees, unlike those of the EFSA (which are made up of independent experts), are composed of Member State-appointed experts, usually members of national authorization bodies. Thus, the Commission's general policy of endorsement is also attributable to the fact that a 'nationally flavoured' element is implicit within the assessments of the scientific committee and the Commission would rather not contradict the Member States.[28]

Whereas none of these factors is a guarantee that the European Commission will automatically adopt agencies' scientific opinions, given the fact that the Commission is not formally bound by these opinions and can deviate from them, these factors do represent strong incentives for endorsement, empowering these formally 'advisory' bodies.

18.3.3 'Strong opinions'

Scientific opinions of European agencies possessing only recommendatory powers thus have a powerful or even decisive impact on the decision-making outcome, often being de facto binding vis-à-vis the decision maker, i.e., the European Commission.

To illustrate, as part of the centralized authorization procedure for pharmaceuticals, the main task of the EMA is to provide the European Commission with scientific opinions on the issuance, suspension or revocation of marketing authorizations. A company files an application

feed, OJ L 268/1, 18 October 2003; see also Article 7(3) of Regulation (EC) No. 1331/2008 of the European Parliament and of the Council of 16 December 2008 establishing a common authorization procedure for food additives, food enzymes and food flavourings, OJ L 354/1, 31 December 2008.

25 Case T-13/99 *Pfizer* [2002] ECR II-3305.

26 Article 10(1) of Regulation EC No. 726/2004, OJ L 136, 30 April 2004, at 1.

27 For a detailed discussion on this, see Krapohl, 'Credible Commitment'; Gehring and Krapohl, 'Supranational Regulatory Agencies'; Groenleer, *The Autonomy of European Union Agencies*, at 154.

28 Permanand and Vos, 'Between Health and the Market', at 23; Gehring and Krapohl, 'Supranational Regulatory Agencies', at 215.

for a marketing authorization of a medicinal product with the EMA, the scientific committee assesses the quality, safety and efficacy of the product(s) and, based on a risk–benefit assessment, the EMA recommends to the Commission whether or not to issue a marketing authorization. If problems arise or an adverse reaction is reported during the post-authorization phase (i.e., after a medical product has been marketed), the EMA can issue a scientific opinion to the Commission, advising for the suspension of the market authorization, in case it considers that further investigations are needed. In other words, the EMA does not adopt decisions or marketing authorizations, but only issues opinions to the Commission in order to support it in its decision making. The final act is the Commission's authorization, suspension or revocation of the marketing authorization. In practice, however, the EMA has substantively gained de facto decision-making powers,[29] and in most instances the agency's recommendation is simply adopted by the Commission.[30] The EMA 'virtually determines the content of the authorization decisions'[31] and 'in spite of its inferior status as an advisory body, the expert committee dominates the authorization process'.[32]

Similarly, in the case of the EFSA, its core task is to provide scientific opinions. Despite their non-binding status, it has been observed that the opinions' 'impact on the outcome of the decision-making procedure is substantial, if not determinant'.[33] EFSA opinions have acquired 'considerable normative authority', can have indirect legal effect and become a source of constraint not only for the Commission, but also for the Member States, private parties and national courts.[34] This 'normative authority' of the EFSA's opinions is evidenced by the fact that 'the actual content of the obligations imposed on institutional actors to meet these objectives is heavily influenced by its opinions'.[35] Although the EFSA's advice is not as

[29] Chiti, 'An Important Part', at 1405.

[30] Craig, *EU Administrative Law*, at 167; F. Sabel and J. Zeitlin, 'Learning from Difference: The New Architecture of Experimentalist Governance in the EU', *European Law Journal*, 14 (2008), 271–327, at 285.

[31] Gehring and Krapohl, 'Supranational Regulatory Agencies', at 209.

[32] *Ibid.*, at 218.

[33] A. Alemanno and S. Mahieu, 'The European Food Safety Authority before European Courts: Some Reflections on the Judicial Review of EFSA Scientific Opinions and Administrative Acts', *European Food and Feed Law Review*, 5 (2008), 320–33.

[34] D. Chalmers, 'Food for Thought': Reconciling European Risks and Traditional Ways of Life', *Modern Law Review*, 66 (2003), 532–62, at 540. This point is reiterated by A. Alemanno, 'The European Food Safety Authority at Five', *European Food and Feed Law Review*, 1 (2008), 2–29.

[35] Chalmers, 'Food for Thought', at 540.

undisputed and authoritative as that of the EMA, as the EFSA's opinions are not always taken up by the European Commission,[36] the latter cannot simply ignore the authority's opinion and has to justify deviations, as explained above. Thus, it has been observed: 'while the EFSA's opinions have not been expressly granted a direct regulatory authority, they are likely to acquire a de facto legally binding value ... and amount to a strong probative authority against private business operators'.[37] Also, it has been reiterated that 'the fact that the EFSA is "only" an advisory body is not determinative of its true role in the Community regulatory process'.[38]

The case of the ECHA raises a similar point. While the agency also has decision-making powers at the registration and evaluation phases of REACH,[39] in the authorization and restriction phases, the role of the agency is that of drafting scientific opinions.[40] The ECHA issues an opinion to the Commission on an application (for authorization or on suggested restrictions) and it is the Commission that adopts the decision through a comitology committee system.[41] The likely weight of its 'opinions' for the final Commission decision has already been emphasized: 'although the Commission appears to be free to deviate from these opinions in the measures it finally takes, these opinions will likely play a very important role in the Commission's decision-making process'.[42]

The weight carried by agency opinions and their impact on the actual decision outcome raise important issues concerning the availability of review and the locus of responsibility. Since formally the agency has only advisory status, does this mean that the opinions of its experts are shielded from judicial probing? As a result of their non-binding character, such measures would not be reviewable under Article 263 TFEU. It is only the final decision of the Commission that is open to an action for annulment. Furthermore, no provisions for legality review of these

[36] Groenleer, *The Autonomy of European Union Agencies*, at 177–211; Permanand and Vos, 'Between Health and the Market'.

[37] Alemanno, 'The European Food Safety Authority at Five', at 20.

[38] K. Kanska, 'Wolves in the Clothing of Sheep? The Case of the European Food Safety Authority', *European Law Review*, 29 (2004), 711–27, at 712.

[39] Regulation (EC) No. 1907/2006 of the European Parliament and of the Council of 18 December 2006 concerning the Registration, Evaluation, Authorization and Restriction of Chemicals (REACH), establishing a European Chemicals Agency, amending Directive 1999/45/EC and repealing Council Regulation.

[40] For an in-depth analysis of REACH, see Bronckers and van Gerven, 'Legal Remedies', at 1829–36.

[41] Everson, Chapter 15 and Schout and Sleifer, Chapter 17, both this volume.

[42] Bronckers and van Gerven, 'Legal Remedies', at 1869–70.

measures are foreseen in the constituent act (i.e., basic regulation) of these agencies. This lack of judicial review is based on the assumption that since these acts are merely advisory, they cannot directly negatively impact upon the position of an individual and, consequently, no special provisions for judicial protection are needed.

This choice, however, has been described as 'problematic' from a judicial protection perspective,[43] amounting to a rather 'rudimentary' judicial protection system compared to the one applicable to agencies with explicit decision-making powers.[44] Potential inadequacies intervene at the interface between agencies' formal powers and the actual weight and nature of these powers. In this context, 'the lack of administrative rule of law principles and judicial review may be seen as a genuine lacuna in European agencies' legal framework'.[45] Below, it will be examined how the issue of review of such opinions has been dealt with by the Court in relevant cases and if the oversight of the legislator has been addressed by the Court.

18.4 Unlawful opinions? Possibilities for judicial review before the European courts

The CJEU has clearly ruled that scientific opinions cannot form the subject of an action for annulment and has repeatedly rejected these actions insofar as they aimed at agencies' opinions. For instance, the issue arose in *Olivieri* v. *Commission and EMEA*[46] with respect to an EMA opinion. The Court rejected the application for annulment against the EMA opinion in question by pointing out that the opinion was an intermediate measure as opposed to a final binding decision. In the words of the Court, 'it is a preparatory measure which does not definitively lay down the Commission's position and is therefore not a challengeable act'.[47] The Court also adopted a similar approach in cases for annulment of the EFSA's opinions. In three orders issued by the Court in cases aimed at annulling an EFSA opinion, the CFI reasoned identically observing that:

> only measures definitively laying down the position of the institution on the conclusion of that procedure are, in principle, measures against

[43] Chiti, 'An Important Part', at 1407. [44] *Ibid.* [45] *Ibid.*, at 1426.

[46] Case T-326/99, *Nancy Fern Olivieri* v. *Commission of the European Communities and European Agency for the Evaluation of Medicinal Products* [2003] ECR II-6053.

[47] *Ibid.*, para. 53.

> which proceedings for annulment may be brought. It follows that preliminary measures or measures of a purely preparatory nature are not measures against which proceedings may be brought.[48]

The CFI then observed that the procedure in question contained three successive stages, with the EFSA's opinion as the second stage, followed by the adoption of a directive or decision in the third stage. On this basis, the Court then concluded that:

> Only the directive or the decision produces binding legal effects capable of affecting the interests of the notifiers. Thus, the contested measure must be regarded as a preliminary step in the procedure ... and, in consequence, it is not a measure against which proceedings for annulment may be brought.[49]

However, the lack of a possibility to bring an action for annulment against agency opinions does not mean that they are altogether removed from the scrutiny of the Court. While being unable to rule in cases directed against agency opinions, the Court has nonetheless found a way to review opinions in cases directed against Commission decisions. Such a situation arose in *Artegodan* v. *Commission*,[50] which dealt with an action for annulment of Commission decisions based on an EMEA scientific committee opinion concerning the withdrawal of the marketing authorizations of several medicinal products used in the treatment of obesity. The CFI recognized from the beginning the 'vital role' of the scientific opinion issued by the EMEA Committee for Proprietary Medicinal Products (CPMP). It observed that since the Commission is not in a position to carry out scientific assessments concerning the efficacy and/or harmfulness of medicinal products, the CPMP scientific assessment is 'essential' to the Commission's ability to make informed decisions, in full knowledge of the facts so as to ensure a high level of public health protection.[51] Thus, the Court held that while the CPMP opinion is not binding on the Commission, it is 'extremely important so that any unlawfulness of that opinion must be regarded as a breach of essential

[48] Case T-311/06 *FMC Chemical and Arysta Lifesciences* v. *EFSA* [2008] ECR II- 0088. See also Case T-312/06 *FMC Chemical* v. *EFSA* [2008] ECR II-0089; Case T-397/06 *Dow AgroSciences* v. *EFSA* [2008] ECR II-0090.

[49] *FMC Chemical and Arysta Lifesciences* v. *EFSA*, paras. 49–50.

[50] Joined Cases T-74/00, 76, 83, 85, 132, 137 and 141, *Artegodan GmbH* v. *Commission* [2002] ECR II-4945.

[51] *Ibid.*, para. 198.

procedural requirements rendering the Commission's decision unlawful'.[52] As such, in order to assess the lawfulness of the Commission's decision, 'the Community judicature may be called upon to review, first, the formal legality of the CPMP's scientific opinion and, second, the Commission's exercise of its discretion'.[53]

Thus, while the Court could not review the scientific opinion in its own right, it nevertheless managed to reason its way into being able to examine the opinion indirectly, while reviewing the legality of the Commission decision. The Court also defined the scope of its review in such cases. In line with its role as a judicial forum rather than a scientific one, it acknowledged that it could not substitute its own assessment for that of the scientific committee and, as such, its review would be limited to three main aspects: the proper functioning of the committee, the internal consistency of the opinion and the statement of reasons.[54] With regard to the statement of reasons, the Court elaborated and explained that it:

> is empowered only to examine whether the opinion contains a statement of reasons from which it is possible to ascertain the considerations on which the opinion is based, and whether it establishes a comprehensible link between the medical and/or scientific findings and its conclusions. In that respect, in its opinion the CPMP is obliged to refer to the main reports and scientific expert opinions on which it relies and to explain, in the event of a significant discrepancy, the reasons why it has departed from the conclusions of the reports or expert opinions supplied by the undertaking concerned.[55]

In other words, the Court regards itself as being able to consider the scientific committee's reasoning process based on the information at hand.[56]

The Court's approach was confirmed in a subsequent judgment, *Olivieri* v. *Commission and EMEA*,[57] which was already briefly mentioned above. In this case, the applicant sought an application for annulment of a Commission decision granting marketing authorization for a medicinal product for human use known as Ferriprox-Deferiprone, as well as of the revised opinion of the EMA. In this case, the applicant sought to annul not only the Commission decision but also the EMA opinion on which the

[52] *Ibid.*, para. 197. [53] *Ibid.*, para. 199. [54] *Ibid.*, para. 200. [55] *Ibid.*

[56] Everson, Chapter 15 and Gruszczynski, Chapter 11, both this volume.

[57] Case T-326/99, *Nancy Fern Olivieri* v. *Commission of the European Communities and European Agency for the Evaluation of Medicinal Products* [2003] ECR II-6053E.

decision was based. As we saw above, the Court rejected the possibility of an action for annulment against the agency opinion. At the same time, however, the Court followed a similar line of argument as in *Artegodan* and indirectly asserted its power to review the opinion in the context of the action for annulment against the Commission decision, given its vital role to the decision. In the words of the Court:

> the contested decision purely and simply confirms the revised opinion . . . The content of that opinion, and also that of the assessment reports upon which it is based, are therefore an integral part of the statement of reasons for the contested decision, with regard in particular to the scientific assessment of deferiprone carried out by the CPMP and its rapporteurs. The content of the revised opinion must therefore be examined in the context of the application for annulment of the contested decision.[58]

In summary, the case law indicates that it is not possible to bring an action for annulment against an agency scientific opinion in its own right, as such opinions are preparatory acts as opposed to final binding acts. Nevertheless, as seen above, the Court has found ways to examine agency opinions and will indirectly scrutinize agency opinions in actions directed against Commission decisions when it constitutes an essential element of the final decision.

This is not the first time that the Court used this type of logic in the case of advisory agencies to ensure applicants' recourse to legal process where the legislator had failed to provide for any. In the case of the EMA, two final agency measures at the administrative phase were challenged in *Thomae* v. *Commission* and *Schering Plough* v. *Commission and EMEA*.[59] These acts were refusals by the EMA of applications for variation of the terms of a marketing authorization. The agency was actually able at the administrative phase of the authorization procedure to adopt a final act without any involvement of the European Commission, despite formally possessing only advisory status according to its basic regulation.

The Court found itself in a tough spot indeed. On the one hand, according to the EU legislator, as provided for in the agency's constituent act, the agency's functions were advisory by nature. On the other hand, the agency was in fact able to adopt a final, binding act. The Court could

[58] *Ibid.*, para. 55.

[59] Case T-123/00, *Dr Karl Thomae GmbH* v. *Commission of the European Communities* [2002] ECR II-5193; Case T-133/03, *Schering Plough Ltd* v. *Commission of the European Communities and European Agency for the Evaluation of Medicinal Products (EMEA)*, order of 5 December 2007.

not reconcile the advisory nature of the agency's powers with the possibility for allowing actions of annulment against such a body. It ruled that the binding measure adopted by the EMA:

> *must be deemed to emanate from the Commission itself.* Since the contested measure is imputable to the Commission, it may be the subject of an action directed against that institution. It follows that the action must be dismissed as inadmissible *insofar as it is directed against the EMEA.*[60]

Thus, in order to ensure that the applicants were not deprived of all judicial protection, the Court reasoned that the EMA decision-making power was an emanation of the Commission's power and upheld the action against the Commission instead.

Given that in these two cases the contested measures were actually binding vis-à-vis third parties, currently such measures (unlike opinions) would be reviewable under Article 263 TFEU. The two cases are, however, illustrative of the problematic issues that arise given the discrepancy between the formally advisory functions of agencies and their de facto decision-making nature. They are also illustrative of the crucial role that the Court has played in trying to shed some light on these problematic borderline areas and ensure that applicants are not deprived of judicial protection.

18.5 Shedding light: the role of the court and beyond

The present chapter has identified a hidden source of agency power: the de facto 'weight' of agencies' scientific opinions. Whereas the separation between risk assessment and risk management was meant to ensure a clear demarcation between science and politics, such a separation has revealed itself to be untenable in practice. By virtue of their highly specialized knowledge, scientists often become the actual decision makers. However, as formally advisory agencies have mutated into decision-making ones and old, formal boundaries have been lost, an accountability gap has emerged in the absence of checks on this de facto exercise of decision-making powers. The CJEU has played a central role in recognizing this gap in judicial protection and has been trying to mend it. Although formally dealing with preparatory acts, the Court has

[60] Case T-133/03, *Schering Plough Ltd* v. *Commission of the European Communities and European Agency for the Evaluation of Medicinal Products (EMEA)*, order of 5 December 2007, paras. 22 and 23, emphasis added.

recognized the significance of agency opinions. It has reasoned its way into reviewing agency opinions, restricting its purview to three main aspects, as outlined above, and in actions directed against Commission decisions based on those opinions. It has demonstrated that it is a vigilant forum with a keen and a watchful eye on the agencification process. It has kept itself synchronized with developments in agency power, delved beyond formal labels and recognized the significance of agency opinions and their impact on decision-making outcomes. In an activist, forward-looking manner, it has indirectly extended its reach over these blurred areas of responsibility.

Despite the best efforts of the Court to shine a light on these grey areas, the system currently in place remains unsatisfactory for several reasons. These reasons are laid out in turn below.

18.5.1 Concealing the real decision maker and the locus of responsibility

First of all, the division of labour between the Commission and the agencies is highly non-transparent in practice, with the boundaries between the advisor and the decision maker, between science and politics, compromised. From the analysis above, the most problematic case is that of the EMA. The Commission has withdrawn from its risk management role in practice: the EMA's powers are de facto decision making, while the European Commission has been merely 'rubber-stamping the agency's opinions, to the admission of the Commission itself'.[61] In fact, commentators are at a loss to find any instance of the Commission diverging from an EMA opinion.[62] The agency has thus long transgressed beyond its formal risk assessment and communication tasks into risk management activities.[63] This belies the Commission's stance that agencies only operate 'in specific areas where a defined technical expertise is required, under clearly and precisely defined conditions and without genuine discretionary power'.[64] Or, as it could be reiterated,

[61] See the internal note adopted on 10 May 1998 by the E/3 service of the Enterprise and Industry Direction General and signed by the chief of unit Patrick Deboyser. See Chiti, 'An Important Part', at 1405.

[62] Gehring and Krapohl, 'Supranational Regulatory Agencies', at 216.

[63] Krapohl, 'Credible Commitment', at 534.

[64] Commission of the European Communities (2008), Communication from the Commission to the European Parliament and Council, European Agencies – The Way Forward, COM (2008) 135 final, at 5.

agencies intervene only in areas where they 'are not called upon to arbitrate on conflicting public interests, exercise any powers of political appraisal or conduct any complex economic assessments'.[65]

Regardless of one's normative stance on the need for it, the separation between scientific advice and political decisions is not being realized in practice. When the Commission simply rubber-stamps the opinion of the agency, the agency is in practice exercising both the role of advisor and of decision maker. Maintaining an illusory formal separation between these roles then becomes an exercise in maintaining an institutional myth, and a costly one at that. What is there to be won by artificially upholding this separation at the formal level? As astutely observed by Dehousse: 'Are decisions that are made (de facto) by the committees and agencies more amenable to judicial or parliamentary control simply because they are formally attributed to the European Commission? Hardly so.'[66] In fact, at this point, this set-up only serves to conceal the real decision maker. It comes with clear risks at the expense of legal certainty, transparency and accountability, and negatively impacts the rights of affected parties.

18.5.2 An emerging gap in oversight

Second, other than breathing ambiguity into the system, this set-up also raises significant concerns about the presence of adequate checks and controls on this source of agency power. It points to a significant gap in respect of the oversight of technical expertise and the inadequacy of current accountability structures to adequately scrutinize expert decisions.

As already observed, the Commission has de facto relegated its risk management responsibilities, which would have allowed it to act as a check on expert decisions. This means that the operative decisions, including the allocation of values inherent in such decisions, are exclusively in the hands of experts. At the same time, as we have also seen earlier in this chapter, even though the CJEU has opened the door for the procedural review, it has also iterated that it will not substitute its own assessment for that of the scientific committee,[67] as the Court had

[65] Commission of the European Communities (2002), Communication from the Commission. The Operating Framework for the European Regulatory Agencies, COM(2002) 718 final, 11 December 2002, at 8.

[66] Dehousse, '*Misfits*', at 18–19.

[67] Joined Cases T-74/00, 76, 83, 85, 132, 137 and 141, *Artegodan GmbH* v. *Commission* [2002] ECR II-4945, para. 200.

already stated in *Pfizer*.[68] This is an understandable judicial stance given the complexity and uncertainty of the issues at stake. The Court will steer clear of actually second-guessing scientific opinions, playing a largely deferential role.[69] Rather than substitute its own views for that of the committee, the Court's role is to check the process through which the decision was made (i.e., as stated in *Artegodan*) as well as to enhance the informational basis of decision making.[70] In respect of the latter, acting as a 'catalyst', the Court has emphasized that it will scrutinize the quality of the scientific evidence according to which the decisions were reached (i.e., *Pfizer*) in the sense that an institution cannot ignore an opinion, without providing reasons 'of a scientific level at least commensurate with that of the opinion in question'.[71] In other words, 'the role of the courts is to prompt new governance actors to generate and rely upon sufficient reliable knowledge'.[72] This approach in fact also further emphasizes the significant role of expertise. Expertise is no longer seen 'as being external to the political process (which may not decide to ignore its suggestions for reasons which the former is not prepared to take into account or evaluate) but rather as something, which is in-built and integral to the "good" political decision'.[73] Therefore, the nature of expertise and how we are able to challenge it becomes a crucial issue of concern.

Yet, the joint result of these approaches, i.e., the Commission's (which is relegating its risk management responsibilities through 'rubber-stamping') and the Court's (which is rightfully steering clear of second-guessing scientific opinions) – is that while experts are sitting in the chair of the decision maker, neither the Commission nor the Court is in a position to scrutinize the measures they adopt.

This gap in oversight is accentuated by the fact that agency scientific opinions are often not strictly 'technical' in nature: value trade-offs and value judgements on the acceptability of risk are often integral parts of

[68] Case T-13/99, *Pfizer Animal Health SA* v. *Council* [2002] ECR II-3305, para. 169.

[69] A. Alemanno, 'EU Risk Regulation and Science: The Role of Experts in Decision-Making and Judicial Review' in E. Vos (ed.), *European Risk Governance: Its Science, its Inclusiveness and its Effectiveness* (Mannheim: Connex Report Series, No. 6, 2008), 37–85, at 69.

[70] J. Scott and S. Sturm, 'Courts as Catalysts: Rethinking the Judicial Role in New Governance', *Columbia Journal of European Law*, 13 (2007), 565–94.

[71] Case T-13/99, *Pfizer Animal Health SA* v. *Council* [2002] ECR II-3305, para. 199.

[72] Scott and Sturm, 'Courts as Catalysts'.

[73] L. Barroso, 'The Problems and the Controls of the New Administrative State of the EU', PhD thesis, London School of Economics and Political Science (2011).

scientific decisions. In this connection, a study of the centralized procedure shows how the EMA performs 'an allocation of values, a balancing exercise', particularly in cases where the benefit/risk balance of the product is very fragile.[74] EMA experts had, for instance, to appraise whether specific anti-obesity medication, which was shown to be moderately effective, yet at the same time was known to be associated with psychiatric disorders, including suicide, should be authorized. Similarly, in the case of an anti-smoking medication, the agency's evaluation involved assessing whether the medicine, which had demonstrated effectiveness in helping patients to stop smoking but had at the same time displayed some serious side-effects, such as suicidal ideation and suicide attempts, should be granted a marketing authorization.[75] In both cases, the EMA recommended granting the marketing authorizations, although in the former case it subsequently recommended the suspension of the marketing authorization.[76]

Such decisions cannot be reduced to a pure technical, scientific assessment, but involve decisions about the acceptability of risk, which are inherently political decisions, involving the balancing of various public interests. Yet, such decisions are being taken exclusively by experts, under the guise of a formal, but in this case de facto meaningless, separation between risk assessment and risk management.

The impact of expertise in decision making has been significantly underestimated, as a result of formal yet illusory labels, which have concealed the actual significance of the powers exercised and the real locus of responsibility. This has created a gap in oversight, with decision-making powers, also involving value trade-offs, being exercised by experts, which neither political accountability structures through the Commission (in its risk management role) nor judicial review or accountability mechanisms by the Court are in a position to adequately scrutinize.

[74] *Ibid.*, at 33. [75] *Ibid.*, at 33–4. [76] *Ibid.*

INDEX